NOT OUR PRESIDENT

People protest against U.S. President-elect Donald Trump in Miami, Florida, November 11, 2016. REUTERS/Javier Galeano

NOT OUR PRESIDENT:

NEW DIRECTIONS FROM THE PUSHED OUT, THE OTHERS, AND THE CLEAR MAJORITY IN TRUMP'S STOLEN AMERICA

EDITED BY HAKI R. MADHUBUTI
and LASANA D. KAZEMBE, Ph.D.

THIRD WORLD PRESS FOUNDATION

PUBLISHERS SINCE 1967

NOT OUR PRESIDENT

Third World Press Foundation
Publishers since 1967

thirdworldpressfoundation.com   facebook.com/ThirdWorldPress

Design by Lasana D. Kazembe

ISBN: 978-0-88378-372-6

Printed in the United States of America

DISCLAIMER
The views expressed in the essays throughout this book are not necessarily the
views of Third World Press Foundation.

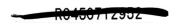

DEDICATION

Wesley Snipes   Danny Glover

Safisha Madhubuti (Dr. Carol D. Lee)

In memory of and more:

Walter P. Lomax Jr., M.D., Maxine Graves Lee,
Gwendolyn Brooks Malcolm X, Ossie Davis,
Dudley Randall, Hoyt W. Fuller, Barbara Ann Sizemore,
Margaret Burroughs, Richard Wright,
Charles Burroughs, Ruby Dee, Derrick Bell, W.E.B. Du Bois,
Paul Robeson, John Henrik Clarke

I work for
My children, grandchildren, cultural children
and
all children

HRM

I dedicate this book to my precious Daughter, **Ella Niani Kazembe**.
My wish is for you to always question critically, critique righteously,
challenge boldly, and raise up the good constantly.

May we all heed the wisdom of Horace Mann:
"Be ashamed to die, until you have won some victory for humanity."

LDK

ALSO BY HAKI R. MADHUBUTI

Non-Fiction
Freedom to Self-Destruct: Easier to Believe than Think - New and Selected Essays (forthcoming)
Taking Bullets: Terrorism and Black Life in Twenty-First Century America
YellowBlack: The First Twenty-One Years of a Poet's Life, A Memoir
Tough Notes: A Healing Call for Creating Exceptional Black Men
*Claiming Earth: Race, Rage, Rape, Redemption: Blacks Seeking a Culture of
    Enlightened Empowerment*
Dynamite Voices: Black Poets of the 1960s
Black Men: Obsolete, Single, Dangerous? The African American Family in Transition
From Plan to Planet: Life Studies; The Need for Afrikan Minds and Institutions
Enemies: The Clash of Races
A Capsule Course in Black Poetry Writing (co-author)
African Centered Education (co-author)
Kwanzaa: A Progressive and Uplifting African American Holiday

Poetry
Taught by Women (forthcoming)
Honoring Genius: Gwendolyn Brooks: The Narrative of Craft, Art, Kindness, and Justice, Poems
Liberation Narratives: New and Collected Poems 1966-2009
Run Toward Fear: New Poems and a Poet's Handbook
HeartLove: Wedding and Love Poems
GroundWork: New and Selected Poems of Don L. Lee/Haki R. Madhubuti from 1966-1996
Killing Memory, Seeking Ancestors
Earthquakes and Sunrise Missions
Book of Life
Directionscore: New and Selected Poems
We Walk the Way of the New World
Don't Cry, Scream
Black Pride
Think Black

Edited Works
Brilliant Fire! Amiri Baraka: Poetry, Plays, Politics for the People (co-editor)
By Any Means Necessary, Malcolm X: Real, Not Reinvented (co-editor)
Releasing the Spirit: A Collection of Literary Works from Gallery 37 (co-editor)
Describe the Moment: A Collection of Literary Works from Gallery 37 (co-editor)
Million Man March/Day of Absence: A Commemorative Anthology (co-editor)
*Confusion by Any Other Name: Essays Exploring the Negative Impact of
    The Black Man's Guide to Understanding the Black Woman (editor)*
Why L.A. Happened: Implications of the '92 Los Angeles Rebellion (editor)
Say that the River Turns: The Impact of Gwendolyn Brooks (editor)
To Gwen, With Love (co-editor)

Recordings: Poetry and Music
RiseVisionComin' (with Nation: Afrikan Liberation Arts Ensemble)
Medasi (with Nation: Afrikan Liberation Arts Ensemble)
Rappin' and Readin'

CONTENTS

2. THE OPTICS OF WHITE NATIONALISM   91

3. EXAMINING AMERICA'S BODY POLITIC

4. ONWARD:ACTIVATING CRITICAL RESISTANCE

FOREWORD

CORNEL WEST

Cornel West is Professor of the Practice of Public Philosophy in the Harvard Divinity School and in the Department of African and African American Studies. *The following remarks were delivered on January 25, 2017—four days after the historic Women's March on Washington—to an audience at Harvard University. View online: hutchinscenter.fas.harvard.edu/spring-colloquium-cornel-west*

THE TRUMP ERA: HOPE IN A TIME OF ESCALATING DESPAIR

Oh, what a blessing. What an honor. What a privilege to be here. But there's no doubt that as I stand here, I am who I am because somebody loved me. Somebody cared for me. Somebody attended to me. It's always a delight to be part of what the Isley Brothers called a *"Caravan of Love."* And that's how I view my calling and my vocation, and I say that in all seriousness in these Trump years, at the beginning of this Trump era. Catastrophe, calamity, monstrosity. But human made. My dear brothers and sisters here have facilitated my coming back [to Harvard] after seventeen years. You're looking at those who were kind enough to bring a cracked vessel like me back to try to tell the truth, and the condition of truth is always to allow suffering to speak and to try to bear witness and be faithful unto death in telling that truth.

I want to dedicate these remarks to two towering figures. One, the closest figure, for me here at Harvard, (though Preston Williams was close, too), is Martin Kilson. And the fact that, at the age of eighty-something, he would come in his wheelchair to hear a student who he first met at the age of seventeen, who has fundamentally changed my life and helped introduce me to the life of the mind and the world of ideas. It was he and Sinclair Drake that served as my models. Drake was at Stanford. I was here at Harvard. And the very fact that our dear brother Martin Luther Kilson, Jr. is here. Give it up, please, for the one and only, the inimitable Martin Luther Kilson, Jr. [APPLAUSE] The one and only, the first black tenured professor in the history of Harvard. [APPLAUSE] And I believe in a Sankofa sensibility. You don't move forward unless you stay in contact with the milestones that constitute the wind at your back. And that's Martin Kilson. That's Preston Williams, and Israel Scheffler, that's John Rawls, that's Stanley Cavell, it's Samuel Beer, Harvey Cox, G. Ernest Wright. They all mean the world to me. They're part of the same caravan of love.

The second person I want to dedicate my remarks to is named Daniel Aaron. He died in April 30, 2016. There was only two vanilla folk who would associate themselves with the Du Bois Institute then run by Preston Williams, and Daniel Baruch Aaron was one. He was the first Ph.D. graduate of the American Civilizations program here at Harvard in 1937 under the powerful leadership of Perry Miller and F. O. Matthiessen. He was a neighbor of Ralph Waldo Ellison in Northampton. Both taught at Smith College. And I was blessed to break bread with my dear brother Daniel Aaron every week. And we give it up to him. He died at 104 years old. Give it up for brother Daniel. [APPLAUSE]

I say all this to say that I have a profound commitment to revolutionary piety. And piety has nothing to do with uncritical deference to dogma. It has nothing to do with blind obedience to doctrine. It has to do with keeping track of the sources of good in your life, in your short move from your mama's womb to tomb. So it's a grounded, a historical consciousness, that keeps you in contact with the best of what has gone into you, that empowers you to be critical of the worst that's been injected into you. It is profoundly Socratic in terms of self-examination, but it's also Gramsci-like in terms of a historically informed critical self-inventory. Situating ourselves in such a way that is first existential; that's what we need to talk about initially here in the Trump era, not just the politics yet, not just the analysis yet, but what kind of human beings are we going to be? What kind of choices are we going to make? What kind of spine will we have? What kind of backbone will we have, given the escalating neo-fascist purposes, or it could be authoritarian populist? It could be right-wing nationalist. We can argue how we characterize brother Trump and his phenomena and the social forces behind him.

But there's no doubt that this is not a time for sunshine soldiers. This is a moment for all seasoned warriors, intellectual warriors, spiritual warriors, moral warriors, academic warriors, athletic warriors across the board. The moment for solely polished professionals is not enough, it's insufficient. It doesn't go far enough. And there's a variety of ways of being a warrior, so let's not think that there's some monolithic model. You don't have to always be in the street. You don't have to go to jail with some of us. Some of us must be willing to die. Because there is no movement for those who Sly Stone calls "everyday", people, for those James Cleveland calls "ordinary people," unless there are people willing to tell the truth and bear witness and, pay the ultimate cost.

That's what we learned in the nineteenth century with the great abolitionists, the Harriet Beecher Stowes and the Frederick Douglasses and the Harriet Tubmans and the Sojourner Truths, and the William Lloyd Garrisons. Tarred and feathered; willing to sacrifice. That's what we learned in the twentieth century with the women's movement. Beat down; that 1913 rally. The magnificent echo we saw this weekend in the Women's March on Washington. Women straightening their backs up in the face of this escalating neo-fascist movement. And that's what we learned in the 1960s and the 1970s, when many of us were blessed to come here to Harvard. It was nearly fifty years ago that I was blessed to set foot. I was just walking past Wigglesworth. I used to clean every toilet in Wigglesworth, and I did it singing Curtis Mayfield songs. [LAUGHTER] I did it with a smile, because I needed the cash. And it was part of my discipline. To do what? To try to be true to my calling.

Let me begin with an epigraph from the greatest of all public intellectuals in the twentieth century. He's got some strong competition, figures like John Dewey—towering, powerful—Edmund Wilson, Susan Sontag, Muriel Rukeyser. We can go on and on. But I'm talking about the one and only, the inimitable W. E. B. Du Bois. I want you to imagine in your minds February 16, 1951, when he's in Washington, D.C. with handcuffs because he is up for conviction—they're trying to send him to jail for life. Two days before he had just married the magnificent Shirley Graham Du Bois who taught here at Harvard. I was blessed to take her course, I'll never forget it. But Du Bois is in handcuffs, the towering figure is eighty-two years old. He's charged with working for a foreign government, being an agent for a foreign government, for the Peace Information Center. And he's looking for comrades, [but they're] hard to find. They had planned to have a major celebration of his birthday, which was February 23rd, just a week later, in the Essex House. Essex House cancelled it. They've got to move to Harlem. The smallest restaurant. And the pullback takes place. Telegrams, Mordecai Johnson, former president of Howard University: *"I can't make it."* Too controversial. Margaret Mead: *"I have nothing to do with this anymore."* Arthur Spingarn: *"No, not me. Nothing to do with it."* Here comes Ralph Bunche, towering figure that he was, we love Ralph. Scared. *"I have nothing to do with Du Bois anymore."* Hmm. Du Bois down and out, down and out.

What would he say? He said, *"Ooh, that was a bitter experience. I bowed before the storm, but I didn't break."* I want you to remember that line in the Trump era. But I did not break. My friends may have got a bit scared. But there are some that stood with me. Albert Einstein said, *"I will speak on behalf of Du Bois and lay bare his high character."* That was brother Einstein. Or brother Bedford Lawford, who was the head of the Alpha Phi Alpha, founded in 1906. I'm Alpha Phi Alpha, so I'm proud of that slice of the house. The Paul Robesons and the Donnie Hathaways and the John Hope Franklins and others. They stood strong. Leonard Bernstein. Shostakovich stood strong. But it was a parting of the waters, not in the sense of agreeing with everything Du Bois said. We're just talking about a commitment to fairness, a commitment to justice, and an acknowledgement that somebody who had given so much of themselves, their bodies, their minds, their energies. Du Bois was isolated, and yet stronger; refusing to break. That's the kind of spirit we need.

And what would he go on to do? Typical Du Bois: *"Let me write a trilogy!"* [LAUGHTER] Here comes *The Black Flame.* And that first novel, *The Ordeal of Mansart.* You turn to page 275 and Du Bois says, I've been wrestling with this life problem. His fundamental questions, these are the questions for the Trump era. This is a love letter Du Bois writes to this generation, especially those under thirty, because if only the folk who had voted in America were under thirty, Bernie Sanders would be in the White House. We ought to be clear about that. There are signs of hope, and it's not abstract. It's concrete. It's on the ground. There's something going on with our young brothers and sisters of all colors and all genders and sexual orientations. It's a beautiful thing. It's just not strong enough at the moment to have prevented neo-fascist elites from taking over—the billionaires, the military generals, and so forth.

The questions Du Bois raised: How shall integrity face oppression? How shall integrity face oppression? This is a question that echoed down through the corridors of time for 400 years, especially of black people who have been terrorized, traumatized, and stigmatized, hated. But in the face of that hate, they taught the world so much of how to love. John Coltrane's *Love Supreme*, Toni Morrison's *Beloved*, the novels of James Baldwin, love so shot-through. Never has there been a figure on the American stage like Mamma written by a genius from the South Side of Chicago named Loraine Hansberry, in *A Raisin in the Sun.* What is it about these Negroes? Hated so, and still dishing out these love warriors? That tradition is getting weak. It's getting feeble these days. And that tradition is the leaven in the American democratic loaf. There would be no American democracy if the Black people who had been terrorized had produced Black versions of the Klan or Black versions of ISIS or Al Qaeda, as opposed to love warriors like Frederick Douglass, A. Philip Randolph, Mary McLeod Bethune, who did stand with Du Bois that night as well.

What a tradition; what a people. Had nothing to do with biology, nothing to do with skin pigmentation. It had to do with integrity, refusing to live a life or cupidity, love of money, or venality, everybody for sale, and everything is for sale, and you'd sell your soul for a mess of pottage, and end up just well-adjusted to injustice and well-adapted to indifference. Oh, what a tradition! I don't know about you, but I'm talking about my grandmother and my grandfather. I'm talking about Irene and Clifton West, who gave birth to me. They were not perfect. They were not pristine. But they taught me to try to be a human being with integrity before the worms get my body. That's the kind of commitment and calling we needed in the Trump era. This is not a game. This is not a plaything. Trump's cabinet is serious.

I get in a lot of trouble on television. In fact, I've got to go on television today. And I've already been trashed, because I said that Trump was a gangster in character and a neo-fascist in content. [APPLAUSE] And they said, Oh, brother West, you're name-calling. No, no. No, I was a *gangsta* before I met Jesus, and now I'm a redeemed sinner with *gangsta* proclivities. So I know what I'm talking about when I'm talking about *gangsta*. To call somebody a *gangsta* is not a subjective expression. It's an objective description of somebody who does not believe that there are constraints, does not believe that there are boundaries, but believes that they can use arbitrary power. When you say you go into Iraq and take their oil any time, that's *gangsta*. When you're grabbing a woman's private parts and think you can get away with it and laugh, that's gangster. Oh, brother West, that's hyperbolic. Maybe for you. But come to my house. Take some of my stuff like you take the oil from Iraq. I'm a Christian, not a pacifist, so I won't get into the details [APPLAUSE]! My sister and my mother and my wife, you grabbing some of her private parts, that's *gangsta*. I know what it is to be *gangsta*. I'm not trying to engage in some kind of denigration of the public discourse, because I'm putting myself on the same continuum. I got *gangsta* proclivities, too!

* * *

Donald Trump is, in part, the failure of each and every one of us in some sense. We're all responsible, and some are more guilty than others, but he's a product of American empire. He's a product of American civilization, the vicious legacies of white supremacy still operating, the vicious legacies of male supremacy still operating, losing sight of our precious gay and lesbian and bisexual and transgender folk, still operating. And then comes the social slippage. Then comes downward mobility in terms of the losers of the neo-liberal order. The neo-liberal chickens come home to roost. That obsession with financializing and privatizing and militarizing, see a project, need big money, big banks, big corporations, massive transfer of wealth from poor and working people to the One Percent, then trash public goods in the name of privatizing, be it prisons or education or any other public institution. And then you militarize. 26,172 bombs dropped by the U.S. armed forces last year. 26,000! Any discussion about it? How many innocent people killed? I come from a tradition that says that a baby in Yemen or Somalia, Afghanistan or Pakistan, have exactly the same value as a vanilla baby in Newtown, Connecticut, or a brown baby on the East Side of Los Angeles, or a Black baby in the South Side of Chicago, a red baby in Standing Rock. Where is the concern? That's integrity. There's more consistency telling the truth in the face of power no matter what color the power-holder is. It's a matter of trying to have some kind of morality, and as a Christian, I would say spirituality, about it. And they will never pay the cost.

And alright, the critiques of brother Trump and his cabinet, and the fellow citizens who at the moment are still excited about him. I'm thoroughly convinced he's going to systematically and chronically betray working people. Wall Street, Goldman Sachs, deregulation, neo-liberal economy on steroids. But the repressive apparatus, that's the neo-fascist dimension of it. It's not just the attack on the press, but he will be coming for some us. We have to say, like Du Bois, like Fredrick Douglass, and like the nameless and anonymous freedom fighters of all colors, we can stand, because these last ten years, as Sly Stone says in his record Stand!: *"we've been sitting much too long / there's a permanent crease in our right and wrong."* I refuse to normalize Donald Trump and his neo-fascist project, and I'm definitely not going to naturalize it. [APPLAUSE] Refuse. Refuse to normalize it.

What do you mean by normalize, brother West? I'm not going to act as if, lo and behold, he's some kind of president because he's got the office that I have to lower, temper my fire and not tell the truth in the name of poor children in Appalachia or poor children in Gaza or poor children in Tel Aviv. Poor children anywhere. Working people anywhere. But we have to acknowledge, in addition to the racism, the sexism, in addition to the downward mobility, is a massive, abysmal failure of the Left. Massive. Weak as presweetened Kool-Aid. [LAUGHTER] All you've got is some isolated voices in a journal here or there. Where's the institutional capacity? I talk about this in my dear brother Adolph Reed who is one of the finest left political scientists. And he and I don't have a history of being lovey-dovey [LAUGHTER]. But I love my brother. He and I did about eight events with brother Bernie Sanders last year. So things change. You've got to be improvisational with these things. [LAUGHTER]

But it had to do with that first question of Du Bois: *"How shall integrity face oppression?"* Again, I'm not talking about purity. A lot of my centric folk say Oh, brother West, you're always into that purity. If they don't fully agree with you, you leave. The Democratic Party Platform Committee. You abstained because it didn't allow for single payer. It didn't allow for wrestling with Israeli occupation. It didn't allow for doing away with fracking. I said, no, it's a matter of taking a stand. I'm on the committees, so that's already impure. [LAUGHTER] I'm willing to dialog, I'm just pushing. But I've got a stand I'm going to take. There's a difference between prudence and opportunism. Martin Luther King, Jr. used to say, I'd rather be dead than afraid. Some of us, we'd rather be dead than be thoroughgoing opportunists. That's slapping Grandmama in the face from the grave. I refuse to do it. But we try again, fail again, fail better. And Samuel Beckett is right. There's no purity.

Second question from Du Bois: *"What does honesty do in the face of deception?"* We live in an age, the Orwellian age of mendacity and criminality. Mass incarceration, that's a crime against humanity in the last forty years. Domestic violence, a crime against humanity. Stagnating wages for forty years for working people of all colors. A kind of crime. And the backlash [from] the xenophobic; they scapegoat the most vulnerable rather than confront the most powerful. It's called spiritual blackout; cowardliness. But it's human, and it's inside of each and every one of us. How to be honest; to be a person of integrity and honesty, in our classrooms? Harvard's going to have a great challenge. Why? Because when the President's first choice for his Secretary of Education was the president of Liberty University rather than someone from Harvard's School of Education, it's a new day in Washington. Liberalism is being decentered.

Harvard's going to have to come to terms with what it's like to be on the margins in the neo-fascist era. That's a compliment. [LAUGHTER] It is. It's a compliment. But the dominant Harvard mentality is that it's the center of the universe. Hey, they're coming to us for advice. We got the wisdom. We can channel our elites, go back and forth and back and forth. Kennedy School's got all of these ex-elected officials, dot, dot, dot. That's over! Liberty University, Jerry Falwell, Jr. was the first choice. And then here comes the free market, charter school obsessed Betsy DeVos. Will we have the spine to deal with our marginal status with integrity and honesty in dialog with each other, disagreeing but recognizing that even as we disagree, we have a larger end and aim? That's what a united front against a neo-fascist project is all about. And we are just at the very beginning of that. We, of course, tremendously buoyed by the massive presence, especially of our sisters of all colors. Beautiful thing. The largest protest rally in the history of the American Empire. That's a beautiful thing. A beautiful thing. [APPLAUSE] Led by sisters of different colors; our Palestinian sister Linda Sarsour, who is being viciously attacked. I've known her for many years. I'd take a bullet for her, for the quality that she has in terms of integrity and honesty.

The third question Du Bois raises is: *"What does decency do in the face of insult?"* What does it mean to be a decent person in a neo-fascist era? First, pointing out what you think is indecent. Decrepit schools. Massive unemployment and underemployment. Oh, brother West, but under the neo-liberals of the Obama Administration, they had jobs every month. But what does Alan Krueger, what does our own Lawrence Katz tell us? Ninety-four percent of those jobs, low wage, contingent, precarious, part-time. Don't brag to me about the numbers of jobs you've got if they're not generating a living wage for our precious fellow citizens of any color. It's better than higher unemployment, yes, but it's far, far, far from enough. That was one of the reasons why the Democrats lost. You're defending a neo-liberal status quo that cannot be defended based on integrity and honesty. And somehow you think by pointing out the underside of Trump, you will win. Even given the brilliance of sister Hillary, even given the smartness of sister Hillary, it's not enough. Truth repressed comes back. The suffering is still there. All the statistics in the world hide and conceal the misery of the human beings beneath those statistics. And of course, large numbers of our fellow citizens just opted out and said, look, the whole thing is rigged. You know that. I know that. It's oligarchy for the most part. Ordinary people do not have any impact with their voices. So, it's oligarchic, plutocratic society for the most part.

The last question: *"What does virtue do in the face of brute force?"* And Du Bois is talking about the enabling virtue, courage. Without courage, all the other virtues are shallow, vacuous, empty. What does courage do with brute force? And that's going to be a crucial one, because brute force is coming our way. And many of us are not used to that. That's why when Du Bois stood there in handcuffs, and they put that picture in Black newspapers, how could the old man be in handcuffs? Brother Kilson and I spent much time at his house, and he talked of the stories and dialogs he had with Du Bois in Chicago and other places. That bitterness that was escalating and intensifying, but at the same time, that conviction that was there. That brute force, the repressive apparatus of the state; our brothers and sisters know about that in Latin America, in Brazil, in Venezuela, in Bolivia. What they know about in the Middle East, what they know about in Africa, what they know about in Asia. Most of us in the U.S. are unacquainted with that brute force hitting us. We're going to have to get used to it. Not fetishize it, not valorize it, but recognize it is a possibility. That's what it is to have a calling in the deepest sense in which Martin Luther as well as Max Weber talked about. And that's what we need, especially among the younger generation. We haven't said anything, of course, about the global catastrophe and the ecological catastrophe awaiting us.

So what do we do? We do exactly what this colloquium represents. We come together in all of our commitments, with integrity and honesty, decency and courage, and recognize that we learn from one another, listen to one another. Most importantly, keep track of those giants and geniuses, the women and men in the past who have known catastrophes we know not of but still were able to straighten their backs up and tell the truth and bear witness. And that means you cut radically against the U.S. grain. And young people, it means that you've got to give up being obsessed with having a brand and find a cause that's bigger than you. [APPLAUSE] Give up using your brand for maneuvering on the market and find a cause that cuts against so much of the mendacity and criminality and the banality and cupidity that is hegemonic. I do believe that we do have a chance.

Now, let me make this point, and I'll sit down. My dear brother Barack Obama, I read his recent reflections on his legacy, and he's got all this optimism, optimism. I said, good God almighty. You sound like a voluntary immigrant who just got here. [LAUGHTER] No matter what happened, men from Ireland and Jewish brothers and sisters from Jew-hating Eastern Europe. They get here like, Oh, my God, New York, Ellis Island, Philadelphia. Let's hit the ground. Then they run into Jamal and Laticia. Been here ten generations. Trying not to get lynched this week. I'm not an optimist. When I heard my brother say, America's a magical land, I said, this brother's going to have a Christopher Columbus experience. He's going to discover America. [LAUGHTER] There ain't nothing magical about America! America is free and democratic to the degree to which each generation fights to keep it free based on the best that came before, and you'll lose that freedom, you'll lose that democracy, if you don't make that kind of commitment with vision and courage. [APPLAUSE] Ain't nothing called automatic, the 'arc bends…' No, no, not at all. Not at all. Blues woman and a blues man who was on intimate terms with catastrophe. Plain truth, it's catastrophe. Nobody loves me but my mom, she might be jivin', too. That's catastrophe.

But prisoner of hope is something else. It has nothing to do with optimism. When you're a prisoner of hope, you're committed to integrity, honesty, decency regardless of what the consequences are, regardless of what the odds are. That's the kind of human being you choose to be before the worms get you, period. That's what's kept Black folk going. We had to wait for the evidence, over 244 years of slavery. We all would have gone to the crack house a long time ago. It was the music that sustained us. It was relations that sustained us. And it was our allies who, with their integrity, honesty, and decency, could come together because they wanted to be decent. They wanted to be human beings who constitute a force for good. To be a prisoner of hope. In some sense even having hope is too abstract for me. People come up to me. Brother West, do you have hope? Not really. But I decide to be a hope. And that's nonnegotiable. Despair is always a vice, a certain form of cowardice. And when you decide to be a hope, that's Curtis Mayfield, Keep on Pushing. It's the choice to be a certain kind of human being, and that by being a hope, maybe it becomes contagious, and you're influenced by those who are, in fact, hopes in their lives. That's what we're talking about.

Thank you all so very much. [APPLAUSE] I appreciate it. God bless you.

THE GOOD FIGHT, AGAIN

NIKKY FINNEY

Nikky Finney is the author of four books of poetry and a collection of short stories including: **On Wings Made of Gauze**, **Rice**, *and* **Heartwood**. *In addition to the National Book Award, Finney has received a PEN American Open Book Award, and the Benjamin Franklin Award for Poetry. She has taught at the University of Kentucky, is currently a professor at the University of South Carolina.*

"I said, I'm gonna fight {Strom} Thurmond from the mountain to the sea."
— **Modjeska Monteith Simkins, Civil Rights Matriarch, 1948.**

You with your little ivory-tipped six-shooter
words, pointed at our dream-filled, churning

up the hill, wanting-to-be-better hearts, you
on your glittering presidential runway,

with your XL holsters of warbling hate,
on both sides of your feeble hips and viewless lips,

your rat-a-tat-tat nickel language of destruction,
cling-clanging in the microphone of our every day,

your worthless cheap silver lingo never adding up,

bulldozing and belittling how far we've come,
pouring your imported gasoline

on our hot-under-the-collar fears, you and your
little Pac-Man hunger games, eating away at

what frightens us, then dangling the live
detritus before us like something we need

to be gargantuan and special,

you and your titanic private jets of hatred
pointed at all who do not share your shock

of thinning blonde hair, you, rising and falling,

a hot air balloon of un-wonder, floating above us,
raining down on us, never looking us in the eye,

tucking dynamite near our homesteads, our heart
forts, our bald eagles, our wheat fields, the heart wood

of our cities, our migrations forward,

you with your trusty little band of loud pointless
aggressives, a rising river of believers, threatening

us, by memorizing together, all the architectural
arpeggio low notes of, "I'll build me a wall,"

your camphored bird-size heart,

you and your kin, with your mean-spirited
manifestoes and hymns, gathered together

at the glorious picnic, ever excited to be witnesses
to the new hanging, of the sovereign kindness

& empathy for each other that is still a work
in progress, you and your kind, standing around

for the photo shoot and then the mailing out,
of the bloody postcard with Wish You Were Here!

scribbled on the back, all while pointing up to the
still swaying branches of all that remains

of what was once a human being, you and your
little Let Me Close the Deal atomic bomb eyes,

threatening a world that refuses to turn the arena
over to you, your orchestra of brass knuckle sound

bites and billionaires, who didn't want you to be
president anymore than I wanted you to be president,

but didn't have the courage to say it to your face,

what a worn out scarecrow of a fearmonger you are,
standing at droopy attention, on momentary display,

all prim-less and prominent in the middle of our sacred
sunflowered field, wearing the same scary and puzzled

look as you loudly ask the Presidential Parade organizers,

"Can I have a tank in the parade? I really want a tank."
Even stopping the cameras to beg, "Please?"

But someone from the last administration (who will be
but has not yet been fired) whispers that a tank

would be very inappropriate.

You turn away disappointed but make a promise
to yourself, that in the next four years, there will be

tanks to play with.

Those who put you where they put you wait with
unspoken worry, unable to fathom, one more

environmental protection order, one more solar
windmill turning on the plains, or the park land,

one more Black president with beautiful Muslim
name, one more Black woman FLOTUS with

Southside Arm(y) muscles. Your true believers
are loud and proud in their stolen election joy.

You aren't a new kind of man. Your kind of man
has been brightly marching across our sweet

yet to be united states with spiked shoes for many
generations, with stink bombs and 1% shrapnel

strapped to AM radio wave microphones, kicking
and poking every newly inflated hopeful thing

we ever dragged to the yet to be finished finish line
of this country. You and your red rooster pompadour,

making your living by strutting into the yard and
looking for the wounded, or the weary, to peck to

death before flying back up to your penthouse
perch to preen, you with your pompous walk,

your empty silk pockets, spouting your latest disregard,

"Look at my African American. There! Over
there! Look! There! That's My African American."

Your extended breath holding my in the air as if
Surprise! Surprise! You happened to look up

from your notes, into the crowd, only to find one
of your exotic dolls, escaped from the Big House,

no longer polishing the silver, but in the front
yard, at your afternoon rally, cheering you on,

alongside others, clinging to your shiny exterior,
with eyes so exquisitely wounded with disregard,

from 400 years of tender constant pummeling,
that they are unable to speak the difference between

a slap in the face,
and a slap on the back.

You bereft and disingenuous lying addict
of TV lights, prisoner of narcissism

and the toys of war, you A student of the quip
and inventor of the bully high bar,

you small-minded new/old stock character
of this our sweet living time,

in the tradition of other great
South Carolina women warriors,

I will fight who you say you are
from the mountain to the sea.

INTRODUCTION

Donald J. Trump is the 45th president of the United States. This happened in 2016, and it is not a hallucination. Trump's political ascendancy, cabinet and judicial appointments, mass appeal among white nationalist extremists, and dangerous unpredictability have expedited feelings of fear, loathing, and endless uncertainty among many Americans – in particular, the poor and working-class. More, Trump's nativist rhetoric and overt fascism synched with the durability of white supremacy (i.e., racism), generational poverty, and U.S. empire-building has imposed newer and more serious life-challenges into the lives of Americans across the socioeconomic and sociodemographic spectrum.

The purpose of this critical anthology is to issue a call-to-action for critical thinking and action, and progressive movement-building among everyday Americans – the vast majority of whom stand outside of Trump's vision for America.

There is nothing normal, natural, or right about White supremacy. It is, in fact, a flawed, noxious ideology built on and sustained through fear(s), ignorance, injustice, violence, looting, and the exploitation and subjugation of hundreds of millions of Black, Brown, Red, Yellow, and White bodies. It is, in fact, the largest criminal enterprise in the history of humanity. The writings presented in this anthology are grounded in the best traditions of activist scholarship engaged in by revolutionary forerunners such as Shirley Graham and W.E.B. Du Bois, Barbara Sizemore,

Asa Hilliard, Anna Julia Cooper, Derrick Bell, and others too numerous to mention. Collectively, that small group of elders represent hundreds years of activism, scholarship, and critical, principled stance against the forces of racism and injustice. Those dynamic women and men committed their lives (quite literally) to the struggle for justice, equality and a more humane existence.

We must do the same.

NOT OUR PRESIDENT

Republican presidential candidate Donald Trump smiles during a campaign stop, Feb. 17, 2016 in Bluffton, S.C. Matt Rourke/AP.

THE AMERICAN MOMENT

New York, United States. April 7, 2017. Protesters converged outside Trump Tower and Union Square for a rally and march, to reject Washington's latest war. Credit: Erik McGregor/Pacific Press/Alamy Live News.

MYTH OR REALITY?

BILL AYERS

*Bill Ayers, Distinguished Professor of Education and Senior University scholar at University of Illinois at Chicago (retired), is a lifelong educator, scholar, and activist. His many books include: **Public Enemy: Confessions of an American Dissident** (with Ryan Alexander-Tanner), and **Race Course Against White Supremacy** (with Bernadine Dhorn). His forthcoming co-edited work is **You Can't Fire the Bad Ones!": And 18 Other Myths about Teachers, Teachers Unions, and Public Education** (2018).*

In the dark times
Will there also be singing?
Yes, there will also be singing.
About the dark times.

— **Brecht**

It's been heartening these last months to gather together with people in city after city across the country, folks who've come out in large numbers, driven by the felt-need to assemble in an available public space, to face one another without masks, and to consider the fundamental questions once again—and with accelerating urgency: who are we? Where are we going? What time is it on the clock of the world? What is to be done? There's a common and compelling feeling from north to south, from east and west that we must somehow muster and unite the disparate forces for peace and justice and liberation into an unstoppable mass force—a love army. Uprising!

There's a wonderful bumper sticker I see now and then, some-times in the form of a banner or a poster: *"If you're not pissed off,"* it reads, *"you're not paying attention."*

It's true. Opening our eyes, paying attention, staying alert—when we see the horrors and the injustices, it ignites indignation; when we notice the unnecessary suffering in all directions, it stirs a sense of outrage and urgency. That emotion is essential—but it's also insufficient. Anger alone cannot create the society we need and deserve; fury by itself will not take us to the place we need to be.

So there needs to be another bumper sticker, right next to that first one: *"If you're only pissed off—if you're not guided by deep feelings of love and empathy—you'll be lost in the wilderness."*

Anger and love. Rage and generosity. Fury and tenderness. Humanity—and the possibility of a humane future—asks us to get it right.

* * *

It was the best of times, it was the worst of times, it was the age of wisdom, it was the age of foolishness, it was the epoch of belief, it was the epoch of incredulity, it was the season of Light, it was the season of Darkness, it was the spring of hope, it was the winter of despair.

— Charles Dickens

The U.S. empire is in steady and irreversible decline, but it's unlikely to exit the world stage, or to relinquish its self-designated role as the "world's only superpower" easily or painlessly—this is where we begin to name this political moment, honestly and unsparingly, a moment unique in history. The end of every previous empire—Ottoman, British, French, Portuguese, Belgian, German—was accompanied by war and mass slaughter at escalating scales. The US is in decline, true, but it's also the greatest military power ever assembled on earth with vast arsenals of weapons of mass destruction capable of wreckage—even extermination—never before seen. This is a precarious, dangerous, and terrifying time.

The decline of empire coexists with renewed patriotic nationalism and deliberately constructed fear; the criminalization of whole communities and the identification of ill-defined enemies—"illegal" immigrants, border violators, Muslims, Arabs, foreigners, queers, Black people, independent women, terrorists—as a unifying cause; the ramping up and cohering of white supremacist forces; the mobilization of secretly financed "popular" movements in the streets based on bigotry, intolerance, and the threat of violence against vulnerable populations and sacrificial scapegoats; the suppression of dissent; military expansion and a state of permanent war; militarized police forces acting as aggressive occupying armies in targeted communities; constant surveillance and ritual searches of everyday citizens and residents; arrogant scorn and disdain for the arts, for intellectual life, and for reason and evidence; and widening disparities between the haves and the have-nots, and the fatal entangling of corporations with government as the "public square" is decimated.

These and other examples of extreme social disintegration are all visible right here in front of our eyes. They are—in brief—an outline of the Trump/Pence political campaign of 2016, and the parameters of the regime's program for the foreseeable future.

Make no mistake: it's a blueprint for a form of friendly-looking and familiar fascism—autocratic despotism with an American face. And it's important to remember and foreground this fact: fascism in the homeland is precisely what empire looks and feels like through the eyes and the bodies of subjugated colonial peoples:

- *Trump's inauguration speech was a textbook: "America first;" depicting the country as damaged—"American carnage"— and in need of radical restoration; claiming legitimacy exclusively from the people who voted for him; stating that he alone stands above the corrupt political class and has a mandate to sweep the slate clean and start over.*

- *Trump issued an executive order denying federal funds to "Sanctuary Cities," and white nationalist and top Trump advisor Steve Bannon was appointed by Trump to a permanent seat on the National Security Council, as the head of the Joint Chiefs of Staff and the Director of National Intelligence were removed.*

- *Trump signed an executive order to build his $20 billion border wall, and promised aggressive efforts to round up and deport millions of undocumented workers and families.*

- *Trump signed an executive order codifying his long-promised Muslim ban, barring indefinitely Syrian refugees from entering the US, suspending all refugee admissions for 120 days, and blocking citizens of seven Muslim-majority countries (Iran, Iraq, Libya, Somalia, Sudan, Syria and Yemen) from entering the US for 90 days. The US is currently bombing five countries (Iraq, Syria, Yemen, Libya and Somalia), has troops deployed and military bases in another (Sudan), and imposes harsh sanctions and frequent threats against the last (Iran). Notably missing from his scapegoat list: Saudi Arabia, Egypt, and the UAE—places where Trump has extensive business dealings. He fired his acting Attorney General when she told him that his travel ban was illegal, and called the federal judge who issued a restraining order a "so-called judge." This from a so-called president.*

- *Trump reinstated and massively expanded the "global gag rule" punishing any foreign family-planning organization that uses its own money to provide, or even discuss, abortion services; millions of poor women will lose birth control access, and thousands will die from unsafe abortions in the name of pro-life.*

- *Trump issued a warning on day one, stating that his is a law and order regime, and anyone who disrespects the police or questions their legitimacy is "on notice."*

- *Trump tweeted: "If Chicago doesn't fix the horrible "carnage" going on, 228 shootings in 2017 with 42 killings (up 24% from 2016), I will send in the Feds!"~~Donald J. Trump (@realDonaldTrump) January 25, 2017.*

- *White nationalist Steve Bannon (Trump's Joseph Goebbels) issued a directive to the press: "The media should keep its mouth shut for a while."*

- *Kellyanne Conway, a top Trump advisor, argued in a televised interview that the administration is looking at "alternative facts" to bolster the bosses' ongoing lie that a million or a million and a half people attended his Inauguration, according to Sean Spicer, Trump's press secretary and official mouthpiece who always looks like his head is about to explode, "the largest crowd in history, period!"*

- *Trump said repeatedly—Big Lie style—that 3-5 million votes were cast illegally.*

- *Trump asked the Department of Energy for the names of climate scientists; told the Department of Agriculture's Agricultural Research Service to put in a ban on "any public-facing documents," including "news releases, photos, fact sheets, news feeds, and social media content;" froze all Environmental Protection Agency grants and suspend its Twitter account; scrubbed the White House web pages of references to climate change or energy alternatives to fossil fuels; deleted Tweets about climate change from Badlands National Park; called the director of the National Park Service to ask why his staff had released data about the inauguration crowd, which Trump insisted was the largest ever, a lie repeated by his terrified press person.*

- *Trump signs orders advancing the dangerous Keystone XL and Dakota Access Pipelines and cancels a federal conference on the health impacts of climate change.*

- *Conservative legislatures from coast-to-coast are introducing legislation that will criminalize protest, turning traditional civil disobedience into felony crimes, sometimes defined as "economic terrorism."*

Of course, the predicament we find ourselves in is no sudden reversal; no shocking disconnect from the path the country's been pursuing for years, and, in fact, we've been on this road—step by treacherous step—for decades now. A deliberate bipartisan effort has brought us to the point of permanent war, mass incarceration, a hollowed-out economy based on "austerity"—privatization, dismantling social safety nets, crushing unions, liquidating jobs—the relentless attack on public education, the devastation of independent media, the eclipse of the public, and more. There are variations to be sure, and they sometimes matter, but too often these amount to a distinction without a difference. The Republicans offer racist dog-whistles and overt white supremacist policies, for example; the Democrats respond with "diversity" and the optics of multiculturalism, but they do not offer what we need and deserve: a program of racial, economic, and global justice.

This is why no one should rely on the Democratic Party to lead the opposition—the Party is ill-prepared, disinclined, and too wrapped up in every policy and program that got us here.

* * *

But the real, authentic opposition is not starting from scratch either—Black Lives Matter, the latest iteration of the centuries-old Black Freedom Movement, has been a leading voice and a powerful force on the ground for progress and against white supremacist power for years now, exposing the never-ending serial shootings of Black citizens and generating innovative programs for comprehensive revitalization; "undocumented and unafraid" youth have been rising and winning; Standing Rock is here, fighting for environmental justice and Indigenous rights; women are not going back to the Middle Ages; "we're queer/we're here" is on the move; and on and on.

Millions of people are enraged and energized right now; many have acted up and spoken out spontaneously; many more have organized and vowed to resist. And be clear: the best preparation for a determined and serious struggle in the long run is to throw ourselves into the fight to stop the Trump/Pence putsch right now. We must refuse to normalize or accommodate to fascism.

And most important, remember that social movements make social change possible, and social movements always involve building fire from below. Our responsibility is to organize, to act, and to transform both ourselves and our world. Even though there's no ready recipe to follow, in a situation like this one, everyone can dive in and find important work to do.

Here's a start:

Gather! We can only build a more powerful movement from the bottom up. Call a meeting of your fellow workers, your neighbors, your faith community, the folks in your building or on your block; begin with questions:

Where are we, and where should we be heading? What can we do together? Don't get too lost in petitioning power—build your own agency, your own collective power.

Learn to Talk to One Another and Forge Unity!

We have to reframe the conversations, and we need to learn to meet one another across issues, organizations, and histories. We may differ among ourselves on strategy and tactics, but we can learn to unite on fundamental matters of principle. We need to go to the root, find the common ground, and discover and articulate the ethical and moral base of our common struggle.

Build a Social Movement!

We must connect economic justice with racial justice and global justice. We can find joy and purpose in living a life of resistance in these troubled times. We can also find ways to live our lives together in beloved community, against materialism, war, violence, and hierarchy. We must join together solidly, and work to forge an unbreakable collaboration.

Make Sanctuary a Reality!

Create spaces to protect the vulnerable, to resist, and to defend the organizers and the activists. Lay down moral markers that illuminate the threats to our humanity and our collective survival. Live the alternatives.

Educate!

We need to educate ourselves and engage in authentic dialogue with friends and strangers alike—each of us committed to listening with the possibility of being heard, and speaking with the possibility of being changed. Form a reading group and share important books and articles, or a movie-going group, or a pot-luck conversation once a month.

Our challenge is to crack the pretense of normalcy in this political moment, to break the conspiracy of silence by which both establishment political parties, the bought media, and the political class mute public debate. Deep and radical change requires the mobilization of an engaged social movement, and the cooperation of an enlightened political leadership emerging from (or empowered by) that movement.

* * *

When all the trees have been cut down,
when all the animals have been hunted,
when all the waters are polluted,
when all the air is unsafe to breathe,
only then will you discover you cannot eat money.

— Cree Prophecy

To be shocked at the outcome of the presidential election is understandable; but to be shocked and disbelieving a few days (or months) later indicates a lack of understanding about the nature of the country we live in, its terrible unresolved history and its living white supremacist base. To gain your balance, channel some of our foremothers and forefathers. Ella Baker was an organizer and a fighter her whole life; she was the mother of SNCC and a major force in the Civil Rights Movement, and she lived long enough to see many of the gains challenged and set back with the Southern strategy and the rise of the right. Frederick Douglass was born into slavery, freed himself and became a leading intellectual and activist of the Abolitionist movement and an architect of Black Reconstruction, and he lived long enough to witness the Hayes Compromise and the unleashing of white terrorism and the rise of the KKK. What did these great freedom fighters do in the gathering dread and darkness? They got up, dusted themselves off, and set out to organize and fight back. We can do nothing less.

Another world is surely coming—greater equality, socialism, participatory democracy, and peace are within our reach, but nuclear war, work camps and slavery, the crushing of dissent and the shredding of civil liberties are also real possibilities. There are still choices and options, and nothing is guaranteed. Where do we go from here? Chaos or community? Barbarism or socialism?

> *History is literally present in all that we do. It could scarcely be otherwise, since it is to history that we owe our frames of reference, our identities, and our aspirations. And it is with great pain and terror that one begins to realize this. In great pain and terror one begins to assess the history which has placed one where one is and formed one's point of view. In great pain and terror because, therefore, one enters into battle with that historical creation, Oneself, and attempts to recreate oneself according to a principle more humane and more liberating; one begins the attempt to achieve a level of personal maturity and freedom which robs history of its tyrannical power, and also changes history.*

— **James Baldwin**

When slavery was formally abolished in the U.S., the former owners felt aggrieved as if they were the victims of a terrible injustice. Many sought, and some even won, reparations for lost property—unlike the formerly enslaved people (the former "property") who instead of reparations got Black Codes, Jim Crow, regimes of lynch-mob terror, red-lining, mass incarceration, occupying police forces, and more. For those who'd been blithely enjoying their privileges while riding on the backs of others, justice and fairness—equality—is constructed as "oppression." It's not—it is instead a cruel if powerful illusion. But privilege works like that.

Today, young people are leading and building a broad and hopeful movement—the next step in the centuries-old Black Freedom Movement—demanding the end of militarized police targeting and occupying Black people and communities, the creation of decent schools and good jobs, the abolition of mass incarceration, reparations for harm done, and simple justice going forward. Black Lives Matter!

To some privileged people, it's as if a terrible injustice has once again befallen them—and of course it has not. To proclaim that "Jewish Lives Matter" in Germany in the 1930s would have been a good thing—those were the lives being discounted and destroyed; to say that "Palestinian Lives Matter" in Israel now would be to stand on the side of humanity, and the downtrodden and the disposable. And to shout out that Black Lives Matter in the U.S. today is to once more to take the side of humanity. Every city hall and every police precinct should hang a large Black Lives Matter banner over the front door, and then get real about the work needed to bring that slogan authentically to life.

It's our duty to fight; it's our responsibility to win.

PRESIDENT AGENT ORANGE

HERB BOYD

*Herb Boyd is a journalist, activist, teacher who has authored or edited 22 books, including, **Civil Rights: Yesterday & Today**. His articles appear regularly in the New York Amsterdam News. Currently, he teaches at the College of New Rochelle and at City College New York. His latest book is **Black Detroit: A People's History of Self-Determination (2017).***

Interestingly, the same day I received Drs. Haki Madhubuti and Lasana Kazembe's "Call for Papers" under the banner of *Not Our President: New Directions from the Pushed Out, the Others, and the Clear Majority in Trump's Stolen America*, a Gallup Poll, tracking President Donald Trump's approval and disapproval rating cited that only 40 percent of Americans said they approved of the job he was doing, while an overwhelming 55 percent said they disapproved of his performance. This approval-disapproval disparity of 15% was a record low for a president with fewer than 10 days in office.

While we are clearly aware of the relative merit of polls, which are but a momentary snapshot; a temporary barometer of an issue, these results are an indication of the increasingly volatile outrage and protests against the Trump regime—and we have no reservation in defining his administration as such.

The urgency I feel to respond to the editors' request comes in the heat of the recent Grammys and the variety of ways the performers and awardees voiced their displeasure about Trump and the confederacy of dunces surrounding him. Most memorable was the appearance of A Tribe Called Quest, kicking down a wall that symbolized Trump's racism, Islamophobia, and misogynistic tendencies, and rapper Busta Rhymes calling him *"President Agent Orange."*

A cursory scan of the proposed topics offered for contributors to this publication from climate change to the deadly role of White Nationalism are spot on. We must oppose Trumpism and resist the lethal menace that is finding expression with each executive order from his poison pen, with each tweet from this twerp of a leader.

Even before Trump's inauguration in January, I was part of thousands of activists, academics, and alarmed citizens who signed a petition and published full page ads in the New York Times and the Washington Post: "NO! In the name of humanity. We refuse to accept a Fascist America!" Our aim was to prevent him from becoming president, but we were not naïve about this possibility, nor was it to be our last effort to keep his feet to the fire and lend our voices to the millions who were soon in the streets of America, particularly after his executive order to block all refugees and immigrants arriving from seven predominantly Muslim countries.

Lately, we at the Amsterdam News, one of the nation's oldest and largest African American newspapers, have begun our editorials on the front page, declaring *"Make America Great Again—Trump Must Go!"* We intend to keep this going, much in the manner of the former publisher, the late Bill Tatum, did in the paper for nearly three years against then New York City Mayor Ed Koch.

Thus far, we've published three editions, beginning with a reference to the great American patriot Tom Paine. I don't think we overstated our case in reciting Paine's "These are the times that try men's souls." His discontent was aimed at the tyranny of King George III and the grip of British colonialism strangling the possibility of a new nation, for all its inadequacies. We were using Paine's call for resistance, his cry to bolster the morale of the flagging Minutemen to remind Americans of a fresh wave of tyranny taking shape on Pennsylvania Avenue.

As I see it, Trump's authoritarianism very much resembles what the British crown was exacting in the eighteenth century on its colonies.

What the nation is currently experiencing are all the plagues Trump promised, and some. Remember, he promised to repeal Obamacare, well, that process is in motion with the enactment of a budget reconciliation measure by a Republican-led Congress. On the heels of this draconian move, Trump, with a stroke of his pen, approved the construction of the Dakota Access pipeline in defiance of the intense protest from Native Americans and others. This means that the Army Corps of Engineers will grant the final approval to complete the oil pipeline, which is a victory for the developer Energy Transfer Partners and a defeat for environmentalists and the Standing Rock Sioux Tribe.

President Barack Obama often talked about America being a nation of laws, a country bound by the Constitution, but neither of these longstanding institutions is given any recognition by Trump, who seems intent to trample any rule or regulation, whether FCC, IRS, Federal Reserve, EPA, or the Appellate Court that interferes with his egotistical and destructive ends.

And where the reach of his executive order is limited or deficient, he has nominated a gaggle of minions who will follow his iniquitous plans until a particular agency no longer exists. His scheme to demolish education as we know it from the nation's public school system to the common core curriculum is evident when he tapped Betsy DeVos for U.S. Secretary of Education. At the top of her agenda, and she makes no bones about it, is privatization with an unhealthy infusion of vouchers and charter schools, all at the expense of public funds. With Jeff Sessions as the Attorney General, the proverbial new sheriff in town, we can expect no safeguard of our civil and human rights. During his tenure as top cop in Alabama he demonstrated that his allegiance is to the Klan and the alt-right denizens.

Sessions, we are sure, will succumb to whatever his boss demands and refuses to do, right down to the continuing concealment of his tax returns and the refusal to relinquish or allow transparency of his business empire. Trump's Attorney General will not for a moment jeopardize the president's power, despite clear violations of the Constitution, including the emolument clause that forbids him to reap benefits or receive gifts while running the nation. It's inconceivable that Sessions would dare charge the president of constitutional infringements, that one of his executive orders had abrogated due process, ignored the First, and Fourteenth Amendments. In this regard, Sessions is an unwavering loyalist who will stand by his man even if Congress, unlikely, vote to impeach the president.

In effect, white supremacy with the likes of Richard Spencer, Stephen Miller, Sean Spicer, Jared Kushner, and Steve Bannon at Trump's beck and call has been formidably bolstered. To find precedent to such a coterie of misfits and malcontents is to recall Goebbels, Himmler, and other Nazis at the table with Hitler. Not a day passes without another element of repression, arrests, harassment, and outright brutality instigated by Trump and those willing to carry out his orders. To say nothing of the general incompetence and falsehoods (otherwise known as "alternative facts") stated by White House counselor, Kellyanne Conway, promoting the president's daughter's products on TV; and the missteps by Mike Flynn, who as Trump's national security adviser was forced to resign after his imbroglio with the Russian ambassador to the U.S.

We are on the brink of an American Crisis, not at all dissimilar from the one Paine railed against. And while there has been signs of resistance from the Democrats, none more vocal than Sen. Elizabeth Warren, much more gumption and resolve, much more determination to challenge the seemingly undoubtable Trumpede is needed. It doesn't help to learn of the dissension in the ranks of the Democratic National Committee on who's to be at the helm. If we are to keep Trump and his legions at bay we need new vision and certitude among the Democrats as well as a critical mass of disaffected Americans, ready to storm the Trump Towers.

As Paine reminded us, *"Tyranny, like hell, is not easily conquered, yet we have this consolation with us, that the harder the conflict, the more glorious the triumph."* To be sure, a triumph over Trump is not going to be a walk in the park. Even setbacks, as with the recent decision by three judges not to support his ban order, only empowers him to invoke another one, with a renewed chilling effect. His moves to bar certain immigrants could in the long run—should they be forever overturned—back fire if one of them becomes the source of or involved in an terrorist attack. Without a doubt you can hear him bleating and tweeting *"See, I told you so."*

Black Americans, except for those quislings lining up for handouts, are well aware of Trump's history of racism, and no amount of citing Frederick Douglass's name, as if he was still alive, will absolve him from those discriminatory practices. Beyond his unrelenting charge that President Obama wasn't born in the United States, it's been discussed on numerous occasions his refusal of Black tenants to his property and the salacious role he played in the Central Park Five rape case in 1989, spending thousands of dollars on full- page ads in local New York papers to bring back the death penalty and execute the young men, all of whom were later exonerated.

During his campaign for the presidency, he was heard encouraging one of his security people to remove a Black participant and supporter of Black Lives Matter. The next day he said the beating of the protester was justified. "It was absolutely disgusting what he was saying," Trump told reporters. Moreover, Trump was reluctant to denounce Klan leader David Duke, a man he had repudiated repeatedly in 1991. However, that was long ago, and Trump told a reporter that he didn't remember ever meeting or knowing anything about Duke. Clearly, a convenient moment of amnesia.

For him to take umbrage for what someone says is simply ironic given the invectives that promulgate and issue from his mouth. Ever since he began his presidential campaign Trump found a way to humiliate or insult Americans, whether they were Muslims, Mexicans, or the disabled. He was, as one commentator noted, an *"equal opportunity insulter."* No one, especially women, were immune to his innuendoes and indecent remarks, and it reached a fever pitch when he charged that Hillary Clinton was a "nasty woman."

In conclusion, and I am glad to be among the contributors assembled here, and I am confident they will tackle the agenda postulated here, excoriate President Agent Orange where I may not have been more forthcoming or severe. We are living in some perilous times with a man in the Oval Office without a clue on how to run a government, insisting it should be run like a business. And if his record of bankruptcies, corruption, and mismanagement are indicators then we are truly on our way to hell in a handbasket, and with a basket case in charge.

As we proposed in our ads with refusefascism.org, the resistance to the Trump regime must grow to millions, this demagogue must be stopped, and this is not the time to conciliate, accommodate, and certainly not collaborate with his incipient, crypto, neo-fascistic worldview.

Make America Great Again—*Trump Must Go!*

PERSONNEL IS POLICY

MICHAEL DATCHER

Michael Datcher is the author of critically acclaimed, New York Times bestseller Raising Fences. He is co-host of the weekly public affairs news magazine, Beautiful Struggle, on 90.7 FM KPFK in Los Angeles, and an Assistant Professor of English at Loyola Marymount University.

Personnel is policy. This may explain why students were still crying two days after the Electoral College victory of Donald J. Trump.

On Thursday, November 10, 2016, sniffles were audible as I walked into my public intellectual class called the Art of the Essay. The innovative course is a hybrid literature/writing course where students study the writings of public intellectuals (James Baldwin, Claudia Rankine, and Ta-Nehisi Coates during the semester in question) then craft their own literary ideas for public consumption. These socio-politically sophisticated students were keenly aware of the implications of a Trump presidency. In this class of young intellectuals, 14 of the 15 writers were women. A leader among the 14 immediately said, *"Many of my friends didn't go to class Wednesday."* The day after an old white man with old white ideas became president-elect, young white women were too devastated to attend class: they pushed pause on education. What these young women had learned about America heretofore didn't cohere with the plausibility of a critical mass of Americans voting for a proudly racist pussy grabber. Several of the black folk in my inner circle were alarmed at the elections results. Few were surprised. None cried.

Walking While Black in America can give you a unique perspective about your countrymen and countrywomen. Walking into a convenience store while Black. Walking into a faculty meeting while Black. Walking behind a white couple on your way to your car while Black. Walking into your daughter's preschool while Black. Walking on the beach while Black. Walking into an elevator while Black. Walking into your bank while Black. Walking into your neighborhood Thai restaurant while Black. Walking at night to clear your head while Black. Walking at night to clear your head, and passing the passenger side open window of a idling police car, occupied by two officers, who watched you approach through their front window, and whose heads both swivel to follow your Black body with its offensive rhythm and pride and confidence enough to turn your own head to meet their stare, to acknowledge their gaze that doesn't see taxpayer, doesn't see citizen, doesn't see American, because Black skin effaces these socio-political markings and makes the Black body morph into a hazy, fuzzy, blurry black mass of unpredictable probable danger, a perfect manifestation of walking probable cause—while Black.

Walking necessitates intimacy. Ambulatory vulnerability. Experiencing a city on foot, circumscribed by other ambling bodies in close proximity—close enough to touch, or judge or stop and frisk—creates kinship. Even when the kinship is fraught with miscommunication and misanthropy, it is still kinship nonetheless. Similar to how a family's dysfunction doesn't stop a dysfunctional family from being family. Ambulating bodies sharing sidewalks is a kind of quasi-quality-time of poor quality for the broken American family. A time to experience the resultant awkwardness that manifests when you publicly encounter Americans who demonize in private domiciles. Denigrate during dinner.

While lecturing on the intersection of race and power, I asked our 15 young intellectuals: *"By a show of hands, who's ever heard someone in your family, maybe around the dinner table or in causal conversation, say something disparaging about black folks?"* Of the 15 students, 14 hands reluctantly raised. The lone hand that remained holstered belonged to the class's only male student—and African American. This doesn't mean that the vast majority of students who attend the Los Angeles university where I teach come from families that are rabidly racist. In fact, the university has a generally progressive reputation and "the promotion of justice" is one pillar of its tripartite Mission Statement. Along with rigorous academics, this progressive reputation and Mission Statement is what attracts students and their families to the institution. As a result, it is unlikely that the 14 young intellectual who raised their hands came from familial or social circles who would self-define as racist.

The significance of those 14 raised hands lies in how normalized anti-blackness is in America. Normalized enough for it to be part of dinner conversation with the family. A racialized aperitif before the main course. Demonization for dessert. For many families, sitting around dinner tables is a ritual to convey family folkways and mores. Furthermore, breaking break around a table is one of the fundamental socialization processes for children. The parental personnel determines familial policy around dinner table discussions.

One of the great dangers of the Trump presidency is that his personnel decisions will set the table for the discourse and direction for the dysfunctional American Family. President Trump's choice for Attorney General, Jefferson Beauregard Sessions III, provides troubling case study into the vision Mr. Trump has for future American policy. First, it may be generative to explore the past to bring the future into replete focus.

On July 17, 1789, the United States Senate passed (by a 14-to-6 vote) "An Act to Establish Judicial Courts of the United States." Signed into law by President George Washington on September 24, 1789, the Act established the structure and jurisdiction of the federal court system and created the position of Attorney General. On June 22, 1870, President Ulysses S. Grant signed a bill into law called "Act to Establish the Department of Justice." The Act imbued the Attorney General with leadership and power over U.S. Attorneys and all other legal counsel employed by the United States of America. In the modern context, the Attorney General oversees an amalgamation of departments, bureaus, offices and divisions that profoundly impact the lives of Americans, especially people of color, including the F.B.I., Drug Enforcement Agency, Office of Tribal Justice, U.S. Parole Commission, Federal Bureau of Prisons, Office of Privacy and Civil Liberties, Office of U.S. Attorneys, Executive Office for Immigration Review, Criminal Divisions—and the Civil Rights Division.

The civil rights record of Attorney General Jefferson Beauregard Sessions III— America's Top Cop—is so disturbing because Mr. Sessions is also the de facto head of America's Prison Industrial Complex. According to the New Republic, as the U.S. Attorney for the Southern District, Sessions aggressively targeted civil rights workers, who were organizing voter registration drives in Alabama. Sessions charged the three workers with voter fraud, after an investigation of black absentee voters produced only 14 allegedly tampered ballots out of 1.7 million cast in the Alabama's 1984 election.

Career Justice Department official J. Gerald Herbert testified that during a conversation between the two men, Sessions labeled the NAACP and the American Civil Liberties Union as "un-American" and "communist-inspired." Sessions asserted that the two seminal civil rights organizations, "forced civil rights down the throats of people." Furthermore, during his failed nomination hearing as a Reagan-appointee for the U.S. District Court of Alabama, Sessions admitted to making the aforementioned statements and admitted to calling the Voting Rights Act of 1965 "a piece of intrusive legislation"— a comment he stood by during his confirmation hearing.

During the hearing, a black former assistant U.S. Attorney in Alabama, Thomas Figures testified that during a 1981 murder investigation involving the Ku Klux Klan, Sessions was heard commenting to several colleagues that he "used to think the [Klan] was okay" until the ardently anti-marijuana Sessions found out that some Klan members were weed heads. Figures also testified that after Sessions overheard him chastising a white secretary, Sessions walked over to him and said, "Boy… Be careful what you say to white folks."

As a woman with deep roots in Alabama, and a long history with Jeff Sessions, Coretta Scott King had planned to testify at the hearing but was unable to attend. She sent a letter instead, which I'll quote at length because of its significance:

> *The irony of Mr. Sessions' nomination is that, if confirmed, he will be given life tenure for doing with a federal prosecution what the local sheriffs accomplished twenty yeas ago with clubs and cattle prods. Twenty years ago when we marched from Selma to Montgomery, the fear of voting was real, as the broken bones and bloody heads in Selma and Marion bore witness. As my husband wrote, 'it was not just a sick imagination that conjured up the vision of a public official, sworn to uphold the law . . . who callously inflicted repeated brutalities and indignities upon nonviolent Negroes peacefully petitioning for their constitutional right to vote' . . . The actions taken by Mr. Sessions in regard to the 1984 voting fraud prosecutions represent just one more technique used to intimidate black voters and thus deny them this most precious franchise. "*

Undoubtedly, Mrs. King's letter played a significant role in scuttling Mr. Sessions nomination to the District Court. During Mr. Sessions nomination hearing to become Trump's appointee as Attorney General, Senator Elizabeth Warren tried to read the Coretta Scott King's letter on the Senate floor and was silenced by her colleagues for allegedly impugning the reputation of a sitting senator. With a 52-to-47 (almost party-line) vote on Wednesday, February 8, 2017, Jeff Beauregard Sessions III was confirmed as the 84th Attorney General of the United States of America. Ultimately, Sessions is now in charge of the Justice Department's Civil Rights Division.

The Civil Rights Division has an outsized importance for African Americans given our historic civil rights battles, including our ongoing battle for voting rights. Officially, the Civil Rights Division enforces:

> *The Civil Rights Acts; the Voting Rights Act; the Equal Credit Opportunity Act; the Americans with Disabilities Act; the National Voter Registration Act; the Uniformed and Overseas Citizens Absentee Voting Act; the Voting Accessibility for the Elderly and Handicapped Act; and additional civil rights provisions contained in other laws and regulations. These laws prohibit discrimination in education, employment, credit, housing, public accommodations and facilities, voting, and certain federally funded and conducted programs.*

After President Trump signaled that he wanted to scale back funding for the Civil Rights Division and reduce focus of civil rights enforcement, he appointed a man as Attorney General with an aggressive anti-civil rights history, who has personally worked against the very concerns that the Civil Rights Division is charged with enforcing. Some Washington insiders call this "ironic staffing."

Personnel is policy.

On November 10, 2017, that first day of public intellectual class post-election, one student, in particular was very disturbed. Just before class, she had received a call from her distraught sister, who attends another university. The young public intellectual informed our class that her sister got involved in a heated debate with a white male student. A debate that should have probably been stopped by the professor before it escalated. When the public intellectual's sister continued to express concern about women's rights under a Trump presidency, the male student with whom she was arguing said, *"Either you shut up, or I guess I'm going to have to grab you by the pussy."* The professor made the male student leave class—but his words remained—like a grotesque Dysfunctional American Family policy—handed down from the head of the table.

TRUMP: COUP WITHIN A COUP

HOWARD DODSON, JR.

Howard Dodson, Jr. recently served as Director of the Moorland-Spingarn Research Center and Howard University Libraries, and was formerly the long-time director of the Schomburg Center for Research in Black Culture in Harlem (1984-2010).

Seven months into the presidency of Donald J. Trump, partisans and opponents alike are still waiting for him to assume the Presidential identity that goes with his office. Twelve weeks after he was inaugurated as the 45th President of the United States, Donald Trump was still as volatile, abusive, insecure and unpredictable as he was throughout the 2016 Presidential Campaign. His serial propensity for lying and dishonesty, his preference for bluster and bullying over statecraft and diplomacy have all made it impossible for anyone to tell where he really stands on any issue. Promises made throughout the Campaign including commitments to his core constituency are not being kept, despite the flurry of Executive Orders he has signed. And his appointments to his staff and Cabinet have been noteworthy for their inappropriateness for their designated positions. Virtually all are opposed to and dedicated to subverting the missions of the Departments they've been hired to lead. Rather than "drain the swamp," Trump has added his list of "Deplorables" to it — shady, rich and super rich, morally and ethically challenged millionaires and billionaires (more than in any Presidential administration in the history of the United States) and rightwing ideologues who have demonstrated no commitment to America or the needs and aspirations of the American people. Wall Street bankers (Goldman Sachs is the banker of choice), corporate moguls, and white supremacist ideologues have taken hold of the reins of power in America and are turning the little Washington swamp Trump complained about so much into an Okefenokee or Everglades of greed and corruption.

Perhaps the most serious violation of Trump's Campaign promises has been his frontal assaults on the foundational principles of American democracy. His commitment to "Make America Great Again" has been repudiated by the daily evidence he displays of his limited, if not total lack of knowledge of and respect for what the America he was elected to lead is and stands for. America, a nation "of the people, by the people and for the people" is not an America he respects or aspires to help create. America's commitment to "liberty and justice for all" is neither in his playbook nor embraced by him and his swamp-dwelling administration. America, a place of refuge for the "tired," the "poor," the "huddled masses yearning to breathe free" has been rejected by his immigration policies. And America, a nation committed to *equality and justice for all* is not the America he is committed to building or sustaining. President Trump has turned his back on the "general welfare" of the American people, declared many unworthy of American citizenship or respect, and committed America's resources to further enriching the one-percenters he has surrounded himself with and seemingly committed his Presidency to. Donald Trump and his administration have seemingly committed themselves to policies and practices that will likely change the America we have been becoming, forever — something he did promise his supporters he would do. But the change he is giving them and us, is a repudiation of the American ideals and principles that have helped rescue the founding American promise from the clutches of slave holders, white supremacists, racists, sexists homophobic and misogynistic white males over the last two centuries — a rescue mission that set America on the path to becoming a more human, more just, more perfect union.

The Barack Obama Presidential Election Campaign of 2008 and

his subsequent two Presidential administrations were deeply rooted in the human-centered principles and values of the promises of America, not its shortcomings. Obama embraced the high ideals of the Declaration of Independence and the Constitution of the United States of America. These values and principles, not America's history of slavery, colonialism, racism and oppression, have made the United States the envy and democratic ideal of the world. Not just the ideals, but the foundations of American democratic institutional life, have been put at risk by the election of Obama-obsessed Donald Trump.

Barack Obama for America

Barack Obama was and is a firm believer in the ideals, principles and values espoused in the nation's founding creed. A former constitutional law professor at the University of Chicago, Obama is also a firm believer in the principles of democracy. Like many of his predecessors, Obama recognizes the fact that the constitutional document that the founding fathers wrote was not perfect, and as he stated recently what gave it life and meaning was *"We the People,"* you and I. While he is an ardent proponent and defender of the Constitution, Obama acknowledged its imperfections and worked to correct them. He expanded the language of the Declaration of Independence that stated *"All men are created equal"* to include all human beings including women. His concept of American democracy embraced all citizens of the United States — native born or naturalized-- regardless of race, class, gender or religion. Obama also recognized the fact that the Constitution was and is a living document, one that has, through 200+ years of practice, struggle, amendments and judicial rulings, expanded the concepts of American democracy, identity and citizenship to include its diverse racial, ethnic, gender and religious communities and peoples.

The coalition that Obama put together in 2008 and again in 2012 reflected this diversity of the American people and sought to extend the rights and protections of American democracy to them all. His Presidency also extended these rights and protections of American democracy to the disabled as well as members of the LGBTQ community. The

Obama Coalition reflected and affirmed the principles of the American creed and tried to apply them equally to all Americans. Its commitment to equality and justice for all of America's people, however imperfect that commitment was, reflected the diversity, changing ideology and values of an America of the 21st century — one that embraced and celebrated ALL of the American people and sought to create policies and practices to make America a more just, more humane and more equitable nation. The waves of freedom and justice unleashed by the social justice movements of the 1960s, 1970s and 1980s came under the defense and protections of Obama's social justice agenda. The Obama Coalition did not produce the imagined post-racial nirvana many thought was announced by Obama's 2008 election victory. Indeed, Obama's election in 2008 and his reelection in 2012 may very well have been the catalysts that sparked the reemergence and coalescence of a latent white nationalist/white supremacist definition of America and Americans that had lain dormant since the latter stages of the Civil Rights movement. Other factors, were involved, however, in the rise of white nationalism and white supremacy that likely triggered this return to some late 19th and early 20th century racial ideologies as definers of Americans as a nation of white people and America as a white man's country. Foremost among these were the changing demographics of 21st century America itself.

Recent census studies and projections have concluded that the United States, which has been predominantly populated by "white" people throughout its national history is on the road to rapidly becoming a majority non-white minority nation. Two years ago (2015) more than half of all Americans aged 5 years or younger were non-white. (Cohn, 2016) By 2020, the majority of American children under the age of 18 will be minorities — nonwhite people of diverse racial and ethnic backgrounds. It is estimated that by 2044, whites of all ages will no longer make up the majority of the American population according to the U.S. Census Bureau. And by 2016, the U.S. minority population will have increased to 56% of all Americans. Millennials who numbered some 83.1 million people and outnumbered the 75.4 million Baby Boomers are the most racially, ethnically and religiously diverse generation in American history. Americans currently speak over 300 languages. 37 million Americans speak Spanish, and 2.9 million Chinese. These changing demographic trends have and continue to challenge every notion that many white Americans have of who Americans are and what kind of nation America is. (Cohn, 2016; Sanburn, 2015).

Many Americans have yet to accept the notion that Black people and other people of color deserve to be recognized as, or are capable of being, equal to whites. The very concept that Black people can or should be equal to whites is repulsive and threatening to many. Even more troubling is the notion that Black people or people of color could or should lead whites and "their" American nation. This fact, in the case of Barack Obama's Presidency, threatened the very foundations of many white Americans' sense of identity, status and self-worth.

A large percentage of white American voters — 43% in 2008 and 39% in 2012 — were sufficiently persuaded by Barack Obama's intelligence, his commitment to the nation's founding creed and his vision of and for America — to become an organic part of his 2008 and 2012 election coalitions and campaigns. (Monteroo, 2012); (Lopez, Mark and Paul Taylor, 2008). They joined with Americans of diverse non-white racial, ethnic, religious, cultural, gender and otherwise marginalized groups to create the Obama Political Coalition. The combination of the two — a Black man as President and Commander in Chief of the United States and a voting majority of Americans of diverse racial and other backgrounds supporting him-- sent white Americans looking for a savior in 2016. Seventeen Republicans (including a woman and a Black) declared themselves candidates after John McCain and Mitt Romney had failed in 2008 and 2012 respectively. Donald Trump's unorthodox, controversy-filled campaign chased them all from the battlefield and unleashed and legitimized the white nationalist and white supremacist ideas and ideology that had lain dormant so long.

* * *

I don't want to suggest or even leave the impression that white opposition to Barack Obama and his Coalition was based solely on race or racism. But racism was rarely if ever not a contributing motivation or operational factor. The shared racial identities of the majority white Republican opposition masked the fact that the ruling elites — the 1% — used their money, lobbyists, think tanks and other power to manipulate the public, politicians and the political system itself to advance and protect their corporate and capitalist interests at the expanse of the interests, needs and aspirations of the American people — whites as well as others. Karl Rove's 2010 plan to win majorities for Republicans in state legislatures across the country by controlling redistricting through its REDMAP (Redistricting Majority Project) was a major factor. Republicans had previously used the Voting Rights Act to gerrymander voting districts putting as many African Americans as possible into one district thereby leaving the neighboring districts more white and more Republican. Aggressive voter suppression campaigns targeting Blacks, Hispanics and other minority voters were also used to increase Republican electoral prospects.

The Koch Brothers — Charles and David — organized a network of some 300 ultra-wealthy Republican donors who donated a minimum of $100,000/year to the network to elect people who shared and supported their political priorities and ideologies. They spent $707 million in 2012 in support of their candidates and policy priorities including opposition to Obamacare, federal spending, more taxes and environmental regulations. In 2016 they spent $750 million including $250 million to think tanks and policy groups working on their policy issues. These and other initiatives were matched with intensive lobbying to define and shape national policy to reflect the elite Republican economic, political and ideological interests rather than those of the American people, including buying and controlling the peoples' representatives in Congress.

Much has been made of the white workers who supported Donald Trump's candidacy. Much has also been made of the notion that Trump "spoke his mind," challenged the elites on Wall Street and in Washington and identified with the plight of poor, displaced men of the white working class. But the average Trump voter earned an average of $70,000 — considerably more than the average worker's salary. Something more drove white male and female voters to Trump. His attacks on Mexicans, immigrants in general, Muslims, Blacks and other minorities appealed to whites who were feeling threatened by the *"rising tide of color."* Trump's continuing and years' long "Birther Campaign" challenging the citizenship of Barack Obama and therefore the legitimacy of his Presidency, reinforced white views of Obama's illegitimacy simply because he was Black. The outright war Trump declared on virtually everything Barack Obama ever did as President played well to some white's sense of authority and power.

The Trump Coup

Donald Trump's campaign slogan, "Make America Great Again" was widely understood to mean "Make America White Again." No one seems to know when America was ever "white." And Trump never said. Blacks, Hispanics and Native Americans have been part of America's racial and cultural landscape since the colonial period in the United States. Finally, Donald Trump's repeated unsubstantiated pronouncements that Barack Obama's Presidency was a failure and a disaster, punctuated the Republicans' eight- year-long Campaign to insure that Barack Obama failed. The Republican Party, joined by its "Freedom" and "Tea Party" cousins committed themselves to making sure that Barack Obama, a Black man of Black and white — European and African ancestry — did not succeed as an American President.

The vision of America that emerged from the Trump campaign was not one that aligned in any way with the nation's founding creed or its centuries long practice as a place of refuge for *"the tired, the poor, the huddled masses yearning to breathe free."* Trump seems poised to deport undocumented workers who were frequently invited into the U.S. to work at low paying jobs to enhance corporate and capitalist profits. He is committed to blocking access to prospective Muslim immigrants. He has shown no respect for women's reproductive or other rights. And sundry other actions and pronouncements are at variance with America's principles and values. He has seemingly identified his "Americans" as whites, with a preference for white male elites and his gestures at solving the problems of the "inner city" with a retired Black surgeon and a band of Black musicians, athletes and media personalities sound bogus at best.

Donald Trump's victory in the 2016 Presidential campaign as the Republican standard bearer was a coup against the Republican Party carried out in broad daylight for all to see. Republican candidates of every stripe — moderate, conservative, evangelical and even liberal — all fell by the wayside as he ostensibly rejected all ties to Wall Street and the "Washington Swamp" and refused to be directed or managed by the official Republican Party and campaign apparatus. Presenting himself as the candidate of the [white] American people through his campaign slogan *"Make America Great Again,"* Donald Trump seemingly marched to his own drummer, violating Republican and American Democratic party principles, attacking opponents, oppressed American citizens and immigrants alike and distancing himself on the Campaign trail from his 16 Republican opponents and his millionaire and billionaire peers. His surprise victory in November 2016, was seemingly his and his alone — a solid electoral college defeat of his chief rival, Hillary Rodham Clinton and in many respects a repudiation of the Republican and Democratic Parties and everything they seemingly stood for. The election was a Donald Trump coup in which he wrested control of the Republican Party from the Republican Swamp Dwellers of Washington, D.C.

Early on during his road to victory, Donald Trump announced that he would self-fund his Presidential Campaign and not accept money from Wall Street and corporate donors and lobbyists. By December 2016, however, he and his campaign had raised in excess of $350 million. It didn't come from his pocket change or other the loose change the purported billionaire had laying around Trump Tower or his Mar-a-Lago residence. Technically, his most critical individual support did not come from Wall Street. It came from one of the richest CEO's in the country — Robert Mercer, the head of the Renaissance Technologies and Long Island Hedge Fund mogul, Robert Mercer and his ultra conservative daughter, Rebekah Mercer. They came at a critical time in the last stages of the Trump Campaign with more than money. They gave Trump big money — and a unique team of largely white nationalist rescuers, armed with alt=right polling technology and their online propaganda campaign apparatus. (Confessore, 2016; Mayer, 2017).

* * *

The Coup Within Trump's Coup

Paul Manafort served as Campaign Chair and Corey Lewandowski, Campaign Manager through the eve of the Convention. But in June, Trump fired Lewandowski and shortly afterward, Manafort came under investigative scrutiny because of his business dealings with Russia and the Ukraine. Into the vacuum stepped Rebekah Mercer with Mercer people and other gifts that she believed could lead Trump to victory. She used the money to negotiate a change in Campaign leadership that would effectively put Robert Mercer's people in control of Trump's campaign and, if he won, the American Presidency. Robert Mercer had been looking for a candidate to carry his agenda since the Republican primaries. Initially, he backed Ted Cruz for the Republican nomination and continued to do so until he dropped out in June. Stephen Bannon, a right wing, Republican and Goldman Sachs alum, convinced Robert Mercer that Trump could win. The Mercer-supported PAC that had underwritten Cruz's campaign had been headed by Kellyanne Conway. She was detailed to the Trump Campaign initially to help him deal with "women's issues". When Manafort resigned, Conway was made campaign manager, the first woman to hold the position in a major Presidential Campaign. Stephen Bannon, another Robert Mercer acolyte, at Rebekah's insistence, was named Chief Executive of the Campaign on Manafort's departure, effectively putting him in charge of election and post- election agenda-setting. Bannon is largely credited with leading Trump's deeply troubled campaign to victory. (Mayer, 2017).

Stephen Bannon had been on the Robert Mercer payroll since at least 2012 — serving as Robert's de facto political adviser, negotiating a $10 million deal between Mercer and Andrew Breitbart that gave Mercer part ownership of Andrew's alt-right Breitbart News Service. When Breitbart, 43, died of a heart attack nine months later, Bannon became Chairman of Breitbart News. Bannon also convinced Robert Mercer to invest in Cambridge Analytica, an alternative polling outfit and purported propaganda apparatus that its owners claim can change individual voting behavior. A year before he joined Trump's staff, Bannon had described himself as Trump's "de-facto campaign manager" because of the positive coverage he had given Trump through Breitbart News (Bouie, 2017). It was a core part of Trump's legitimacy with many conservative Republicans. During his tenure at Breitbart, Bannon was politically aligned with Jeff Sessions and Steve Miller in Republican efforts to block passage of Barack Obama's comprehensive immigration bill. Miller and Bannon would also author the ill-fated Muslim ban Executive order, a high priority on their Trump agenda. (Mayer, 2017).

A third Mercer surrogate, David Bossie, was named Deputy Campaign Manager. Bossie had, with Robert Mercer support, initiated the 2010 Citizens United lawsuit that resulted in the controversial Supreme Court ruling that effectively removed all limits on how much money corporations and nonprofit organizations can give to political-action committees.

This Mercer rescue team — Bannon, Bossie and Conway — coupled with Rebekah Mercer, who served on the Executive Committee of Trump's Transition Team, and Steve Miller, an alt-right idealogue who had become an advisor to Trump during the Campaign, have shaped Trump's post-election agenda. (Harkinson, 2016).

For a time, it had appeared as though the Mercer/Bannon-led coup within the Trump coup was working. Bannon and his right-wing partner in crime Steven Miller drafted the doom and gloom view of America that Trump presented in his Inaugural Address. But the clearest manifestation of the coup came in the selection of Trumps administrative and staff leadership. Bannon's self-professed agenda of "deconstructing the administrative state" — which is Bannon- speak for destroying the federal government — was most directly expressed in Trump's choices to head major government agencies and programs. With the exception of the military and certain fiscal management and security agencies, virtually all of the individuals chosen to lead federal Departments in Trump's government were people who were ideologically opposed to their existence and committed to outsourcing or "deconstructing" them. Bannon and Steven Miller also took the lead in drafting Trump's other signature Executive Orders. Announced with great fanfare, they called for, promised or authorized studies that would suggest that Trump was acting on some of his myriad Campaign promises. The Muslim travel ban (twice stymied by the courts) was there. So was the deportation of illegal aliens and the Wall. One order sought to reverse Obama's "Clean Power Plan", part of his global warming initiative. High on the list was one designed to eviscerate the Affordable Care Act. Others were extremely big-business friendly — approval of the Obama vetoed the Keystone XL and Dakota Access pipelines; a halt on regulations of the U.S. financial system; and a revocation of the Obama authored federal contracting orders.

Bannon seemingly reached too far, however, when he had Trump sign an Executive Order putting him on the National Security Council without Trump's knowledge or approval. In addition, Bannon was getting too much press for Trump's liking. He was especially perturbed that Bannon appeared on the cover of TIME Magazine and was being credited with making Trump. Stories and comedic stunts about "President Bannon" suggesting Trump is just Bannon's puppet, have also drawn The Donald's ire. (Chang, 2017). When Trump removed him from the National Security Council position, Rebekah Mercer reportedly had to intervene to keep Bannon from resigning his position as the Chief Strategist of the Donald Trump administration. His ouster was reportedly orchestrated by Jared Kushner, Trump's son-in-law and Senior Advisor to the President. Kushner and his wife (Trump's daughter), Ivanka, are the most trusted pillars of "Team Trump", that incestuous and internecine center of Trump power at the White house and in Trump's administration. Other people hold larger titles and positions than Jared and Ivanka but Trump has, throughout his campaign trusted Ivanka, Jared and his family's opinion second only to his own. His family has provided whatever grounding and stability the Trump political journey has travelled. Though officially only working in an advisory capacity, Kushner has amassed an impressive portfolio of duties and responsibilities in the Trump administration that, at an operational level, superceded Bannon's. Bannon had begun to realize this and was not a happy camper. With Ivanka moving into the West Wing as a volunteer employee, additional power shifts in the White House are likely to continue. The struggle for power over the definition of the Trump Presidential agenda continues.

In the meantime, opposition to Trump's anti-American agenda is still alive and well in America. Or, I should say, the majority of American's have never embraced the white nationalist agenda embraced and promoted by Stephen Bannon and exploited by Donald Trump. The majority of American's — by 3.5 million voted for Hillary Clinton. They are still very much committed to the principles and values articulated and embraced by Obama and the Obama Coalition. At no time was this more obvious than on the occasion of the "Women's March on Washington" which took place on January 14, 2017, the day after Trump was sworn-in as the 45th President of the United States.

References:

Bouie, J. (2017, February 6). Government by white nationalism is upon us. Online: slate.com/articles/news_and_politics/cover_story/2017/02/government_by_white_na-tionalism_is_upon_us.html

Carter, P. (2017, February 24). The Trump administration's not so-benign neglect. Online: slate.com/articles/news_and_politics/politics/2017/02/while_we_re_watch-ing_the_scandals_trump_is_dismantling_the_federal_government.html

Chang, C. (2017, February). President Bannon is starting to get on Donald Trump's nerves. *The New Republic Magazine*. Online: newrepublic.com/minutes/140437/presi-dent-steve-bannon-starting-get-donald-trumps-nerves

Confessore, N. (2016, August 18). How one family's deep pockets helped reshape Don-ald Trump's campaign. *The New York Times*. Online: nytimes.com/2016/08/19/us/poli-tics/robert-mercer-donald-trump-donor.html?_r=0

Cohn, D. (2016, June 22). It's official: Minority babies are the majority among the na-tion's infants, but only just. Pew Research Fact Tank. Online: pewresearch.org/fact-tank/2016/06/23/its-official-minority-babies-are-the-majority-among-the-nations-infa nts-but-only-just

Gans, Herbert J. (2017, February 13). This is how the republican party plans to destroy the federal government. *The Nation*. Online: thenation.com/article/this-is-how-the-re-publican-party-plans-to-destroy-the-federal-government

Harkinson, J. (2016, December 14). Trump's newest senior advisor seen as white na-tionalist Ally. *Mother Jones*. Online: motherjones.com/politics/2016/12/trumps-newest-senior-adviser-seen-ally-white-nationalists

Harkinson, J. (2017, January 30). The dark history of the white house aide who crafted trump's muslim ban. *Mother Jones*. Online: motherjones.com/politics/2017/01/stephen-bannon-miller-trump-refugee-ban-islamophobia-white-nationalist

Mayer, J. (2017, March 27). The reclusive hedge-fund tycoon behind the Trump presi-dency. *The New Yorker*. Online: newyorker.com/magazine/2017/03/27/the-reclusive-hedge-fund-tycoon-behind-the-trump-presidency

Sunburn, J. (2015, June 25). U.S. steps closer to a future where minorities and the majority. *Time*. Online: time.com/3934092/us-population-diversity-census

Toronto, Ontario, Canada. November 19, 2016. Hundreds of Canadians take part in a massive protest against American President-elect Donald Trump at Nathan Philips Square.

TRUMP'S WAR ON DANGEROUS MEMORY AND CRITICAL THOUGHT

HENRY A. GIROUX

Henry A. Giroux is a Contributing Editor for Tikkun magazine and the McMaster University Professor for Scholarship in the Public Interest and The Paulo Freire Distinguished Scholar in Critical Pedagogy. His most recent books include: **Dangerous Thinking in the Age of the New Authoritarianism** *(2015), coauthored with Brad Evans, and* **Disposable Futures: The Seduction of Violence in the Age of Spectacle** *(2015), and* **America at War with Itself** *(2016). His website is henryagiroux.com*

The ideal subject of totalitarian rule is not the convinced Nazi or the dedicated communist, but people for whom the distinction between fact and fiction, true and false, no longer exists.

— Hannah Arendt

People living in the United States have entered into one of the most dangerous periods of the 21st century. President Donald Trump is not only a twisted caricature of every variation of economic, political, educational, and social fundamentalism, he is the apogee of an increasingly intolerant and authoritarian culture committed to destroying free speech, civil rights, women's reproductive freedoms, and all vestiges of economic justice and democracy.

Trump is the fascist shadow that has been lurking in the dark since Nixon's Southern Strategy. Authoritarianism has now become viral in America, pursuing new avenues to spread its toxic ideology of bigotry, cruelty, and greed into every facet of society. Its legions of "alt-right" racists, misogynists, and xenophobic hate-mongers now expose themselves publicly, without apology, knowing full well that they no longer have to use code for their hatred of all those who do not fit into their white-supremacist and ultra-nationalist script.[1]

Trump's victory makes clear that the economic crisis and the misery it has spurred has not been matched by an ideological crisis— a crisis of ideas, education, and values. Critical analysis and historical memory have given way to a culture of spectacles, sensationalism, and immediacy.[2] Dangerous memories are now buried in a mass bombardment of advertisements, state sanctioned lies, and a political theater of endless spectacles. The mainstream media is now largely an adjunct of the entertainment industries and big corporations. Within the last 40 years training has taken the place of critical education, and the call for job skills has largely replaced critical thinking. Without an informed public, there is no resistance in the name of democracy and justice; nor is there a model of individual and collective agency rising to such an occasion. Of course, power is never entirely on the side of domination, and in this coming era of acute repression, we will have to redefine politics, reclaim the struggle to produce meaningful educational visions and practices, find new ways to change individual and collective consciousness, take seriously the need to engage in meaningful dialogue with people left out of the political landscape, and overcome the factionalism of single-issue movements in order to build broad based social movements.

Manufactured ignorance erases histories of repression, exploitation, and revolts. What is left is a space of fabricated absences that makes it easy, if not convenient, to forget that Trump is not some eccentric clown offered up to the American polity through the deadening influence of celebrity and consumer culture. State and corporate sponsored ignorance produced primarily through the disimagination machines of the mainstream media and public relations industries in diverse forms now function chiefly to erase selected elements of history, disdain critical thought, reduce dissent to a species of fake news, and undermine the social imagination. How else to explain the recent Arkansas legislator who is pushing legislation to ban the works of the late historian Howard Zinn? How else to explain a culture awash in game shows and Reality TV programs? How else to explain the aggressive attack by extremists in both political parties on public and higher education? Whitewashing history is an urgent matter, especially for the Trump administration, which has brought a number of white supremacists to the center of power in the United States.[3]

The great novelist, Javiar Marias, captures in a recent interview why memory matters, especially as a resource for understanding the present through the lens of the past. He writes:

> *I do not know what I might say to an American young person after Trump's election. Probably that, according to my experience with a dictatorship – I was 24 when Franco died – you can always survive bad times more than you think you can when they start, when "thus bad begins." Though the predictions are terrible, I suppose we must all wait and see what Trump does, once he is in office. It looks ominous, indeed. And [Vice President Mike] Pence does not seem better, perhaps even worse. It is hard to understand that voters in the United States have gone against their own interests and have decided to believe unbelievable things. One of the most ludicrous interpretations of Trump's victory is that he represents the poor, the oppressed, the people "left behind." A multimillionaire, and a very ostentatious one to boot? A man who surrounds himself with gilded stuff? A guy whose favorite sentence is, "You're fired!"? A bloke who has scorned Blacks, Mexicans, women, and of course, Muslims in general? He is the elite that he is supposed to fight. Indeed, it is a big problem that nowadays too many people (not only Americans, I'm afraid) don't know anything about history, and therefore cannot recognize dangers that are obvious for the elder ones (those with some knowledge of history, of course, be it first- or second-hand).[4]*

As Marias suggests, historical legacies of racist oppression and dangerous memories can be troublesome for the neo-fascist now governing American society. This was made clear in the backlash to Ben Carson's

claim that slaves were immigrants, Trump's insistence that all Black communities are crime-ridden, impoverished hellholes, and Education Secretary Betsy DeVos's assertion that historically Black colleges and
universities were "pioneers of school choice."[5] Memories become dangerous when exposing this type of ideological ignorance aimed at rewriting
history so as to eliminate its fascist and poisonous legacies. This is particularly true of the genocidal brutality waged against Native Americans and
Black slaves in the United States and its connection to the memory of
Nazi genocide in Europe and the disappearance of critics of fascism in
Argentina and Chile in the 1970s.

Dangerous memories are eliminated by political reactionaries in
order to erase the ugliness of the past and to legitimate America's shop
worn legacy of exceptionalism with its deadening ideology of habitual optimism, one that substitutes a cheery, empty Disney-like dreamscape for
any viable notion of utopian possibility.[6] The Disney dreamscape evacuates
hope of any meaning while attempting to undercut a radical utopian element in the conceptual apparatus of hope that speaks to the possibility
of a democratic future very different from the authoritarian present. Jelani
Cobb is right in insisting that *"the habitual tendency to excise the most tragic
elements of history creates a void in our collective understanding of what has
happened in the past and, therefore, our understanding of the potential for
tragedian in the present."*[7] The revival of historical memory as a central political strategy is crucial today given that Trump's white supremacist policies not only echo elements of a fascist past, they also point to the need
to recognize as Paul Gilroy has observed "how elements of fascism appear
in new forms," especially as "the living memory of the fascist period
fades."[8] What historical memory makes clear is that subjectivity and
agency are the material of politics and offer the possibility of creating
spaces in which "the domestic machinery of inscriptions and invisibility"
can be challenged.[9] Catherine Clement is right in arguing that *"Somewhere every culture has an imaginary zone for what it excludes and it is that
zone we must try to remember today."*[10] Historical and dangerous memories
inhabit that zone in today's neo-fascist social order.

While it would be irresponsible to underestimate Trump's embrace of neo-fascist ideology and policies, he is not solely answerable for the long legacy of authoritarianism that took on a frontal assault with the election of Ronald Reagan in 1980. This neoliberal attack was later embraced in the Third Way politics of the Democratic Party, its expansion of the mass incarceration state, and solidified under the anti-democratic, war on terror, permanent war policies of the Bush-Cheney and Obama administrations. During this period, democracy was sold to the bankers and big corporations. Whistleblowers were sent to prison. The financial elite and the CIA tortures were given the green light by the Obama administration that they could commit the gravest of crimes and act with impunity. This surge of repression was made possible mostly through the emergence of a savage neoliberalism, a ruthless concentration of power by the ruling classes, and an aggressive ideological and cultural war aimed at undoing the social contract and the democratic, political and personal freedoms gained in the New Deal and culminating in the civil rights and educational struggles of the 1960s.

Trump's unapologetic authoritarianism has prompted Democratic Party members and the liberal elite to position themselves as the only model of organized resistance in such dark times. It is difficult not to see such moral outrage and faux pas resistance as both comedic and hypocritical in light of these centrist liberals have played in the last forty years—subverting democracy and throwing minorities of class and color under the bus. As Jeffrey St. Clair observes, *"Trump's nominal opponents,"* the Democrats Party are *"encased in the fatal amber of their neoliberalism"*[11] and they are part of the problem and not the solution. Rather than face up to their sordid history of ignoring the needs of workers, young people, and minorities of class and color, the Democratic Party acts as if their embrace of a variety of neoliberal political and economic policies along with their support of a perpetual war machine had nothing to do with paving the way for the election of Donald Trump. Trump represents the transformation of politics into a reality TV show and the belief that the worth of a candidate can only by judged in terms of a blend of value as an entertainer and an advertisement for casino capitalism.[12] Chris Hedges gets it right in revealing such hypocrisy for what it is worth – a carnival act. He writes:

> *Where was this moral outrage when our privacy was taken from us by the security and surveillance state, the criminals on Wall Street were bailed out, we were stripped of our civil liberties and 2.3 million men and women were packed into our prisons, most of them poor people of color? Why did they not thunder with indignation as money replaced the vote and elected officials and corporate lobbyists instituted our system of legalized bribery? Where were the impassioned critiques of the absurd idea of allowing a nation to be governed by the dictates of corporations, banks and hedge fund managers? Why did they cater to the foibles and utterings of fellow elites, all the while blacklisting critics of the corporate state and ignoring the misery of the poor and the working class? Where was their moral righteousness when the United States committed war crimes in the Middle East and our militarized police carried out murderous rampages? What the liberal elites do now is not moral. It is self-exaltation disguised as piety. It is part of the carnival act.*[13]

The production of dangerous memories and critical knowledge and the democratic formative cultures they enable must become central to resisting the armed ignorance of the Trump disimagination machine. While such knowledge is the precondition for militant resistance, it is not enough. A critical consciousness is the precondition of struggle but is only the starting point for resistance. What is also needed is a bold strategy and social movement capable of shutting down this neo-fascist political machine at all levels of government through general strikes, constant occupation of the political spaces and public spheres under the control of the new authoritarians, and the creation of an endless wave of educational strategies and demonstrations that make clear and hold accountable the different ideological, material, psychological, and economic registers of fascism at work in American society. This is a time to study, engage in critical dialogues, develop new educational sites, support and expand the alternative media, and fight back collectively. It will not be easy to turn the tide, but it can happen, and there are historical precedents.

The main strategies of change and political agency, in part, have to focus on both the young and those most vulnerable to the dictates of neo-fascism. Young people, workers, and those now considered disposable, especially, are the driving force of the future and we have to both learn from them, support them, contribute where possible, and join in their struggles. At the same time, as Robin D.G. Kelley argues in his *Boston Review* article, After Trump, *"we cannot build a sustainable movement without a paradigm shift. Stopgap, utilitarian alliances to stop Trump aren't enough. … So where do we go from here? If we really care about the world, our country, and our future, we have no choice but to resist."* [14] This would also suggest building up unions again and putting their control in the hands of workers; working to build sanctuary cities and institutions that would protect those considered the enemies of white supremacy – immigrants, Muslims, Blacks, and those others considered disposable. Politics has to be revived at the local and state levels, especially given the control of 56 percent of state legislatures by right-wing Republicans. There is also a need to make education central to the formation and expansion of study groups throughout the country and to further a public pedagogy of justice and democracy through the alternative media and when possible in the mainstream media. Central to the latter task is expanding both the range of dialogue regarding how oppression works focusing not merely on economic structures but also the ways it functions ideologically, psychologically (as Wilhelm Reich once argued), and spiritually as Michael Lerner has pointed out in his book, *The Left Hand of God: Taking Back our Country from the Religious Right.* [15]

It is not enough for progressives and others to examine the objective forces and underlying conditions that have pushed so many people to give up on politics, undercut acts of solidarity, and dismantle any viable notion of hope in the future. It is also crucial to understand the crippling emotional forces and psychological narratives that cripple them from the inside out.

It is worth repeating that at the core of any strategy to resist the further descent of the United States into authoritarianism, progressives must recognize that stopping Trump without destroying the economic, political, educational and social conditions which produced him will fail. In part a successful resistance struggle must be both comprehensive and at the same time embrace a vision that is as unified as it is democratic. Instead of reacting to the horrors and misery produced by capitalism, it is crucial to call for its end while supporting a notion of democratic socialism that speaks to the needs of those who have been left out of the discourse of democracy under the financial elite. At stake here is the need for both a language of critique and possibility, a rigorous analysis of the diverse forces of oppression and a discourse of educated hope. Such a task is both political and pedagogical. Not only do existing relations of power have to be called into question, but notions of neoliberal commonsense learning have to be disconnected from any democratic sense of political agency and notion of civic literacy. As Michael Lerner insightfully observes, rather than engaging in a politics of shaming, progressives have to produce a discourse in which people can recognize their problems and the actual conditions that produce them.[16] This is not just a political but a pedagogical challenge in which education becomes central to any viable notion of resistance. Making education central to politics means the left will have to remove itself from the discourse of meritocracy that often is used to dismiss and write off those who hold conservative, if not reactionary, views. Not doing so only results in a discourse of shaming and a self-indulgent congratulatory stance on the part of those who occupy progressive political positions. The hard political and pedagogical work of changing consciousness, producing new modes of identity, desires, and values conducive to a democracy doesn't stop with the moral high ground often taken by liberals and other progressives. The right-wing knows how to address matters of self-blame and anger whereas the left and progressives dispense with the pedagogical challenges posed by those vulnerable groups caught in the magical thinking of reactionary ideologies.[17]

While it is crucial to address the dramatic shifts economically and politically that have produced enormous anger and frustration in American society, it is also important to address the accompanying existential crisis that has destroyed the self-esteem, identity, and hopes of those considered disposable and those whom Hillary Clinton shamelessly called a *"basket of deplorables."* The ideological mix of untrammeled individualism, self-reliance, a culture of fear, and a war against all ethic has produced both a profound sense of precarity and hopelessness among not only immigrants, poor people of color, but also among working class whites who feel crushed by the economy and threatened by those deemed other as well as demeaned by so called elites.

Resistance will not be easy and has to take place on multiple fronts while at the same time enabling a view of politics that understands how a new class of financial scavengers operates in the free flow of a global space that has no national allegiances, no respect for the social contract, and exhibit a degree of power that is unparalleled in its ability to exploit, produce massive inequality, destroy the planet, and accelerate human suffering across and within national boundaries. Resistance is no longer an option, it is now a matter of life or death. The lights are going out on democracy across the globe and the time to wake up from this nightmare is now. There are no guarantees in politics, but there is no politics that matters without hope, that is, educated hope. This is not merely a call for a third political party, progressives need to create a new politics and new social and political formations. For instance, instead of mounting resistance through a range of single issue movements, it is important to bring such movements together as part of a broad-based political formation.

Any vision for this movement must reject the false notion that capitalism and democracy are synonymous. The crisis of democracy has reached its tipping point, and once again the possibilities for reclaiming the ideals and practices of democratic socialism seem capable of moving a generation of young people and others to act. Under the reign of Trump, the words of Frederick Douglass ring especially true:

> *If there is no struggle, there is no progress. ... This struggle may be a moral one; or it may be a physical one; or it may be both moral and physical; but it must be a struggle. Power concedes nothing without a demand. It never did and it never will."*[18]

Trump's election is surely a tragedy for democracy and a triumph for neo-fascism and it must be challenged and stopped on a variety of levels. Yet, making clear Trump's anti-democratic ideology and practices will not put an end to the current stage of neo-fascism in the United States, especially when memory no longer makes a claim on our understanding of the past. Trump's election has unleashed a brand of savage capitalism that not only has and will continue to have horrible consequences, but is deeply rooted in a mode of historical and social amnesia that eliminates its relationship to an authoritarian past. Memory loses its role as a vehicle of liberation when policies that produce savage modes of austerity, inequality, racism, and contempt for public goods become frozen in historical time and consciousness and as such become normalized. Under such circumstances, organized structures of misrecognition define and legitimate memory as a threat.

Memory, reason and thoughtfulness have to awake from the narcotizing effects of a culture of spectacle, consumerism, militarism, and the celebration of unchecked self-interests. A society that enshrines the war of all against all, elevates self-interest as its highest ideal, reduces responsibility to a solely individual undertaking, makes distrust a virtue, and turns love and compassion into a pathology points to a social order that has lost its memory of self-worth, dignity, justice, and compassion. Evil in politics is no longer a figment of the past but a present day reality enshrined in the ethos of neoliberalism. The body of democracy is on life support and the wounds now being inflicted upon it are too alarming to either ignore or normalize.

Notes:

[1]See, for instance, Ned Resnikoff, Rep. Steve King: 'We can't restore our civilization with somebody else's babies.' *ThinkProgress* (March 12, 2017). Online: thinkprogress.org/steve-king-white-nationalist-tweet-5f43c687902a#.uh1yf1p8m. Also, see Chris Hedges, "The March of Death," *Truthdig* (March 12, 2017). Online: truthdig.com/report/item/the_dance_of_death_20170312

[2]I take this up in great detail in Henry A. Giroux, *America at War with Itself*, (San Francisco: City Lights Books, 2017).

[3]See, for instance, Emily Bazelon, Department of Justification. *The New York Times*, Feb. 28, 2017 Online: nytimes.com/2017/02/28/magazine/jeff-sessions-stephen-bannon-justice-department.html

[4]Gregg LaGambina interviews Javier Marías, The World Is Never Just Politics: A Conversation with Javier Marías. *Los Angeles Review of Books*, (February 9, 2017). Online: lareviewofbooks.org/article/conversation-javier-marias

[5]On DeVos's incompetency and racist understanding of history, see Anthony Dimaggio, "DeVos and the 'Free Lunch' Flimflam: Orwell, Neofeudalism, and the Destruction of the Welfare State," *Counterpunch* (March 7, 2017). Online: counterpunch.org/2017/03/07/devos-and-the-free-lunch-flimflam-orwell-neofeudalism-and-the-destruction-of-the-welfare-state

[6]Jelani Cobb, "Ben Carson, Donald Trump, and the misuse of American history," *The New Yorker* (March 8, 2017). Online: newyorker.com/news/daily-comment/ben-carson-donald-trump-and-the-misuse-of-american-history
[7]Ibid., Jelani Cobb.

[8]Paul Gilroy, *Against Race: Imagining Political Culture Beyond the Color Line*, (Cambridge: The Belknap Press of Harvard University Press, 2000), pp. 145-146

[9]Joao Biehl, *Vita: Life in a Zone of Social Abandonment* (Los Angeles: University of California Press, 2005), p. 10.

[10]Cited in Cited in Helene Cixous and Catherine Clement, *The Newly Born Woman*, trans, Betsy Wing Theory and History of Literature Series, vol 24 (Minnesota: University of Minnesota Press, 1986), p. ix.

[11]Jeffrey St. Clair, "Fools on the hill: Trump and Congress," *Counterpunch*, March 3, 2017 Online: counterpunch.org/2017/03/03/fools-on-the-hill-trump-and-congress

[12]The classic commentary on politics as show business can be found in Neil Postman, *Amusing Ourselves to Death: Public Discourse in the Age of Show Business*, (New York, NY: Penguin Books, 1985, 2005).

[13]Chris Hedges, "Donald Trump's Greatest Allies Are the Liberal Elites," *Truthdig*, (March 7, 2017) Online: truthdig.com

[14]Robin D. G. Kelley, "After Trump," *Boston Review* (November 15, 2016). Online: bostonreview.net/forum/after-trump/robin-d-g-kelley-trump-says-go-back-we-say-fight-back

[15]Michael Lerner, *The Left Hand of God: Taking Back our Country from the Religious Right* (New York: HarperOne, 2007).

[16]This issue is taken up in great detail in Michael Lerner, "Overcoming Trump-ism: A New Strategy for Progressives," *Tikkun* (May 16, 2017). Online: tikkun.org/nextgen/overcoming-trump-ism-a-new-strategy-for-progressives.

[17]Ibid., Lerner, "Overcoming Trump-ism"

[18]Cited in Frederick Douglass, "West India Emancipation" speech at Canandaigua, New York on August 3, 1857. Online: blackpast.org/1857-frederick-douglass-if-there-no-struggle-there-no-progress#sthash.8Eoaxpmo.dpuf

THE WEAKNESS OF THE U.S. PRESIDENCY AND THE IRRELEVANCE OF DONALD TRUMP

EDMUND W. GORDON, Elder

Edmund W. Gordon's career spans professional practice, minister, clinical and counseling psychologist, research scientist, author, editor, and professor. Gordon was recognized as a preeminent scholar of African-American studies when he was awarded the 2011 Dr. John Hope Franklin Award. He is author of **Pedagogical Imagination: A Conceptual Memoir**, a trilogy on psychology, educational leadership, and social action.

There is no difficulty for me in understanding the election of Donald Trump to the office of President of the United States. It can be argued that the position of President of the U.S. has been stripped of much of its power, as is evident in the greater use of executive orders by both President Bush and President Obama. In the eight years of each of these administrations, the Chief Executive's power to lead legislative action had been restrained, albeit for different reasons. Bush may have lost the respect and confidence of his party, while Obama may have never had the respect nor the support of his party. Even when the Congress was controlled by Democrats, Obama had to severely compromise his legislative program. In his later years in office, the Republican controlled congress did not support his program and greatly curtailed his power to act, some of us feel because members did not want to see a Black man succeed as President.

In the case of Bush, it may have been significant changes in the political economy of the nation and shifts in the seat of control of the corporate capitalist interests that determine federal and state economic policy decisions, along, of course, with problems in differences in perspective within the Republican party. For Obama, the impact of corporate capital controlling federal governance was, many of us think, combined with racism.

It appears that the political system simply refused to take leadership from even enlightened Black leadership. Two of our country's most respected journalists, David Brooks and Paul Krugman, each writing independently for the New York Times, gave Obama high marks for his intelligence and competence in the office. Krugman ranks Obama as one of the most able persons to have occupied the White House. The head of the U.S. Senate openly stated his intent to immobilize Obama as President, or to deny him a second term.

Following the logic of the honorable Richard Gordon Hatcher, whom the U.S. political system permitted to be elected first Black Mayor of Gary, Indiana, by the time of the election of Obama to the office of the President of the U.S.A., that office was either powerless or no longer considered to be of significant importance. According to Hatcher, then writing in Freedomways Magazine in the late 1970s, he, Hatcher, was permitted to run for the office of Mayor and occupy it only after the office had been stripped of its authority and power. Hatcher reported that he felt that he had the power to make minor appointments, to influence inconsequential policy decisions, and to make decisions concerning modest budget items. He reported feeling powerless to impact or control issues that were then being settled at the level of state or national government, if not made in national or international corporate capital offices. The political power structure seemed to care little about who occupied the position of Mayor of Gary, by then a city in great decline. Thatcher felt that he was permitted to go through these motions as chief executive, but what he actually controlled was relatively miniscule. Fiscal policy and political decision control had been stripped from the nation's cities, and Gary was a prime example of the decline of such power in the nation's cities. National urban city decline followed, as did growth in the representation by people of color in urban city politics. For the prime shakers and movers there was simply not enough to be bothered. This pattern continued, extended across the nation to national politics, and reached a peak with the election of Barack Obama to a relatively neutered presidency of the nation. Where even with the presence of many of the symbols of power, he was rendered relatively powerless, first by the members of his own party, when they controlled congress, and rendered impotent by the republican congress and a national political economy that I feel was now under the control of a global political economy that is controlled by internationally based corporate capital - an arena in which Russia under Putin's leadership, apparently some of Trump's cronies, China, possibly India and potentially South Africa appear to me to be trying to establish their positions. In that view of the world, the presidency of the United States may appear to be powerless and for someone who is thought of and also ran—a nobody. Under that view of the world, I can see people with bigger fish to catch agreeing that they can let a person of color, or a White person lacking competence, or a clear compass by which to fly, occupy the position.

I concede that I may have had too much wine for dinner, but how else do we explain the outcome of the contest in the Republican party for its 2016 nomination for the party's candidate for president. We can begin with the pool from which they were to select a candidate. I could not get excited by anyone in that pool, save Jed Bush, who at least appeared competent. But for good or bad reasons, it was clear early on that he was not going to be a serious contender. I think that it was an insult to people of color that an unprepared but otherwise accomplished Black physician was in the pool, but clearly out of his depth. Mr. Trump easily and quickly became front runner, with the Republican Party Leadership apparently unable to stop him, despite the fact that the party rules were designed to protect the party from permitting the nomination process from getting out of control. As I watched that process, I was convinced that the action proceeded by the intent of at least a powerful few. There is no way, in my estimate, that competent people in the know and supposedly in control did not understand the latent power of the mixed bag of Trump supporters, the nature of his appeal, and the hollowness yet destructiveness of his program. I thought the process as allowed was the result of their embrace of chaos by intent, and a recognition that the nation's executive leadership role was no longer considered important or worth the effort. After all, the nation had survived a controlled presidency for 16 years (eight under Bush II and eight more under Obama). Why not try another four under a president whose program was insufficiently defined and whose style was sufficiently chaotic to allow fascism to be substituted for democracy?

Obviously I do not think President Trump is the most important problem. I think our nation has become accustomed to a weakened presidency. I think our nation has become accustomed to behind the scenes control of our executive, and for that matter legislative government. Many of us struggle to retain confidence in our justice and judicial systems. We often assume the operation of a shadow government, actually run by folks whose agenda is determined by interests other than those of the people of our nation. To me this state of affairs is too reminiscent of the years of fascist rule in Germany. Recall that Hatcher suggested that this first became obvious to him when representatives responsive to local and populist interests lost control over our cities to corporate capitalists' interests. Du Bois argued that it began with the betrayal and defeat of the Black Reconstruction following the Civil War, when monopoly industrial capital gained control of a compromised progressive capitalist class and culture and a disgruntled and defeated slave based capitalist class of the Southern U.S., where government was established and maintained for the purpose of protecting white supremacy and the right of capitalist exploitation. To achieve these ends control of government in the north and the south was seized and controlled.

I trace our nation's preparation for a Trump presidency through the geographic and colonial expansion of our nation and its repeated capitulation to the capitalist class that led us into and through World Wars One and Two and the Great Depression, ever consolidating its position and control of the nation and its political economy in the name of democracy. That capitalist democracy was saved and rehabilitated by F. D. Roosevelt, whose progressive capitalism and collaborating Labor Movement came to see its interest better served by fusion with the politically conservative political forces than with the more progressive populists. (See Patrick Moynihan's classic essay on the marriage between the U.S. labor movement and racist conservative forces.) As I see it, these forces have emerged as the corporatized capitalist class, which protected, preserved and learned from the experiment in fascism and racism in Germany, Italy and Spain in the middle of the 20th Century. My reading of history suggests that the U.S.A. protected and preserved the wealth of those fascist states and restored its fiscal leadership to power as a democratic capitalist Europe, which together with a defeated Japan became, later in that century, the core of a globalized capitalist international corporate-driven political economy, answerable to no single nation, but under control of a virtual corporate executive committee or cabal. I see this cabal as being in position to challenge heads of governments and the nations they head, if not control them.

Now this is my (possibly jaundiced?) vision of the world in which our nation and its leaders must play. I think Bush/Cheney tried to exploit it in the interests of the U.S. capitalist oil-based class. It was this international corporate capitalist dominated political economy, to which Obama tried to bring some humane order, but never really stood a chance. He was out powered by the cabal and was made neutered by a racism-sickened U.S. Congress.

I think Trump is a naive, pompous figurehead who has been allowed to assume the office of President with the assumption that he will be prevented from doing too much harm and will lack the know-how and sophistication or moral character to stand in the way of the continued consolidation by the fascist operators on the world scene in Russia, China, India or even the oil-rich Arab world. I worry about the abuse he may be able to impose on the weaker members of our nation and world society. I do not see him as a friend of the common man or marginalized minority groups. We are likely to be neglected during his term in office. But I am more worried about what these very powerful forces may force him to do, or even worse, that they may be free to do on his watch and to our nation, which has been reduced to his level in the name of democratic tolerance of difference of perspective and old fashioned ignorance. Flying the banner of populism while exercising the even limited powers of national government, concerning which no one with power cares, but orchestrated and directed by an impersonal anonymous international corporate capitalist cabal. What can a sane populist do?

I think the democratic well of communal humanist values has been poisoned by our worldwide concern for optimizing personal gain and profit, even the legitimation of exploitation and greed. In the evolution of the human species we see repeatedly the emergence of collective and cooperative human agentic strategies. As I read history, when human cultures get close to destroying themselves, they forced cooperation onto some, while they also join hands with others in order to prevent their destruction. Others have elected to turn to consideration of others, protection of the other, and collective action with the other. This survival action has often required that we broaden, rather than narrow, the criteria for we - out of necessity we have become more inclusive. In the history of our own nation we embrace the slogan *E Pluribus Unum* (Out of many, One).

What alternative have we but to join the hands of our neighbors and their neighbors, and theirs, in organized resistance, to recognize that humankind is one, that the earth is shared, that my survival depends on your survival, and that those who advocate for selfishness, exploitation and hate are our false leaders. That will be a hard message to deliver in a world where powerful forces thrive on its denial. But I believe that it was in the process of caring for each other that we became human animals.

ART OF THE DEAL: HOW TO GRAB A NATION BY THE PUSSY ONE VOTE AT A TIME

ALLYSON HORTON

*Allyson Horton is is a native of Indianapolis, Indiana. Her poetry will be featured in the anthology **It Was Written: Poetry Inspired By Hip-Hop** (2017). Her first book of poetry published by Third World Press, Foundation (Chicago, Illinois) is forthcoming and will be available in 2018. Currently, she teaches and resides in her hometown.*

"All of the women on The Apprentice flirted with me – consciously or unconsciously. That's to be expected."

— Donald J. Trump, host of NBC's Celebrity Apprentice

"If the head of state can treat women like objects, why should any other American man feel he should behave differently?"

— Jean Hannah Edelstein, *The Guardian*, 2017

Just when you thought that there were some things a candidate for the highest office in the country should never be heard saying on or off the record and still be able to seal the deal at the end of the day—surprise, surprise. By now, it is no secret that during the 2016 U.S. presidential election, the patriarchal construct known as "locker-room talk" reached an all-time *what the hell* when Donald J. Trump was caught on a hot mic discussing his peculiar way with women. Step One: "Just kiss. I don't even wait." Step Two: "And when you're a star, they let you do it." Step Three: "Grab them by the pussy. You can do anything."

Well, ladies and gentlemen, there you have it—a first class clown showing his true "upresidential" colors. Orange you glad that during his circus of a campaign, we got to to see the reality TV superstar live and di-rect. Up close and might I add--just a wee bit too personal for my blood or ballot. But then again, I've never had my pussy grabbed like that before, in private or on national television. With no foreplay, forewarning, and no permission. Come to think of it—I've never had my attention grabbed like that before during a United States presidential election process.

It is important to note, that over the course of my politically en-gaged life, I've survived one "Tricky Dick," another actor in office, two Bushes and a two-term-two-timing-Arsenio Hall- "Late-Night"-Televi-sion-sunglass-wearing-saxophone-playing-Whitehouse-womanizer. This is just to say, I have seen it all. So I thought. The year is 2016 and in walks "the Donald": businessman and television personality before landing his latest gig as the 45th and current (but not my) president of the United States. I want to be clear that none of them were, all things considered. Therefore, I am less inclined to simply grin and patriotically bear this po-litical atrocity calling itself American democracy.

With that being said, I can hold my head up unashamedly and declare—I am not a part of the 8% of us who did in fact cast our vote in Trump's direction in a botched effort to make America great again. Yet, there is no historical reference for such a time cultural landscape, climate, or collective memory. And while clutching the pearls between a woman's legs may seem as good a place to start as any (In the beginning was the womb....), the act alone is a violation of every woman's constitution. A proverbial slap on the ass. A political power play, if you will. To be more precise—a pussy power play. After all, that is where our power lies, right? —on our backs, between our thighs—if we even possess it then, right?

Furthermore, by commandeering the "P" one is able to shift the power from one hand to another. To literally have it at one's fingertips. Thereby, inflating the ego of a very insecure, and most likely, small penis individual, one who is in constant and reckless pursuit of control and power. It doesn't matter if the woman likes it, or has signaled that she wants it, or perhaps signaled she doesn't want it—according to the infamous audio recording in which the current president elect is heard advising former Today and Access Hollywood host, Billy Bush, on how to ignore all such messages: *"Just kiss"* her he encourages. He then goes on to admit that in those particular situations he doesn't 'even wait.' The fact that this kind of documented rape culture can be casually passed off as "locker room banter" is actually more unsettling than any measure of actual locker room talks. Implicit in such behavior is the belief that white male supremacist thought and action, even when perverse, obtuse and unpresidential will seldom, if ever, be met with the kind of scrutiny one might assign to the first Black, all-American, well-spoken, well-mannered and highly-qualified Commander-in-Chief.

As double standards come and go, so too does political pressure for then-candidate Donald Trump to release tax returns, a slew of criminal lawsuits, and other character flaws and unanswered questions. Say, whatever happened to his other "locker room" remarks regarding women as "pigs and dogs"? Yes, his misogynistic political trail would rival hip hop's any day. For example, his "beautiful" daughter, Ivanka might be the best woman for the job for confronting her father on being referred to as "a piece of ass." After all, he agreed adding that "if Ivanka wasn't my daughter then perhaps I'd be dating her" (The View, ABC 2006). Creepy is an understatement. Not my president is the clarion call and response for such a disgusting display of wealth, male whiteness, power, privilege and yes—presidency.

However, there is something about the white male privilege that affords the recipient the luxury of protection by any means necessary. Although "the Donald" expressed these sentiments nearly twelve years ago, he had already put in his bid for presidency in 2000. With that said, by the time he was on record engaging in lewd conversation about women in 2005 and later in 2006 (in regard to his own flesh and blood), his character should have already been in question. Character is a developing trait. It is not some magical or fleeting possession. We, the people, should be able to dial back ten years on any presidential candidate and see them acting in the best interest of themselves, their families and others. Aren't these and other factors part of the qualifying components of a potential POTUS.

Collectively, pussy possessors make up 50.8 % of the population. Therefore, powerless, we are not, i.e., until we relinquish it. Otherwise, it is, or could be, a woman's world in a blink of a ballot. Instead, 54% of non-white women saw another woman as more enemy than the devil, himself. It would seem that more white women identified with Trump than his white male counterparts. Had more women decided to stand together and declare 'not my president' as so many are currently yelling from the mountaintops of Washington and other cultural spaces, we would be having a totally different conversation and culture. Not at all a great one, but certainly a far less dysfunctional, destructive and diabolical one.

ON THE REMOVAL OF CONFEDERATE MONUMENTS IN NEW ORLEANS

MITCH LANDRIEU

Mitch Landrieu *is the current mayor of New Orleans. This is the full text of the remarks delivered on May 23 by the mayor, upon his removal of the last of the city's several Confederate monuments.*

Thank you for coming.

  The soul of our beloved City is deeply rooted in a history that has evolved over thousands of years; rooted in a diverse people who have been here together every step of the way — for both good and for ill. It is a history that holds in its heart the stories of Native Americans — the Choctaw, Houma Nation, the Chitimacha. Of Hernando De Soto, Robert Cavelier, Sieur de La Salle, the Acadians, the Islenos, the enslaved people from Senegambia, Free People of Colorix, the Haitians, the Germans, both the empires of France and Spain. The Italians, the Irish, the Cubans, the south and central Americans, the Vietnamese and so many more.

  You see — New Orleans is truly a city of many nations, a melting pot, a bubbling caldron of many cultures. There is no other place quite like it in the world that so eloquently exemplifies the uniquely American motto: e pluribus unum — out of many, we are one. But there are also other truths about our city that we must confront. New Orleans was America's largest slave market: a port where hundreds of thousands of souls were bought, sold and shipped up the Mississippi River to lives of forced labor of misery of rape, of torture. America was the place where nearly 4000 of our fellow citizens were lynched, 540 alone in Louisiana; where the courts enshrined 'separate but equal'; where Freedom riders coming to New Orleans were beaten to a bloody pulp. So when people say to me that the monuments in question are history, well what I just described is real history as well, and it is the searing truth.

And it immediately begs the questions, why there are no slave ship monuments, no prominent markers on public land to remember the lynchings or the slave blocks; nothing to remember this long chapter of our lives; the pain, the sacrifice, the shame... all of it happening on the soil of New Orleans. So for those self-appointed defenders of history and the monuments, they are eerily silent on what amounts to this historical malfeasance, a lie by omission. There is a difference between remembrance of history and reverence of it.

For America and New Orleans, it has been a long, winding road, marked by great tragedy and great triumph. But we cannot be afraid of our truth. As President George W. Bush said at the dedication ceremony for the National Museum of African American History & Culture, "A great nation does not hide its history. It faces its flaws and corrects them." So today I want to speak about why we chose to remove these four monuments to the Lost Cause of the Confederacy, but also how and why this process can move us towards healing and understanding of each other. So, let's start with the facts.

The historic record is clear, the Robert E. Lee, Jefferson Davis, and P.G.T. Beauregard statues were not erected just to honor these men, but as part of the movement which became known as The Cult of the Lost Cause. This 'cult' had one goal — through monuments and through other means — to rewrite history to hide the truth, which is that the Confederacy was on the wrong side of humanity. First erected over 166 years after the founding of our city and 19 years after the end of the Civil War, the monuments that we took down were meant to rebrand the history of our city and the ideals of a defeated Confederacy. It is self-evident that these men did not fight for the United States of America, They fought against it. They may have been warriors, but in this cause they were not patriots. These statues are not just stone and metal. They are not just innocent remembrances of a benign history. These monuments purposefully celebrate a fictional, sanitized Confederacy; ignoring the death, ignoring the enslavement, and the terror that it actually stood for.

After the Civil War, these statues were a part of that terrorism as much as a burning cross on someone's lawn; they were erected purposefully to send a strong message to all who walked in their shadows about who was still in charge in this city. Should you have further doubt about the true goals of the Confederacy, in the very weeks before the war broke out, the Vice President of the Confederacy, Alexander Stephens, made it clear that the Confederate cause was about maintaining slavery and white supremacy. He said in his now famous 'cornerstone speech' that the Confederacy's

> "cornerstone rests upon the great truth, that the negro is not equal to the white man; that slavery — subordination to the superior race — is his natural and normal condition. This, our new government, is the first, in the history of the world, based upon this great physical, philosophical, and moral truth."

Now, with these shocking words still ringing in your ears... I want to try to gently peel from your hands the grip on a false narrative of our history that I think weakens us. And make straight a wrong turn we made many years ago — we can more closely connect with integrity to the founding principles of our nation and forge a clearer and straighter path toward a better city and a more perfect union.

Last year, President Barack Obama echoed these sentiments about the need to contextualize and remember all our history. He recalled a piece of stone, a slave auction block engraved with a marker commemorating a single moment in 1830 when Andrew Jackson and Henry Clay stood and spoke from it. President Obama said, "Consider what this artifact tells us about history... on a stone where day after day for years, men and women... bound and bought and sold and bid like cattle on a stone worn down by the tragedy of over a thousand bare feet. For a long time the only thing we considered important, the singular thing we once chose to commemorate as history with a plaque were the unmemorable speeches of two powerful men."

A piece of stone — one stone. Both stories were history. One story told. One story forgotten or maybe even purposefully ignored. As clear as it is for me today... for a long time, even though I grew up in one of New Orleans' most diverse neighborhoods, even with my family's long proud history of fighting for civil rights... I must have passed by those monuments a million times without giving them a second thought. So I am not judging anybody, I am not judging people. We all take our own journey on race.

I just hope people listen like I did when my dear friend Wynton Marsalis helped me see the truth. He asked me to think about all the people who have left New Orleans because of our exclusionary attitudes. Another friend asked me to consider these four monuments from the perspective of an African American mother or father trying to explain to their fifth grade daughter who Robert E. Lee is and why he stands atop of our beautiful city. Can you do it? Can you look into that young girl's eyes and convince her that Robert E. Lee is there to encourage her? Do you think she will feel inspired and hopeful by that story? Do these monuments help her see a future with limitless potential? Have you ever thought that if her potential is limited, yours and mine are too? We all know the answer to these very simple questions. When you look into this child's eyes is the moment when the searing truth comes into focus for us. This is the moment when we know what is right and what we must do. We can't walk away from this truth.

And I knew that taking down the monuments was going to be tough, but you elected me to do the right thing, not the easy thing and this is what that looks like. So relocating these Confederate monuments is not about taking something away from someone else. This is not about politics, this is not about blame or retaliation. This is not a naïve quest to solve all our problems at once.

This is however about showing the whole world that we as a city and as a people are able to acknowledge, understand, reconcile and most importantly, choose a better future for ourselves making straight what has been crooked and making right what was wrong. Otherwise, we will continue to pay a price with discord, with division and yes with violence.

To literally put the Confederacy on a pedestal in our most prominent places of honor is an inaccurate recitation of our full past. It is an affront to our present, and it is a bad prescription for our future. History cannot be changed. It cannot be moved like a statue. What is done is done. The Civil War is over, and the Confederacy lost and we are better for it. Surely we are far enough removed from this dark time to acknowledge that the cause of the Confederacy was wrong.

And in the second decade of the 21st century, asking African Americans — or anyone else — to drive by property that they own; occupied by reverential statues of men who fought to destroy the country and deny that person's humanity seems perverse and absurd. Centuries old wounds are still raw because they never healed right in the first place. Here is the essential truth. We are better together than we are apart.

Indivisibility is our essence. Isn't this the gift that the people of New Orleans have given to the world? We radiate beauty and grace in our food, in our music, in our architecture, in our joy of life, in our celebration of death; in everything that we do. We gave the world this funky thing called jazz, the most uniquely American art form that is developed across the ages from different cultures. Think about second lines, think about Mardi Gras, think about muffaletta, think about the Saints, gumbo, red beans and rice. By God, just think.

All we hold dear is created by throwing everything in the pot; creating, producing something better; everything a product of our historic diversity. We are proof that out of many we are one — and better for it! Out of many we are one — and we really do love it! And yet, we still seem to find so many excuses for not doing the right thing. Again, remember President Bush's words, "A great nation does not hide its history. It faces its flaws and corrects them."

We forget, we deny how much we really depend on each other, how much we need each other. We justify our silence and inaction by manufacturing noble causes that marinate in historical denial. We still find a way to say 'wait'/not so fast, but like Dr. Martin Luther King Jr. said, "wait has almost always meant never." We can't wait any longer. We need to change. And we need to change now.

* * *

No more waiting. This is not just about statues, this is about our attitudes and behavior as well. If we take these statues down and don't change to become a more open and inclusive society this would have all been in vain. While some have driven by these monuments every day and either revered their beauty or failed to see them at all, many of our neighbors and fellow Americans see them very clearly. Many are painfully aware of the long shadows their presence casts; not only literally but figuratively. And they clearly receive the message that the Confederacy and the cult of the lost cause intended to deliver.

Earlier this week, as the cult of the lost cause statue of P.G.T Beauregard came down, world renowned musician Terence Blanchard stood watch, his wife Robin and their two beautiful daughters at their side. Terence went to a high school on the edge of City Park named after one of America's greatest heroes and patriots, John F. Kennedy. But to get there he had to pass by this monument to a man who fought to deny him his humanity.

He said, "I've never looked at them as a source of pride... it's always made me feel as if they were put there by people who don't respect us. This is something I never thought I'd see in my lifetime. It's a sign that the world is changing." Yes, Terence, it is and it is long overdue. Now is the time to send a new message to the next generation of New Orleanians who can follow in Terence and Robin's remarkable footsteps. A message about the future, about the next 300 years and beyond; let us not miss this opportunity New Orleans and let us help the rest of the country do the same. Because now is the time for choosing. Now is the time to actually make this the City we always should have been, had we gotten it right in the first place.

We should stop for a moment and ask ourselves — at this point in our history — after Katrina, after Rita, after Ike, after Gustav, after the national recession, after the BP oil catastrophe and after the tornado — if presented with the opportunity to build monuments that told our story or to curate these particular spaces... would these monuments be what we want the world to see? Is this really our story?

We have not erased history; we are becoming part of the city's history by righting the wrong image these monuments represent and crafting a better, more complete future for all our children and for future generations. And unlike when these Confederate monuments were first erected as symbols of white supremacy, we now have a chance to create not only new symbols, but to do it together, as one people. In our blessed land we all come to the table of democracy as equals. We have to reaffirm our commitment to a future where each citizen is guaranteed the uniquely American gifts of life, liberty and the pursuit of happiness.

That is what really makes America great and today it is more important than ever to hold fast to these values and together say a self-evident truth that out of many we are one. That is why today we reclaim these spaces for the United States of America. Because we are one nation, not two; indivisible with liberty and justice for all... not some. We all are part of one nation, all pledging allegiance to one flag, the flag of the United States of America. And New Orleanians are in... all of the way. It is in this union and in this truth that real patriotism is rooted and flourishes. Instead of revering a 4-year brief historical aberration that was called the Confederacy we can celebrate all 300 years of our rich, diverse history as a place named New Orleans and set the tone for the next 300 years.

After decades of public debate, of anger, of anxiety, of anticipation, of humiliation and of frustration. After public hearings and approvals from three separate community led commissions. After two robust public hearings and a 6-1 vote by the duly elected New Orleans City Council. After review by 13 different federal and state judges. The full weight of the legislative, executive and judicial branches of government has been brought to bear and the monuments in accordance with the law have been removed. So now is the time to come together and heal and focus on our larger task. Not only building new symbols, but making this city a beautiful manifestation of what is possible and what we as a people can become.

Let us remember what the once exiled, imprisoned and now universally loved Nelson Mandela and what he said after the fall of apartheid. "If the pain has often been unbearable and the revelations shocking to all of us, it is because they indeed bring us the beginnings of a common understanding of what happened and a steady restoration of the nation's humanity." So before we part let us again state the truth clearly.

The Confederacy was on the wrong side of history and humanity. It sought to tear apart our nation and subjugate our fellow Americans to slavery. This is the history we should never forget and one that we should never again put on a pedestal to be revered. As a community, we must recognize the significance of removing New Orleans' Confederate monuments. It is our acknowledgment that now is the time to take stock of, and then move past, a painful part of our history.

Anything less would render generations of courageous struggle and soul-searching a truly lost cause. Anything less would fall short of the immortal words of our greatest President Abraham Lincoln, who with an open heart and clarity of purpose calls on us today to unite as one people when he said: "With malice toward none, with charity for all, with firmness in the right, as God gives us to see the right, let us strive on to finish the work we are in, to bind up the nation's wounds...to do all which may achieve and cherish — a just and lasting peace among ourselves and with all nations." Thank you.

DONALD TRUMP: THE GREATEST FRAUD OF AMERICA'S NEW CENTURY, HIGHLIGHTING CRIMINAL INTENT AND DOUBLE-DOWNED IGNORANCE

HAKI R. MADHUBUTI

Haki R. Madhubuti—*poet, publisher, and educator*—*has published over thirty books including* **YellowBlack: The First Twenty-One Years of a Poet's Life,** *and* **Liberation Narratives: New and Collected Poems 1967-2009.** *He founded Third World Press in 1967, and is a co-founder of four independent schools in Chicago. His teaching career spanned 42 years, included Chicago State University and DePaul University. His latest book is* **Taking Bullets** *(2016).*

Bernie Madoff, the so-called 'Wizard of Wall Street', the man who pulled off one of the greatest, most notorious Ponzi schemes in recorded history of this nation—to the unbelievable sum of 65 billion dollars—will have to take a backseat to the current president of the United States, Donald Trump. That Madoff, for years without any serious oversight from local, state or federal regulators could openly and brazenly hoodwink, outfox, deceive, and dupe many of the most sophisticated financial and intelligent minds in the nation and the world has nothing on Donald Trump.

Mr. Trump just stole the nation. That his "criminal" record which is extensive was not used against him in any meaningful way, represents a "legal" and election Ponzi scheme that the Republican Party and its Big Money enablers and corporate elites will never own up to. Why? Even after extensive lying to the public, running as a Republican, talking like a

Democrat, Mr. Trump in his own way hoodwinked, outfoxed, deceived, conned and duped the American people by running as a Republican and campaigning like a Democrat. He promised to all who would listen that he would not eliminate any of the social safety nets that the Democrats fought to create over the last fifty years: healthcare, voting rights, strict environmental protections, Dodd-Frank banking regulations, free community college, moving to make state universities more affordable, establishing a living wage for the working poor and middle class and much more. He lied and moved as quickly as possible to try to reverse his campaign promises in his first 100 days in office.

Rather than drain the swamp, he hired the swamp: his family, current and former Goldman Sachs executives, a cabinet full of men and women who are on the record for being anti- or totally against progressive policies of the departments they are leading. Most of Mr. Trump's cabinet members who required senate confirmation are white and male. The exceptions are four women, one Hispanic and two Negros. All of them are anti-policies that would benefit the majority in the nation. Six members who have negatively affected the general population upon walking in their offices on the first day are Attorney General-Jeff Sessions, Agriculture Head-Sonny Purdue, Health-Tom Price, Housing-Ben Carson, Energy-Rick Perry, Education-Betsy DeVos, and EPA-Scott Pruitt. This in no way minimizes the rest of his cabinet, especially those appointed members such as his chief strategist and openly white supremacist in residence Stephen K. Bannon. Senior advisor, son-in-law in charge of everything Jared Kushner, Carl Icahn-Regulatory Czar, Chief Corporate Rader, and corporate takeover artist Kellyanne Conway-the Alt-facts counselor who has perfected the art of lying before she is told to lie.

Even though Donald Trump ran on a platform of not cutting social security, Medicare and Medicaid, these benefits are now in serious danger of losing new funding. For the last six years or so, the Republican Party has half-heartedly attempted to repeal Obamacare. However, they mainly used its existence as a state and national fundraising ploy, that fooled the largely uninformed white, working poor and middle class. The recently passed Republican led "health" bill pushed through the House by Paul Ryan is essentially a tax cut for the rich.

Biography does not lie; it is one's documented personal journey, is history, is story, confirmed narrative, representing a serious clue to one's future. A deep study of Mr. Trump's biographies details a dishonest, entitled, intellectually compromised, privileged, discredited, and dishonorable life. That such a man could rise to the highest office in the land and occupy one of the most powerful positions on the planet is a sad commentary on the nation's politics and its people. As noted in Jane Meyer's *Dark Money* and Bruce Berlin's *Breaking Big Money's Grip*, the Republican Party has sold its body and soul to corporate elites and big money who now gives the Republican Party its dancing orders. A recent *Newsweek* cover article "The Billionaires March on Washington" (April 14, 2017) by Nina Burleigh also makes this point.

However, it is the obvious criminality of Mr. Trump that goes unnoticed, excused and hidden. His thug-like actions—legal and otherwise—against those whom he has done business with over the last three decades are breathtaking and embarrassing for the President of the United States. *USA Today Network* provided the country with a clear example of what investigative reporting is all about at the highest levels for print journalism. Starting in June of 2016, the paper provided its readers with an extensive exposé of Mr. Trump (at that time Republican primary candidate) in its cover story "Trump and the Law." Writers Nick Penzenstadler, Susan Page, and others provided ample evidence as to why this man should not have been allowed to be anywhere in the vicinity of the White House.

Their work documented 3,500 lawsuits against Mr. Trump. These "legal actions in federal and state courts…range from skirmishes with casino patrons to million-dollar real estate suits to personal defamation lawsuits." They go on to find that Mr. Trump "doesn't hesitate to deploy his wealth and legal fire power against adversaries with limited resources, such as homeowners. He sometimes refused to pay real estate brokers, lawyers, and other vendors." The best known litigation, that he was forced to pay 25 million dollars was that of the Trump University fraud. It can be argued that the only reason that fine was paid was because he was destined to be the Republican candidate for the presidency.

* * *

Trump and Black People

Black people are the magical faces at the bottom of society's well. Even the poorest whites, those who must live their lives only a few levels above, gain their self-esteem by gazing down on us. Surely, they must know that their deliverance depends on letting down their ropes. Only by working together is escape possible. Over time, many reach out, but most simply watch, mesmerized into maintaining their unspoken commitment to keeping us where we are, at whatever cost to them or to us.

—Derrick Bell

Professor Derrick Bell was one of the great lawyers, educators, legal scholars, lightning quiet minds, lover of Black people and the righteous others, that I've had the pleasure to interact with. No longer with us, but as we contemplated this book—like Du Bois—who lives daily in my consciousness, professor Bell sent me back to two of his many books: *And We Are Not Saved* and *Faces at the Bottom of the Well*. The quote above is very small insight into his vision and work. His analysis, passionate and lived displays an awareness of the racial, economic, and human divide that this nation still faces today. His alter-ego, the lawyer-prophet Geneva Crenshaw is always on point for now and the future. Professor Bell and the hundreds of lawyers and non-lawyers that he taught and mentored over his short life would be on the attack against the many crimes and actions of Mr. Trump.

Professor Bell is indeed missed.

Donald Trump's maltreatment of Black people is in keeping with the history of the nation. Any serious study of the founding and conquering of this land, which is not accurately taught at any educational level must be understood, if the ascendancy of Trump is to be comprehended. Black people in America, after that of Native Americans have been the object of pure and constant contempt and hatred for centuries. The greatest success of white-nationalist-supremacist philosophy is the acculturation or more accurately seasoning of an entire people, enslaved Africans, into believing that they are not who they really are, and by extension they have become a people who have actually ended up hating themselves, period. Obviously, there are brilliant exceptions; however, for the most part, this brain alteration worked. This reality speaks volumes to our current condition.

Mr. Trump's description of the national Black community is not only ill-informed and ignorant, it is insulting and small-minded. His only association with Black people is one of an employer (a few) or as gopher (for any of his many needs). Mr. Trump not only does not want Black people "counting his money," he does not want them living in any of his properties. Truth be told, any examination of New York court records would show that he and his father have been charged repeatedly with housing discrimination. Two other glaring examples of his hatred and disdain for Black people can be seen in his fight to criminalize five young Black and Brown men who had been accused of rape and thus labeled the Central Park Five. Trump used his power and privilege and spent $85,000 to take out full-page ads in all four major New York daily newspapers, claiming their guilt, which aided in their conviction. After years of imprisonment, they were found "not guilty" and released. To this day, he has not acknowledged their innocence or pray tell issued an apology.

The most glaring example of his disrespect for Black people is his birtherism fight against the citizenship of former President Barack Obama. That this travesty, this big lie, this insult to the intelligence of the people who elected Barack Obama president went on for almost seven years and ultimately propelled Trump into the White House, is a lesson for serious historians to comment on as to the lack of integrity of the U.S. electoral process.

Black Lives Matter helped keep alive the Black Struggle advanced in the Sixties and Seventies. They have positioned in the minds of today's young and not-so-young that we are still fighting in many ways the same battles. That which forced me and millions of others into the streets, state houses, halls of congress, universities and workplaces have not changed that much today. That which has changed and is consequential, is the technology: our phones, iPads, computers, and many other phases of new communication such as film, video, community radio, photography, and all mediums of art. To highlight that the many struggles my and Derrick Bell's generation experienced remains very much the same are two recent examples. One, Alexander Nazaryan writes the cover story in *Newsweek* (May 10, 2017) about the re-segregation of the nation's schools that have largely gone unnoticed. He explains:

> *"Regardless of what happens in Gardendale, Birmingham and its suburbs are an example of what happens when communities diminish the scope of public education creating their own fiefdoms, funded by public dollars but effectively functioning as private institutions that guard against intruders... Those borders are frequently created as suburbs that want to use their property taxes to fund their own schools, without having to share with poorer inner-city neighborhoods in many ways the explicit teetering of taxation to education is a deep motivating factor for school secession movements, allowing citizens to act like dissatisfied customers and take their tax dollars elsewhere."*

Mr. Nazaryan asks *"Is integration only the job of working class whites?"* Enter Donald Trump with the answer for the poor and working class whites. It is the Black and Brown people's fault for your condition. No mention of Mr. Trump's class, the richest 1%, led by the likes of Robert Mercer, Sheldon Adelson, Carl Icahn, and multitudes of others who helped to fund his political ascension. Second, a recent story in *USA Today*, "Black Troops as Much as Twice as Likely to Be Punished" by Tom Vanden Brook burst the bubble that the military was the answer to upward mobility for Black people (mainly men). Yes, limited "integration" of the armed forces helped millions of Black people, I was one of them. However, this latest report is devastating in its indictment of the Air Force, Marine Corps, Navy, and Army. Mr. Brook writes:

> *"Black service members were as much as two times more likely than white troops to face discipline in and average year, according to an analysis by Protect Our Defenders (POD) an advocacy organization for military justice and victims of sexual assault. The group combed through Pentagon data from 2006 to 2015 for its report... 'over the past decade, racial disparities have persisted in the military justice system without indications of improvement."*

Mr. Brook makes it clear that these "disparities" are for Black service members. That they faced general or special court-martial far in excess of white service members. He also points out, "In 2016 about 78% of military officers were white and 8% were Black. This study needs to be read by all people who wish to understand that discrimination against Black people is not only in the civilian society, but also has permeated the nation's military.

The Reality of America

Who loves Black people?
Who loves poor people?
Who loves all children?
Who loves all young people?
Who loves the elders of our nation?

These are the central questions facing the nation that is quickly losing its core identity, its purpose, its direction, its meaning, its highly compromised and conflicted history.

In America, Black people are no longer needed as a critical labor force. Our population of 40 million is not significant to the continued development of the United States with the minor exception of fighting in foreign and domestic wars (yes, we will kill our own people). We are not needed to pick cotton, vegetables or fruit (Latinos), as skilled laborer (Eastern Europeans), to rebuild the nation's infrastructure, (the trade unions are still highly tribal and racist to the bone). The current population of the United States as of 2014 is about 310.1 million making it the largest in the world far behind China and India. The white poor in the U.S. is about 10 percent of the population, which makes it in real numbers about 31 million. The Black poor is approximated to be 10.9 million, about 28 percent of the Black population. The Hispanic percentage of poor people is 25 percent, its population which roughly translates into about 50 million. The point I'm making here is that the white poor, if we look closely at their voting records in 2010 and 2014, voted against their own self-interest, casting their votes in concert with the likes of the Koch Brothers, corporate classes, and big banks This should tell us exactly what we need to see and hear. Black people, by and large in the economic sphere beyond consumers do not matter in the United States other than as uninformed consumers.

If we seriously look at who runs the United States in all of the determinant areas of human activity, we see white people. Or we may see a measured and manageable number of Blacks and others who think and often act white. If we survey the universities and colleges that many white and Black people graduate from such as the Ivy Leagues, the Big Ten, Pac-12, the Top Southern schools like Duke and Emery, the top state schools, the standalone independents like Chicago, Stanford, Massachusetts Institute of Technology, and several state schools like University of California, Berkeley and Los Angeles and hundreds of others you will notice that the Black students and teaching faculty have receded significantly. This should tell us something.

Central to any people's tomorrow is memory. Deny a people's past, and you put them at the mercy of those who are in the business of imposing their past, present and future upon others. One's history of oppression, misadventure, and suffering is too often a victim's history and people cannot build a future on the history of the enslaver. The centrality of memory and the gladness and hope of measureable accomplishments must be larger and must encompass the worldview of the majority of any people who seek liberation and a bright future on their own terms. For Black people, the right memory, accurate memory, long memory, history-based memory can be fuel, the clean protection that jump starts a recalibration of a liberation narrative. And, historically, this has always been the case. Remember, the people who control and shape the narratives decide the conversation. History, according to winners, is always quickly and solely recorded, written, published, taught, and studied. Black boys and men, girls and women need new love, Black unconditional love and security, need a deep earth rooted love based upon Black cultural knowledge that we (Black families, communities, institutions and people) are our own answer to any bright future.

That which has the power to save lives, to change lives, to give birth to imagination that can power questions from unknown spaces of one's expanded brain, while unlocking the mystery of misunderstood relationships and loves, all while celebrating the highs and lows of one's undisciplined, careless, clueless, narrowly focused vision until it truly becomes a vision, thereby, humanizing all future growth of a person's production is art.

Black people, young people—exposed early and often to the magic and discipline of art-making—can and will see another world and other possibilities. Art, in the many forms and cultural rooms of making a life, can also give a life. To be young and in the grips of creation, after all is said, done, and acknowledged, is to be in search of something self-directing that is forever thirsting for beauty, breath, truth while fighting hourly the many temptations leading Black boys and girls towards ordinariness, sameness, and predictable failure all accompanied by the loneliness and isolation of having lived ones' life on the assembly line of anti-knowing and anti-wanting to know.

Art opens the avenues of the unasked questions and denied gifts and fuels life's energies in one's ability to say yes to tomorrow and yesterday. We can be saved and elevated by the unique beauty of a child's—any child's smile—running toward full laughter having viewed, read, experienced, listened to, showed and located something wonderful and at peace with itself, Art. Art works and illuminates.

The big question is, who is Donald J. Trump? The answer is he is a man without a center, especially, if one's center is measured merely by money and wealth. This fact would have gone largely unnoticed if he had not become president and his many lies and ignorance of his new position had not become his Achilles heel. Clearly, there is a lack of any knowledge of civics or humanities in his educational upbringing: literature, music, art, language, history and philosophy which leads to intellectual conversation about the world are missing. Other than money, and the "art of the deal" you have a man incapable of speaking intelligently for more than five minutes. His concept of the truth is *his* concept of the truth. His warped perception of making America great again actually translates to making America white again. So actually when he and other Republicans state that America is the richest nation in the world, they are actually correct if they mean for the richest people in the world. When it comes to the seriously rich white people there is no rule of law. Big money and power always trumps poverty, goodness, fidelity and all that is human— add to this, any nation that works for the majority.

Indeed, in looking at the totality of Mr. Trump's life, he can be defined as a sociopath and a clear example of American exceptionalism. He is a man who has never been hungry, never without the best of everything, never without heat, electricity or the most advanced technologies (communication, transportation, housing, etc.); he is actually a traitor to his office and the country, where he put his family and party ahead of the nation. All of this back and forth, whether he is in bed with the Russians would go away within 24 hours, if the congress would subpoena his taxes, therein lies the answer to his many lies. His dedication to corporate personhood, personal wealth, and family enrichment is more important than the Constitution or the Office of the President of the United States.

No one with any knowledge of this country's history, with as many wars, especially that of the Civil War, and the entire legacy of racial divide should have any respect for this president. He has placed his family, the Republican Party, his economic class, his warped sense of rightness above the nation. The most patriotic act that he could do and save the country from further turmoil, expense and division is to release his taxes over the last 18 years. The sad reality of this catastrophe is that if former

President Obama, or former candidate Hillary Clinton had committed 1/1,000th of what this man has been accused of they would have not only been taken seriously as president or candidate—but they would be in prison.

Yes, America may be the "richest nation in the world" for the richest people in the world, clearly not for the majority of the population who do not enjoy that which the rich and the rulership take for granted. The only answer to this hellhole in which we find ourselves is resistance at every human and political level possible, and to actually realize that corporations are not people and money is not speech, and the supreme court is not a monarch. If indeed this is a nation of laws, why do they function differently for the white rich?

References:

Arvedlund, E. *Too Good to Be True: The Rise and Fall of Bernie Madoff.* New York: Portfolio, 2009.

Barrett, W. *The Greatest Show on Earth: The Deals, the Downfall, the Reinvention.* New York: Regan Arts, 2016.

Bell Jr., D. A. *Faces at the Bottom of the Well: The Permanence of Racism.* New York: Basic Books, 1992.

Berlin, B. *Breaking Big Money's Grip on America.* New York: Our Times Books, 2006.

Brown, E. *The Web Debt: The Shocking Truth About our Money System and How We Can Break Free.* 5th revised ed. Baton Rouge, LA: Third Millennium Press, 2012.

Chomsky, N. *Who Rules the World?.* New York: Metropolitan Books, 2016.

Chomsky, N.. *Requiem for the American Dream: The Ten Principles of Concentration of Wealth and Power.* ed. by Hutchison Peter, Nyks, Kelly and Scott, Jared P. New York City: Seven Stories Press, 2017.

Clarke J. H. *Who Betrayed the African World Revolution? and Other Speeches.* Chicago: Third World Press, 1994.

Clarke J. H. *Notes for an African World Revolution: Africans at the Crossroads.* Trenton, NJ: African World Press, Inc. 1991.

Henriques, D. B. *The Wizard of Lies: Bernie Madoff and the Death of Trust.* New York: Henry Holt & Company, 2011.

Herbert, B. *Losing Our Way: An Intimate Portrait of a Troubled America.* New York: Double Day, 2014.

Madhubuti, H. *Taking Bullets: Terrorism and Black Life in Twenty-First Century America Confronting White Nationalism, Supremacy, Privilege, Plutocracy, and Oligarchy.* Chicago: Third World Press, 2016.

Madhubuti, H. *Black Men: Obsolete, Single and Dangerous.* Chicago: Third World Press, 1991.

Mayer, J. *Dark Money.* New York: Double Day, 2016.

Nader, R. *Breaking Through Power: It's Easier Than We Think.* New York: City Lights Publishers, 2016.

Obermaier, F. and Obermayer, Bastian. *The Panama Papers: Breaking the Story of How the Rich and Powerful Hide Their Money.* UK: Oneworld Publications, 2016.

Painter, N. I.. *The History of White People.* New York: W. W. Norton & Company, 2010.

Sander, P. *Madoff: Corruption, Deceit, and the Making of the World's Most Notorious Ponzi Scheme.* Guilford: The Lyons Press, 2009.

West, C. *Race Matters.* New York: Vintage Books, 2001.

West, C. T*he Cornell West Reader.* New ed. New York City: Basic Civitas Book, 1999.

Williams, C. T*he Destruction of Black Civilization: Great Issues of a Race from 4500 B.C. to 2000 A.D.* 3rd ed. Chicago: Third World Press, 1989.

Periodicals, Newspapers, Magazines and Quarterlies:

The Nation, New Republic, MotherJones, In These Times, Z Magazine, Newsweek, Yes, The Guardian Weekly (UK), *Forbes* (Annual Billionaire's Issue), *The American Prospect, Ad Busters* (Canada), *New Internationalist* (Canada), *USA Today, New York Times, The Washington Post, Wall Street Journal, New York Review of Books, London Review of Books, The Atlantic, Harper's, The Crisis, Foreign Affairs, The African Report, Forward, Moment, BookForum, The Economist, New Yorker, ISR (International Socialist Review),* and *Pacific Standard.*

TRUMP'S MEAN IRISHMEN

ISHMAEL REED

Ishmael Reed is a poet, novelist, essayist, songwriter, playwright, editor and publisher, who is known for his satirical works challenging American political culture, and highlighting political and cultural oppression. A MacArthur Genius Grant recipient, he has authored over thirty publications including his latest, The Complete Muhammad Ali (2015).

In the 1960s, I was like Muhammad Ali, indifferent to whether I possessed non-African genes. Ali's position was that if he had a European heritage it was because a slavemaster raped a female ancestor. A few years before he died, Ali traveled to Ireland to meet his Irish relatives, the Gradys, members of his great-grandfather Abe Grady's family. Grady left Ireland in the 1860s. Since race mixing is the principal horror of American race relations, little attention was paid to this visit by the American media; it was covered by the Irish press.

I found out about the Europeans in my background during a casual conversation with my grandmother, who was in her eighties at the time. I asked her a question that I had never asked before. Who was her father? She said that he was Irish and that he had to leave Chattanooga because of his effort to organize the pipe workers. He left my great-grandmother, Mary Coleman, to support 5 children one of whom was named "Riley," who perished when a child. To feed and clothe them, she operated a food stand in the front yard of her home, a business sense that was passed down to the current generation, my sister, Linda, and my brother Bennie Reed, Jr.'s siblings. This was not the only jaw dropping answer that I received when I began to explore my ancestry. I sat my mother and her cousin Elizabeth Pope down and turned on the tape recorder. Mrs. Pope said that her grandfather was a "mean Irishman." This might be Pleasant Hopsin. Why mean? Just as some have speculated that the experience of slavery lingers in the psyche of the descendants of slaves, the Irish Famine, the result of the British genocidal policy against the Irish has affected the generations of the Irish that followed, and Jews are suffering from post-traumatic as a result of the Holocaust. Dissolving into Whiteness has provided both with an escape chute. It was when James Baldwin wrote in Dan Watt's *The Liberator* that Jews had become White Christians that he was abandoned by his sponsors. His novel, *Tell Me How Long The Train Has Been Gone*, severed these ties, permanently. Many American Jews weren't the only group to abandon their heritage for a bland Whiteness.

In connection with my new novel, *Conjugating Hindi*, I studied the British Occupation of India, which led to the murder and starvation of millions of people. I discovered that Churchill helped to faminize these millions by exporting their rice to the British and Australians. This was the Churchill who had contempt for both Indians and the Irish, yet "White nationalist" Steve Bannon and other Irish Americans sit in the Oval Office where Churchill's bust is on display. This is how it would look if former president Barack Obama had a bust of Jefferson Davis on display in the Oval Office.

President Trump's mother, a domestic, Mary Anne MacLeod Trump, was born in Scotland, who, like the Irish, were enslaved by other Whites. She arrived in the United States in 1929, yet Trump wants to expel Hispanics from the country whose ancestors have dwelled in the now American West for hundreds of years. Of course, going Churchillian, or Anglo represents an improvement in status for Trump, Bannon, Mick Mulvaney, Paul Ryan and other members of the president's Irish mafia. As with the Blacks who are profiled by Professor Houston Baker Jr. in his *The Betrayal* and Professor Martin Kilson author of *Transformation of The*

African American Intelligentsia,1880-2012--both American Book Awards winners--, White ethnics, who were members of ethnic groups that were formerly regarded as "garbage," have earned status from the establishment by attributing the low station of the less fortunate among their group to their personal behavior, as J. D. Vance does in his book *Hillbilly Elegy: A Memoir of a Family and Culture in Crisis.*

Despite two scandals exposed by WikiLeaks, and his principal sponsor questioning his morals, Henry Louis Gates, Jr. remains the designated leader of Black Intellection. One of the reasons for his rise has been his insistence that the plight of the Black underclass is attributable to their personal behavior. He goes after 35-year-old grandmothers living in the projects and commented that the election of a Black president would not end substance abuse among Black Americans, when most all of the heroin and meth seems to be located in White states like Maine. This is one of the reasons for a rise in mortality rates among Whites:

> "Two years ago, two married Princeton professors, Anne Case and Angus Deaton, released an alarming study, showing that white middle-aged Americans were suddenly dying much more frequently than in the past. The results were surprisingly given that mortality rates for the U.S. population had in general been falling since 1900. The authors partly blamed what they called 'deaths of despair'—deaths from alcohol and drug poisoning, suicide, and alcoholic liver disease…"

J.D. Vance's, a Scots Irishman, goes Gates one further. He even exhibits tough love by refusing to aide his mother whom he finds has become homeless. "J.D. visits his mother in Middletown. At this time in the story, she is homeless but sleeping in a decrepit hotel. J.D. contemplates his mother's situation, his situation, and his Christian faith. He also thinks about the parent-child relationship, even though he remained emotionally detached from his mother. He decides not to help her financially."

Another Scots Irish writer, the powerful and influential Charles Murray, abandoned the less fortunate among his group by coasting along on the old canard and tabloid academic hustle that Whites are smarter than Blacks, a leftover from the French Enlightenment. His "research" was financed by the Pioneer Fund, a foundation established by a Hitler admirer. His own ethnic group, the Scots Irish, are the "crackers," and the "White trash" group of the South. While he was entertaining the Establishment and providing them with ammunition with warnings about the Africanization of American culture like the intellectual court jester he is, signs of the deterioration of his own group, the Scots Irish was evident when The Bell Curve was published. The Scots Irish have been pitted against Blacks by management, politicians and the media since both groups encountered each other. All of the founders of the Klan were Scots Irish. Daniel Rosenberg in his *New Orleans Dockworkers, Race, Labor, and Unionism 1892-1923*, writes that the interracial general strike that brought New Orleans to its knees in October of 1907 was formed because the "whites" in this case were southern Europeans and not Celts like Murray, and Vance.

The clique surrounding the president are like Representative Paul Ryan, an Irish American who wants to strip millions of their health care, or Mick Mulvaney, director of the Budget office, who sees "Meals on Wheels" as a luxury and wishes to end Medicaid and SSI, even though it might hurt Trump supporters, the White working class, who are made chumps of again. Ryan's a disciple of Charles Murray, whose values are reflected in the president's budget, which, if passed, would leave 23 million people without health insurance. Paul Ryan is also an Ayn Rand fan. She was a Russian Jew who was influenced by the Nazi philosopher Frederick Nietzsche, in whose home in the Swiss Alps I lived in 2015. Nietzsche was a groupie of the ruling class and blames Jews for advocating that the poor have equal status with those who are referred to in this country as "the job creators," the radical egalitarianism that is despised by the Neo-Nazi clique surrounding the president in the White House. He writes:

> *"It was the Jews who, with awe-inspiring consistency, dared to invert the aristocratic value-equation...saying "the wretched alone are the good; the poor, impotent, lowly alone are the good; the suffering, deprived, sick, ugly alone are pious, alone are blessed by God, blessedness is for them alone—and you, the powerful and noble, are on the contrary the evil, the cruel, the lustful, the insatiable, the godless to all eternity; and you shall be in all eternity the unblessed, accursed, and damned!"*

Scots Irish writer Charles Murray calls the American version of the European ruling class "the creative minority," the rich, whom he scolds for accepting the Africanization of American culture instead of opposing it. "When Tipper Gore, the wife of senator and later vice president Al Gore, attacked the incontestable violence and misogyny of rock and rap lyrics, why was she so roundly scolded by so many of her social and political peers? Why were four-letter words, which formerly were seen by the upper-middle class as déclassé, appearing in glossy upscale magazines? How had 'the hooker' look, become a fashion trend among nice girls from the suburbs?"

Paul Ryan, so removed from his origins, said that the Irish came to the United States because they couldn't grow potatoes. Even I know that the British played a role. Tony Blair even apologized. "In 1997, the British Prime Minister, Tony Blair, belatedly acknowledged that the all-powerful British government had 'stood by' while the Irish people starved in the years after 1845." As the poet Speranza, Oscar Wilde's mother put it, *"Stately ships to bear our food away, amid the stranger's scoffing/They guard our masters' granaries from the thin hands of the poor."*

Steve Bannon an Irish American who is the president's chief of staff, in his Vatican speech cites the Victorian Period as the pinnacle of the West's achievement. The Irish famine occurred during the Victorian period!! What an example of self- loathing! Bannon believes that he has better quality genes than Blacks. Someone should direct him to the cartoons in the old Harper's Weekly, in which the Irish were depicted with simian features. Irish senator, Aodhán Ó Ríordáin, calls him and the other Irish Americans surrounding the president, "Irishmen without hearts." He writes:

> *"What we're really conscious of... is that quite a number of Irish-Americans surround Trump — Bannon, Conway, Pence, Spicer, Flynn, Kelly — these are all Irish-Americans, these are all Irish names — Ryan," Ó Ríordáin said, referring to top Trump administration officials and House Speaker Paul Ryan (R-Wis.). "These are all people that in my judgment have completely forgotten their family history, because the Irish story is one that has been replicated now by other people... We were once the people who came to America as refugees.*

We were viewed by the British as being terrorists. We were people who suffered sectarian discrimination in the United Kingdom and in the U.S. as well."

Paul Ryan doesn't know this. He is far more dangerous than the president, a nihilist. Ryan has a philosophy. He and other Irish Americans of humble origin--he wants to end Social Security even though at one time he was a recipient of funds from this program--can always be relied upon to serve as enforcers for the "creative minority," the rich. When John Quincy Adams was deemed too soft on Native Americans, they brought in a Celtic thug, Andrew Jackson. Donald Trump followed President Obama who was considered feminine. Notice the number of Irish names, whether they be the police or the prosecutors, who refuse to indict the police,who are connected to the killing of unarmed Blacks, Hispanics and Native Americans. And what has the loyalty to the "creative minority," in the name of racial solidarity, gotten millions of Celtic Americans? The "creative minority" otherwise known as "the job creators," stash trillions in offshore accounts instead of creating jobs and their hirelings in Congress eliminate social programs that benefit them the most.

Another thinker who has influenced those who have the ear of the president is Raymond Bernard Cattell, a pro-Hitler thinker who was almost awarded a prize by the American Psychological Association until he was exposed by the Anti-Defamation League. Cantrell's theory of the nonviolent extermination of undesirables, Genthanasia, is the guiding philosophy of this administration or as Richard Spence, a member of the Alt Right put it, non-violent ethnic cleansings. This explains Katrina, Flint, the removal of funds for the treatment of lead poisoning, the indirect murder of Black prisoners whose symptoms are not treated, or are even ridiculed by prison authorities, the arrest of thousands of Black school children and the threat from Ayn Rand and Murray follower Paul Ryan to end health services to millions. Colonel Jeff Sessions wants to bring back mandatory minimum sentencing.

Since the Black experience is under occupation by people who have never been racially profiled, or experienced redlining and their Black surrogates whose ideology is exposed in Professors Baker and Kilson's books,

Black, Brown and Native Americans are obligated to open up spaces where their opinions can be voiced. "Dysfunctional" White ethnics need their own Baker's and Kilsons, who will challenge those who have betrayed them in order to court favor with "the creative minority."

References:

Online: irishcentral.com

Grady, A. Online: irishcentral.com/culture/the-greatest-muhammad-ali-was-very-proud-of-his-irish-roots

Leeming, D. (1994). *James Baldwin: A Biography*. New York: Alfred A.Knopf.

Online: wikileaks.org/sony/emails/emailid/132247

Online: nytimes.com/2015/06/25/business/media/citing-ben-afflecks-improper-influence-pbs-suspends-finding-your-roots.html

Online: fortune.com/2017/03/23/death-rates-white-americans-rising

Vance, J.D. (2016). *Hillbilly Elegy: A Memoir of a Family and Culture in Crisis*. New York: Harper, 2016.

Online: splcenter.org/fighting-hate/extremist-files/group/pioneer-fund

Online: amazon.com/Writings-Nietzsche-Modern-Library-Classics/.../0679783393

Murray, C. (2012). *Coming Apart: The State of White America, 1960-2010*. New York: Random House, 2012.

Online: irishcentral.com/roots/the-spoilers-93278889-237694361

Online: the-american-catholic.com/2016/11/18/remarks-of-stephen-bannon-at-a-conference-at-the-vatican/

Online: irishtimes.com/news/world/us/trump-is-a-fascist-and-i-m-embarrassed-by-the-government-s-response-1.2873639

Online: splcenter.org/fighting-hate/extremist-files/individual/raymond-cattell

U.S. presidential hopeful Donald Trump speaks in New York September 3, 2015. REUTERS/Lucas Jackson.

THE OPTICS OF WHITE NATIONALISM

TRUMP, AFRICAN AMERICANS, AND AFRICA: HYPOCRISY, LYING, AND CONTRADICTION IN THE WHITE HOUSE

MOLEFI K. ASANTE

*Molefi Kete Asante is the author of 83 books including **The History of Africa** (2014), **The African American People: A Global History** (2011), and **Revolutionary Pedagogy** (2017). He teaches in the Department of Africology at Temple University. His websites are: asante.net; mkainstitute.com; dyabukam.com*

It does not take clairvoyance to see that Donald Trump is the newest in a line of anti-African presidents. Black people have lived through the antics and attitudes of many racist presidents from the slave-holding George Washington to Donald Trump.

Africans in America have seen a parade of racist presidents. Thomas Jefferson's statement that *"I advance it therefore as a suspicion only, that the Blacks, whether originally a distinct race, or made distinct by time and circumstances, are inferior to the whites in the endowments both of body and mind"* set the presidential tone while he slept with Sally Hemings, a fourteen-year old enslaved girl. We know that Andrew Jackson held 200 Africans living at Hermitage and became known as Sharp Knife because of his slaughter of native people on his way to inciting the First Seminole War. Jackson, the so-called Indian Fighter President, set a mark for injustice and cruelty that stood for decades. We suffered through the insane racist years of James Polk, the "slaveholder's slaveholder" who mercilessly separated African people from their families out of spite and greed, maimed the complainers, had those who resisted his mystifying cruelty killed, and sent General Zachary Taylor to invade Mexican lands as a ruse for war. Even in the 21st century, the progressive students at Princeton University have protested racist Woodrow Wilson's image and name at the university where he became president. Franklin D. Roosevelt's incarceration of Japanese Americans must be classified as a racist action. Dwight Eisenhower was known to be unhappy with the decision of his appointee Earl Warren's Supreme Court decision in *Brown v. Topeka Board of Education.* Ibram Kendi's award-winning book, *Stamped from the Beginning: The Definitive History of Racist Ideas in America*, cites a sorry litany of even more racist American presidents.

Trump and African Leaders

So Trump is of the same ilk as other racist presidents; he is a white nationalist with the aim of demonstrating white superiority in relationship to African and other people. For him, only winners can be trusted because winning is a sign of superiority in his narcissistic mind. This cannot be good for Africans despite Mr. Trump's embrace of Black athletes and entertainers and phone calls to Nigeria's President Mohammed Buhari and South Africa's President Jacob Zuma during the second week of his presidency.

I am convinced that Trump's rapacious mendacity always yields one lie after another, or one damning insensitivity on top of one, or one rude tweet after another. He asked, for example, a Black reporter if she were a friend of the Congressional Black Caucus and did not understand how naïve and racist he sounded when he thought that all Blacks knew each other. A few days later he demanded that a befuddled Jewish reporter who wanted to ask about anti-Semitism "sit down" thinking that the young man wanted to question him about his personal stance on anti-Semitism. Then again, this man prancing as president has managed to anger the nation's friends, upset his own party, spout propagandistic lies that would make the Nazi *propagandaministerium* proud.

So, I have concluded that we African Americans, with a history of setting the moral compass of this nation, have a duty to educate Donald Trump to the character of this pluralistic society, not simply because we have been here longer than his two generations, but because we have an intimate understanding of the nature of racist attitudes and policies; and we always fight vigorously against them. We are not chumps when it comes to understanding the nature of racism; we genuinely know this place and have known it for generations.

The United States of America is a dynamic idea, and it cannot be left to Donald Trump to make a static, racial or regressive definition of nation. However, for the moment the impact on Donald Trump's election to the presidency of the United States reverberates around the world, but most of all it re-energizes the African population in this country.

The rude and crude chants of victory punctuating every pronouncement of the Trump Administration demonstrates superficial self important madness and almost unhinged mental contortions of a little man about an election where he lost the popular vote by three million. The fact that he did not win the popular vote and immediately began a long slide toward being the most unpopular president in history during the first month of his presidency caused him to become the most distracted and petulant president in recent memory.

Trump became president like Rutherford B. Hayes and George W. Bush became presidents; that is, the Electoral College gave each one the victory, despite the popular votes in favor of the opposing candidates. Each close election cries out for a change in this obsolete idea. Nevertheless, as democracies go, you often get your most representative people in office. If he or she is a bigot, a racist, a misogynist, a nativist, or a fascist and the people elect the person then they are reflecting their own fears and interests. Racist nations elect racist presidents. In ascending moments there are interplays of progressive tendencies but these are often aberrations.

Trump's serious non-engagement with Africa represents the invisibility of Africa in the American imagination at a time when the fastest growing economies are on the African continent and the Chinese have made a play for sharing the resources of Africa. Trump's disregard for the heroic history of resistance of African Americans is a telling sign of his lack of knowledge of American history. After all, what does a man, only interested most of his life in making profits, know or care about morality, harmony, and justice? Had he the slightest interest in the African narrative, it might have tamed his insensitivities for there is no greater story on this land than the resistance and resilience of African Americans.

The White Nationalist President

I said earlier that America is an idea, but like all ideas it is corruptible, and can become irrational, racist, sexist, and bigoted. Trump has proven that with the emergence of white nationalism sitting in the White House that Breitbart's Steve Bannon, Trump's Commissar, and Trump's crew of financial *guarimbas* can drive a wedge between the traditional liberal pluralistic and multicultural vision of society that was the marquee idea of America and the idea of a white nationalism that is a throwback to the past. Trump has managed to either abuse or neglect Latinos and African Americans during his first weeks in office. Attempts to destroy our ambitions and visions by pushing us toward the fringes of the society will not work. African Americans, like the Mexicans and Native Americans, are woven into the sinews of whatever this nation is to become.

One cannot speak about America without talking about African people. So where is Africa in Trump's rhetoric and administration?

How can a Stephen Miller, Steve Bannon, and Kellyanne Conway have anything to say worthwhile about relationships with Africa? Who are these people who somehow have come to believe that they alone are entitled to express themselves as white nationalists in a multicultural, pluralistic, and complex country. The fact that some who bellow with loud voices and demonstrate profane sensibilities have corrupted the idea is no reason to think that the facts have changed. And we know the facts.

The land we call America is powdered with the ashes of the First Nations who entered the land thousands of years before the English, German, French, Dutch, and Swedes stepped foot on this soil as nationals.

The blood of the natives fertilized the land upon which the Europeans set their plows often oblivious to what had gone on before they discovered the earth beneath their feet or crossed the streams and rivers whose banks yield millions of artifacts of civilized life.

Donald Trump and the Exceptional Nation

No nation is exceptional in isolation and no nation can be talked into exceptionalism. Donald Trump claims to speak for the nation; sometimes his speeches are staged with dumb Black people holding stupidly orchestrated and coordinated signs behind his podium as he speaks. They make themselves look like ducks lined up in a row to be slaughtered. I guarantee you that they have no understanding of their history or that of white nationalism. They are often misguided, self-deprecating, and dislocated Africans who claim that they, too, are fighting for Trump's America. It is sad but real; it is unfathomable to many of us, but certainly a part of the rhetoric of chaos that has brought about open hypocrisy and contradictions.

What is the nation? Who constitutes it? What are the unrecorded or underreported narratives of other nations on this land like the Diné, Muskogee, Iroquois, Illinois, Shawnee, Lenape, and Apache.

Who invented the Lone Ranger and why was he alone when Tonto was said to be alongside him? Whose blood and tears and foottracks through the thickets as runaways made topographical history and shaped the architecture of this nation's soul? Who are the made mixed and the trying to mix who created courage and bravery both personal and collectively to overcome America?

How does Trump deal with the racial divide, the class divide, the cultural divide, the education divide, and the electoral divide? Who speaks for my nation if it is not the African American female voter? No, Trump does not speak for the nation and he does not speak for me on democracy, generosity, humility, grace, mercy, valor, intelligence, or international appeal to the best human instincts. He is not my president; as Black people, there have been far less white men who can be called our presidents than those who have been elected. Most of the elected presidents, unfortunately, have been corrupted by white racial nationalism often feigning populism, another name for playing to the basest instincts of white Americans. If racism enters the picture as stains on presidents, only Lyndon Johnson, John F. Kennedy, Abraham Lincoln, Franklin D. Roosevelt, and Barack Obama can claim some of our allegiance; the rest have even deeper crevices of deceit than these five. I cannot claim, as whites do, that George Washington, Thomas Jefferson, Ronald Reagan, or Dwight Eisenhower were great. They wrote and said things that showed me their disdain for Africans. Even Roosevelt did terrible things to Japanese and Abraham Lincoln did not believe in our equality with whites. In Trump's case, African Americans are probably seen as dispensable and easily fooled. He loves the quality of our showmanship, athletic prowess, entertainment, and musical value, but he could only find one position for a Black in his cabinet and that one Black, Ben Carson, exudes cultural confusion and historical simplicity.

How could Trump or any of his supporters with any sense of time and space claim on this land that it belongs to them or to them alone? What elements of education are missed? Who would have the audacity to challenge facts? There are other questions, perhaps more serious that must be asked but for now we must assume that the answer lies in lack of information, ignorance of national existence and inexperience of the global political infrastructure. What could you really expect from someone who claims to be a businessman—a new term for those who have mastered the technique of cheating, lying, and deceiving in order to win at any cost? The aim of the "businessman" is to be for himself, not for others, not for the collective; and this spirit runs counter to the best ideas of African philosophy and morality.

Something bad is going on in a society when the people who should know better are neither knowledgeable nor ethical. Yet we must know, but *"How are they to know when they have been fed the poisonous diet of white nationalism and have eaten at the table of the doctrine of white male supremacy and hegemony?"* There are no nutritional values in close-mindedness and one cannot feast on lies without feeling hungry all the time. It is an insane insatiability that like a beast cradles the worst fears of people.

Trump Speaks to the Presidents of Nigeria and South Africa

I did not consider it a victory for Africa when Donald Trump phoned two African presidents on February 13, 2017. Trump's idea of cutting a deal with the leaders of those two large African nations would not serve the benefit of either Nigeria or South Africa. In fact, I am not even certain that Trump is able to turn the phone meetings with the African leaders into something positive for both sides. The reason for my pessimism is that Trump's philosophy, as led by Steve Bannon, is for a ruthless white nationalism that seeks only the interests of the 62% of the American nation that is of European heritage. Ok, I agree that telling President Muhammadu Buhari that the United States would assist with fighting Boko Haram in Nigeria sounds good, but it is not extraordinary since the United States under AFRICOM (United States Africa Command) has already been assisting in that fight. While we can say that it is gesture, it is really all that we can say now. Selling weapons to Nigeria in return for Nigerian oil may be on the table but does Nigeria really need more weapons? President Obama was not a friend to Africa either, and he certainly blocked the sale of Cobra Helicopters to Nigeria from the Israeli government on the ruse that the U.S. was against Nigeria having the weapons because of the latter's lack of protection for civilians when the army conducted military operations. One could surmise (I have no knowledge of this factually), but I speculate that the lack of sale to Nigeria of the Israeli helicopters made in America had to do with the relationship between President Obama and Netanyahu. Now that Trump is President of the United States, he is said to have a much better relationship with Netanyahu. Let the sale go on!

One could ask, *"Why can't the Nigerians build their own helicopters?"*

On the other hand, when Trump spoke to President Jacob Zuma of South Africa right after speaking with the ailing president of Nigeria it was reported that Trump stressed trade and peace on the African continent. There are more than 600 American companies doing business in South Africa. I personally know that there are some African American entrepreneurs in the country but clearly there is nothing in Trump's rhetoric, history, or background to insist that he will encourage African Americans to partner with South Africans. Trump never spoke about Africa during his presidential campaign and has no real African policy. This makes him dangerous because he could be easily swayed by the most nefarious characters operating on the African political landscape. Who is to say that he will not support, as other Republicans have, the most deleterious, sinister, and reactionary characters in Africa?

Clearly, these conversations were mandatory protocols and not clearly meaningful in terms of policy since the only use Africa has for Trump is to be a part of the American campaign against Islamic extremists. If Rex Tillerson, Trump's Secretary of State, is to be seen as important to Trump's view of the world, then one has to know that for more than forty years Tillerson's Exxon Company invested in Equatorial Guinea, Chad, Nigeria, and Angola despite the corrupted nature of several of these governments. Exxon got richer, the politicians that gave them access got rich, and the poor masses got robbed of their potential for wealth. Even now, only Nigeria, of the four nations where Exxon has multimillion-dollar investments, has open elections. Chad, Equatorial Guinea, and Angola might be models for the Trump administration where the governments allow no free press, no opposition parties, and maintain authoritarian rule.

Should Secretary Tillerson be allowed to dictate African policy, it will be a security and commercial one, not one that cares about the masses of poor people. Indeed, the liberal democratic ideas of good governance and free elections that once had the hollow ring of American imposition now seem to be quite progressive given what might be coming in the Bannon-driven White House of Trump.

It is too early to really know what the Trump Administration will do on the Africa question. But, given what we can garner from the Trump Transition Team's questions about Africa to the State Department it might not be too early to say that there will be a lessening of USAID support to African nations. Some of my colleagues have argued that this might not be a bad thing. They believe that African nations have not examined their own possibilities and potentialities because of the heavy reliance on external aid. When African nations fail to develop capacity for their citizens, they invite intrusions and interferences into their internal affairs from the United States and other powerful nations.

Our task is simple: African Americans have to hold both the government of the United States under Trump and all corrupt African governments under the microscope of good and decent governance. Take Equatorial Guinea, for example, the country where Exxon is the largest oil investor. The country produces more oil than all countries but three in the whole continent of Africa. It is often compared to Kuwait. It is the richest country per-capita income in Africa, a middle-upper income atenation, according to the World Bank, yet its population lives in entrenched poverty of less than $700 a year. The family of the president, Teodoro Obiang Nguema Mbasogo, whose son, Teodorin Obiang, is the vice president, has become one of the wealthiest families in the world with homes in California, France, and South Africa. Obiang drives Bugatti and Ferrari sports cars and owns private jets, yachts, French Impressionist paintings and a crystal-studded glove that Michael Jackson used to own. Now the French are trying him in their courts for stealing $115 million from his country. Of course, they know they have him on this because the French and perhaps Exxon helped him to steal the money.

One of the first acts of Trump's presidency was the order banning Muslims from traveling to the U..S Of the seven banned majority Muslim nations (Iran, Yemen, Iraq, Syria, Sudan, Libya, and Somalia), the last three are all African nations. These are neither the most populous Muslim nations nor yet the nations that have terrorized the U.S.. In fact, Saudi Arabia, Afghanistan, and Pakistan may be considered, given past history, most likely to create issues for Americans, not Libya, Somalia, and Sudan.

Libya may now be a failed state, but its condition is in direct relationship to the killing of Muammar Gaddafi by the Obama regime. One can actually trace the decline of free education, free health and hospital care, and abundant housing under Gaddafi to the utter disaster of Libya after the all-out attack on the country by the United States, France and Britain. Sudan is a racist state with wars of Arabs against Africans, Muslims against African traditions, and African languages against imposed Arabic, but it is not a state that has brought terror to the United States. Somalia is a failed state by years of clan wars and external intrusions and invasions and internal conflicts since the attempt by the United States to make Somalia its base at the Horn of Africa. One does not have to know the full extent of African history to understand that after Somali made an attempt to unite the Somali-speaking Ogaden with Somalia under President Siad Barre, the Soviet Union, once the sponsor of Somalia changed sides and supported Ethiopia against Siad Barre and Somalia. Barre then asked for and got United States support on the side of the Somali people. Because Somali had been supplied by the Soviet Union and then by the United States, Somalia built the largest army in Africa during the 1970s and 1980s. In 1992 and 1993, the United States led an unsuccessful attempt to restore stable government to Somalia and the failure produced still more conflict and the creation of Al-Shabaab, a militant Islamic group responsible for numerous attacks in East Africa. Trump has rolled over all sensibilities of political decorum and international diplomacy.

Trump's Banning of Muslims

Trump's dictatorial executive order on January 27, 2017 to ban people from seven Muslim countries is one of the most un-American political action against foreign-born individuals in the past fifty years. It was an irrational, almost knee-jerk response, to a perceived threat. In fact, Americans have committed most mass killings in the country since September 11, 2001. None of the initially banned countries produced terrorists that have come to the United States to commit terror.

My negative assessment of Trump's intentions is not out of bounds because I think that a virulent anti-Muslim, anti-African, anti-Asian, and anti-Latino rhetoric driven by white nationalism sits at the door of an out-of-the-closet negativity enthroned next to the presidency in the White House. If you cannot understand that this twisted vision of nation and international relations is the principal contradiction and the meme most infected with the virus of national disaster then you will never understand the need for the people to correct the coordinates. Traveling down this path, the one that other nations have followed to their own ruin, is sure to be rocky, bumpy, disconcerting, and depressing, but it will lead ultimately to historic ruin. Hence, Trump is not the president of progressive values; he is the anti-president, the white ghost of fear and anger, sinking deep into the depression of a bygone era. When white racism ruled in this country.

The Trump Nation Needs Education

There is something to be said about education, not schooling. I do not get the impression that Donald Trump has ever been educated. Schooling sends you through a system where you are introduced to certain ideas and civil notions of how to act in a society but in the end schooling rarely changes the opinions you had when you entered the system. There are some significant ideas that you ought to master as a president:

- If you believe that history on this land did not begin until the pilgrims landed on the rock they named Plymouth, then you are a victim of misinformation.

- If you think that whites civilized the Native Americans, then your education has betrayed you.

- If you have no idea of what wampum belts were used for, then you are sadly less than educated.

- If you believe that African people, the mothers and fathers of humanity, have made no contribution to world history, then you are truly in need of more information.

- If you believe that your religion is better than that of someone else's, then you have no idea of how inventive the myth-making human mind can be.

- One cannot expect people to make proper decisions if they have no true understanding of the facts of their own history.

- The imperceptible crack in the Liberty Bell has grown to become much larger over time as will the break caused by the abrasions inflicted by Trump's disinformation and misinformation.

There is something good to be said about the nature of proof, that old quality that we used to claim was important to determine what was true or not. I am not talking about the abusive and brutal tests of endurance, strength or pain inflicted by those who sought to determine witches and shamans but proof as determined by what is real according to the rubric of a logic based on what we know as fact. I am shocked by the insanity and inanities of Trump's discourse, if one can call it discourse, as he attacks every conceivable liberal idea.

I have seen nothing in Donald Trump that suggests that he knows Africa. He probably has the same limited understanding that most schooled Americans have about Africa. There are those who see Africa as a "a big country" where Black people came from to America. Pushed to explain a little more many they would probably say *"Africans sold their people to whites who brought them to America to civilize them."* Asked for further clarification, they might say, *"If Africans were not already enslaving their own people there would not have been any slaves for Europeans to buy."* Of course, this is nonsense, but we live in an era of nonsense.

First, Africa is a continent with 55 countries. These countries represent many nationalities and ethnic groups. Africans speak more languages than are spoken on any other continent. So it is not one country, but many countries and more than 2000 languages.

Second, before the coming of Arabs and Europeans to the continent, there is no history of slavery in Africa. No African nation ever used slavery as a primary mode of economic production. This is unknown to Africa, as far as I know, largely because of kinship and lineage philosophies of African people.

Third, Africa is the original home to both humanity and to civilization. This means that the DNA of every people on the earth goes back to Africa. It also means the first people to organize societies, tame the forests, build bridges across streams, plant villages in the desert, and decide what was edible and what was not, had to be Africans.

I would love to have the opportunity to teach Trump and his human trumpets that before 70,000 years ago, all the people on earth were Black because color differentiation did not occur until some Africans left the continent. Three-fourths of the time of *homo sapiens* on the earth was spent on the continent of Africa. How is it that the younger brothers and sisters of humanity have come to claim a civilizing heritage? It is like your little sister whom you taught to ride a bicycle claiming when she is an adult that she actually taught you—although you are ten years older!

Because Trump is ignorant of most of the world, despite his claim of business acumen, he is not fit to be a president that I respect. I have never understood anyway how someone who produces nothing, creates nothing, who adds nothing to the betterment of the human condition, can claim to be a good business person. Trump is a chump, a fake, a pretender to greatness, because his ambitions are individualistic and not collective. He thinks that he is absolutely the savior of America when, in fact, he demonstrates the end of the doctrine of white supremacy.

The truth is that neither Trump nor his most ardent followers understand their own history. Already by the turn of the 16th century, the European template for beguiling themselves and others had been set in place and the account of conquest solidified into a racist ideology supported by church, state, and official historians.

Thus, the lack of specificity about explorations of adventurers lingers in the hinterland of foggy imagination and questionable hearsay without clarity. Few students who go through the American educational system from kindergarten to twelfth grade could give a coherent account of the European conquest without getting lost in the fog. What actually did Columbus do? De Soto? Ponce de Leon? Cortez? How many people did they kill? How many women did they rape? What were their personal motivations for adventure, outside of the tired notion of looking for a route to India?

A Brief Context of Africans in America

The enslavement of Africans is history, whether seen as an aberration or not, and there have been many odd human actions on every continent, set in motion by the integrated forces of greed, technology, and ideology. Each aspect of this cauldron of animus reinforced the other until racism became a palpable idea supported by the allegiances of priests, prophets, and profiteers.

By the time twenty Africans were landed in the Jamestown town of Port Comfort in Virginia in 1619, Europeans had been carrying on the raiding of coastal Africa for Africans to enslave for more than one hundred years. The first Africans brought by Europeans did not come to the English colony but to the Spanish and Portuguese colonies. Approved by the Pope, and authorized by the King of Spain, enslaving nations and companies competed for *asientos* that would allow them to have unilateral control over certain region of Africa for the purpose of capturing and bargaining for captured Africans.

The record of hundreds of African battles with Europeans over the capturing of Africans has been largely underreported leaving the impression among some that Africans were sold rather than kidnapped by Europeans. So, how much would I be sold for? To whom would the European pay this sum? Would the slave ship captain bring enough "money" to pay for 800, the average number of enslaved people on a boat?

This tortured brutal story has a simple truth. Millions of Africans were uprooted from their homeland against their wills and brought across the ocean to the Americas at gunpoint to build, plant, mine, harvest, and develop the lands taken from the Natives by Europeans. The fact of the matter is that there were Africans who collaborated with the Europeans in many instances, some even becoming agents for the Europeans assisting them in capturing and holding Africans. However, collaborators did not initiate the slave trade and collaborators had no knowledge or idea or interest in sending other Africans to the Americas. This was not within their historical or ethical system of knowledge.

The guilty parties for the European Trade Slave were Europeans just as the guilty parties for the Arab Slave Trade were Arabs. It is a euphemism to speak of Atlantic Slave Trade or Sahara Slave Trade and it is a curse to speak of African Slave Trade. This "business" was other people's business for their own greedy and heinous purposes. Once we call it for what it is, then it becomes easier to deal with the implications of enslavement for Africans and European descendants in the United States.

Europeans quickly became white in the context of the enslavement of Blacks. To be Black meant to be a slave or to be a descendant of those who were enslaved; to be white meant to be an enslaver or those who were the descendant of the enslavers. America was not Europe as James Baldwin, the brilliant essayist, had observed when he wrote that *"In Europe there are no white people; the only white people are in America and South Africa."* The view expressed by Baldwin was that Europe had nationalities. One could be French, German, English, or even Turkish, but not white. America (as the great melting pot) started off with English, German, Swedes, French, and Dutch but quickly found ways to identify as white, a term that seemed elastic as new immigrants made their way from Eastern and Southern Europe. At one time Irish, Italians, Armenians, Greeks, Hungarians, and Jews were not a part of this super construction of white, but after the 1924 Asian Exclusion Act, which included southern and eastern Europeans the melting pot ideas came to include these groups but not Chinese and Japanese. A few decades later the question of Hispanics would be raised by the US Census and the decision to speak of Hispanics who were white and Hispanics who were Black would further enlarge the white classification. By the time the Office of Budget Management declared that a person born in North Africa was white, the term had come simply to mean anyone other than Africans with a history of being enslaved in America.

The Election of Donald Trump

We are at a critical juncture for how we communicate dissatisfaction with a president leaning toward fascism as a way of expressing, not condemnation, but something more hopeful, about what it is that we do not know, but should know.

The election of Donald Trump in the 240th year of the American nation which is still less than the 246 years we spent enslaved in the bosom of this country, is one last tweet of a dying racism. As I watched on January 21, 2017 as thousands of women filed by my house in Philadelphia on the way to demonstrate against Trump's election, I saw a sign that read *"I can't believe this shit."* I know that the anti-Trump views I hold are shared by millions and will torment us until the nation coughs up this foreign body buried in its soul.

Reactionary Republican sentiment is illusive and has all of the elements of delusion when it is expressed. Those who believe in their own realities created out of the thin air of imagination will fall victim to every whim of a dictatorial impulse.

I am not convinced that Donald Trump is legitimate as a president of the United States because I do not believe he honors the Constitution. He has violated the emoluments clause in the Constitution, demonstrated a rare ignorance of good judgment when it comes to diplomacy, raised the curtain on the most vile and obscene notions of torture, and refused to reveal his taxes which could show to whom he gave money and from where he received his money.

Trump presents us with a despicable narrative of conquest. His words follow the same pattern of lying that we see in the schoolhouse story that Columbus discovered America. As the first "explorer" to arrive in the Americas, Columbus is given credit for opening the way for future Europeans to arrive and settle in the Americas. Honor to him is a part of the defining narrative of what it means to be a European in this land. Of course, there is the narrative of the Native People who first interacted with the European travelers. What the Caribs, Arawak, and Taino, and their descendants tell is a different account, often verified by the written records of the Europeans themselves. Columbus murdered many of the native leaders at a banquet. The account of this murder of the native leaders who had gathered to eat harks back to so many tales of betrayal from the Greek Period.

Progress in the social accommodation of the peoples of the United States of America has been defined by the degree to which whites have become less white because in a real sense it is this whiteness, this illusion, that has given rise to the many privileges and problems of whiteness. The narrative is slowly being rewritten by brave historians who see a revolutionary way to change the habits of hate and the dictates of meanness, all brazen helmets to protect whiteness from the falling sky. Trump will not be able to turn back history; the future is inexorable.

You cannot go around believing that you are superior to other people and be real in the 21st century whatever desire there is for a notion of Trumpian exceptionalism. The only privilege that one should have is because one has earned it by being named a wise elder, an honorable person because of virtue, a gifted artist or scientist, an inspirational teacher, or a good human. This is not based on color, racial background, religion, or shape of your eyes.

It is not my place to correct all of this history, but it is necessary to set the record straight so that information becomes more available to larger groups of masses that will understand why a white nationalist parading as a populist can be elected president in the United States. Our posture must remain as it has always been in this nation when we have been confronted with hypocrisy and ethical contradictions; we must resist because in resistance there is political awakening and redemption.

People protest against U.S. President-elect Donald Trump in Berlin, Germany, November 12, 2016. REUTERS/Axel Schmidt

AGENT ORANGE: DONALD TRUMP AS POLITICAL CHEMICAL WARFARE

JARED A. BALL

Jared A. Ball is a father and husband. After that, he is a Professor of Media and Africana Studies at Morgan State University. He produces multimedia for imixwhatilike.org

"President Agent Orange, for perpetuating all of the evil that you been perpetuating throughout the United States, I want to thank President Agent Orange for your unsuccessful attempt at the Muslim ban... when we come together... We the people! We the people! We the people!"

— **Busta Rhymes**

The election of Donald Trump speaks to the precarious state of radical activism and organization and to the trappings of electoral politics and specifically the Democratic Party. Our inability or refusal to develop genuine alternatives to existing political structures that capture and galvanize the majority of us who are beyond fed up with this place and an almost psychotic, irrational and imposed obeisance to the Democratic Party must be obliterated. Notions of pragmatism and of being "mature" have stunted our ability to even dream properly of a world we need to create. I want to, as Bob Brown has said, *"shotgun that idea,"* because in a twist of what Jamilah Lemieux tweeted recently, *"I've run out of maturity minutes... My adulting plan is done."*

It is appropriate that the man that gave us *Extinction Level Event* would take also the occasion of a recent event to level a blow against our extinction – or at least, prove worthy of extinction existing formations, protocols and encouraged patterns of behavior. Now, I doubt I can prove at this point the extent to which I have argued for years that Busta Rhymes is an underrated top 5 or 10 emcee, but I have. His anthemic hook to *Everybody Rise* would often be featured during the many iterations of our broadcast radio and mixtape work. I mean, his name says it! He Busts Rhymes! Longevity. Check. Massive hits. Check. Legendary collaborations. Check. Undeniable recognizable flow. Check. Fully energetic, top flight live performance. Check. Subtle wisdom (via the Five-Percent Nation and elsewhere). Check. And lets not discount, which I think often happens, his lyricism. But now, with his most recent Grammy appearance alongside A Tribe Called Quest, I can add to that list, overt radical political critique! Check. It was measured for Busta Rhymes, but clear and strong. Donald Trump, he said, is "Agent Orange." Its more than funny. Like many of Rhymes' rhymes, it's a loaded and deeply-packed label.

The line got gobs of media attention, retweets and likes. However, missing from most of the media praise (and some criticism), was a sufficient look at the depth of the claim. It is a brilliant and cavernous pun, that Donald Trump is Agent Orange. Yes, yes, his manicured hair and complexion are ripe for commentary and jokes. But, the pun and comparison it offers us is brilliant. Agent Orange is, of course, a chemical warfare agent, developed and deployed as military weaponry by the United States as part of its imperial campaign primarily during Operation Ranch Hand in its invasion of Vietnam. Agent Orange is meant to aggressively attack and devastate the environment of an enemy, creating havoc and destabilizing their ability to defend themselves. It is also meant to cause post-deployment, permanent damage via the lingering effects of harmful chemicals in the natural environment of the target population. But even after the initial (and subsequent) devastation there still remains a need to judge its context, purpose or conditions of development and to asses reasons behind its deployment if for no other reason to better understand an enemy that would produce such a weapon or use such a tactic.

Agent Orange, like any product comes as a culmination of a process, and like its front man president, turned eponym by Rhymes' genius, a process marked by an often overlooked ruling-elite, particularly its relatively liberal wing, which hides behind more easily consumed in unsophisticated symbolic forms. That is, while variations of U.S. imperialism are at play their popular representations are often reduced to childish renditions packaged for mass distribution intending to create an imposed confusion. White supremacy is reduced to old southern tropes about Confederate flags, "No Colored" signs, hillbillies and spaghetti western fantasies. Capitalism is condensed into "reality television," and epic myths about home remodeling or fame. Imperial war is passed off as a patriotic duty to spread a democracy abroad sold to us via popular film often itself a result of an incestuous Pentagon-Hollywood relationship, or we get this fed to us as cop and court room television dramas suggesting an undo legitimacy for the domestic and international "the rule of law."[1] And leadership or authority is apparently arrived at every four years in a fully produced propagandized spectacle known to us as presidential elections but which are more appropriately described by Noam Chomsky as "quadrennial extravaganzas."[2]

Despite an abundance of and variations taken on the theme of a rising fascism and radical or "Alt Right" as a leading reason for Trump's victory, I see his win resulting more from the failures (or complicity) of the liberal-wing of the nation's ruling-elite. As is often the case, ensconced power, ruling classes and even the deep state-within-a-state go unnoticed, or, at worst, go lightly scathed as atrocities are tabulated. But the continuing effects of and inequality fostered by – and of course the establishment and maintenance – of African enslavement were not developed, carried out, codified by Constitutional law and maintained as a legal business for centuries by the Confederacy. Jefferson Davis was a Democratic Representative and Senator, then U.S. Secretary of War before his inauguration as President of a seceded Confederacy in 1861. He flew the stars and stripes long before he flew the stars and bars, and the Confederacy has never, then nor now, been the national governing body. Jim/Jane Crow were not maintained under a Confederate government nor run by red necks who need Prilosec. The extension of enslavement through schooling and prisons did not occur under the auspices of the Confederacy, nor have their modern equivalents in school-to-prison-pipelining or imperial war policies.

To that end, that of "perpetual war for permanent peace,"[3] it has not been a Confederate or Klan government driving a military-industrial-complex which produced an Agent Orange (and worse) and the ongoing war for global hegemony into which it was deployed. Much of all this and the rest of what exposes North American hypocrisy, including the worsening material conditions today of Black, Brown and working communities, occurred under the auspices of the liberal-wing of the ruling-elite. It is not the overtly racist Klansman, or the brash and loud "Alt-Right" who establish policies the late Ron Walters described as "White Nationalism,"[4] it is the seemingly rational, the sophisticated, mature and often liberal ruling-elite who create these conditions and who, worst of all, are presented as an only option for well-meaning people looking for redress of the very conditions caused by those policies.

It may be that Donald Trump won the presidential election as a Republican, but it is the existence and behavior of the Democratic Party – the most overt and organized body of the liberal wing of the ruling elite – which as many have noted, "paved the way" for a Trump presidency and many of the policies he has or intends to enact.[5] While, again, presenting themselves as the only rational choice for the sane, it was the Democratic Party that most recently gave us two terms of Barack Obama and then attempted to follow that hustle with an even worse option, Hillary Clinton. After the empty symbol of a pretty Black family, Obama mostly just gave us mass deportations, expansion of "wars against terrorism," an expansion of the Africa Command (AFRICOM), drone strikes, increased Wall Street bailouts, refusals to prosecute bankers, increased police funding post-Ferguson uprisings, record-setting targeting of whistleblowers, refusals to protect net neutrality, support for the privatization of both healthcare and education, a full back-turn on his initial campaign promise to help workers unionize (remember the Employee Free Choice Act or EFCA? No? Neither apparently did he since Obama never said it again once elected), plenty of condescending speeches to Black people and blame for continental African poverty on African corruption as opposed to anything having to do with historical and contemporary forms of European imperial exploitation, assassination, theft and military conflict.

More specific to the Trump victory were the Democratic Party's twin pillars of self-destructive futility; wreck Bernie Sanders and promote Donald Trump. Here is where I suggest that the fraudulence of what is considered Left in the U.S. and the Democratic Party – the most popular and organized formation of the liberal wing of the ruling elite – as an option for progressive hope is further exposed.

As millions of people attempted to make an electoral political advance by pushing the relatively more progressive Sanders to the Democratic nomination and demonstrated him as the more likely than Clinton to defeat Trump in a general election, the party worked feverishly to hamper their best option in favor of something and someone far worse. Rather than have their political apparatus behave in a fashion consistent with its claims as an electoral home for the people, the Democratic Party chose the risk of dirty tricks in an attempt to sway their party back to Clinton rather than supporting a more likely party victory with Sanders, who they saw as too far left.

It was the Democratic Party that rigged and then stole their primary from Sanders while helping to develop a Trump campaign that would delegitimize the Republican Party making it easier for the uninspiring Clinton to defeat. The Democratic National Committee (DNC) was actively frightened by the popularity of Sanders, more specifically the popularity of the ideas he encouraged audiences to believe he represented. It wasn't that Sanders was a real socialist, or that he, indeed, advanced a national understanding of what that means. It was more that Sanders symbolized a general will among many to redistribute society's benefits downward and its (economic) pain upwards, to stop wars (even if it wasn't understood how much money Sanders was taking from defense contractors) and to spread broad, even vague, messages of openness and humanity. In short, the DNC took this as a threat and a challenge to its unwillingness to be what it claims it is, so they worked to deny Sanders media time and to characterize him and his ideas as unfit. We learned (via WikiLeaks) of an overall campaign within the DNC to engage in an effort against Sanders which "undermined democracy":

> In its recent leak of 20,000 DNC emails from January 2015 to May 2016, DNC staff discuss how to deal with Bernie Sanders' popularity as a challenge to Clinton's candidacy. Instead of treating Sanders as a viable candidate for the Democratic ticket, the DNC worked against him and his campaign to ensure Clinton received the nomination.[6]

Further, the DNC attempted to discredit Sanders as an "atheist," and engaged in a wide array of tactics which included the very early/premature selection of Clinton by her party's superdelegates to:

> … planning debate schedules to ensure the lowest possible viewing audience; widespread voter suppression through registrations being dropped, party registration being changed, or receiving incorrect ballots; manipulating voter registration rules; forged signatures on voter registration sheets; scandalously high discrepancies in many states between exit poll results and actual voting tallies (disparities that were not evident in either the Republican primary or the 2008 Democratic primary); officials conspiring to paint Sanders as an atheist, as revealed in the recent WikiLeaks email dump; and the list goes on…

> Her campaign's collusion with the DNC (not to mention her corporate media allies, lobbyists and tech industry cohorts) to undermine Senator Sanders' bid for the nomination – to any rational, thinking person who'd paid even the slightest bit of attention to the unfolding race – was as obvious as it was incensing. The party's hierarchy, working with their establishment counterparts at state and local levels, did everything they could to sabotage and stifle the Vermont Senator's burgeoning campaign.[7]

Then there is also the lesser-discussed research demonstrating further that possibility that the DNC worked to rig the very voting machines (among other tactics) to assure Clinton, not Sanders, won their party's primary:

> The existence of stored digital images of the ballots cast in most US precincts was recently discovered by election integrity activists, who last summer charged that the results of the 2016 Democratic primaries were riddled with evidence of fraud. The activists and experts, one of whom includes the 100th president of the American Statistical Association, suggest that Bernie Sanders actually won the Democratic nomination. In the report *"Democracy Lost: A Report on the Fatally Flawed 2016 Democratic Primaries,"* the authors called for: "decertification of the 2016 Democratic primary results in every state in which we have established a reasonable doubt as to the accuracy of the vote tally."[8]

Trump was among the shortlist of the DNC's strategy to develop straw candidates against whom Clinton could more easily win in a national general election. Her deserved unpopularity, coming on the heels of 8 years of a nearly useless Obama presidency, had made Clinton all but anathema to her apparent constituency most of whom were defecting to Sanders' camp. So the party engaged in a media campaign to bolster Trump as a "Pied Piper" who would drag his party farther to the right making them less likely to gain mass support nationally, while also scaring as many as possible into the Clinton campaign fold.[9]

The success, in other words, of Donald Trump's candidacy is intimately tied to and is the result of the work of the Democratic Party – or established, liberal, monied, ingrained power. It was not poor or disaffected White laborer or college student any more than it was the every woman and man Black voter that lofted Obama to office twice.

It was the DNC and Clinton campaigns that encouraged, promoted and supported the eventual rise of Trump. It was their allies in mainstream commercial media who, while admitting to not liking Trump, could not deny their DNC friend's requests or the ratings and ad revenue the man generated.

Trump's candidacy, "may not be good for America," said CBS Chairman Les Moonves, "but it's damn good for CBS."[10] And it would not just be the so-called "liberal media" – which may be operated by liberals but are undoubtedly owned by far more right-wing and conservative major stockholders, conglomerates and private equity groups – who have made Trump so pervasive, it has been also a friendly media environment provided him for so many years.

Even a quick Wikipedia refresher reminds of just how much time we've spent being inundated with Trump by a media ecology that have long loved and provided him with mentions, references and appearances, assuring that for us he became a kind of ever-present and yet easily dismissed entity.[11] Even before *The Apprentice*, from comics, television and film references to even at least 50 separate hip-hop tracks referencing him over a "25 years of Donald Trump mentions in hip-hop,"[12] Trump has been imposed on us to a point where, as Theodor Adorno said long ago, *like* is confused for *recognition*. Even where these pop cultural references are critical they speak to the fact that his presence was not at all inconsistent with the routine order of things any more than news organizations would find it inappropriate to suspend coverage of bad news. And as reported, it was the previously existing media biases against Muslims (among many others) that have, again, "paved the way" for Trump's ban.[13]

It was the DNC and Clinton campaign who scuttled their own frontrunner and apparently stole the primary from Sanders.

Clinton and her supporters may well point to FBI director James Comey and his "October surprise," but it was her campaign, her personality, and mostly her center-right, hawkish, and neoliberal political track record along with mostly the machinations of her own party that backfired and caused her defeat. It then was also fitting that it would be the Democratic Party, the nominal best option for the Left and for peace, that would see both its leading candidates, Hillary Clinton and Bernie Sanders, become the largest recipients of 2016 defense contractor campaign financing.[14] Once again, Agent Orange is unleashed upon the world by the United States' permanent power structure, its deep state, via its most liberal major political party.

The post-deployment and extrapolated suffering of Agent Orange is in some ways already visible most notably in national tendencies toward fear and liberalism. Fear encourages apathy and stagnation while liberalism encourages further attempts to revive or save the Democratic Party. Were it not enough that the Dems perpetrated this primary fraud (extending their very foundational purpose) the Clintons and Obama then came right back to assure their man Tom Perez held off any hope that a Keith Ellison might continue the popularity of Sanders' platform (or at least energy). But Ellison had his Blackness dragged through the "anti-Semitic" mud – probably more for his tendency to support single-payer healthcare than anything he once said regarding the Nation of Islam or Zionism while in college – by a "…very reactionary, very reactive opposition…" who were "…incredibly worried about the progressive wing of the party having access through the chair."[15]

Agent Orange should be one of many final straws that create a permanent fissure in the Democratic Party scattering its devotees toward more radical winds. Practically, this would mean developing other electoral political formations and committing to move beyond electoral politics altogether. Psychologically, this would mean an important, necessary break with the state as currently formed. There is no salvation here and those wedded to reformist fantasies have to, in this moment in particular, be vigorously challenged. For, it is in this moment that there is a new attempt being developed to cajole (corral) potentially disaffected voters back into the fold under the guise of national unity and respect for the office of the presidency. Either it's a direct call for reinvigorating the Democratic Party or a more broad and vague, but equally damaging, call for support of the current administration. For example, the liberal mainstream media standard-bearer MSNBC, specifically the Morning Joe program – who prided themselves as leading Trump critics – began immediately after Trump's first inaugural address on the morning of March 1, 2017 to praise the president for his calm and measured tone and repeatedly made the point that it was a speech that Ronald Reagan, Bill Clinton or Barack Obama could have given.[16] Exactly.

But, I much prefer the calls from folks like Kamau Franklin, Kali Akuno, and Rosa Clemente that we become Ungovernable and develop new formations that do not necessarily even involve electoral politics.[17] I am inspired by the position taken by Dhoruba bin-Wahad that rather than be cowed by the election of Trump that we form a more aggressive national united front against fascism.[18]

Cynthia Mckinney has argued for a "DemExit," that we all break with all parties and become independent voters who organize in blocks to vote our interests, not a party.[19] This sounds good to me provided there is an organized movement with accountable leadership whose goals are, to the extent possible, to use the concept of voting to galvanize and organize on a large scale while also challenging the contradictions inherent to electoral politics and the pursuit of political power.

I have said we can call this effort The After Party. The phrase "after party" has always connoted an advance, a move to a new and better setting that will enhance previous efforts to party. What follows the abject failures of the two dominant parties? The After Party. But the goal, as I understand McKinney, would be to develop a front that operates (perhaps more broadly but along similar political lines) more akin to how Malcolm X once described the Organization of Afro-American Unity's approach to voting:

> ... We the [OAAU] will start immediately a voter-registration drive to make an Independent voter; we propose to support and/or organize political clubs, to run Independent candidates for office, and to support any Afro-American already in office who answers to and is responsible to the Afro-American community.[20]

The encouragement of Busta Rhymes that we see Trump as Agent Orange can be turned into one of those accidental pop cultural occurrences that crashes the intent and purpose of such commercial spaces. Let it be the call to which we refer when we think back to when we broke with convention saying finally, "Ya Basta!" Enough! Agent Orange has been deployed as an assault on our environment, but this is not an ascendence of a mad right-wing. This is the result of the success of the left-wing of the ruling-elite to assure that progressivism dies within its own ranks. Its lingering post-deployment intended effect must be seen as a kind of collaborative assault between competing circles among those who currently rule meant to terrorize us into stagnation or repeated patterns of behavior.

No currently formed organizations or political parties are viable at this point for the kinds of action required. No one is coming. As Busta's ATCQ comrades put it, there is no currently acceptable plan for us, its time to *"Move on to the stars" of new political formations because, "… there ain't a space program for niggas…"*[21]

References:

[1]Laura Nader and Ugo Mattei, *Plunder: When the Rule of Law is Illegal*, Wiley-Blackwell, 2008.

[2]Noam Chomsky, The Disconnect in US Democracy, *Khaleej Times*, October 29, 2004, Online: chomsky.info/20041029/

[3]Gore Vidal, amazon.com/Perpetual-War-Peace-How-Hated/dp/156025405X

[4]Ronald Walters, *White Nationalism, Black Interests: Conservative Public Policy and the Black Community*, Detroit: Wayne State University, 2003, 23.

[5]Do a simple web search for "Democrats paved the way…" and you will find dozens of articles accurately making variations of this claim.

[6]Michael Sainato, "Wikileaks Proves Primary Was Rigged: DNC Undermined Democracy," observer.com/2016/07/wikileaks-proves-primary-was-rigged-dnc-undermined-democracy/, 7/22/16

[7]Charlie Musgrove, "How Hillary Clinton TOOK the nomination (and why she'd better pray they DON'T dump Trump)," August, 9, 2016, markcrispinmiller.com/2016/08/how-hillary-clinton-took-the-nomination-and-why-shed-better-pray-they-dont-dump-trump

[8]Ralph Lopez, "We can PROVE if there's election fraud this Tuesday—but officials nationwide won't let us!," November 6, 2016. Online: markcrispinmiller.com

[9]Podesta Emails, "2016 GOP presidential candidates," Wikileaks Cable: 1973MADRID01251_b, dated April 7, 2015. Online: wikileaks.org/podesta-emails/fileid/1120/251

[10]Eliza Collins, "Les Moonves: Trump's run is 'damn good for CBS'," February 29, 2016. Online: politico.com/blogs/on-media/2016/02/les-moonves-trump-cbs-220001

[11]Wikipedia, "Donald Trump in Popular Culture," Online: wikipedia.org/wiki/Donald_Trump_in_popular_culture

[12]"25 years of Donald Trump mentions in hip hop." Online: youtube.com/watch?v=m3PDW6g1ceU

[13]"How Corporate Media Paved the Way for Trump's Muslim Ban," FAIR. Online: http://fair.org/home/how-corporate-media-paved-the-way-for-trumps-muslim-ban

[14]Alexander Cohen, "The Defense Industry's Surprising 2016 Favorites: Bernie & Hillary," April 1, 2016. Online: politico.com/magazine/story/2016/03/2016-election-defense-military-industry-contractors-donations-money-contributions-presidential-hillary-clinton-bernie-sanders-republican-ted-cruz-213783

[15]Héctor Figueroa, DNC member, president of the 163,000-member SEIU Local 32BJ and an Ellison supporter quoted in, Cole Stangler, "How the Democratic Establishment Beat Back Keith Ellison's DNC Bid." Online: inthesetimes.com/article/19958/keith-ellison-dnc-chair-tom-perez-political-revolution

[16]MSNBC, Morning Joe archives, March 1, 2017. Online: msnbc.com/morning-joe

[17]Ungovernable 2017. Online: ungovernable2017.com

[18]Dhoruba bin-Wahad, "'Don't Be Scared: Organize A National United Front Against Fascism": Dhoruba bin-Wahad on the 2016 U.S. Elections." Online: imixwhatilike.org/2016/11/09/dont-be-scared-organize-a-national-united-front-against-fascism-dhoruba-bin-wahad-on-the-2016-u-s-elections

[19]Cynthia McKinney, RT, March 7, 2017. Online: rt.com/shows/rt-america/379799-rt-america-march72017

[20]John Henrik Clarke, *Malcolm X: The Man and His Times*, p. 339, Trenton, NJ: Africa World Press, 1990.

[21]A Tribe Called Quest, "The Space Program," *We Got It From Here... Thank You 4 Your Service* (2016), Epic.

NUMBER 45 AND THE PERSISTENCE OF WHITE NATIONALISM

KELLY HARRIS

Kelly Harris is an Associate Professor and coordinator of African American Studies at Chicago State University. His areas of expertise include Black politics, African politics, and Black political thought.

"But let's be honest: some groups commit more crimes and use more welfare, other groups are mainly unskilled and illiterate illegals, and some religions inspire violence and don't value human life."

— **Ian Haney Lopez**, *Dog Whistle Politics*[1]

The March 27, 2017 issue of *The New Yorker* features an essay by Jane Mayer "The Reclusive Hedge Fund Manager Behind the Trump Presidency."[2] Mayer provides a rich description of Robert Mercer and his influence on the far-right movement.

Mercer, a billionaire hedge-fund investor, was not satisfied simply making philanthropic donations to a variety of right-wing groups and candidates. He sought an avenue to transform American politics and saw an opportunity in Steve Bannon and Breitbart News, a radical right online news and opinion juggernaut. Bannon has championed Brietbart as the voice of the Alt-Right. From the moment Bannon joined the Trump campaign as chief strategist and was elevated to White House Chief Strategist, the Alt-Right movement has taken center stage in American discourse. However, as is often the case, the Alt-Right movement is more old wine in new bottles than a new revolutionary ideology.

The presidential election of 2016 was supposed to be Hillary Clinton's for the taking. Newsrooms certainly prepared stories of the first woman president in U.S. history after the results of the election. What few people expected was for Donald Trump, political novice, to upset the apple cart. Although the election of Trump was met with widespread awe and derision, he had support from a vocal White base. Trump, by claiming Barack Obama as a foreigner, Hillary Clinton as a Criminal, Black people as having nothing to lose, declaring what amounts to war against Islam, and a plethora of politically incorrect statements, effectively endeared himself to the Alt-Right movement - a movement that unabashedly embraces White nationalism and White supremacy.

White Nationalism Renascent

The Alt-Right movement has been discussed as if it is a radically new approach to politics. Though the term is new, White nationalism, which undergirds the Alt-Right movement, has a long history in America. Shorn of its manifold titles (conservatism, Alt-Right, radical right, etc.), the movement is rooted in a few core beliefs that have stood the test of time: American culture is the legacy of White men, anti-immigration, anti-government, anti-social programs, and anti-liberal arts education. Bypassing the obvious that America began as an experiment in White supremacy, the White nationalist movement that currently exists in America, has dotted the American landscape since the turn of the 20th century. Thomas Dixon, Jr. did as much as any writer at the turn of the 20th century to revitalize the White Nationalist movement with his publication of *The Leopard's Spots* (1902) and *The Clansman: A Historical Romance of the Ku Klux Klan* (1905). Both works idealized the Klan as heroic defenders of the American (White) way of life. Sandwiched between Dixon's work was Woodrow Wilson's *A History of the American People*. All three-works (two by Dixon and one by Wilson) informed the grand 1915 production of D.W. Griffith's *The Birth of a Nation*, a decidedly racist rendering of Reconstruction and the birth of the Klan. Griffith's film lingers as a testament to the power of propaganda.

According to Cedric Robinson, Wilson's book, "in its treatment of the Civil War, Reconstruction, and the Ku Klux Klan…was so profoundly negative towards Blacks and solicitous of 'White civilization' that Griffith would unabashedly borrow from its structure *The Birth of a Nation*."[3] The film was really the culmination of America's version of the *"White Man's Burden."* The Spanish-American War of 1898 and ensuing colonies led to W.E.B. Du Bois' spectacularly prescient "The Problem of the twentieth century is the problem of the color line." The White Nationalist movement that ushered in the 20th century by justifying American forays into land occupied by Black, Brown, and Yellow people ignored the contradictions inherent in America's own documents by retreating to White privilege. The idea of White privilege became embedded in conservative thought and is particularly strong among its most radical elements.

Like the manner that Griffith's *Birth of a Nation* mythologized American history, Trump's campaign slogan to "Make America Great Again" was rooted in the art of propaganda rather than any historical context useful to groups outside the domain of Whiteness. Indeed, his campaign was one long marketing ploy to construct a narrative about America that privileged whiteness. Similarly, his Nixonesque call for law and order reinforced the narrative he was constructing.

In discussing the significance of social construction on target populations, Ronald W. Walters, in *White Nationalism, Black Interests*, points to the work of Helen Schneider and Anne Ingram:

> The social construction of target populations refers to the cultural characterization or popular images of the persons or groups whose behavior and well-being are affected by public policy. These charac-

terizations are normative and evaluative, portraying groups in positive or negative terms through symbolic language, metaphors, and stories.[4]

The renascent White Nationalism of the early 20th century reflected a white fear of Black movement. Throughout American history White nationalists have always been threatened by the movement of African Americans – literally and symbolically. Every instance of White backlash to perceived losses is a response to symbolic and literal Black movement. Slave rebellions (planned or carried out), development of a Black counter-public, Reconstruction, the Great Migration, development of the radical Black press, the Civil Rights and Black Power Movements, and the election of Barack Obama. Each instance was met with a counter response by White supremacists determined to maintain their power. While there is a consistency of White recalcitrance to Black progress in American history, Cedric Robinson to contextualizes the import and significance of Griffith's work:

> What Griffith consciously had served as midwife for was the birth of a new, virile American Whiteness, unencumbered by the historical memory of slavery, or being enslaved, undaunted by the spectacle of racial humiliation so suddenly manufactured by the shock of poor white immigrants arriving in the cities…No force in the world was its equal. No moral claim would dare challenge the sovereignty of race right.[5]

The Radical Right as Precursor to Alt-Right

In 1964, Daniel Bell edited *The Radical Right*, an expanded edition of the 1955 text of the same name. Bell and authors who contributed to the book were responding to McCarthyism and a growing fundamentalism. Nineteen fifty-five was also the year the National Review was first published. Under the leadership of William F. Buckley the magazine would become somewhat of a standard-bearer for the new right. Efforts to grapple with the election of Donald Trump and rise of the Alt-Right would do well to go back and read Bell and his colleagues work. While one must always be careful not to oversimplify contemporary political phenomena as an extension of past movements, the Radical Right roots of the Alt-Right is so glaringly obvious that it cannot be ignored.

Prior to the uproar caused by McCarthyism during the 1950s and the *Birth of a Nation* in 1915, a "backlash" tradition had already developed in America. The de jure end of the Civil War was quickly met by the birth of the Klan and the end of Reconstruction was met with White redemption of the south. In fact, by 1880, the redemption of the south was in full bloom. This idea of redemption has been a constant presence in American politics since its first appearance and is a feature of the current White nationalist movement. To be sure, Justice Taney's majority opinion in the Dred Scott decision of 1857 that the framers of the constitution did not have Black people in mind when they thought of citizens' rights, captured the sentiment of, if not most 19th century White Americans, then a good portion of them.

Because the Dred Scott decision is so ingrained in the White nationalist psyche, Black progress, symbolic or real, can only be understood by the Radical Right as a zero-sum game. There is no room for mutual progress. In fact, Robert Mercer, the primary investor in the Alt-Right movement and the Trump campaign, views the Civil Rights Act of 1964 as a terrible mistake.

By the time Bell published *The Radical Right*, he could speak to the confluence of forces that energized the movement. By doing so, he anticipates Robinson's *Forgeries of Memory* even though he came from a different perspective. Bell discussed the formation of a national culture that developed from the invention of the automobile, motion pictures, and the radio.[6] While Bell does not use the phrase "White nationalism" he effectively describes the same crusade:

> Until the mid-1920s, America in its top and middle layers had been, politically and culturally, a fairly homogenous society...But in time its dominion was challenged, and principally from the cities. The year 1920 was the first in American history when a majority of persons lived in urban territory.[7]

Bell was describing the Great migration coupled with the influx of immigrants to urban areas. Black migration from the South increased during the same year Woodrow Wilson premiered Birth of a Nation at the White House. At the same period White Nationalism received a boost from the film, anti-communism and fear of immigrants was stoked because of WWI. The International Workers of the World and the emerging Black Press became primary targets for the growing American intelligence industry. As a result, the Espionage Act (1917) and Sedition Act (1918) were passed to curtail the Red Scare.

In retrospect, the race riots during the late teens were predictable. While African Americans were eager to assert their newfound status as "New Negroes" by developing an independent press, White Nationalists read their activity as a part of a larger communist conspiracy. A myth that reverberates through the conservative movement today.

By the time of the first edition of *The Radical Right* in 1955, there had already been a long tradition of anti-communism and a concern that the New Deal placed the United States on what Freidrich Hayek called *The Road to Serfdom*. Hayek along with Ayn Rand were the two most important scholars on the influence of the early Radical right movement. A large part of their appeal was the idea of Western exceptionalism.

Hayek from the very beginning of his work sets the terms of debate that conservatives would use up to the present. The choice becomes one between slavery and freedom and the war of ideas is hammered home throughout the text. Additionally, Hayek emphasizes the need to protect Western values, which became another staple of the conservative movement, particularly its most radical elements. Hayek's work became popular among select businessmen in the U.S. and led to the founding of the Mont Pelerin Society – a society where "businessmen could work with scholars in a common political and ideological struggle, defending the market against the incursion of New Deal Liberalism."[8] The group of intellectuals and businessmen that came together to form Mont Pelerin Society created a model for the later success of the conservative. A model where intellectuals and their ideas would receive significant financial backing from businessmen seeking to preserve White nationalism.

Kim Phillips-Fein examined how businessmen crusaded against the New Deal from its inception and how Hayek provided the intellectual cover the movement had longed for. But it was not until the 1960s that the Radical Right came to full bloom. By "donating money to think tanks and by reading the studies those think tanks produced," businessmen helped shape a force in American politics that continues to inform the far right. One of the flagship organizations for the Radical Right, the John Birch Society, was formed in 1958. Fred Koch and Robert Welch were two of the more prominent founders. Limited government and anti-communism were the guiding principles of the society. Robert Welch even accused Dwight Eisenhower of being a communist agent. Eisenhower's error? He Accepted the New Deal and the role of government in "hop[ing] that twentieth-century capitalism could be reformed so that America was no longer divided by class or economic conflict."[9] But, as Hofstadter pointed out, the radical right allowed no room for dissension. True conservatives had to either conform to their understanding of American values or risk being labelled a traitor, communist, spy, or revolutionary.

The Radical Right and Dog Whistles

Donald Trump is not original or unique. While it is understandable that Trump's histrionics can lead to overstatements about what he represents. The reality is that he is the latest in the line of presidents that use dog whistles to amplify White Nationalist sentiments. Trump most notably utilized this strategy when throwing his hat in the "birther" ring. Questioning Barack Obama's bona fides as an American citizen was a signal to White Nationalists that he was of the same mind. The subtext of the far-right birther movement was that the presidency was occupied by a radical whose allegiance is more to the communist and Black Power movement than to the United States. "Birthers" were the latest addition to the new radical right that espoused the same anti-communist sentiment of the past in addition to the tropes of big government, states' rights, and American values.

However, it was not simply Obama who was being rejected and cast as public enemy number one. In the same way that adherents of the radical rights attacked Eisenhower, the new Alt-Right movement portrayed the conservative movement as represented by congressional republicans and the Bush administrations as betraying White nationalism. As an example of continuity, we can turn to Richard Hofstadter in his 1955 essay *"The Pseudo-Conservative Revolt"* where he explains:

> The restlessness, suspicion and fear manifested in various phases of the pseudo-conservative experiences in his capacity as a citizen. He believes himself to be living in a world in which he is spied upon, plotted against, betrayed, and very likely destined for total ruin. He feels that his liberties
> have been arbitrarily and outrageously invaded. He is opposed to almost everything that has happened in American politics for the past twenty years.[10]

Hofstadter could easily have been discussing Donald Trump and his assertion that the Obama administration wiretapped his phones. Although Trump was widely denounced for his unfounded claims, his suspicion resonated with the Alt-Right since they view U.S. political and cultural landscape as attacks on their liberty. This is in large part due to the Alt-Rights embrace of political incorrectness, which is, again, not new for American politics. A deep sense of foreboding and fear-mongering is evident daily on Fox News and the online Breitbart News Network. The Koch brothers, who initially did not support Trump's campaign (nor did they initially support Ronald Reagan in his campaign for president) have a long history of fear-mongering. Jane Mayer in *Dark Money: The Hidden History of the Billionaires Behind the Rise of the Radical Right* reports:

> In a 1960 self-published broadside, A Business Man Looks at Communism, Koch claimed… "The Colored man looms large in the communist plan to take over America" …welfare in his view was a secret plot to attract rural blacks to cities, where he predicted they would foment "a vicious race war."[11]

The loudest dog whistle of the Trump campaign was in the slogan *"Make America Great Again."* African Americans and White Americans both recognized the slogan for what it was – a thinly veiled appeal to racism. Hence, the raucous Trump rallies where in Raleigh, NC March 2016, a White Trump supporter punched a Black man in the face. Critics of Trump argued that he encouraged acts of violence on the campaign trail. While the Trump campaign defended itself by claiming "free-speech," a judge in Louisville, Kentucky "rejected Trump's free speech defense."[12]

White Nationalist Persistence

The biggest difference between White nationalist movements of the past and today is the presence of social media. Before, the radical right's primary means of spreading propaganda was think tanks, magazines, and television. The Alt-Right movement was largely generated online, with the one large exception of Fox News. But the presence of Steve Bannon and Kelly Ann Conway in the White House gives the Alt-Right unprecedented access to the highest office in the land. Thus, Breitbart News and Alternativeright.com are two examples of how the Alt-Right has become

Radical Right	Alt-Right
Anti-communist	Anti-communist
Limited government	Anti-government
American exceptionalism	American exceptionalism
Semi-politically correct	Anti-political correctness
Hawks	Isolationists
Rejects overt far-right appeals to White Supremacy	Embraces White Supremacy
Prioritizes Free Markets	Prioritizes Western Culture
Anti-social legislation	Anti-social legislation

a significant player in national politics. Their stock in trade is to appeal to White Americans, particularly men, who believe they have been under attack. They have an alarming way of holding to their beliefs, even when confronted with contradictory evidence.

Their tactic of waging war against the media speaks to a long-standing-belief on the far right that the media has been coopted by leftists. Indeed, the infamous Powell Memorandum of 1971 by future Supreme Court justice Lewis Powell, was a 10-page tome against communists, leftists, and the media. Powell was writing in the service of the Chamber of Commerce and his memo served as a call to arms and helped spur the growth of conservative think tanks.

I have attempted to show that the presidency of Donald Trump and his embrace of the Alt-Right movement is nothing new. This is simply the latest example of the persistence of White Nationalism on the American political landscape. Presidents before Trump all in one way or another nodded and winked to White nationalists during their campaign. Nixon had Law & Order (as did Trump), Reagan conjured up the "welfare queen," George H.W. Bush used the specter of Willie Horton, Bill Clinton Welfare reform, and even Barack Obama chastised Black men about responsibility in a Father's Day speech. These were all thinly-veiled attempts to speak to far right White voters. Trump, therefore, inherits a tradition of race-baiting in the American presidency.[13]

However, the fact that the Trump administration is in many ways like other administrations does not mean that it poses no danger to African Americans and other groups.

The Trump administration and their surrogates have contextualized the media, Muslims, urban areas, and immigrants as "the other." Doing so paves the way for not only a rollback in Civil Rights but also Civil Liberties.

During the early 1900s, the "threat" to America that White nationalists alleged was first legitimized by the nascent Bureau of Investigation (BOI). By 1919, J. Edgar Hoover penned a report *"Radicalism and Sedition Among Negroes as Reflected in their Publications."* The BOI had already begun a covert campaign against Hubert Harrison by the time of Hoover's report. Counterintelligence against Black activists and intellectuals, immigrants, union organizers, and communists was justified in no small manner because of the fear stoked by Dixon, Wilson, Griffith and others. Such that in 1925, the BOI had Langston Hughes, Claude McKay, Marcus Garvey, and an immense number of men and women under surveillance. In addition to individuals, the Black press was especially targeted. *The Messenger, The Crisis, Boston Guardian, The Negro World, Chicago Defender*, and *The Crusader* are just some of the papers targeted by the BOI. The Bureau made a concerted effort to control, repress, and eliminate the radical Black press.

Because of the history of repression against the Black freedom struggle, African Americans and their allies must be ever vigilant. This book is a good first step in contextualizing the meaning and potential impact of the Trump presidency. Despite Trump's plea to the Black community that we had nothing to lose, a declining social safety net, winnowing of resources for urban development, corporate driven public school policy, and the trope that dissent amounts to treason, all adds up to Black people having a lot to lose. Tellingly, the Trump presidency really speaks to the interests of a select few in America. The White working-class and poor prospects of benefitting from the Trump era are slim. But the Alt-Right is successful because they appeal to Whiteness rather than class. Which is another example of the Alt-Right overlapping with the Radical right. When Thomas Frank wrote *What's the Matter with Kansas*, he wrote it to analyze the phenomenon of working-class Whites voting against their interests. Trump won the election in large part because White voters in the rust belt states were disaffected voters who were turned off by the democratic party and traditional republican party candidates. They identified with Trump's desire to 'take the country back." He never had to say from who they were taking it back and how he could *"Make America great again."* Somehow his audiences understood exactly what he meant.

References:

[1]Ian Haney Lopez, *Dog Whistle Politics: How Coded Racial Appeals Have Reinvented Racism & Wrecked the Middle Class* (Oxford University Press, 2014), 3-4.

[2]Jane Mayer, "The Reclusive Hedge-Fund Tycoon Behind the Trump Presidency: How Robert Mercer exploited America's populist insurgency," *The New Yorker* (March 27, 2017).

[3]Cedric Robinson, *Forgeries of Memory and Meaning: Black Regimes of Race in American Theater and Film Before World War II* (University of North Carolina Press, 2007), p. 89.

[4]Ronald W. Walters, *White Nationalism, Black Interests: Conservative Public Policy and the Black Community* (Wayne State University Press, 2003), pp. 1-2.

[5]Cedric Robinson, *Forgeries of Memory and Meaning: Black Regimes of Race in American Theater and Film Before World War II* (University of North Carolina Press, 2007), p. 108.

[6]Daniel Bell, ed., "The Dispossessed," in *The Radical Right* (Anchor Books edition, 1964), p. 26.

[7]Bell, 25

[8]Kim Phillips-Fein, *Invisible Hands: The Businessmen's Crusade Against the New Deal* (NY: W. W. Norton & Company, 2008), p. 44.

[9]Ibid, p. 56.

[10]Richard Hofstadter, "The Pseudo-Conservative Revolt, 1955. Reprinted December 1, 2006. Online: theamericanscholar.org/the-pseudo-conservative-revolt

[11]Mayer, Dark Money: *The Hidden History of the Billionaires Behind the Rise of the Radical Right* (Anchor Books, 2017), p. 39.

[12]Online: amp.theguardian.com/us-news/2017/apr/01/judge-rejects-trump-defense-claim-incited-violence-protesters

[13]Kenneth O'Reilly, Nixon's Piano: Presidents and Racial Politics from Washington to Clinton (Free Press, 1995).

THE RECKONING: DONALD TRUMP AND THE GENERAL CRISIS OF WHITE SUPREMACY

GERALD HORNE

Gerald Horne is Professor of History and African American Studies at University of Houston. Author of over 45 books, his research addresses issues of racism in a variety of relations involving labor, politics, civil rights, international relations and, war. His latest books include: **The Counter–Revolution of 1776: Slave Resistance and the Origins of the United States** *(2014) and* **Rise and Fall of the Associated Negro Press: Claude Barnett's Pan-African News and the Jim Crow Paradox** *(2017).*

The election of Donald Trump was unsurprising mostly to those who have not paid attention to the history of this former slaveholder's republic, whose chief executives before 1860s were—mostly—slaveholders. It is fair to assume that the electorate that chose the likes of John Tyler and Andrew Jackson (whose chilling visage now hangs quite appropriately on the walls of the Oval Office in the White House and whose gravesite Trump visited in March 2017) were not—contrary to what you might have inferred from the maunderings of today's liberal historians—incipient followers of John Brown or even Frederick Douglass.

Thus, this 2016 election of this nation's Gorbachev—a man selected to rescue a system that he will inadvertently weaken—represents a reckoning, as history settles the overdue account of this moral spendthrift now known as the United States of America. It has taken a while for this inexorable process to assert itself, which only serves to ensure that the inevitable decline will be even more precipitous than many now suspect. The election of Trump represents, in short, an ideological crackup, whereby the liberal and conservative consensus alike have become exhausted, unable to either explain how we reached this point of no return and certainly unable to direct even a remedial reform.

One can espy this in the heterogeneous makeup of the anti-Trump coalition. The mainstream press—notably the *New York Times* and *Washington Post*—have conducted a holy crusade against the U.S. Imperialist-in-Chief, Mr. Trump, but at the same time refuses to retreat from its ongoing and relentless effort to destabilize left-wing regimes in the hemisphere—particularly Venezuela—without even a hint of recognition that this misguided path only serves to pave the way for the kind of caveman politics that the Profiteer-in-Chief so artlessly represents.

Unfortunately, the much-beleaguered left-wing forces in the anti-Trump coalition have their own deep-seated flaws. Future historians—assuming that the latest incompetent "white" man in the White House does not destroy the planet—will either conclude that many among these forces either were hopelessly opportunist, reluctant to risk further marginalizing by courageously critiquing the liberal/conservative consensus that delivered the Vietnam War among other debacles or so bedraggled by the meat grinder that has developed almost effortlessly from the bowels of the former slaveholding republic that they have been simply unable to mount an effective resistance.

I realize that I will be accused of "playing the race card"—the latest rhetorical evasion that joins the miserable ranks of "political correctness" and "identity politics"—but I am hard-pressed to think of one Euro-American analyst (or those influenced by them) who has come to grips with the basic rudiments of U.S. elections: e.g. that 9 of 10 Euro-American voters in the Deepest South cast their ballots across class lines for the right wing and have done so repeatedly for more than a half-century; that the GOP routinely wins a majority among the descendants of those with roots stretching from the Atlantic to the Urals in Europe. To bruit about these fundamentals leads to the charge that one is "playing the race card" or engaged in "identity politics"—not that those who vote in such a metronomic fashion are "playing the race card" or are engaged in the latest iteration of the original "identity politics" (uniting often warring European ethnic groups across class and gender lines in the invented identity that is "whiteness") which seized a continent via militarized means, displacing indigenes and enslaving Africans in the process.

This blundering idea of "identity politics" is—not surprisingly—akin to what occurred in apartheid South Africa where the concept of "whiteness" was viewed as monolithic (despite the none too latent antagonisms that exploded in the so-called "Anglo-Boer War" more than a century ago), while seeking to fragment "blackness" by dint of accentuating the perceived and actual uncommonness that divided Xhosa and Zulu and Sotho, et. al.

On this side of the Atlantic, "whiteness" remains "un-raced", uninterrogated and made to seem invisible and normalized, while those not part of this ruling category are said to be immersed in 'identity politics" and fierce guardians of "political correctness" in the bargain.

The way things stand now we of the left will have plenty of time to debate this at length in the dankest recesses of internment camps in Yankee Stadium and Fenway Park

The misfeasance of the left—and their liberal and conservative enablers—begins with their miscomprehension of 1776, routinely described as a "great leap forward for humanity" or—if they consider themselves sophisticated—an "incomplete bourgeois democratic revolution" (which is like describing apartheid in South Africa in 1948 which sought, inter alia, to uplift poorer Afrikaners, as an "incomplete reform", which somehow neglected or forgot inadvertently to uplift millions of Africans).

These would-be cosmopolitans in a staggering example of nonfeasance choose not to compare the settlers' revolt of 1776 with that of Algeria in the 1950s or that of Rhodesia in the 1960s and 1970s or even the so-called Anglo-Boer War of the late 1890s, all of which are remarkably similar, with the chief difference being the North American republicans attained a more sweeping victory—which leads us back to opportunism as an explanation for the inability of "progressives" to come to grips with the dispossession of indigenes and mass enslavement of Africans as the motive force for creation of the nation now known as the USA and how such a development makes the election of a huckster and con man like Trump virtually unavoidable.

Then there is the misunderstanding of the basic notion of secession; i.e. there are conspicuous blindspots within the dominant liberal cum conservative ideology that—unsurprisingly—hinder basic understanding of the trajectory of this former slaveholder's republic. Yes, the 1861 secession is rejected—though liberals have surrendered generally to the flawed idea that their conservative counterparts should be allowed to honor their traitorous ancestors by littering the landscape with monuments to their bloodthirstiness, on the widely accepted "marketplace of ideas" fallacy, which evades the question of power and conveniently equates those with lack of capital and those who control capital.

But what about the secession of Texas from Mexico in 1836, driven in no small measure to evade the logic of abolitionism south of the border (or the startling rise of Mexico's president of African descent, Vincente Guerrero who ascended to the highest office in the land in the immediate decade preceding the faux heroics of Stephen F. Austin, Sam Houston and the other brigands whose names continue to besmirch this vast region)? And what about the secession of the Dominican Republic from Haiti in 1844, a maneuver as I suggested in my recent book on the topic adroitly engineered by Washington, mimicking its own 1776? Neither the U.S. left nor the malfeasant historical profession generally have deigned as a general proposition to contextualize the 18th and 19th century phenomenon of secession as a mode for avoiding abolition, nor how enslaved mainland North America Africans were in the vanguard of opposing such ruthless cynicism and how that correlates with how we continue to be pulverized to this very day as a direct result.

Given such an evasion, is it really surprising that a Trump could be elected? Indeed, much of what passes for the U.S. left are akin to the mythical French intellectual who concludes with mock sagacity that *"I know what you are saying makes sense in praxis—the question is, does it make sense in theory?"* In other words, because of a misreading of the basic dynamic of settler colonialism—a stock phrase hardly and scandalously visible in their vocabulary—and despite the obvious implication of measures e.g. the Homestead Act, which bluntly seized the land of indigenes to distribute to European settlers, the notion that those defined as "white" should receive emoluments at the expense of rest of us is deeply imbedded in this society with the failure and reluctance to underscore this garish reality only compounding the utter sin.

Given the failure to scrutinize the basic dynamic of settler colonialism, which complicates class solidarity tremendously, is it really shocking that too many in the Euro-American working class and middle class voted for Trump on the premise that history has not ended and that— once again—those not defined as "white" could be looted on behalf of those so defined, with that process simply extended beyond the boundaries of this continent to the planet—perhaps other planets??

How can one understand the effectiveness of Reagan's insulting and sexist "welfare queen" trope, meant to denigrate African American women most notably without understanding the basic dynamic of settler colonialism? Thus, to continue the analogy from the hexagonal republic, the U.S. left is often reduced to the ridiculousness of the naïve and uncomprehending U.S. tourist in Paris, who assumes that if he simply speaks English slowly and with precise enunciation, the storekeeper will understand. If one can speak slowly and simply explain that a single payer health care system—ala Canada—will benefit the Euro-American working class and middle class, then one can evade the difficult questions of racism compounded with sexism and buttressed by the history of settler colonialism that makes it difficult for retrograde elements to divine their presumed class interest. I say presumed because history has taught many of these folks that alignment with the ruling elite of the 'race' trumps (pardon the expression) alignment with those of one's class of a different "race."

It seems to be part of the birthright of the much-beleaguered

U.S. left to parse the numbers diligently so as to ignore that majorities defined as "white" routinely vote for the right, which—sadly—has led many within the Black Liberation Movement to conclude that *"A Marxist is a liberal who purports to be a Socialist."* Is this unfortunate trend simply a derivative of so much happiness at one's ancestors being able to escape the barbarism that too often has characterized European battlefields that this has led to extreme giddiness making it difficult to see the abject misery inflicted on indigenes and Africans in the process? Perhaps the rise of Trump and the specter of fascism will roughly induce insight—if not, perhaps the forced seclusion of internment camps will do so.

Yes, there are those who furrow their collective wrinkled brows and stroke their rapidly doubling chins and pontificate about how the real and imagined failures of the Democratic Party to take a more class-conscious approach, contributed to the efflorescence of neo-liberalism and compelled the "working class" to vote for Trump. Obviated in the jumbled process is that the African working class, which has suffered more than most, did not pull the lever for President "Agent Orange." Why the difference? Those of the furrowed brow do not say.

This misanalysis at once racializes class as "white"—we, of course, are "race"—misreads the basic dynamic of settler colonialism, and, quite conveniently, exculpates those who (we are told) voted for the embodiment of neo-fascism, denying these voters "agency." This does not bode well.

Part of the many problems with the bankrupt concept of "American Exceptionalism" is—not accidentally—it tends to isolate the U.S. from the rest of the planet since it is (supposedly) entirely *sui generis* (beyond category), as was once said correctly of Duke Ellington's musical genius. Again, even if the left does not bring Algeria or Rhodesia or even Canada and Australia into view (the latter two did not rebel against the Crown and, yet, are by most measures better places to live for the working class and poor in contrast to the alleged "revolutionary republic) when considering the former slaveholding republic, it remains stunning that the U.S. has turned the concept of "permanent revolution" on its head by pursuing relentlessly a policy of "permanent counter-revolution", as its foreign policy suggests.

This evasion makes it difficult to "connect the dots" and see truly how, for example, the Cold War was more than a simple crusade against the so-called "Evil Empire" in Moscow but, instead, was a relentless Javert-style pursuit of those who were seeking to redistribute wealth from top to bottom—instead of the preferred U.S. mode: bottom to top—that claimed Paul Robeson as an early victim, which paved the way for debacles on the Korean peninsula and Vietnam and Grenada and Panama and Central America generally and Iraq.

Of course, Afghanistan is a continuing victim of this blinkered process, as Washington began in the late 1970s to interfere grossly in this nation's internal affairs in order to destabilize the left-leaning Peoples Democratic Party. The PDP was to be ousted despite a massive Soviet intervention to forestall this result but, in the process, U.S. imperialism aligned with religious zealots, who were to come to power, then incubate Al Qaeda which was then accused of murdering thousands of U.S. nationals in New York and Virginia on 11 September 2001. This, in turn, led to a U.S. military intervention that same year, which seems to have no end in sight, making for one of the longest wars ever embarked upon by a nation that is well versed in fighting long wars.

Naturally, misanalysis has been accompanied by a dearth of analysis. Understandably and justifiably considerable optimism has been invested in the massive women led marches that rocked Washington mere hours after the day that will forever live in infamy—the inauguration of the Plunderer-in-Chief in January 2017. My sources tell me that notwithstanding the hundreds of thousands that descended upon Washington, D.C., the demonstration in Los Angeles was even larger.

And yet, it is said that 53% of Euro-American women voted for the Sexual Predator-in-Chief. More than that, the *New York Times* of 3 March 2017 reported at length on the disturbing trend that the U.S. may not be alone in this regard in that the leaders of European far right and neo-Nazi parties are women. This lengthening list includes Marine Le

Pen of France; Frauke Petry of Germany; Siv Jensen of Norway; Pia Kjaersgaard of Denmark—and, if the reporter had been more expansive, space could have been devoted to Pauline Hanson of Australia. Why is this so? Liberal, conservative and even many "radical" analysts have presented no analysis of this disturbing trend, perhaps acting like the infant who assumes if she covers her eyes, the horror will disappear.

No, hypothesis was put forward to explicate this troubling trend though it is possible that the rise of China—more of which anon—has compelled many women of European ancestry to be the weathervane sensing that the easy pickings of white supremacy and imperialism are receding, necessitating a circling of the wagons and sterner measures to retain the status quo. In any case, if the U.S. left bungles the analysis of "race" and class, why should gender be different?

* * *

Perhaps the ultimate commentary on the early administration of U.S. President Donald Trump is the reassurance in the 15 February 2017 *New York Times* from Dr. Allen Frances, a retired medical professor at Duke University, that the present occupant of the Oval Office is not "mentally ill." Dr. Frances should know since he wrote the *Diagnostic and Statistical Manual of Mental Disorders IV (DSM-IV)* upon which professionals rely to diagnose narcissistic personalities and its accoutrements e.g. grandiosity, self-absorption and, most of all, lack of empathy.

Maybe Dr. Frances is correct and President Trump is not mentally unbalanced. Yet, the very fact that this point is being debated—the president is bonkers—is indicative of a larger crisis that soars far beyond the psyche of one man. The election of Trump is symptomatic of a wider crisis that points to a New World Order but not of the type that former president, George H.W. Bush predicted after the crumbling of the Berlin Wall in 1989, which seemed to augur an invigorated U.S. imperialism bestriding the planet like a latter-day Colossus.

More to the point, charging that Trump is crazy, once again elides the point of the competency of the tens of millions that voted for him.

As shall be suggested, was it not crazy for the U.S. ruling elite to think it could conduct a domestic and global crusade against class-based projects without creating objective conditions for the rise of right-wing populism and xenophobia as now embodied in the Huckster-in-Chief?

However, reality has intruded and it is evident that Washington misplayed its cards and will soon be overtaken by events. It was left to Chen Weihau of the Beijing based *China Daily* to deliver the bad news— for U.S. imperialism and white supremacy—on 13 February 2017. Citing a report from the leading accounting and consulting firm Pricewaterhouse-Coopers (PwC), he observed that by 2050, six of the world's 10 largest economies will be mostly Asian nations. The question for U.S. imperialism is not only how can white supremacy be maintained in the old way, on a planet dominated by the world's majority but, as well, how can the swagger and braggadocio of the Pentagon —which was based on a hegemonic economy—continue in the old way given such a correlation of forces?

According to PwC, China and India will have the leading economies (both giants have spent considerably on space exploration, the next frontier) with the U.S. in third place, followed in order by: Indonesia, Brazil, Russia, Mexico, Japan, Germany and the United Kingdom. Strikingly, Nigeria-which has just surpassed South Africa as the leading economy in Africa—is ranked at fourteenth in this analysis.

Similarly, London's *Financial Times (FT)* of 6 March 2017 reported that "China's banking system has overtaken the Eurozone's to become the world's largest by assets, a sign of the country's increased influence", signaling the direction of future investments and importance, and is also indicative of the direction of prevailing winds. In that regard, the *FT* of 8 March 2017 reported that a top economic advisor of the Pillager-in-Chief, Peter Navarro bemoaned China's rise which—he contended—created a world where "we are all likely to be owned by foreigners." Washington's "rapidly militarizing rival" was "intent on hegemony," was "buying up our companies, our technologies, our farmland and our food supply chain and ultimately controlling much of our defence industrial base." Wailing uncontrollably, he went on to wonder, "how might this alternative version of conquest by purchase end for us and our sons and daughters.... might we lose a broader cold war for our freedom, prosperity and democracy not by shots being fired but by cash registers ringing? Might we lose a broader hot war simply because we have sent our manufacturing and defence industrial base offshore on the wings of a persistent trade deficit?"

Perhaps that morning Mr. Navarro had encountered the *China Daily* of 28 February 2017 which—rather gleefully—reported that Hollywood's top movie, *"La La Land"* was financed largely by a Chinese company, Hunan TV & Broadcast Intermediary, which cost $30 million and to that point has earned $368 million globally. This is part of a larger trend in that China's Dalian Wanda Group has purchased a controlling interest in numerous U.S. movie-houses and has MGM, the studio with the roaring lion as a symbol, in the potential grasp of the presumed rapacious dragon.

Compounding Navarro's angst, a *CD* columnist on 15 February 2017 warned Washington bluntly that the Exploiter-in-Chief "will not win a trade conflict" with China and would only serve to harm the interests of the numerous U.S. corporations dependent on the Asian giant's goodwill, including Apple, Boeing, Walmart, KFC, etc. Remarkably, this same line was repeated on 28 February, just in case the initial message was not received.

This rise of China is a direct result of Washington's co-optation of Beijing in the early 1970s in an anti-Moscow venture, which led to massive foreign direct investment by U.S. corporations in China and the creation of this rival now in the passing lane. This Copernican process is akin to London appointing Tokyo as its watchdog in Asia in the late 19th century, a decision which backfired spectacularly by 8 December 1941.

Yet, younger comrades might be surprised to ascertain that many on the left—including some who deemed themselves to be radical—were supportive of the allied Afghan and Chinese overtures of the 1970s while others in our movement were merely silent.

The fact that—per usual—the Republican Party vote nationally was comprised overwhelmingly of Euro-Americans (more than 90%), and embodied Mr. Trump's slogan, "Make America Great Again", harkened back to a long gone post-1945 era with Washington as Colossus and when Jim Crow was the law of the land and naked racist privilege prevailed. But post-1945 the world began to change dramatically as the colonialism that undergirded Jim Crow began to retreat with Sudan surging to independence in 1956 and Ghana in 1957. As Africans snapped the chains of colonialism and began to speak out vigorously against U.S. apartheid, Washington found it difficult to charge Moscow with human rights violations when legalized racism stained the national escutcheon: Jim Crow had to go as a result as favorable conditions were created for the rise of a movement pushing desegregation and Black Power.

The problem was that as a direct result of the horrors of lynching and Jim Crow, a goodly number of the best and the brightest in Black America had been attracted to the cause of socialism, which was then thought to mean that they were little more than pawns of the "Evil Empire": the Soviet Union. This lengthy list included Paul Robeson and his closest comrades, William Patterson and Ben Davis—excellent attorneys both—not to mention Caribbean born Communists e.g. Ferdinand Smith of Jamaica and Claudia Jones of Trinidad & Tobago, not to mention the leading left-wing couple: Shirley Graham Du Bois and W.E.B. Du Bois.

Sadly, the NAACP leadership backed this purge, which only served to place these "moderates" in the crosshairs to their detriment.

In other words, concessions on the anti-Jim Crow front were crudely coupled with givebacks on the class and ideological front. For African Americans, this meant gaining the right to check into a hotel but not having the wherewithal to pay the bill. This paradoxical and confusing result—a head fake to the left, while plowing ahead mercilessly to the right—also made it easier for demagogues to convince too many Euro-American voters that the ruling elite was more interested in Negro advance than their rapidly deteriorating plight. The lesson they should have gleaned is that if many of them had seemed to be turning leftward or, at least supporting avidly those who had, e.g. the Hollywood screenwriter and activist, John Howard Lawson, they too may have been rewarded with concessions instead of being bludgeoned with the iron fist of class rule.

Instead, the U.S. labor movement—the AFL-CIO—went overboard in ousting left wing leaders e.g. Ferdinand Smith and the Australian born leader of the West Coast stevedores, the heroic Harry Bridges and endorsing every cockamamie anticommunist intervention devised, which served to grease the skids for exporting jobs to low wage havens abroad ruled by dictators buoyed by the misguided AFL-CIO foreign policy.

Though a sound argument can be maintained that desegregation improved the overall economy, as enhanced income for African-Americans, for example, allowed this group to make purchases from non-Black entities creating a virtuous circle for all, this is not how many Euro-Americans saw things. Some may have recalled Pete Gray, the one-armed outfielder for the old St. Louis Browns baseball team, who was able to play regularly in the 1940s—until the arrival of Jackie Robinson and his Negro counterparts in 1946 and the market for one-armed white outfielders shrank accordingly. This perceived setback for Euro-Americans led to a so-called "white backlash" after the passage of the Civil Rights Act of 1964 and Voting Rights Act of 1965, with Euro-Americans across class lines defecting en masse to the Republican Party and abandoning the Democratic Party of then president, Lyndon B. Johnson. This retrograde tendency was thought to have reached a zenith in 1991 when a Klan and Nazi leader, David Duke, received a majority of Euro-American votes in running for governor of Louisiana.

In some ways, the victory of Donald Trump in November 2016 was simply a continuation of the Duke near-triumph. However, part of the problem is that reigning liberal mythology hampers the ability to see the nation as it is, instead we are force fed a view of the nation that tends to downplay a discernible reactionary thread that has coursed through this continent ever since the first Europeans invaded over 500 years ago.

The problem today is that the Euro-American majority that has been a condition precedent for sustainable white supremacy is crumbling. California, where the GOP is a minor player, is Exhibit A in this regard. Despite strenuous efforts by former governor Pete Wilson, to delimit the Latino population—especially that of Mexican origin—in the 1990s, today that group's numbers now exceed that of the so-called "Anglo" population and, predictably, the GOP's fortunes have crumbled accordingly. During the 2016 presidential race, Hilary Rodham Clinton won the Golden State by millions of votes—and this margin largely accounts for her victory in the popular vote nationally. Similarly, the Euro-American majority voted to eviscerate affirmative action but this backfired too; before this maneuver, those defined as "white" comprised about 70% or more of the student population at the flagship campus of the University of California, sited in Berkeley; after this maneuver, their number dropped to about 30% with the majority now being those of Asian and Pacific origin.

Tellingly, despite California not voting for the victor in the presidential race of 2016, in this case certain Californians reaped the spoils nonetheless, as a significant percentage of Trump's closest advisors have roots in Southern California—including former Hollywood producers, Steve Bannon and Steve Mnuchin; White House henchman, Steve Miller of Santa Monica High School; "Bannon's Bannon", Julie Hahn of the ritzy Harvard-Westlake School on the Westside of L.A.; failed Labor Secretary nominee Andrew Puzder of a fast food chain with roots in Los Angeles, et.al. It seems as if their arrival in Washington is designed in no small measure to insure that what transpired in California in recent decades will not occur nationally. Hence, the laser-like focus on immigration, particularly from south of the border—while ignoring the legions of undocumented Poles and Irish to be found in cities e.g. Chicago and New York and Boston—and circumscribing women's reproductive freedoms. (Translation: white women should wholeheartedly embrace natalism.)

Of course, in comprehending how and why Trump became president it would be folly to under-estimate the viscerally negative reaction by many of his supporters to this predecessor. Cornell Belcher, a long time Democratic pollster who worked on both of Barack Obama's presidential campaigns, details this disturbing phenomenon in his book, *A Black Man in the White House: Barack Obama and the Triggering of America's Racial- Aversion Crisis.* He deftly exposes the canard that this Chicagoan's triumph marked the onset of a "postracial society." Instead, it ignited the polar opposite, which further exposes the banality and misdirection of liberal mythology. Obama won by garnering about 40% of the so-called "white" vote nationally, a victory facilitated—again—by the changing demographics of the nation, which Trump's anti-immigrant psychosis addresses frontally.

Not to be forgotten is Trump's trumpeting of the "birther" movement, which purported to show that Mr. Obama was actually born in Kenya, not Hawaii, and thus was elected illegitimately. (Interestingly, that Senator John McCain was actually born in what is now Panama did not ignite a similar controversy about the constitutional provision mandating that a president must be born in the U.S.). And, again, Trump's anti-immigrant stance does not extend to closer scrutiny of the roots of his British born advisor, Sebastian Gorka or the bona fides of Joel Pollak, a former spokesman of South Africa's neo-apartheid party now touted as Washington's next chief envoy in Pretoria.

In short, Trump's victory is not a bolt-from-the-blue, wholly unanticipated and inconsistent with past national praxis. No, it is a logical outcome of the post-1945 scenario which forced Washington to beat a hasty retreat from the more egregious Jim Crow practices. But just as U.S. imperialism routinely chided the leaders of socialist Yugoslavia in the 1990s for not dealing forthrightly with nationalism but, instead, driving it underground, the same accusation could easily be leveled at the myrmidons of U.S. imperialism, who bowed to global pressure and a Black-led movement from below without winning over the broad masses of Euro-Americans.

* * *

The Reckoning has arrived. China's rise is circumscribing the leeway for white supremacy leading U.S. imperialism to compensate by seeking to heighten exploitation at home, which bodes ill for the African population not least. Yes, a global anti-Trump is the order of the day but this would mean our "moderate" leadership rethinking their now questionable relationship with a wing of the U.S. "liberal" elite that is now seeking to save its own hide, while the much-besieged U.S. left would similarly have to rethink its past and present so it can advance in the future.

Still, our leadership would be well-advised to start sending delegations immediately—if not sooner—to confer with counterparts in Mexico City, not to mention our allies in the Caribbean Community (CARICOM) and the African Union in Ethiopia and even the European Union in Brussels since U.S. imperialism may be considering a renewed post-Brexit Anglo-American alliance targeting Germany (already fencing with pro-Yankee regimes in Poland and Hungary and an embittered Britain miffed with the divorce bill it will have to pay to leave the EU and a Russia furious about Berlin's enforcement of sanctions in the wake of the Crimea intervention). Berlin needs allies desperately and about a century ago during World War I, hired Negro agents to sabotage the U.S. economy. Now all we need is help in sabotaging the mis-leadership of the Ignoramus-in-Chief: Donald J. Trump.

Toronto, Ontario, Canada. 19th Nov, 2016. Hundreds of Canadians take part in a massive protest against American President-elect Donald Trump at Nathan Philips Square in downtown Toronto, Canada. Credit: Creative Touch Imaging Ltd./Alamy Live News

THE CATASTROPHE CALLED TRUMP: RESISTING THE MONSTER SIDE OF AMERICA

MAULANA KARENGA

*Maulana Karenga is Professor/Chair of Africana Studies at CSU Long Beach, and the Creator of Kwanzaa and Nguzo Saba. He serves as Executive Director, African American Cultural Center (Us); Co-Chair, Black Community, Clergy and Labor Alliance. He is author of numerous publications including **Essays on Struggle: Position and Analysis** and **Kwanzaa: A Celebration of Family, Community and Culture.***

It is the righteous teachings of our ancestors who left us this awesome legacy and culture of struggle that we must never collaborate in our own oppression. On the contrary, they teach us, we must "Let our motto be resistance" and live our lives in righteous and relentless struggle (Walker and Garnet, 1969; Karenga, 2016). Thus, honoring our ancestors and the legacy of struggle and sacrifice they left us, we refuse to accept Donald Trump as our president, to participate in rituals of recognition and legitimation for him. For we could not and cannot in good conscience legitimize the wrong, evil and injustice he practices, promises, and represents.

Indeed, even though we were asked and urged to accept elected evil, pray for its success in office, attend its official ritual of recognition called inauguration and give it a chance to prove itself, we refused.

It was argued that his election and inauguration represented the "peaceful transfer of power" which is essential to democracy. But again, we would not collaborate in our own oppression nor did we fail to see that the transfer of power is among the elites; and that the power of the people is yet to be achieved.

Therefore, it was good and within our moral and struggle tradition for Congressmember John Lewis to stand up and speak truth to power in the midst of silence, muted voices and constant calls for compromise and collaboration in the interest of an agenda we have not defined and don't share. Rep. Lewis dared to declare to this country and the world that Donald Trump is *"not a legitimate president"* and *"You can't feel at home with what is wrong, not right"* (Blake, 2017; Remnick, 2017). Surely, we cannot feel at ease with evil, if we have any sense of the moral and any concern for human good and the well-being of the world.

There are three basic ways to understand illegitimate, i.e., as illegal, unreasonable and immoral. Rep. Lewis points to the legal issue in that Trump's election was a tainted process, involving intervention by the Russians and the FBI in favor of Trump, and if democracy is about the rule of the majority, Trump lost by 3 million votes. And, it is an unreasonable assumption that a person who is willfully and arrogantly uninformed, professionally unprepared, pathologically self-focused and embarrassingly temperamental can be president, if president is to mean anything more than just being in the position and having a title.

But even if legally and reasonably he passed the criteria established, the most definitive disqualifying criteria are the moral problems he poses for the vulnerable, the country and the world. These moral issues expressed by Trump, himself, include his commitment to reestablish state sanctioned torture; killing of whole families to get at suspected or designated "terrorists;" mockery of the disabled; contempt for the poor; racist indictments of peoples of color; hostility toward Muslims as personal attitude and public policy; degrading conceptions and treatment of women; exploitative practices toward workers; warmongering threats and promises; encouraging the worst in those prepped, prepared and prone to hate, howl and harm the vulnerable, different and disadvan-taged, and recklessly doing away with environmental protections and accords.

Then, some told us we should or they will pray for Trump's suc-cess because his success means the success for the country. But Trump's concept of success will not be success for the country, but for himself, his associates and his class. Thus, if we pray for success it should be for the success of the people, and if he acts in the righteous interests of the people, the people and the country will be successful and he will be also. But if he doesn't, he should and will fail by any moral measure of success and justice. Clearly, then, we have no alternative but to set aside illusions, keep the faith, honor the legacy and continue this beautiful, righteous and re-lentless struggle that is our honored legacy and self-defining way of life.

And we should also concede that the polluted rivers, rutted roads, bloody streets and dark alleys that lead to Trump have passed through Fer-guson, Flint and flooded New Orleans; through Baltimore, Los Angeles, Philadelphia, Mississippi and Pennsylvania, Charleston, New York, Cleveland and other well-known sites of lynching, killings, hatred, hos-tility, systemic and police violence and man-made disasters, peddled and posed as necessary, normal and justifiable in racial, religious and realpolitik terms. There is also a blood-red line of history that runs through Haiti, Palestine, Iraq, Afghanistan, Hawaii, the Philippines, Australia and all other places coveted, conquered and occupied by the U.S. and its most fa-vored and lavishly funded allies and associates.

Trump is a real-time representative of a society that privileges profit over people, especially over people of color and the poor, and evi-dences a ruthless callousness and addiction to assumptions of racial and religious superiority and a parallel practice of violent imposition on others. Therefore, it is dishonest and self-deceptive to pretend that the U.S. gov-ernment, its corporate collaborators and favored allies have not already done and are doing, in various ways and places, what Trump proposed and promised if elected and now is doing. Nor are his Republican rivals proposing a different road or route to *"making America great again."* So, let's face it; Trump is not the first to propose or build an apartheid wall of separation which this country condoned and helped fund, nor the first to justify torture and propose its legalization. Nor is he the first to propose killing the families of suspects and nor is he the first to do it. Indeed, it has been practiced unannounced by this country and by its allies of various so-called democratic and dictatorial kinds. Sometimes, it is called collateral damage when discovered or a mistake, a technological misreading in targeting the ever-present and useful "terrorists". But whatever it is called, it is always deadly and destructive to its victims and their way of life.

Trump comes from a mindset and culture that has a deep and abiding affinity for wealth, war and power over others, and having declared persons, groups and peoples enemies of God, country and corporations; it can and does, without moral reflection or flinching, mercilessly bomb hospitals, schools, religious institutions, wedding parties, men and women at work, children at play and whole cities. It is all rooted in a racist, classist and anti-human conception of human life, a perversity of perception that devalues the different, posits the vulnerable as prey, and sees any disability, disadvantaging, disease, death or disaster of others as self-inflicted and unworthy of recognition or remedy.

Moreover, Trump finds a kindred "soul" in the corporate media which during his campaign gave him unlimited and continuous opportunities to whip up the White masses, playing on their racial and religious fears and hatreds, their social and economic insecurities, and their penchant for a racial and religious patriotism of suppression and supremacy. It is racialized and racist fare, peddled at bargain prices not only at rallies, but in the media which advertised the spectacle of racial fire-feeding during Trump's campaign as merely an angry populace—read White people—clamoring to rid itself of the established group and trying to let people know they are afraid, feel left out and are hurting, However, such explanation is not justification, especially no justification for injury and injustice imposed on others more vulnerable.

Surely, it is not sacrilegious to assert or even unpatriotic to affirm what history and current practice already prove: that "America the Beautiful" has an ugly side, indeed a monster side, in spite of its songs, tweets, Facebook "likes" and general propaganda of self-praise. Such a Janus-faced, two faced, character was present at the beginning of America's creation, but its "beautiful" side was put forth as the whole of what it was. The image was cultivated with racial and religious arrogance, untruth and exaggeration, recruiting religious language and leaders to support its claims to other peoples' lands, lives and resources through conquest, colonization, enslavement and occupation. And in the midst of all this destruction, there was/is a studied denial of the devastation being imposed on the targeted people in these systems of suppression and slaughter, whether at home or abroad.

Thus, in spite of fake and feeble attempts to define Donald Trump as rich White trash, a rogue, renegade or rare occurrence as he trashes the world, he mirrors the monster side of "America the Beautiful", which we must confront with righteous and relentless resistance. Trump mirrored the monster side of America first in political campaign costume, unmasked and without subterfuge, reality TV raw and on primetime, straight out and straight down dirty, nasty, mean-spirited, racist, religiously chauvinistic, constantly seeking an easy kill. And he continues to do it with the arrogance, insensitivity, and know-nothing cockiness of the uninformed and small-minded who are sure of what they claim to know, because they know so little and could not be less concerned with complexity, deep thought or truth, or the human tragedy such devoted ignorance, delusionary arrogance, and destructive actions impose on the world.

His money and ruthlessness have made him (and too many in America) respect this more than other peoples' lives, lands, rights, needs or aspirations also for a good life for themselves and their children. Trump's appeals have not only been to the racist and anti-immigrant audience who feel the immigrant, refugee, residents and citizens of different colors and kind are taking their jobs, changing their country and ruining their lives. Equally important, he carries the water and "let-us-prey" position of the predatory billionaire class to which he belongs. These ruling class billionaires want to make the world safe, not for pretensions of democracy, but safe for their wealth and power and the predatory ways they acquire them.

Trump has directed his attacks against the vulnerable and different—African Americans, Mexicans and other Latinos, Asians, Arabs and Muslims, disabled people and women. He will not say interning Japanese Americans was wrong and is determined to build a racial and religious apartheid wall at the border, register all Muslims, surveille their mosques and ban Muslims from entering the U.S., and his recent court losses on this issue will not deter him. He claimed America "has become a dumping ground" for undesirables and he wants to end this. His language is America's language of an unrestrained violence by self-proclaimed racial and religious superiors, i.e., attack, torture, kill, destroy, "shock and awe", "bomb them to hell" and kill the whole family of "suspects". He contrasts the White, winner, wealthy and powerful with those of another color, characterized as losers, weak, poor and unworthy of respect.

During the presidential campaign, the Republican politicians, self-declared guardians of the realm and guides to the patriotic and perplexed, tried for some time to out-Trump Trump in cultivating fear, hatred, and the will to violence against the vulnerable and different. From among them came this language and discourse of racial and religious supremacy, calling for carpet bombing, making the sands glow with radiation, indicting and ruthlessly attacking Islam and its adherents, and urging and approving governors' closing the border to refugees fleeing from the chaos and killing in Syria, which is a product of the U.S.' arrogance and disastrous policy of regime change and attempting to police and parent the world. If Dr. Martin Luther King called his country, America, *the greatest purveyor of violence in the world*" in the 1960s, what would he say of it now with its enhanced technology of war and the demonstrated will to use it (Washington, 1986:233)?

Even in efforts to distance from or disavow Trump, what is stressed is not what these calls for hate, fear and violence against the vulnerable and different do to its human targets and victims, but more of what they do to damage America's reputation, the image of its beautiful side. This fits well within America's monster side morality where what is hated and condemned is not so much untruth and injustice, but being caught and being unable to justify it, turn it around on the victim, win the gullible to endorse and/or excuse it, and explain it away with another virtue or value one is perceived to have.

Thus, it is said during his campaign: yes, he lies, but he is consistent; yes, he is irrational, but he speaks from the heart; yes, he wants to kill whole families in pursuit of suspects, but he is concerned about our security; yes, he is mean-spirited, narrow-minded and petty, but he wants to make America great again. And yes, he's, irreparably flawed, but look at the polls—he's winning. Having helped sow such seeds, can his collaborators honestly be surprised by now having to reap this arctic whirlwind of incompetence, corruption, callousness and catastrophe?
Trump and his trumpeteers say he wants to "make America great again". But what does this mean and down what road of ruin will it take the country? He sounds like historical counterparts whose road to "greatness" was fascism, i.e., a system of fear, hatred, scapegoating, grievance and violence toward the different and vulnerable; racism; suppression of all opposition;, sacrifice of human and civil rights and democratic rule for a false sense of glory, security and supremacy; worship of technological weapons within a religion of war; and practice of aggression and the cultivation of conditions and consciousness that unreflectively support and even demand it.

And when he and they speak of "making America great again" are they conjuring up an imaginary and ideal time when White was right and without question; when imperial aggression, colonization, genocide and enslavement took on a religious tone and texture and claims were made of a "Manifest Destiny", a "divine right" of conquest and a "divine gift" of a "promised land", unjustly and savagely dispossessing its original inhabitants? Or do they dream with drones of the long period of White terrorism dressed in Christian clothes and claims; of the physical, legal and psychological lynching and imposition of social death and other savage practices of White segregation of and against Black people; as well as other people of color, in varied forms?

It is in this period of American history that Mrs. Fannie Lou Hamer stood up among the millions of oppressed and struggling African Americans and called on us to question America through criticism and struggle, question its self-congratulatory claim to be "the home of the brave and the land of the free" in the midst of so much cowardice, unfreedom, injustice and official evil and struggle to radically change it (Hamer, 2011:45, 62). And it is time for us in this same spirit, to ask and answer with other oppressed, progressive and struggling peoples and groups how do we move forward at this particular juncture of history, and then, with earnestness and audacity dare to do it (Johnson and Marians, 2017).

And it is good also to remember always the ethical teachings of our ancestors in the midst of current and continuing confusion of wealth, power or even technological knowledge with greatness. For they teach us to focus instead on what we should do with these capacities, i.e., use them to improve the human condition and enhance the well-being of the world. Thus, they teach in the *Husia, "the wise are known by their wisdom but the great are known by their good deeds"* in and for the world (Karenga, 1984: 48). It is good to struggle and good to serve, then, and this, our ancestors reassure us, is the real and righteous road to greatness and shared good in the world.

There is clearly a rising arctic winter wind blowing our way, ravishing the rights, lands and lives of the people all over the world. And it is an irony of history that the people who are denying climate change in nature and backing out of international climate control accords are causing a climate change in society with similar devastating and disastrous effects and parallel denials of their destructiveness. And if we rightly read the signs and lessons of history, which Malcolm (1965:8) assures us *"is best qualified to reward our research,"* we cannot help seeing signs already of a coming Ice Age, a prevailing condition of deadly cold and bone-breaking callousness that is normalized and called "necessary" for the "common good" or to "make America great again" with no moral meaning attached to it.

Certainly, Trump's celebration at the White House of the passage of a bill that among other things would deny or make prohibitive health coverage and treatment for those with pre-existing conditions reflects the coldness and callousness of the changing climate. After all, how can lessening the possibility of preventable death and suffering merit celebration in a normal human mind and moral system? Billed as a victory celebration, the White House huddling and hurrahing resembled a death dance for many who see their lives and futures now hanging in the balance. What other than an ice age "morality" could justify or even explain a celebration of the denial of health care and health coverage for the poor and vulnerable while the rich rejoice in the Rose Garden?

Surely, we can only make sense of this senseless and immoral conception of victory and celebration, if we realize Trump and his cohorts and the society in which they do their dances and deeds of death are carriers and perpetrators of pre-existing conditions themselves, diseases of heart and mind that diminish and distort their sense of humanity, morality and fellow-feeling. It is pre-existing conditions of racism, classism, sexism and other forms of oppression and an accompanying moral numbness to others' death, disease and suffering established at the very founding of the country. It is in this context of pre-existing social savagery and sickness that the issue of adequate health care for all becomes a problem rather than its being accepted and embraced as a human right and moral obligation.

But again, it is too easy and grossly inadequate to focus on Trump alone, for nobody and nothing comes into being by themselves or itself. Everyone and everything is rooted in a history and current condition that ground them. So, Trump could not be Trump without the sanction and support of the society that provided "the swamp", to use his words, from which he and his mean-spiritedness, ruthlessness, and irrational and amoral proposals, plans and policies emerge.

Thus, if we are to survive and end this coming Ice Age of Trump-ism unfolding in full blast in front of us, we must quickly admit the problem is not only Trump himself, but also society and his openly out-of-control supporters, his complicit enablers of various kinds and commitments and the pre-existing conditions that existed and brought him into being as president. The man, himself, though regularly offering a monstrous display of real ignorance and self-delusionary arrogance, did not elect himself, create the racism, classism, sexism, xenophobia, immigrant-bashing, religious chauvinism, Islamophobia, and all the other morally repugnant and humanly disastrous policies, proposals and practices with which his administration is infected and seeks to impose.

It is the context and the wide spectrum of Americans who have elected him, and that have given him the sanction and support that allows him to make claims without evidence, ramble on without reason and do his speech and acts of evil and injustice, and peddle them as worthy all-day news. And only a relentless and righteous resistance can halt the spread of the cold and callous things planned and reverse all those evil and ugly things already put in place.

The media never tires of vainly trying to give importance to Trump and those who follow him. Often they try to explain him away and his coarseness, callousness and abysmal lack of knowledge about almost anything relevant to the office he occupies or to the problems he proposes and pretends he's going to solve. Tied to the philosophy of the media owners, these journalists justify Trump and his practices, refusing to seriously criticize and condemn the sick, insane, inane and other disordered words and actions emanating from his mouth and mind. And likewise, they don't report or discuss the massive resistance to Trump in any meaningful and extended way. Nor do they speak assertively and critically of issues of poverty, suffering and social pain caused by structured social and racial injustice he proposes and practices or the real and destructive impact it will have on the lives and future of the people, the country or the world.

And so, it is up to us to refuse to be cowered or concede to the normalization of human coldness, callousness, evil and injustice that now so pervade the climate of this country. It is up to us to take responsibility for ensuring a righteous and relentless resistance in the coming Ice Age. This means we must remember Malcolm's (1970:12) teachings that we must be responsible in our people's eyes and assessment, not in our oppressors'. And it means that we must act responsibly for our people and outrageously toward the oppressor, interrupting and disrupting his planned business-as-usual, and putting another agenda on the table—an agenda more humane, dignity-affirming, just and contributive to the health, well-being and rightful flourishing of all.

We must stand up in the midst of the social madness and moral numbness around us and audaciously and defiantly reembrace our mission of serving as a moral and social vanguard which our ancestors, heaven and history have assigned us. We must fulfill our sacred mission of working and struggling to bring an inclusive and shared good in the world, creating places and spaces where freedom for all is a lived reality rather than an empty and hypocritical claim of a dominant race, class or elite, and where justice is a normal process and product of our daily practice and exchange, and moral sensitivity, empathy and caring are understood and embraced as both normal and necessary to any real claim to being human (Karenga, 2008). Thus, as Mary McLeod Bethune (2008:128) teaches us, *"We must remake the world. The task is nothing less than this."*

To live is to choose and to act in ways that will day by day determine the course and quality of our lives and form the contours of our future. Therefore, in the face and context of oppression, we cannot honorably or responsibly choose other than struggle, righteous and relentless struggle. As our ancestors instruct us, we must defiantly and boldly "bear witness to truth and set the scales of justice in their proper place, especially among those who have no voice", little visibility and ultimately less value in the eyes of the icemen, huddling in air-conditioned caves to develop ways to deny them the rights and well-being they deserve.

Indeed, we must, as the ancestors teach us, bear witness to their poverty and pain, their suffering and suppression, their hunger and homelessness, and condemn and resist the bitter cold and bone-breaking callousness that defines the coming Ice Age in which we already and in great part live and struggle. And even when the icemen and women criminalize our criticism, prosecute our practice of active and defiant dissent, demonize and ostracize us and capture us and put us in prison on "Trumped-up" charges, we must still dare to struggle and dare to win, opening up the way to a new world and history of African people and humanity as a whole.

Our task, then, is world-encompassing, as the Maatian ethics of ancient Egypt teaches us. It is a practice of *serudj ta*, repairing, renewing and remaking the world (Karenga, 2006:397ff). This, then, is the instruction and counsel of our ancestors:

> *Continue the struggle. Keep the faith. Hold the line. Love our people and each other. Seek and speak truth. Do and demand justice. Be constantly concerned with the well-being of the world and all in it. And dare rebuild the overarching Movement that prefigures and makes possible the good world we also want and deserve. Hotep. Ase. Heri.*

References:

Bethune, Mary McLeod. (2008). *Mary McLeod Bethune: Words of Wisdom*, edited by Chiazam Ujo Okoye, Bloomington, IN; AuthorHouse.

Blake, Aaron. (2017). "John Lewis says Donald Trump Isn't a Legitimate President, and Trump Hits Back Hard," *The Washington Post*, (January 14).

Hamer, Fannie Lou. (2013). *The Speeches of Fannie Lou Hamer: To Tell It Like It Is*, edited by Maegan parker Brooks and Davis W. Houck, Jackson: University Press of Mississippi.

Hutchinson, Earl Ofari. (1972). *Let Your Motto Be Resistance: The Life and Thought of Henry Highland Garnet*, Boston: Beacon Press.

Johnson, Dennis and Valerie Merians, (eds.) (2007). *What We Do Now: Standing For Your Values in Trump's America*. Brooklyn, NY: Melville House.

Karenga, Maulana. (2016). *Essays on Struggle: Position and Analysis*. Los Angeles: University of Sankore Press.

Karenga, Maulana. (2008). *Kawaida and Questions of Life and Struggle*. Los Angeles: University of Sankore Press.

Karenga, Maulana. (2006). *Maat, The Moral Ideal in Ancient Egypt: A Study in Classical African Ethics*, Los Angeles: University of Sankore Press.

Karenga, Maulana. (1984). *Selections From the Husia: Sacred Wisdom of Ancient Egypt*. Los Angeles: University of Sankore Press.

Malcolm X. (1970). *Malcolm X on Afro-American History.* New York: Pathfinder Press.

Malcolm X. (1965). *Malcolm X Speaks.* New York: Grove Press.

Remnick, David. (2017) "John Lewis, Donald Trump and the Meaning of Legitimacy," *The New Yorker.* (January 15).

Walker, David and Henry Highland Garnet. (1969). *Walker's Appeal in Four Articles/Garnet's Address to the Slaves of the United States of America* (reprints). North Stratford, NH: Ayer Company.

Washington, James M. (ed.) (1986) *A Testament of Hope: The Essential Writings and Speeches of Martin Luther King, Jr.*, San Francisco: Harper & Row Publishers.

TRUMP'S ADMINISTRATION: THE NAZIFICATION OF A NATION

UGOCHI NWAOGWUGWU

*Ugochi Nwaogwugwu is a poet, singer, and dramatist. Her one-woman show, **Seasons of Separation** (2018), chronicles her family's immigrant experience. Her poetry is featured in several anthologies including, **A Storm Between Two Fingers**, and **Golden Shovel**. Her spoken word albums include: **African Buttafly**, **A.S.E.**, and **Love Shot**. Her website is: **ugochi.com***

With every election, someone must lose. That is inevitable. But somehow, this time, the emotion lingering in the streets is different, more menacing. Although, I'm sure conservatives experienced a similar disdain with the first election victory and subsequent second term of President Obama and antagonism aimed at George Bush was severe, this time it IS different. Even though Trump doesn't believe in climate change, the climate is changing. There is a difference in the attitude of the people of America and the altitude of the title of President. Culturally, American citizens have grown more cautious and fearful in terms of how they view and interact with one another. Growing numbers of white nationalists wear their unapologetic attacks like paraphernalia and seem to engage in frequent marches through American streets carrying progeny as their parents did before them during the Civil Rights/Jim Crow era. Some so brazen, allowing racial slurs to hang in the air like nooses, clamoring out of their white robes, committing hate crimes on an almost daily and consistent basis. White male terrorism is at an all-time high.

Is this mainstream America? Has it always been a gaggle of Anglo-Saxon liberals who find it extremely difficult to take a long, hard look at themselves without internalizing the shame of their choices? The blatant white supremacist microaggressions that hold Africans in America hostage every day needs proper acknowledgement to promote healing to manifest. This old behavior is unhealthy for the human family. The symptoms of the dynamics of racism have been critically analyzed and linked to various issues including mental health issues, housing disparities, disparities in sentencing, school failures/closings, gentrification, unemployment, drugs. However, the root of the problem is poorly identified.

Americans believe in the idea of democracy, like they believe in patriotism, baseball and cold beer. The illusion of this institution has hit a homerun with the people and is revered as sacred politics. But is it just a notion? Under a democratic system, the majority is supposed to rule, yet stand frozen, invisible to the likes of Betsy DeVos and her cabinet comrades. America's founding fathers found no contradiction in declaring. "all men were created equal," while they also owned slaves who were considered three-fifths of a person. The White house was built on black backs. Blood, sweat and spirit mixed into mortar stories set in the cobblestone streets of this land. Indigenous culture birthed America, born through barbarism, spilled blood and sacrifice. Africans could build your White House but remain grossly under represented when it counts by your electoral colleges and institutions.

Gentrification is raging like a wildfire around the globe, displacing Brown and Black people, forcing them out of their homes and communities. Donald Trump, has managed to disrespect every minority group in existence. He has also appointed Stephen Bannon, former CEO of Breitbart News, an alt-right/white nationalist newspaper, as his senior political strategist. Juxtapose this reality with the memory of Obama who was vilified and advised to denounce his longtime Pastor, Reverend Jeremiah Wright, for comments he made concerning race during the 2008 Democratic presidential primary.

Surely this couldn't happen in a true democracy. This could only happen within a system of racism/white supremacy. It seems there are many potholes in the White House lawn where the American people find themselves stuck and (seemingly) powerless.

I know I am not the only person who goes to sleep at night in any town, USA and awakes feeling like a stranger in a strange land. Many American liberals are trudging along in a state of disbelief trying to make sense of the state of our union. *"How could this have happened?"* we ask ourselves. However, are we fully prepared for the answer when it presents itself? America is not just a country ripe with lush land and waterways for commercial use and exploitation. It is also a living, breathing body. Like the corporations operated by humans who eat gourmet from its vibrancy then focus on ways to capitalize on its growth and decline.

Trump (a German-American) and his cabinet comrades are an assortment of unsavory characters who find themselves at the helm of America. This sinking ship has been plagued by scandals since the start of Trump's presidential campaign. Who are Trump supporters? The same alt-right press who gave him the initial platform to spew his white nationalist jargon and rally supporters. The Trump victory has made a large percentage of the residents of the United States experience what Africans in America and indigenous people internalize all too often. Feelings of helplessness that (in some cases) lead to hopelessness and depression. Just another day for the person of color who by now, probably has PTSD (post-traumatic stress disorder) as a result of this American life. A cyclical condition many disgruntled Americans may suffer from during the next four years. Believers have decided if you can't beat them, then build a Resistance! Do your work, only you know what that looks like. Being active and visible with protest efforts can assuage the mass of voters who claim Trump is not their president reconcile their American pride with their disgust at the current direction of American leadership.

As with Frankenstein, Trump is the monster CNN, FOX & CBS created, giving him new life as a political candidate. In private newsrooms, they sought more interesting ways to increase ratings and entertain American people. Trump admittedly never needed to pay for advertising because these major networks gifted Trump's ministry, offering him constant, unpaid, million-dollar access to primetime viewers. "Make America Great Again," was the core rhetorical idea of his campaign. None of the pundits thought to question him concerning the moment in American history to which he was referring. Trump was speaking to a specific demographic, very squarely, in coded language. Trump's administration fans the flames of fires born of church bombings and race riots. Much like in the horror films, it is only once the monster begins to destroy his surroundings and his creators that his destructive nature is exposed. By then, it is usually too late.

Entertainment and news media outlets neglected to characterize Donald Trump in his true image, an unqualified candidate, megalomaniac and failed business man with a long list of bankruptcies under his belt. When he initially entered the race for the Presidency he was given valuable air-time. Trump stood on his wealth, class and was presented as a potential candidate Americans could consider without any explanation as to why. As the days turned into months, more Americans were not just entertained but thrilled to binge watch the sideshow that was Donald Trump's presidential campaign. No one thought he would be taken seriously, much less get the Republican nomination, yet, here we are. Since his inauguration, he has been caught in lies on numerous occasions. As well as his advisor Kellyanne Conway, who introduced the world to another style of important information gathering called, "alternative facts."

Our sadness as Africans in America is that we were told that we're in a democracy, and a democracy is supposed to work in such a way that people are treated as equal and they have equal opportunity across the board, but that is a distorted way of looking at the situation. Global inequality is not by accident, it is by design. We live in a system of racism, white supremacy. We should have learned this by now. The uncomfortable truth is that our world has been created in the founding fathers image of racism/white supremacy. Not one President in American History has taken the plight of the stolen African and made it part of their presidential plan of service to improve the condition of the African in America. Not even the African President. Nor did we as a collective group of Africans in America make any special request of "our" then President, Barack Obama. The reality is that there hasn't been one president in U.S. history that has had the best interest of the black man, woman or child since the birth of this nation. So, what did we really expect from Donald Trump? He never promised us rose gardens.

In an article for the *Los Angeles Review of Books*, Mr. Rosenbaum offered this brief historical look at how the Nazi party rose to power. "Hitler's method was to lie until he got what he wanted, by which point it was too late," Mr. Rosenbaum, author of *Explaining Hitler, The Search for The Origins of His Evil*, explained adding there is no comparison between Hitler and Mr. Trump in terms of scale. But, he said, it was important to see that, like Hitler, Mr. Trump is *"defining mendacity down by normalizing lies and lowering expectations of truthfulness."* He also explained how calling news sources who don't agree with you, "fake news" is a tactic right of Hitler's playbook. Hitler was considered by Rosenbaum to be a mountebank, a con-man. *"Hitler used the tactics of bluff masterfully, at times giving the impression of being a feckless Chaplinesque clown, at other times a sleeping serpent, at others yet a trustworthy statesman…"*

When you compare, and contrast the personas of both men you find remarkable similarities. Both men used their poker faces and bag of tricks on the media to bluff their way into power, baffling their massive audiences who didn't know what to make of them. The press shined their omnipotent cameras on Trump making him newsworthy, not only in the entertainment section of your local newspaper but eventually sitting at the table in the political discussions as well, masquerading as an informed nominee. In Weimar Republic and America, Hitler and Trump were validated by local media and electoral lists in an act of what he called "democracy destroying itself democratically." The American people are slowly being desensitized to the foul play that is becoming politics as usual for the Trump era. Indoctrinating the masses into a new manner of interacting with one another and digesting information that leaves a bitter taste in the mouth of large number of registered voters. "While marchers and the courts have put up a fight after the Muslim ban, each new act, each new lie, accepted by default, seems less outrageous," Mr. Rosenbaum said. Nazi's also limited immigrant travel with the similar rhetoric that birthed Trump's travel ban. History of Nazi Germany started with moving against foreigners. Racism/white supremacy at its finest. Isolate all the people then divide and conquer. The genocide of Jewish people began with politicians attempting to divide people, intolerance and hate speech. Once the people became desensitized to the regimes way of life, they turned over their neighbors, friends and in some cases, family members.

The late Frances Cress Welsing, author of the *Isis Papers, Keys to The Colors* and a renowned, African-centered psychiatrist, was no stranger to the *Mein Kampf* mentality lurking latent in the psyche of certain human beings. Dr. Welsing specialized her practice to focus on what she described as "white supremacy culture." In 1957, 12 years after the second world war, Dr. Frances Welsing asked her parents to be given a trip to Germany as her undergraduate graduation present. She wanted to live with the German people and ask them if they understood what they allowed to have happen to their neighbors and friends. Whenever she would ask the question they would always look down, which Dr. Welsing recognized as an awareness of their actions. But that didn't stop them from allowing it to happen. Dr. Welsing recalled how on the surface they appeared nice but those supposedly nice people let their neighbors be killed. As Dr. Welsing stated in a 2015 radio interview with journalist Carl Nelson, *"Adolph Hitler understood, the way you destroy a people is to program the other group to have negative images of the people you want to destroy."*

There is no one more diabolical than a shady, political salesman on his march to power. One who desensitizes the American people to fraudulent political leaders while simultaneously polarizing the people they are expected to serve. Outraging the masses even as you manipulate them. Hitler and Trump share(d) an understanding of the effects of mind-control and the strategy of targeting a group for marginalization, de-huminizatin, and, ultimately, elimination. Fear-mongering, scapegoating and race-baiting are some of the tools always left sharpened and in the Trump bag of tricks. The First Family is fostering a new trend of complete disrespect for 99% of the human family.

On June 6. 2017, Eric Trump spoke with Sean Hannity on Fox News insulting his fathers' critics saying, *"I've never seen hatred like this... to me they're not even people."* This is actual Nazism. Any president or First Family member who speaks of or about their constituents like this in a public forum is demonstrating deplorable demeanor. Behavior such as this is divisive, dismissive and disrespectful.

The Trump Era is one rife with insensitive and unseemly comments, tweets and interviews. He is general public relations failure and an international embarrassment for even the most patriotic of Americans. The Trumps are altering the manner in which politicians should engage the American people and conduct themselves as a First Family. I have news for you, Eric Trump: There are more than 65,844,610 Americans who didn't vote for your father and we ARE real people, real voters.

Donald J. Trump is *not* our president.

AFRICAN AMERICANS, RACIST COUNTER-REVOLUTION, AND TRUMP

MICHAEL SIMANGA

Mchael Simanga is an activist cultural worker, artist and scholar who has written, edited and published fiction, poetry, drama, essays and memoir. His publications include: **Congress of African People: History and Memory** *(2014),* **Brilliant Fire! Amiri Baraka: Poems, Plays, Politics for the People** *(co-editor, 2017).*

"there is no place on this earth without my fingerprint, and my heel in the skeleton of skyscrapers, and my sweat in the brilliance of diamonds!"[1]

Africa's human and natural resources were extracted through atrocity to build the wealth of the white western world. The trans-Atlantic slave trade and European colonialism are the economic and cultural foundations of the global power of the white western world. To justify the atrocities of slavery and colonialism a mythology was created, a story told, a culture built and governments created around the idea that Europeans and their descendants are superior to the rest of the world, especially Africans and their descendants. In the context of a traditionally white supremacist's society like the United States, where white men have traditionally held power almost exclusively, it is not difficult to comprehend their ferocious opposition, the violent response to any idea or movement that challenges that authority. We are witnessing and experiencing it today.

From the first minute and every second of every minute since the atrocity began, we have been engaged in a long struggle, spanning generations, to free Black humanity from people and systems that deprecate us for the purpose of satisfying their greed or their need to assert dominance over us. Our history of resistance to oppression and our assertion of our humanity is the framework for contextualizing and organizing in the 21st century as it has been for all previous generations of African Americans. This knowing is critical in the storm of a white racist counter-revolution that culminated in the election of trump and the takeover of the federal government by the right wing of the Republican Party.

The mythological political narrative of the United States begins with a story of noble ideas and noble white men creating a new nation where the human rights of all people would be respected. From that premise those noble men with noble ideas created a government of the people, for the people and by the people. They established law, policy and practice to form a participatory and inclusive democracy, moving steadily toward a more perfect union.

Euro-descendant genocide against indigenous peoples to facilitate the theft of their land, the subjugation and exclusion of women and the enslavement of Africans and their descendants are some of the obvious problems with that narrative. Critical complications also exist in trying to reconcile the enterprise of slavery and the ideas of freedom when at significant moments in US history, times when those with power could have moved the country toward the idea of a government that respected and protected the human and civil rights of all people, they chose to do the opposite and preserve undeserved power and unwarranted profit.

Throughout the entire history of this country a significant and intransigent section of the white population vehemently opposes any attempt to create a legitimate, inclusive, participatory democracy, an equitable economy and a government dedicated to both human rights and civil rights. They rebel against any attempt to abolish the mythology and culture of white supremacy and the privileges it renders them, even if those privileges ultimately do not give the majority of them the resources or opportunities they desire and need for a better life. Rich and powerful white men, have long understood that an appeal to white supremacist entitlement still resonates deeply within white America. The 2016 presidential campaign and election of trump is the most recent proof. It is evidence of the temporary success of the white right-wing counter-revolt against the civil rights and social justice revolution that dismantled Jim Crow and has steadily pushed American culture, its public and private institutions, toward equitable inclusion and participation in the economic, political and social life of the country.

Historically, the tendency within the white community has been to acquiesce to the white supremacists while condemning their ideology. As with previous white right revolts, the success of the current revolt will be temporary, although it has the potential to have a negative impact for years or even generations. As an example, the consequences of conceding to the racist plantocracy in the founding of the US still reverberates in every aspect of society today.

The writing and ratification of the US Constitution was the first opportunity to create a governing structure on the basis of human rights codified as law. Instead, the founders of the United States chose to not only protect but promote the most egregious violation, the enslavement of Black people. The so-called 3/5 compromise was an agreement to engage in a scheme to protect and extend the power of the white plantation class in the south. The enslavers would be allowed to count African men as 3/5 of a man while also denying them any rights expressed in the new nation or its constitution. By falsely boosting eligible population figures in southern states the plantocracy was granted more representation in Congress, cementing their ability to protect their profits and their white supremacist culture. This practice continued through the Jim Crow era where Black people were counted for political representation but denied the right to vote and other rights.

Instead of creating a polity with unequivocal, absolute opposition to slavery, the US constitution gave legal authorization and also cultural justification for a 77-year extension of slavery, a system that "…would disgrace a nation of savages."[2] A system that brutalized African Americans while its perpetrators professed piety.

> "Women are considered of no value, unless they continually increase their owner's stock. They are put on a par with animals. This same master shot a woman through the head, who had run away and been brought back to him. No one called him to account for it. If a slave resisted being whipped, the bloodhounds were unpacked, and set upon him, to tear his flesh from his bones. The master who did these things was highly educated, and styled a perfect gentleman. He also boasted the name and standing of a Christian, though Satan never had a truer follower."[3]

The 3/5 compromise was a constitutional embrace of white supremacist ideology and practice and deepened its infection into all American institutions and throughout its culture where it has remained intractable into the 21st century. As historian Gerald Horne points out, *"Whatever the case, it is evident that there is a disjuncture between the supposed progressive and avant-garde import of 1776 and the worsening conditions for Africans and the indigenous that followed upon the triumph of the rebels."*[4]

The U.S. constitution became the law of the new nation by betraying Black people. Slavery endured in the south and the north nursed on it with blood dripping from its mouth.

Reconstruction, that brief period after the Civil War, presented the second major opportunity to turn toward a human-rights based democratic society. It was born from the defeat of the plantocracy's attempt to establish a new confederate nation on the noble idea that slavery was God's divine order and Black people were created to serve white people. Their defeat was the result of a two and a half century, multifaceted resistance of Black people to American slavery, the support of indigenous and white allies and the violence of the Civil War which the north won with a Union Army that included 180,000 Black soldiers fighting for Black freedom.

Creating a new anti-slavery south, a democratic south where they could live as free people on the land they had cultivated for generations, finally felt possible for the African American community. The 13th, 14th and 15th amendments seemed to present the potential to create a pathway into full first class citizenship for Black people. To exercise their rights as citizens, Black men registered to vote, ran for and were elected to local, state and national office. The newly free four million descendants of Africa pursued empowerment with education, guns from the war, land that many now owned, Reconstruction courts and laws that enforced their rights and a federal government that remained in the former confederate states to suppress the plantocracy. It seemed as if freedom fought for had finally been won.

The enslavement of Black people in the US and the colonies that preceded it lasted 246 years from 1619 to 1865. Reconstruction lasted 12 years, 1865 to 1877. The project to create a democratic south where the descendants of enslaved Africans would be equal citizens building a life for their families and a future for their children came to a terrifying end with the Tilden-Hayes Compromise. The contested presidential election of 1876 between Republican Rutherford B. Hayes and Democrat Samuel Tilden was resolved through a compromise between the two parties. Tilden conceded the presidency and Hayes agreed to withdraw federal troops from the former confederate states allowing the plantation class to retake power. When the troops left, the space they had occupied was filled with a 90-year reign of terror by white supremacist vigilantes like the KKK and southern state and local governments who enforced the subjugation of Black citizens. The power of rich white people to exploit and abuse them was restored and the monster Jim Crow ruled the south for the next nine decades with the explicit or implied complicity of US presidents, congress and the courts, churches, media and other institutions south and north, east and west. "The South resented giving the Afro-American his freedom, the ballot box and the Civil Rights Law."[5] That resentment was evident in the rules, laws and customs to humiliate and remind Black people of their absolute vulnerability within the white supremacist system and their place beneath even the poorest, most ignorant white person. Black resistance deepened and continued, fashioning a conception of freedom for the future.

In the tradition, 20th century African Americans fought oppression on all fronts. By the mid-1950s through the 1970s the fight had created a movement with the unshakeable faith of Black ancestors, the unbreakable tradition of Black resistance and the unmovable force of a Black warrior generation determined to be free.

On Tuesday, November 4, 2008, African American democrat Barack Hussein Obama was elected president of the United States. With a broad coalition that included Hispanics, young people, Asian Americans, women and labor Obama won the election with 53% of the votes over Republican John McCain's 45%. At the center of the coalition were African Americans who cast 95% of their ballots for Obama. It was not the first time they were responsible for electing a Democratic president. John Kennedy ('60), LB Johnson ('64), Jimmy Carter ('76) and Bill Clinton ('92) all owe their elections to the overwhelming support of the Black community. The 2008 election was different, its meaning deeper and more powerful for Black people and for the United States.

The election of Barack Obama was a result of the long freedom movement of enslaved Africans and their descendants who stood and fought for centuries never accepting our dreadful condition as our destiny. His election was also directly the result of the impact of the political and social changes forced by the battles and victories of the Civil Rights/Black Power Movement and the consciousness of self-determination it created. Other movements, women, Hispanics, native peoples, LGBTQ communities, Asian Americans, young people were inspired by and often aligned with Black people who were also inspired by them. As those movements grew in strength and influence, American institutions were challenged to reject the old idea of this country as a white supremacists Christian nation and become more inclusive of all the Americans.

The social justice revolution and its movements forced changes in law, social practice, politics and culture. As a result, the United States of the 21st century does not look like the same country it was in 1950 when white men held almost all power exclusively and benefitted first and the most from available resources and opportunities. As the social movements won victories and challenged the culture, the privileged position of white men was diluted and their traditional structures of white supremacy were weakened. Civil rights, women's rights, LGBTQ rights, inclusiveness, recognition of a multi-cultural America and more equitable sharing of power enraged the white traditionalists, especially in the south. They pushed back and a counter-revolution grew with their discontent.

"White Democrats will desert their party in droves the minute it becomes a black party."[6] Leaders of the Republican Party saw the outrage of southern Democrats as their party under Kennedy and Johnson was forced by the Civil Rights Movement to oppose segregation. Understanding the growing white opposition to Black empowerment, Republicans welcomed them with assurances they would uphold traditional white American values. Nixon spoke to and for those he called the silent majority. Later Ronald Reagan solidified their loyalty by assuring them when he launched his 1980 campaign for president in Philadelphia, Mississippi the site where civil rights workers James Chaney, Mickey Schwerner and Andrew Goodman were murdered in 1964 assisting Black people registering to vote. Reagan spoke nostalgically about the old south and proclaimed his preference for state's rights (a battle cry of confederate apologists and segregationists) confirming to the supporters of the old America, the defenders of the old white power, that Reagan would help them take their country back.

At the time of Reagan's 1980 election the growing strength of the white counter-revolution was evident in politics but not yet powerful enough to take and hold control of the federal government. Reagan was president for two terms and pushed the agenda forward. The Republican Party embraced the right-wing counter-revolution, even convincing the less conservative members that they could win elections by appealing to the white discontent. The Republicans supported and mounted legal challenges to affirmative action. They developed and supported the "culture wars" launched by the white Christian evangelical movement and public campaigns to challenge ethnic studies programs and diversity in education, Hispanic immigration and multiculturalism and attacked women's reproductive rights. They became skilled at propaganda, built networks of speakers, launched talk radio and television programs that appealed to white racist discontent and relentlessly attacked the progress of the social revolution. Slowly, state by state, they elected candidates who promised fidelity to their cause. They captured positions on school boards, county commissions, city councils, state legislatures, governorships and congress. They also elected two presidents, both named Bush, neither hard right but both willing to placate the hard-right wing to get elected.

In 1984 and '88, Jesse Jackson ran for the Democratic nomination for president and although he didn't secure enough votes, he succeeded in pushing the Democratic Party to remain committed to a platform that was more aligned with the past demands of the social justice movement agenda. Between the two Bushes, Bill Clinton was elected president as a centrist in the Democratic Party and began to pull the platform from the left and toward the center right. Before his tenure as president ended and with his wife and political adviser Hillary, he led the country to accept a culture of mass incarceration that devastated African American communities across the US and fed the racists' narrative of the necessity to manage Black people through violence. It was a revitalization of the narrative created during slavery to justify the brutalization of enslaved Black people.

In 2001, George W. Bush was handed the presidency over Al Gore by the Supreme Court in a contested election, it was a signal of the growing strength of the Republican right-wing. They were marching steadily toward an ultimate goal, control of the entire federal government to enact their right-wing agenda. Meanwhile the Black social justice movement was no longer leading a powerful united front making change. The coalition was trying to defend what had been won but didn't have the deep national grassroots movement that had been the foundation of social justice change. Veteran and emerging organizers, were in communities working heroically everywhere, but not with the national effectiveness of the previous period. Meanwhile, the Republican right was consolidating and expanding its power on the local and state level. They gerrymandered congressional districts, launched a national strategy to dismantle the Voting Rights Act and implemented a strategy to suppress African American voting rights.

The 2008 presidential campaign represented a confrontation of the political and social forces that had been struggling over America's future. The Civil Rights/Black Power movement had successfully challenged the old order of white supremacy and along with other social movements had pulled the US from its past and toward a future possibility of an inclusive participatory democracy. The candidacy and campaign of Barack Obama galvanized progressive forces in a way that had not been seen in a long time. The united front, a broad coalition of many different interests, came together around an agenda of change to elect the first African American president of the United States and send the first African American family to live in the White House.

African Americans rightly felt enormous pride in an experience that represented a victory in our long, continued struggle to be citizens in the country of our birth and choice. For us Barack and Michelle were a familial and familiar part of our story. Representing the arc of our striving, they were Black woman and man grown from the foundation, the complex bottom of color and class. They were our people succeeding at the highest levels while facing seemingly insurmountable odds. To many they carried the spirit of the Black national anthem "full of the faith that the dark past has taught us…full of the hope that the present has brought us."[7]

We basked briefly in the hope that the unique moment represented a new day for us, for this country, for the future. We had little time to ponder the possibilities because shortly after the election our historical memory coughed up the reality of the relationship between America and its African American citizens. With every victory, in every generation, we are always acutely aware of the specter of white supremacy, its violent manifestations standing in the shadows sharpening its teeth, looming long and large in our consciousness. Within hours after the 2008 election, it leapt from the shadows and a surge of the ugly truth began to roll in and over the possibility that this country was ready and willing to break with its past.

> "Cross burnings. Schoolchildren chanting 'Assassinate Obama.' Black figures hung from nooses. Racial epithets scrawled on homes and cars. Incidents around the country referring to President-elect Barack Obama are dampening the postelection glow of racial progress and harmony, highlighting the stubborn racism that remains in America."[8]

In the wake of Obama's election, the Southern Poverty Law Center expressed hope and issued a warning:

> "Even as we embark on a new national adventure, the signs are worrying. It may be that the hatemongers are wrong, that Americans' better angels will prevail and the changes that are sweeping America will not result in a growing rage on the right. But experience tells us that while we hope for the best, we also must prepare for what could be a dangerous, racially motivated backlash of hate."[9]

Black people braced for the storm we knew was coming, whispering concern that the mysterious racist "they" would assassinate Obama. Or that the violence of racism would become a pandemic again, a sickness growing strong enough to spread quickly. We heard the Republican pledge to destroy the Obama presidency, to insure its failure. We saw the open disrespect by white elected officials and the growing hate in traditional and social media directed at the Obamas including their daughters. We understood it was not about them as individuals it was about us, Black people, collectively. They were the easy target, the obvious symbols of our struggle for civil and human rights and they, we had to be denigrated, diminished, damned. We witnessed trump lead a racist campaign questioning our legitimacy as US citizens by challenging President Obama's citizenship and we could smell the putrid breath of the ante-bellum Supreme Court as it read its Dred Scott decision:

> *"In the opinion of the Court the legislation and histories of the times, and*

the language used in the Declaration of Independence, show that neither the class of persons who had been imported as slaves nor their descendants, whether they had become free or not, were then acknowledged as a part of the people nor intended to be included in the general words used in that memorable instrument.... They had for more than a century before been regarded as beings of an inferior order and altogether unfit to associate with the white race, either in social or political relations; and so far inferior that they had no rights which the white man was bound to respect; and that the Negro might justly and lawfully be reduced to slavery for his benefit. He was bought and sold and treated as an ordinary article of merchandise and traffic whenever a profit could be made by it. This opinion was at that time fixed and universal in the civilized portion of the white race...."[10]

During the campaign of 2008, the Republican Party objective was not just to win the presidency but to expand its dominance over the entire federal government. They wanted the majority in both houses of congress, the presidency and a majority on the Supreme Court. They understood that they could not succeed unless the network of right wing activists and donors were fully committed. Their presidential candidate John McCain, in his ambition to be president at all costs, was willing to compromise with the racist right wing by signaling, like his predecessors Nixon, Reagan and both Bushes that he and the modern Republican Party were committed to support their agenda if elected. Although McCain had been seen and touted as a maverick senator unwilling to fall in lock step with peers in his party, that image was shattered when he chose Sarah Palin, the right-wing governor of Alaska, as his running mate. McCain lost to Obama. Although he was ultimately defeated by a significant margin, losing both the popular vote and the Electoral College, McCain had unleashed the ugly racist right wing elements of the Republican Party and called them to the surface.

McCain's compromise, backed by the Republican establishment, elevated Sarah Palin and the racist right wing of the Republican Party to a position of national acceptance as a legitimate and public force in American politics. That group organized themselves into the Tea Party and in 2010 sent more than 80 of their movement to Congress. Determined to dismantle every gain of the social justice movements and destroy the legacy of the first Black president, they helped Republicans capture the House of Representatives where they not only waged war against the Democrats but also those moderate Republicans who opposed them.

By the 2012 election, there was no longer a moderate Republican voice being heard. As in the past, they conceded power to the most racist elements of American politics. Republicans in the center either left congress or shut-up and fell in step with the right wing. Sarah Palin helped give voice to them but she could not lead them. A megalomaniacal real estate developer and reality TV personality with wealth and a high media profile, could. Donald Trump took over the task of promoting the lie that President Obama was not an American, endearing himself to Nazi's, white nationalists, Tea partyers, evangelical Christians, and others in the alternative right. He became their leader and he prepared to lead them into Washington D.C. after President Obama left office.

The election of Barack Obama and his relationship to Black liberation veterans is complex. It has to be understood in relationship to the relative strength or weakness of the Black liberation movement, the political forces vying for power in society and especially for control of the instruments of power. Obama is a center-left Democrat. There is a drastic difference between him and the racist right-wing which is evident now. In discussing the 2012 re-election campaign Angela Davis said, "We learned a lot from that election. It was actually quite incredible. Even more so than the first election. During the first election most people were myopically focused on the individual who was the candidate, right? This time around, many of us were really afraid that the Republican candidate would win, which would mean disaster with respect to political issues."[11] His election was clearly important to African Americans and others in the coalition that elected him. He was also president of the American imperialist empire. Analyzing the phenomenon of his election and his presidency is important to our understanding of how to organize against the counter-revolution.

The 2012 reelection of President Obama demonstrated that the coalition that elected him in '08 had held in the presidential race but was steadily losing in state and congressional races. Shortly after the second Obama inauguration we begin to see the forces that had been unleashed. We felt it first when an American teenager walking down an American street, eating American candy on the way to his American family's home, is stalked and murdered by a racist vigilante. A Black son was dead, and there was no justice for his family. A wave of black deaths, lynchings, murders of African American women and men followed. In our grief, we were reminded of a history that was not the past. In the second decade of the 20th century a Black person was being killed every 28 hours at the hands of the police or vigilantes.[12]

It wasn't just the vigilante murder of Trayvon or the jail hanging of Sandra Bland or the police shooting of Mike Brown. It wasn't blood spilt on the floor of our church and hymnal. It wasn't the violence against all those children and all those women and all those men and all that agony and all those tears of all those families grieving in all those communities all over this country. It wasn't all those lies and all those excuses and all those people who choose to subvert justice. It wasn't all those anonymous cowardly hateful, white people who killed by telephone when they called the police to falsely report Black people with toy guns or walking suspiciously. It wasn't social media that allowed us access to the images and video and live streams of bloody assaults on Black bodies. It wasn't the brutes choking us, punching and kicking our elders, slamming our partners into concrete. It wasn't schools handcuffing our children, body slamming our girls and shocking our boys with Tasers. It wasn't where we lived or how much education we had or whether we were poor or rich. It was the bile of America's history retching into 21st century Black life.

Our rising anxiety grew in proportion to our increasing rage because we knew what this was. We understood instinctively that evident in our historical presence in America was the unrelenting violence we'd experienced for centuries and in the grief caused by every incident of state violence and each vigilante attack we saw the old scars we wore on our backs, our minds and on our souls. We knew this 21st century escalation was the sickening sound of a quickening all-out war on Black people. It was also being waged on women, people of color, non-Euro immigrants, Muslims. We knew what it was, American capitalism, especially its most right wing racist elements, depends upon the mythology of white supremacy.

We could feel this ghost rising up from the basements and creeping from the closets of families yearning for an American past that granted them an unearned and undeserved privilege. It was the racist army of southern slavers and northern accomplices rising up from the underworld where it had retreated to regroup from the battles it lost to the African American mass movement for Civil Rights and Black Power. It was America's institutional power aligning to assault us, again. It was James Weldon Johnson reminding us, "We have come over a way that with tears has been watered. We have come, treading our path through the blood of the slaughtered."[13]

Contrary to the racist narrative of passive acceptance of our oppression, Black people resisted and fought enslavement, Jim Crow and every other form of oppression from the first day, the first minute of contact with those intent to steal our humanity. From the 1950s into the 1970s their descendants stood up in the spirit of those resisters and liberators and formed a mighty army that marched on the bastions of our oppression. The warrior generation, thousands of women and men, domestic workers and laborers, teachers, sharecroppers and preachers, students, artists and lawyers, elders, parents and children engaged in battle after battle for justice in what came to be known as the Civil Rights/Black Power Movement. They joined or formed the NAACP, SCLC, CORE, SNCC, the Mississippi Freedom Democratic Party, Women's Civic organizations, the Black Guards of Monroe North Carolina, the Deacons for Defense in Louisiana and the Lowndes County Freedom Organization (the Black Panther Party in Alabama). They created the Revolutionary Action Movement and the League of Black Revolutionary Workers, the Black Panther Party for Self Defense, the Us Organization, the Republic of New Afrika, the Congress of African People and the African Liberation Support Committee. They held Black Power Conferences and convened the National Black Political Convention. They forced American education to include Black people's story through their own eyes and demanded an end to sexist and patriarchal ideas in society and within the Black Freedom Movement. They created the Black Arts Movement, drafted the Gary Declaration and the Cohambee River Collective Statement. They challenged the legal forces of oppression and discrimination, worked in the labor movement, built independent institutions of education, culture and politics. Opened clinics and community organizations. Reclaimed and reconnected our consciousness with Africa and demanded its importance be recognized. We called ourselves beautifully Black and African American, claiming both histories and experiences.

And there was progress. We had dismantled Jim Crow, transferred power to our communities, educated more Black people than ever before and grew a college educated middle class. Black people broke down discriminatory barriers in the public and private sector, became mayors and elected representatives to congress, built businesses and climbed into the executive level of corporations. With the election of Barack Obama, it seemed as if that progress would eventually lead to an eradication of the white supremacist foundation of American culture. We were wrong. While we had rightly focused on consolidating and expanding the gains of our struggle, the warrior generation was aging and our battle tested organizations in civil rights and Black liberation had also aged, weakened or no longer existed. We were not ready for war, but there were people working for social justice in communities and building organizations. In our mobilization in the Obama campaigns we were also preparing.

The 21st century counter-revolution of white supremacist capitalism had begun marshalling their forces 40 years ago. Their strategy to retake power and to "take our country back" included an above ground plan using the legal structure, politics and vast sums of money from sectors of the billionaire class to create institutions, non-profits, think tanks and organizations advancing the take America back agenda. It also included an underground mobilization of white supremacist groups that were not yet able to come out of the shadows. They would emerge in the 2016 presidential campaign, but not on the fringes, in the center of the Republican primaries and then more forcefully in the trump campaign.

The growing assertion of the white right presence, the rise in state and vigilante violence against Black people and the hardened opposition to the Obama administration put African Americans on the defensive. We begin organizing in our mourning and marching and making our way to where we knew it was going. We'd seen it coming, building since 2008 and the election of O. The violence, the rise of racism in the public discourse, the continuing surge of mass incarcerations, the permission given by politicians to openly denigrate black people. And if we were confused about it, we could see it on social media or talk shows every day. We knew it was coming, the storm that is never still inside of us. It is sometimes held back, hidden beneath hope it will not be necessary to feel it explode beyond our grief, our tears our generations of scars passed on in the quiet discussions of how to stay alive when being hunted by ogres. We knew it was coming, beyond our reasoning and theory, beyond our prayers and attempts at reconciliation, it was coming, an explosion of unstoppable force, the heat that races through our blood into our brains reminding us that there is no one else, there is nothing else except our own fire that can back up these monsters. They called it out and it came roaring with courage, conviction and commitment from young voices and old wisdom. Black Lives Matter the sisters said as they gather and lead us to build new armies. In Jackson, MS and in Newark, NJ the Black radical tradition of grassroots organizing was the foundation of the successful mayoral campaigns of Chokwe Lumumba and Ras Baraka. A new movement has been taking shape and learning, growing from protest to governing to the structural changes that Martin Luther King called for.

The election of trump shocked many in 2016. But it is not sudden or accidental. It is the successful realization of the white counter-revolution strategy. It is the product of a history that makes the choice to betray Black people, women and others in favor of a white male power and narrative. By 2016 the white supremacist counter-revolution had gained enough strength to capture the federal government. They control the White House, both houses of Congress and the Supreme Court. They also have control over all federal agencies, the military and the state department. Nazi's, the KKK and other terrorists are in and now have access to the white house and openly parade around the internet and in communities carrying confederate flags and torches. They don't have to hide and they will not retreat unless forced to. They believe trump and his sycophants are all powerful. They are not.

As with the birther movement, Trump and his band of racists are furiously attacking the power and accomplishments of the Black community by eradicating any legacy of President Obama. Executive orders from Trump rain from the White House pushing back environmental protections and consumer protections against bankers. Attorney General Sessions has ordered the Justice Department to seek maximum penalties against drug offenders taking the country back to policies that led to the mass incarceration of Black and Brown people. Republicans are silently complicit with the destruction of health care and public education. There is a huge surge in open racist acts of violence and attacks on multi-cultural education and inclusion. The right wing wants war and Trump is a warmonger seeking to make himself look powerful by sending the daughters and sons of Americans who are not his children to war. The Trump administration is filled with criminals engaged in all manner of criminal enterprises. They look all powerful but they are not.

Black people and our allies are in a fight for the future of this country, again. We have to build a broad united front that includes every sector of the Balck community around an agenda of our concerns and objectives. We have to build a broad united front with our allies around an agenda that includes our concerns and objectives. We are in a fight not unlike the one to end slavery which seemed invincible. We are in a fight not unlike the one to defeat Jim Crow and other forms of oppression in the 20th century. We must organize in every way necessary including protests and elections. We will win. White supremacy is a lie. The people and structures that depend on it will be defeated by the truth. *"Truth is on the side of the oppressed..."*[14]

References:

[1]Cesaire, Aime. Notes on a return to the native land in *The Negritude Poets: An Anthology of Translations from the French*. Ellen Conroy Kennedy, Ed. Viking Press, 1975.

[2]Douglass, Frederick. The meaning of July fourth to the Negro in *The Essential Douglass: Selected Writings and Speeches*. Nicholas Buccola, Ed. Hackett Press, 2016.

[3]Jacobs, Harriet Ann. Incidents in the Life of a Slave Girl in *A Will to be Free, Vol 2*. Wilder Publications, 2008.

[4]Horne, Gerald. *The Counter-Revolution of 1776: Slave Resistance and the Origins of the United States of America*. New York University Press, 2014.

[5]Wells, Ida B. *Crusade for Justice: The Autobiography of Ida B. Wells*. University of Chicago Press, 1970.

[6]Phillips, Kevin. *The Emerging Republican Majority*. Princeton University Press, 2014.

[7]Johnson, James Weldon. Online: poetryfoundation.org/poems-and-poets/poems/detail/46549

[8]Online: nbcnews.com/id/27738018/ns/us_news-life/t/obama-election-spurs-race-threats-crimes/#.WRr042jys2w

[9]Online: splcenter.org/fighting-hate/intelligence-report/2008/radical-right

[10]loc.gov/rr/program/bib/ourdocs/DredScott.html

[11]Davis, Angela. *Freedom is a Constant Struggle*. Haymarket Books, 2016.

[12]Online: operationghettostorm.org

[13]Johnson, James Weldon. Online: poetryfoundation.org/poems-and-poets/poems/detail/46549

[14]X, Malcolm. *Malcolm X Speaks*. Pathfinder Press, 1965.

PRESIDENT CHEETO AND THE DEATH OF THE SCHOOLHOUSE

DAVID O. STOVALL

*David O. Stovall is a Professor of Educational Policy Studies and African-American Studies at University of Illinois-Chicago. His research interests include critical race theory, school-community relationships, youth culture and the relationship between housing and K-12 school systems. His latest book is **Born Out of Struggle: Critical Race Theory, School Creation, and the Politics of Interruption** (2016).*

We are in an absurd moment. I should be able to end the account here, but there is much we need to understand in the current absurdity. Right now, the order of the day is chaos. More importantly, said chaos is accepted as order. Neely Fuller remains prophetic in his statement, *"if you do not understand White supremacy everything else will confuse you."* At the same time, some of us are not confused. White supremacy is absurd conceptually, but fatal in reality. The difference this time might be that some White folks are seeing it for the first time. For the rest of us, we've seen it all too often.

This same group of people live in recognition of the fact that the current onslaught by the Trump administration is just an iteration of what a lot of his minions (i.e. children, cronies from previous/current business ventures, appointees at the executive branch, etc.) have been clamoring to do in the open for years. For some, there is shock value to the fact that the Trump administration, along with Republican members of congress and everyday White residents, feel emboldened to act on their racial animus with impunity.

Instead of engaging in a diatribe about the numerous tentacles of the ridiculousness of the Trump administration, the focus of this meditation is on the future of education and what communities are doing to self-determine despite the odds. We must be honest that the moment can at sometimes appear daunting, but now is actually the moment to be the most diligent, tactical and cunning.

I submit my offering from Chicago. A city where the mayor gets away with covering up a murder to win an election, while the state is in its third year without a budget. Over 150 schools have been closed or repurposed since 2004. Forty-nine were closed in the summer of 2013, resulting in the largest single set of school closings in the history of the United States. The city's municipal bond rating has been reduced to junk in 2017. Chicagoans endured 762 homicides in 2016. Simultaneously, the city has built over 100 skyscrapers in the same period of time (since 2000). All of this predates Trump.

I make this point to put forward the fact that the move to end the public commons in education has been on a slow, but direct pace. Before Trump's election and his subsequent appointment of Betsy DeVos as Secretary of Education, the neoliberal surge in education moved to privatize under the rhetoric of competition, market viability, and "data-driven" success (Lipman, 2013). Under these conditions, Trump and DeVos just expedite the process.

As the expedition of this process is rapid and filled with derision, there is also a ridiculousness that is coupled with it. DeVos has fueled her process of "delivering the kingdom of God" through a numbing series of quotes that are beyond head-scratching. Without going into detail, the audacity of a person stating that HBCUs are one of the "greatest" examples of school choice is an example of the racist, out of touch, delusional perversion of the history of Black life in the U.S.

At the K-12, level, vouchers are positioned as examples of choice, when the reality is, that if a family has multiple children, there is little-to-no guarantee that all of the young people will be able to utilize the voucher. Additionally, vouchers in most instances only pay partial tuition for private schools. When vouhcers are not in play, charter schools fill the void of what is accepted as "choice". What is rarely mentioned, however, is that many policies of charter schools run by corporate entities utilize policies that are more reminiscent of prisons than they are of institutions of learning. Rules that force students into silent lunches, force them to walk on lines for risk of punishment or fines for receiving demerits or being out of uniform are situated around the punishment of the Black body as normal, right, and good. The racist notion of bringing Black and Brown youth to heel to the desires of White supremacy has become the order of compliance. Instruction and engagement is muted by rules that make it "safer" for White women to control the bodies of youth of color that they fear. Again, Trump and DeVos bring this dynamic closer to becoming the rule than the outskirts of the exception.

Survival, Resistance, and the Will to Build

More dangerous than any of the aforementioned realities is the politics of desperation that plague our communities. For some, because the education condition is deemed so drastic, charters and vouchers become viable options for communities of color. These new educational "options" pitch educational "innovation" through special themes (Science Technology Engineering Arts Mathematics—STEAM, performing/visual arts, military, etc.) that are enticing to parents who view their educational options as limited.

Fortunately, through organizing, there are collectives of organizations that resist this trend through popular education for parents through community dialogue and political action. Collectives like the Grassroots Education Movement in Chicago (facebook.com/gemcoalition) and New York (and gemnyc.org) along with the Journey for Justice Coalition (j4jalliance.com) and the People's Education Movement (peoplesed.weebly.com) make the effort to self-determine to meet community educational needs.

As many of the authors in this edited volume have been part of community-driven efforts to self-determine, the current Trump moment brings a critical issue back into the fold—because we know the US public education system was never intended to educate the populace (especially Black folks) what will we do for the young folks and families who continue to suffer? This isn't positioned to be polemic, but is instead posited as a challenge to us all. Because the work to reclaim what has been stolen from Black people in the Western Hemisphere (primarily our humanity and culture), is layered, multifaceted and riddled with contradictions, there are no easy answers. The "gift" of the current administration is that it awakens some of us from our Obama administration-era slumbering. It is confirmed that we are not post-racial. The multitudes of us have not "made it over." Now is the moment to recalibrate and engage in our position and build with one another. In our fugitive space we must engage a commitment to work in-between the "rules" and "compliance" while making the decision to take what works while rejecting what does not.

We are in the resistance, even though some us don't know it. But that's okay. Continuing to do the work on the ground will allow those who have decided to sit the fence to make a decision. In this moment elders cannot forsake the young folks while the young folks must continue to learn the lessons from history with a commitment not to repeat it. President Cheeto is *not* our president, but none of them before him ever were. He's a fraudulent, misogynist, racist, pathological liar.

To wallow in despair in this moment is futile. For these reasons, I have sided with those who demand justice. In this Movement for Black Lives I see young people making a decision on Fanon's treatise to fulfill their destiny. I am trying with everything I have to meet them where they are to join them.

References

Fuller, N. (2010). *The united-independent compensatory code/system/concept textbook: a compensatory counter-racist code.* Chicago: Third World Press.

Lipman, P. (2013). The new political economy of urban education. New York: Routledge.

THE DEADLY ROLE OF WHITE NATIONALISM, SUPREMACY, AND PRIVILEGE

SANDRA TURNER-BARNES

Sandra Turner-Barnes *is a poet, spoken word artist, and children's author from New Jersey. In 2002, together with her jazz ensemble 'Mysterious Traveller', Sandra released her first poetry and jazz CD,* **September Will Never Be the Same.** *In 2010 she published her second children's book,* **Beyond the Back of the Bus,** *a tribute to Rosa Parks.*

"In America, bigotry is bequeathed and legislated…"

That direct quote was made on a mid-October morning in 2012, to me, a Black woman, while at work, in what I believed to be a somewhat safe and secure position of power. The speaker, a white man in his late sixties, was my immediate supervisor at the small community college where I was employed between 2012 and 2015. This man was actually half-smiling as he matter-of-factly made this statement; his evil, softly spoken words delivered with such precision and sacredness, as if whispered every day, like a prayer, like a pledge. His blunt declaration was in fact, his response to me advising him that someone else on his staff was attempting to treat me, his only Black employee, in a rude and disrespectful manner which was racially motivated.

As my pen began flying across the page of my notebook, I asked, *"Are these your words?"* And he replied, *"oh no, I would never say anything like that!"* Laughing, I replied, *"Oh, but you just did, and so eloquently, you've said these words before!" I need to know, if they're not yours' whose words are these?"*

No longer at ease, and attempting to change the subject, he finished with, *"I don't know where I heard those words..."*

Apparently, my supervisor was attempting to put my mind at ease, so that I'd have a better understanding of what was happening to me, and why. (At least that's what he later implied in 2016.)

Now, having served as an EEO officer and diversity trainer in the past, I've been surprised, perhaps even startled by the ignorance and insanity of the racist mindset; Lord, twice in my life, I've been shocked by the blatant stupidity of white supremacy, or the perceived legitimacy of white privilege. Throughout my career, I've even been forced to take a bigot to court on occasion, but I must admit, I was still unprepared for this level of audacity and disregard within this institution, especially the second and third time.

My first introduction to the white conspiracy within the bureaucracy of this small county college occurred in August of 2012, and presented me with a ridiculous, almost laughable situation that I was also not prepared for. After six very successful years, after being told that it was not possible to close the Commission, the County Freeholders determined that in order to save money, they would transfer the Cultural Commission to the college, so, as Executive Director, I was extremely busy attempting to run a smooth operation, and pull off a successful move. When I finally arrived on campus to view the new offices, I was greeted by the clerical support person, a white woman my own age, assigned to work for me, in my offices, while still reporting directly to the Vice President. After I walked through the three office suite and nodded my approval, this woman announced that because I was Executive Director, my office would be in the receptionist area, because, after all, if anyone came to the office, they would be coming to see me, so, this arrangement would make it easier for everyone. She, on the other hand, simply to answer the phone and make copies, would have the private window office with its own bathroom, and private entrance. I simply smiled and asked, *"So, was this your brilliant idea and decision?"* to which she replied, *"Oh no, you'll learn that no one makes any decisions around here, except the supervisor."* So, I told her, as politely as I could, *"you do know that this is not going to stand?"* And she replied, *"Well, it's already done, there's nothing that can be done about it before the move."* I walked out without another word and went to the supervisor's office, he wasn't in, but one of his secretaries arranged for me to meet with him on the Camden Campus the following day, so I returned to Hopkins House. When I met with the supervisor the next day, I was still livid, but I wore the mask, and didn't let my anger show; I also didn't address the issue of the office right away, I talked about several other pressing issues, and put him at ease by chatting as if nothing was wrong.

Then just before the meeting was over, I advised the Vice President that I had seen the Blackwood offices, and that if all college department heads, including himself, sat in the receptionist area, I'd be happy to join right in; but, that if, as the only African American department head, I was being singled out and asked to do something so out of the norm, something so demeaning, and uncharacteristic for leadership, then there was going to be a huge problem, and that I wanted the situation corrected before I was scheduled to move on campus next week. He protested, and explained everyone was so busy and that he might not be able to get it done for another 2 or 3 months; I simply smiled and stared him right in the eye. Well, the office set up was corrected before the move, and I never had to speak on it again. Of course, this woman assigned to spy on me was a little disappointed upon moving in, but she got over that, and a few other things. In retaliation though, the supervisor and his staff began to spread the rumor that the furniture, telephones and computers for the Commission had to be reconfigured simply because I didn't like the original arrangement. Every time someone asked me about it, I just told them the entire truth.

Now, it is important to note that although my offices had been relocated within this small county college in 2012, I held the same title and position I was appointed to in May of 2006, which was that of a county Administrator. At the college, during the day, I served as the

Director of Cultural Affairs for the entire county, and I was responsible for providing critical funding to grassroots organizations, as well as planning and implementing cultural, artistic and educational programs to enrich the lives of the county's 550,000 diverse residents; programs which consistently won "Citation of Excellence" awards from the State of New Jersey, as well as National recognition. Additionally, as an award-winning poet and published author, I taught a poetry & creative writing class in the evenings. I was often asked to speak on campus, and throughout the county at various schools and organizations, my books were sold at the Barnes & Noble bookstores on campus, and the college and county libraries carried my books, as well. I know for a fact that any of these individual roles would have been greatly honored and highly respected by this institution and my county, had I, like my predecessors, been born white. Another very sad fact is that when I was appointed to my position in 2006, I was not only the first African American to hold this position at the county level, I was the first in the State of New Jersey, which has 21 counties. Oddly, in this day and age, in an environment like this, my position, skills, abilities, or numerous awards and accomplishments, meant nothing, and earned me only contempt, not respect, simply because my skin, as well as my lovely soul, is forever, beautifully Black. I am so very proud to be an accomplished woman of color, I can trace my rich ancestry back to the year 1787, and I am a direct descendant of the William Still and Joshua Sadler families, so I tend to smile and carry my head a little high, especially when I pass by a bigot.

On that particular October morning, I arrived at the supervisor's office to discuss the offensive, and intentional back-stabbing actions of yet another one of the clerks on the supervisor's staff, another middle-age white female. You see, as the only Black, and the "Executive Director" ceremoniously lumped into a department of approximately 25 to 30 mostly administrative white females, I needed to be acclimated. I also had to contend with that deep-seated secret fear that surfaces when racists begin to realize that their colorless skin has not righteously earned them the privileges they enjoy, even worse; the fear that not only are they not better, they are most often not even as good!"

My offender this time was a grant writer, charged with assisting me in the grant writing process for the Commission now that I was part of the college. I was applying for funding from the State of New Jersey to expand opportunities for historic projects for county organizations, and although it was my role to identify appropriate grants and then to provide the operational, financial and narrative requirements, the grant writer's only role was to submit the paperwork, after I prepared it for her, so that the college and that individual could receive credit for the grant, once awarded. Ridiculous right? I wasn't crazy about this arrangement, but always attempted to work within the confines of the college. Oddly, I did not receive this grant. Knowing the individual personally responsible for managing the State grant program because we served on two New Jersey State Boards together, I called to question why, and was told that upon receipt, the application did not include many of the key components that I had worked so hard to include. I forwarded a copy of my original draft, and was told that there would definitely be another funding opportunity in about six months that the Commission would qualify for. So, I shared this information with the Vice President and the grant writer, who's cubical wasn't far from my office. The grant writer, instead of calling me, or visiting my office to ask me for further information, called the State program director and demanded to know what I was talking about. I considered this insubordination and wanted this situation addressed and corrected. Needless to say, the supervisor and other individuals within the Institutional Advancement department attempted to convince me that the grant writer, while sabotaging my grant and attempting to undermine and discredit me, was simply doing her job, and I was over-reacting. The grant writer, on the other hand, had simply stared blankly at me, and would not respond as to why she took the steps she did; oh she wanted to respond, but instead quickly retired. I documented the incident, because I knew there would be more issues. After all, like millions of other African Americans throughout these Un-United States, I had suffered much as a result of racism throughout my 40 plus year career, throughout my life. But now, I had just gained some deeper insight into a bigot's psychology. Up to this time, I just thought racists were not very bright people, somewhat sick in the head, ruled by jealousy or envy, but mostly fear that their past actions, and the lies they've been living their entire lives would reverse and prove them even more foolish, render them useless human beings. But this "bequeathed and legislated" nonsense implies a serious permanent commitment; people willing to lie, live and die as well as do everything possible to pass on the lie to future generations in order to ensure perpetual racism, bigotry and mistreatment of Blacks in America, F O R E V E R! How sick is that?

* * *

My relationship with the county and the college actually began back in 2006. I wasn't looking for a job, then, as a matter of fact, this particular job came looking for me. You see, I was minding my own business while serving as Director of Development and External Affairs at Camden, New Jersey's Walt Whitman Arts Center, making a decent wage, actually a better wage, directing the literary programs there, while writing, performing and pursuing my own art; my plate was full. I was surrounded by like-minded African American, Latino and White artists who loved and supported each other and the arts; and I was content!

Then, I started to receive telephone calls advising me that I was the ideal candidate for this position at the county, reminding me that I was already serving the community, and that this position would simply allow me to serve at a higher level. I knew the current executive director at the time, and when I ran into her at a cultural event in February, Ruth told me, *"Sandra, you'd be excellent at this job, in many ways you're already doing the job, and I'm going to retire in April!"* So, I started to connect the dots. I learned the job was a civil service position, and when I reviewed the requirements, I found I had the exact qualifications and background for this position, so I paid the fee and submitted an application online.

Within a month I received notification from the State of New Jersey that I had placed number one on the Civil Service test for the position, and then I heard from the county and was requested to complete their application, and scheduled for several interviews. After visiting historic Hopkins House on the Cooper River (built in 1724) where my offices would be located, I realized I was called to do this work, so I prayed and marched around Hopkins House seven times, and then waited to see what God had to say! I interviewed several times, always being evaluated by 3 to 5 individuals at a time. By the second week, I was elated, I was the number one candidate, and was actually offered the job, but was then told the interview process had to continue because one of the applicants felt they had not received appropriate consideration, so the top five candidates would all have to be re-interviewed.

I was told that someone with connections wanted to edge me out of the number one spot, so, the day before my final interview, I was divinely inspired to make some special preparations. The next day, I was being interviewed by the President of the Board and 5 other individuals when the question was asked: *"Should you be hired, give us a few new goals and/or procedures you will establish and/or implement within the first 2 years in order to make the Commission a success?"* So, I reached into my briefcase and pulled out 7 printed and bound copies of a comprehensive five-year plan I had written and prepared the night before, the cover page included my name as the Executive Director. Well, I simply passed copies out to each evaluator, and proceeded to conduct a step-by-step review of my goals for the Commission. Needless to say, this was a very successful interview, and I was hired, ratified by the Freeholder Board, and began working on May 15, 2006.

From day one, the job proved extremely challenging, but also rewarding in that education and participation within cultural and artistic programs actually have the ability to impact and enrich individual lives. As an artist, I knew that, and, as God would have it, I was the ideal candidate for this position! I began taking a serious look at the problems of education, poverty, and at risk kids within the many diverse communities that made up the County of Camden, and decided to throw some art at the pain. I created a literary project for youth in danger of dropping out of school entitled "Success is in the Bag" which was funded by the state of New Jersey, and was designed to teach our youth to write their own success stories, before they were faced with failure. 5 high schools with high dropout rates were selected for this project, and nearly 300 students received bright and beautiful backpacks with the bold logo, "Success is in the Bag" -- inside the bag was a journal and a pen and came complete with a teaching artist who taught a four-week writing and empowerment class on envisioning a successful future.

I learned something else truly important that first year, "Our Art is Our Humanity" art touches hearts, and gradually, art changes hearts, through poetry, literature, music, painting and sculpture, hearts connect and lives change. By partnering with organizations like the Katz Jewish Community Center, Chinese Musical Voices, the Pilipino-American Community, Latin Community Center, and many other groups, people throughout the community ultimately came together, and respected each other's differences, rather than the distrust and disdain I first witnessed. One diversity project, "The Gray in between Black & White" a partnership between Muslim and Jewish, Black and White, musicians, poets, and artists of all kinds, truly had a tremendous impact on the artist community throughout Camden County.

But while the artists community was thriving, a political change brought about a change in leadership and suddenly I was under attack for doing my job too well, bringing too much attention to the Commission and myself through my work, while someone else wanted that limelight. For two years I tolerated the racist games and attacks until this younger, very inexperienced white woman decided she wanted to suspend me for 3 days without pay because one of my subordinates had called her to tell her I was 15 minutes late in September, 2008. Now I suggested that she not do this, that I could prove that her charges were in violation of all kinds of workplace rules and regulations, and just wrong, in general. But, she wouldn't listen, and proceeded to put this foolishness in writing; so I notified my union and charged her with violating my rights and creating a hostile working environment and she was found in violation. This woman was even reprimanded by her own Board of Directors and the county's legal department, for issuing me a letter threatening my job, however, because she was so well connected through nepotism, and protected; she wouldn't stop. I had no other choice but to file a discrimination & harassment suit with the Division of Civil Rights.

That 2008 matter was settled out-of-court in 2010; and then after the standard 2 year retaliation statue expired in 2012, I was again under attack and transferred to the county college and forced to suffer additional racial attacks and harassment there, under the deceitful disguise that the overall community would benefit from this collaboration. Then, in January of 2015, the college decided to eliminate me from my position without notice, or cause, two years before my scheduled retirement, simply to place one of the supervisor's unqualified white females into my position to prevent this individual from being displaced for the third time. This final ridiculous action by the college, which personally caused me undue financial and emotional harm, impacted my pension and benefits, also impacted the entire arts and culture community by eliminating 90% of the programs and services once offered as a result of the residents' tax dollars. This action demonstrates the supervisor's, and therefore the college's deadly disregard for equal opportunity for all its staff, faculty and other employees, or adherence to appropriate State and Federal rules and regulations; resulting in yet another legal action.

At the same moment I was being terminated the college was placing the supervisor's white female into my position, and calling that position something else; but it was still my job. This white female was the same individual who scheduled my evening classes for me; she was incapable of performing the vast and complex duties of my job, but, obviously white privilege somehow qualified her for my civil service position. Within a year, this individual was let go, anyway, as she had been twice before, so another white female was assigned to oversee the commission, while doing other clerical duties. Now, there's a rumor that the college is trying to force a minority to take on this position, either an African American or Latino female, to further cover up their obvious wrongdoing... We'll see!

What I do see now, and certainly better understand is "The Deadly Role of White Nationalism, Supremacy and Privilege" in this Country. Although I've only lived "Up North" in the Southern New Jersey area of the Country, where it is supposedly safe from the mindset and actions of southern bigots, this is where my pain began, and continues to this day. The State of New Jersey was the last Northern State to relinquish its cruel confinement and mistreatment of slaves, and Black folk continue to suffer here as a result of racism, bigotry, white supremacy and privilege in this day and age. It's a little known fact that the city of Camden, New Jersey, from the year 1766 to 1800, actually allowed not just one, but three slave blocks to operate; on the Waterfront, accepting stolen human cargo from European ships and reselling them to the highest bidder for shipment down south, or enslavement right here in the North.

These more recent racist actions which all occurred in the great state of New Jersey, remind me of still others from my past. Another unexpected, ridiculous racist incident that shocked me, occurred back when I was the Business Manager for an early, pre-Comcast cable television system, back during 1988 thru 1991. This system covered four of the most racist small towns of southern New Jersey. One such town, Gloucester, NJ, often held KKK Rallies on Broadway in broad daylight. Well, there I was, the only Black with a staff of 16, and while there were 2 or 3 truly great folk, informed, kind and fair; there were others at the bottom of the barrel, intellectually, spiritually, emotionally & morally, who believed, that they were somehow superior to everyone with a natural tan, like mine. Back then, there was this one young girl, I'll call her Molly because I can't remember her name. Well one morning, Molly comes running into my office just as the clock struck 9:00am and asked to borrow money for a donut and coffee; instead I just gave her the $1 and told her not to worry about repaying it. I then assigned her to the front register to accept cable payments from walk in customers. At noon, Molly was relieved for lunch, but, she returned an hour later with several shopping bags, which was an immediate danger sign, how do you go from flat broke to pockets full that quickly.

I shut down Molly's register to validate payments and cash; the drawer was $240 short; I took Molly into my office and asked her to explain the shortage; she simply shrugged her shoulders; she never said there must be a mistake, I'm a good person and I like my job, she just sat there staring at me as if I had done something wrong. When I pressed her again, she finally said, "Well, I was broke and my kids needed some things, so I just took the money!" I had her empty her pockets and purse to find only about $70 which I confiscated, and then I told her to leave the bags, she was fired and had 5 minutes to remove herself from my sight, or she would go to jail. Molly stared me right in the eye, half smiled and said, *"Oh, but you can't fire me, I'm white!"*

This was so very foolish to me, it actually shocked me, but I literally laughed out loud. Then, it occurred to me that she might be in shock or under stress, and that I probably needed to slap her upside her head a few times, real hard, in order to save her life. But, although I might enjoy helping her, that probably wouldn't go over very well in that environment. So I marched over to the Regional Director's office, who only visited once, perhaps twice a week, but who just happened to be in that day. Now, mind you, I wasn't quite sure how this would turn out, but I quickly told him what happened and suggested that he speak with Molly, and then sent her in. I'm not exactly sure what he said to her, but she went running out of the office in tears, never to be seen again.

Twenty-seven years later, the question remains, where was Molly getting her information and direction? From the same kind of people, the same evil places as Dillan Roof, the racist 21 year old who marched into that historic African American church near Charlotte, North Carolina? This demented man then prayed with the congregation for over an hour before suddenly shooting 9 beautiful Black souls to death. Roof was unapologetic, and literally felt justified for this heinous murders because of the lies he'd been told since birth. This same sick justification is being used by the likes of George Zimmerman, who murdered Trayvon Martin, and the countless white men dressing in blue who are intentionally murdering our sons and daughters every day. And now it would appear that

Bigoted white people are all in on this plot to diminish and murder Blacks in America? Together? And have been, since the very beginning? There are countless good and decent white people in the world, but how can we recognize who and what, they really are?

It is so obvious that #45, Donald J. Trump, in his efforts to "Make America Great Again" is a product of White Supremacy. It is frightening how many mind-blind supporters he has and how little is expected of this man, as a man, let along President of the United States, simply because he's white. He's not even expected to tell the truth, and he could never be my President. The centuries-old "White Lie" is the only reason someone like this Trump could ever come to power; that lie that causes Bigotry to flourish; the "White Lie" that Whites are superior to Blacks! This "Bequeathed and Legislated" nonsense puts a new spin on the racial problems in America. Bigots are not born, therefore, millions of innocent white children are being indoctrinated into ignorance, into hate, at a very early age. They are being fed evil by the spoonful at the breakfast table as if nourishment, like a sacred tradition, or family recipe! Young whites are being taught to reimagine a deadly, deceitful and hateful history of would-be heroes, constant cowards, seeped in lies of perceived greatness and power, in hopes that this "White Lie" like a fairy tale you wish upon a star for, will someday become truth.

What do we do? What can we do? We must resist racism, ignorance, and each and every violation of our rights, in our schools, on our jobs, our communities, anywhere in the world. We must tell our own stories, and teach our children the proud truth of our true role and survival in America. And even though it seems sad we must teach our sons and daughters the truth about bigots; prepare them to protect themselves, to remain alert, on guard against a mindset of evil because they are the ultimate target.

In order to diminish our greatness, our "Black seed" is under attack because our seed is what makes us strong and beautiful and creative and intelligent and talented and soulful. Through the worst possible conditions we survived being brought to America by force; forced to build this Country from the ground up; a job no other people could have accomplished; something no other people would have survived. So we must teach our beautiful "Black Seeds" that in America, not only do Black lives matter, Black lives are essential, because there would be no America without us...which, in reality, makes Blacks superior!

Republican presidential candidate Donald Trump speaks during a campaign rally at the American Airlines Center on Sep. 14, 2015 in Dallas, Texas. Tom Pennington—Getty Images.

EXAMINING AMERICA'S BODY POLITIC

SURPRISES THAT ARE NOT REALLY SURPRISES: AMERICA AND THE WORLD IN THE TRUMP ERA

ARTHUR ADE AMAKER

Arthur Ade Amaker is an English professor, poet, writer, and activist. His work has appeared in In Defense of Mumia (1996) and Role Call: A Generational Anthology of Social and Political Black Literature and Art (2002). He is the founding editor or Oyster Knife Publishing and has edited What It is: Poems and Opinions of Oscar Brown Jr. (2005).

First, let's analyze how we got into this situation. The fact is, overall, the Democratic game was weak, marred by a smug over-confidence and dismissiveness of the legitimate concerns of a large portion of the U.S. electorate—particularly those affected by the decline of blue-collar jobs in rural areas, and a porous southern border, allowing illegal workers from Mexico to come into the country, driving down wages. Even some Hispanic voters agreed with this assessment, voting in larger numbers for Trump than they did for Mitt Romney in 2012 (Schmidt 2016).

Hillary Clinton was not as strong a candidate as she thought she was, and she did not expect how much her past email scandal would affect her campaign, as well as how her perception as a corrupt Washington insider tied to the shenanigans of husband Bill Clinton, (whose Clinton Foundation was under investigation for unethically accepting donations from foreign governments while Hillary Clinton was Secretary of State) would lose her votes. The Clintons thought that the average American voter would ignore these slights, and smugly assumed that popularity and reputation alone are enough to win elections. But, to borrow a line from Gershwin's *Porgy and Bess: "it ain't necessarily so."*

It is undeniable to me that the deathblow to the Clinton campaign was its underestimation and disregard for Democratic presidential nominee Bernie Sanders. Sanders' support came mostly from large numbers of young people – the same young people who twice-elected Barack Obama to the White House. These young people are bright, and—despite popular belief—quite attentive to the news, which they mostly get from Facebook, Twitter, and cable "satirical" news shows like Real Time with Bill Maher and The Daily Show. I stood in line for hours to attend a Sanders rally in Chicago, and I was shocked by the size of the turnout. They were legion. This multitude did not take kindly to Sanders' treatment by the Democratic National Committee and high-ranking Democrats.

The most egregious treatment came from Debbie Wasserman Schultz, the former DNC chairperson who resigned from that post when it was alleged she rigged the Democratic primaries in favor of Clinton by reducing the debate schedule between Sanders and Clinton, and even going as far as to denying Sanders' campaign access to an online voter database (Treyz, 2015). Then, news came out that Nevada State Democratic Party Chair Roberta Lange Young modified party rules to ensure that Clinton had more delegates than Sanders in the National Democratic Party Convention. Sanders' supporters were livid; some went as far as to threaten violence during the convention. Schultz was replaced by Donna Brazille, who lost her spot as a commentator for CNN when it was learned that she fed debate questions beforehand to Clinton after Clinton won the primary and debated several times against Donald Trump. All of the top brass of the DNC were in line for Clinton, never giving Bernie a chance. Young people paid attention to this. When Hillary got to the top spot due to these ill-gotten gains, former Sanders supporters did not switch over to her side, nor did they vote Republican. They just didn't vote at all. Trump stepped into the breach left by an increasingly corrupt and inefficient Democratic party.

So, now we have President Trump—a man with a mercurial personality. A reality show celebrity who even New York's rich, white elite look at with disdain for his antics. Trump is like a trickster, the embodiment of Esu-- the traditional Yoruba spirit or Orisa of the unpredictable; a deity imbued with the power to completely harmonize or disrupt, but who will always definitely cause change. Trump is neither all good, nor all bad. He is just, well, confused--off balance because he doesn't know how to balance. We have to continue to prepare ourselves for a term of surprises in both domestic and foreign policy, and-- as of the moment of this writing-- Trump's first one hundred days has been anything but consistent (some would say consistently bad) and is a preview of what it to come. He is trying to make sense of his own confusion; this comes from someone who is just making things up as he goes along. He is like a bad jazz improviser who has no knowledge of melody, harmony, or anything on which to base his "spur of the moment" music.

Trump arrogantly promised he was going to repeal Obama Care. He signed an executive order to ban Muslim immigrants from certain countries that faced legal challenges, but has so far been unsuccessful. However, his most jarring notes come in foreign policy. It is very important that we pay attention to Trump's foreign policy because it can affect us here at home. For example, if Trump withdraws from the North American Free Trade Agreement (NAFTA) between the U.S., Mexico, and Canada, the prices of goods imported from Mexico and Canada could go up due to increased import tax. Even though his impetus behind this withdrawal would be to bring back jobs to our country, the reality is U.S. manufacturing corporations do not want to pay U.S. workers a competitive wage. In that case, the corporations would be forced to raise prices to keep up with increases in workers' pay. This would have a negative impact on the American working class (which voted for Trump in large numbers), and for certain "minority groups" (particularly African Americans). In the long view, an American withdrawal from NAFTA could negatively affect working class African American's pocketbooks and further drive more Black families into generational poverty.

In the so-called Middle East, Trump is faced with an even more complicated set of questions from those who follow international politics: was the Trump administration's recent attack on Syria executed solely for humanitarian purposes, or was it a distraction tactic to show the American population that he is not in support of Russian Prime Minister Vladimir Putin, an Assad supporter, and someone whom the CIA claims could have helped Trump win the election? Is Trump really a humanitarian in that sense? Why would he seek to turn away from his Alt-Right supporters (the White Nationalist, White supremacist groups who reject mainstream conservatism and who reject the idea of American intervention abroad) by making such a move in Syria? Trump spent most of the election stating that he would focus on the "homeland"—a word the Alt Right likes to use and that is reminiscent of Nazi Germany. Ironically, to date, there has been no major protest from this demographic in response to Trump' emerging foreign excursions. We will see how they react in the upcoming year as Trump makes more decisions; the Alt-Right is not ready for unpredictable, "unsafe" White supremacy. They may act out as a result.

I believe that, undeniably, Trump used Syrian bombing campaign as a "reality show moment" to bolster his image as an international tough guy who will bring back American military might. However, the reality is that the U.S. has been bombing Syria for months in order to hit strategic Al-Qaeda targets. Hundreds of Syrian civilians have died because of U.S.-caused "collateral damage." These are bombings that the average American citizens have no idea about. This action on behalf of Trump will not improve anything. In fact, some analysts believe that there really isn't a way to stop the mass killings in Syria by the Syrian government outside of the U.S. and Russia negotiating a deal to stop NATO expansion in exchange for the Russians withdrawing their support of the Assad regime. (Narin interview, DemocracyNow, 2017)

So, Trump is doing—essentially-- a "for show" foreign policy. I would not call it a pure "wag the dog" move. I don't think he is that sophisticated to do that intentionally—even though some in his cabinet might try to move him in that direction. My perception is that Trump is surrounded by generals and foreign policy experts who feed him a variety of conflicting viewpoints, and he is simply trying his best to synthesize information that he really does not have the foundation to understand. He will go with any choice that makes him look good and makes it appear like he knows what he is doing. If it is a distraction tactic, it is a distraction away from his incompetence, not a larger issue.

In terms of North Korea, Trump was caught in a lie when he stated that the U.S. was sending an "armada" of ships in response to North Korea's recent nuclear tests. The ships were actually near Australia, and never arrived near North Korea's waters. The South Koreans (historical U.S. allies) now have serious trouble trusting what Trump says (O'Connor, 2017). We are entering an era where many of our foreign allies will no longer trust the words of an American president, or his competence. Recently, in a meeting with the President of China, Trump told a Wall Street Journal reporter that Korea had been a part of China. This, historically, has never been the case (O'Connor, 2017). He does not seem to have the patience to actually learn the extensive history of a region before he makes major life or death decisions concerning it. Such a cavalier attitude toward foreign policy will definitely sully the United States' international image and have disastrous consequences down the line. Our nation can little afford such inconsistency from its national leader.

When Trump was elected, there were protests throughout the country. Kids started fires and smashed windows. The country was thrown into shock. However, now that the smoke has cleared, the biggest questions I have are why there is such a shock that the U.S. is now in the state that it is in politically and that someone like Trump could have won the presidency? It would seem to me that most Americans do not have a sufficient grasp of history to realize that we have seen bad presidents before—several who were put in office as a "violent" reaction to the rise of progressive forces. (I use the word "violent" in quotes here because, like Chairman Fred Hampton from the Chicago Black Panther Party once said in the sixties, "politics is nothing but war without bloodshed." I would add to that and say that indeed, politics is the bloodiest game of all, much harsher then shooting someone dead in the street).

If I could be permitted to use the classic analogy that the recently deceased legendary poet Amiri Baraka was fond of—we are in a situation that mirrors the Greek myth of Sisyphus. Sisyphus was damned by the Gods to the underworld– his eternal punishment to toil strenuously to roll a boulder up a hill. As soon as he thinks he is done and comes to rest at the top of the hill, the evil gods roll it back down again. Sisyphus is forced to repeat this process, and the same thing happens again, and again and again. This *"Sisyphus Cycle"* repeats itself in U.S. history continuously, and the ones who feel the "weight" of the boulder the most are always the most vulnerable, historically-marginalized groups. We have former U.S. presidents who have always been like those cruel Gods in the Sisyphus myth. For example, James Buchanan and Andrew Johnson were presidents during the 19th century who allowed the spread of slavery and blocked progressive legislation respectively for the rights of African Americans. Richard Nixon created the War on Drugs to specifically target the antiwar Left and Black people. (Nixon later resigned under the threat of impeachment due to the Watergate scandal, but the damage had been done to Black people). Ronald Reagan was hostile to Civil Rights, appointing such figures as Clarence Thomas to the Supreme Court to aggressively attack Affirmative Action.

What we are witnessing is another Reconstruction Era circa post-Civil War; a period in which rights that were fought for were rolled back by the Federal State. They will most likely be rolled back again during this era. The freedom for which progressives have striven during the past eight years under the Obama administration is now tenuous under Trump. Trump is not unique in the larger span of American presidential history. There is no surprise here. He himself is full of surprises and controversy, not because he is trying to be so innovative or revolutionary, but simply because he is confusing the world of reality television with the even realer world of national administrative politics. These two realities, apparently, are causing him a lot of cognitive dissonance. He doesn't know his right from his left, his up from his down.

The questions we have to answer are: how are we going to maneuver this chaotic cycle during (at least) the next four years? How can we become balanced in the midst of regressive forces that would hope to keep us off-kilter? (I am one of those who, personally, do not believe Trump will be impeached before then, despite the projections of pundits. However, I also concede that when Esu runs things, anything can happen. The key is to maintain balance and make sure that we come out of this with our benefits and our hat still on our cool heads. This political rain is unpredictable. Better have our umbrellas ready.

Ultimately, we are going to be all right. Rapper Kendrick Lamar sounded the anthem. (Pick up his album, *To Pimp A Butterfly* and read the lyrics). There is no reason to scream inside our hotel rooms; to want to self-destruct, the answers we are running for can be found in this dialogue we are having right now. This anthology is just one collection of voices. There will be more. We need to use our voices to get ready for the next big change, refusing to let whoever is in power dim our shine. It may seem like we are in the midst of disaster. Perhaps we are. Perhaps we are not. But, that does not mean that we cannot transform politically from a still and silent caterpillar to a moving, brilliant butterfly. We will not allow to ourselves be pimped. Not this time.

References:

Narin, Allan. (2017) Only mass disruption from below can stop right wing revolution. Online: democracynow.org

O'Connor Tom. (2017 April 21). Trump threatens North Korea, but his mistakes upset U.S. ally South Korea. *Newsweek.* (online edition) Online: newsweek.com/trump-threaten-north-korea-mistake-upset-ally-south-587966

Schmidt, Steven (2016, Nov. 14). How did democrats lose in 2016? Let me count the ways. *The Gazette.* Online: thegazette.com/subject/opinion/guest-columnists/how-did-democrats-lost-2016-let-us-count-the-ways-20161114

Treyz, Catherine et. al. (2015, Dec. 21). Sanders campaign sues DNC after database breach. CNN. Online: cnn.com/2015/12/18/politics/bernie-sanders-campaign-dnc-suspension

CHASING THE AMERICAN DREAM: A CHALLENGE TO VALUES OF MERITOCRACY AND CHARITY

ANN M. AVILÉS

*Ann M. Aviles is an Assistant Professor at University of Delaware whose teaching experience spans educational foundations, child development, child advocacy, and education policy. She is an advocate for educational and housing equity/access, and anti-racists systems/practices. She is the author of several publications, including her recent book, **From Charity to Equity: Race, Homelessness and Urban Schools** (2015).*

"I think poverty to a large extent is also a state of mind. You take some-body that has the right mindset, you can take everything from them and put them on the street, and I guarantee in a little while they'll be right back up there...And you take somebody with the wrong mindset, you can give them everything in the world, they'll work their way right back down to the bottom."

–Dr. Ben Carson, HUD Sectretary

When one has access to ample financial and material needs, no one asks if they "deserve" access to education, housing, food, etc. Children that come from wealthy homes are supported in their academic/emotional endeavors, whether or not they "work hard" for it. Rarely, if ever, do we question if the children of the wealthy "deserve" second chances, access to tutors, healthy food or any of the other amenities that accompany wealth.

But somehow, if one is not born into wealth, stability and access, their deservedness is constantly under scrutiny. It is well documented that economic disparities in the U.S. continue to widen. The U.S. has seen an increase in tent cities; according to the Department of Housing and Urban Development (HUD) more than half a million people are currently identified as experiencing homelessness, including hard working veterans. An examination of root factors contributing to issues of poverty and housing instability are needed; not more deficit commentary from Donald Trump or Benjamin Carson. Their rhetoric continues to feed into classists and racists understandings of poverty, as noted in the opening quote where the U.S. Secretary of Housing and Urban Development espouses that poverty is a mindset rather than a social condition. He has also expressed that affordable housing should not be too cozy for poor individuals already struggling to maintain stability. Is anyone questioning whether Melania's housing is too lavish?—It is government funded after all. The reality is that the problem isn't Melania's government funded housing or public housing itself—they are simply distractions to the fundamental issues that create conditions of poverty and homelessness. Simply stated, these fundamental issues stem from the lack of affordable housing to the lack of living wage jobs, and there is almost always an assumption or denial about who affordable housing and living wage jobs will impact—mainly (undeserving) poor folks (of color).

As a young person, I was always told to work hard in order to get ahead. My parents did not only espouse this narrative, they lived it. My father managed, and was part owner of a retail store in Chicago, working seven days a week to provide our family with shelter, nourishment and safety. My mother also worked at the store, and would often leave in the late afternoon in order to make it home around the same time my siblings and I arrived from school. She would oversee that our school work was done while she cooked dinner. While my family faired pretty well in the big picture of society—we were never without food, housing or most of our basic needs—my parents hard work has not done much to significantly change their economic position in society. In fact, most folks, including my parents, and many friends/family members work hard. Really hard. Yet, most of us continue to live check-to-check, always working (extra hard) to make ends meet.

As it relates to the American Dream of owning property and/or a home, housing advocates contend that households should not spend more than 30% of income on housing costs, still, many individuals and families spend a significant portion of their income to cover the basic costs of housing. Most of these individuals work hard, and despite their hard work, continue to experience significant levels of (intergenerational) poverty, although the American Dream promises the opposite. The failure of big businesses in providing living wages, coupled with the lack of affordable housing, and further compounded by the disparities of income based on gender and race, result in far too many folks perpetually stressed about whether or not to pay rent or make sure their families eat. In these cases, we hold the individual accountable, but continually let the systems that contribute to these social conditions go unquestioned, unexamined and unaccountable. Focusing on the individual, and in many cases the communities in which individuals experiencing poverty and homelessness reside, solidify the American values of meritocracy and charity, a model not only written into our constitution but also preached by many governmental and religious practitioners.

While many would argue that values of meritocracy and charity are inherently "good," I urge readers to consider the complexity and contradictions inherent in meritocratic and charitable narratives—narratives that convince us of the need to continue working hard in a system that is rigged. A system that allows exceptions to the rules (e.g corporate welfare and $700 billion banking bailout of 2008), but rarely, if ever, changes the rules that result in a great majority of "losers" with very few "winners." This meritocracy is inherently biased towards those who have consistent stable housing, supportive families, access to top tier academic institutions and financial resources. I am well aware, that what I am expressing here has been shared before. These values have become even more salient given this current socio-political moment. For example, many refer to Ben Carson's hard work and determination as the primary factors of his success, as noted in his hearing confirmation to Secretary of HUD in which his accomplishments were referred to as "remarkable;" his life story being an "inspiration and testament to the American Dream." However, I would argue, he is an exception to the rule, given the small percentage of Blacks and low-income individuals that are able to ascend economically, as well as in the medical field. As noted by Senator Brown during the confirmation hearing for the U.S. Secretary of Housing and Urban Development, only 1 in 13 Americans will move from the lowest income quintile to the highest over a lifetime. Furthermore, in relation to race and gender, there are also disparities, given Johns Hopkins didn't accept its first Black female neurosurgeon resident until this past March (2017).

According to Association of American Medical Colleges (AAMC), African-Americans/Blacks make up only 4% of the physician workforce in the U.S., despite making up 13% of the U.S. population. Overall, physicians of color (Black, Latinx, Asian, Indigenous) are 8.9% of the workforce; it is critical to emphasize that these numbers have not kept pace with the demographic shifts of the U.S. Are we to believe that approximately 90% of people of color are not capable, smart enough, or work hard enough to become physicians? For the most part, if someone is born into wealth and/or poverty, they are likely to remain there. According to a study by The Pew Charitable Trusts, for individuals/families born into poverty, only 4% made it into the highest income bracket, with approximately 70% remaining in the lower income bracket, and 24% making it to the middle or upper middle class. Further, it is well documented that most households receiving public assistance are led by a working adult. These statistics underscore and challenge the dominant narrative that hard work and determination will ensure access, social mobility, or desired employment. We must ask ourselves, how will the fallacy of meritocracy continue to shape societal beliefs and dispositions about peoples "deservedness?" How will the rhetoric of hard work and "grit" shape the trajectory of individuals who are struggling with mental illness, addiction, incarceration, economic instability, food insecurity, housing instability, and various other physical, and mental differences? Further, who really benefits from (the fallacy of) meritocracy?

A narrative that compliments and reinforces the notion of meritocracy and "getting ahead" in society is charity. If you happen to be down on your luck, find yourself in a compromising position, aren't perceived as smart or strong enough, no fear, people will have empathy for you and your situation. And those with the financial means and resources to do so will donate to an organization/cause that addresses the poor hand you've been dealt and/or the poor decisions you've made in life. A charity model focuses on the individual, and is also biased. Charity, the notion of giving back or helping the "less fortunate," while virtuous in theory, only works to sustain the structure of capitalism, and other forms of marginalization/oppression; it does not work against social hierarchies or the dismantling of systems that create and sustain conditions of poverty/wealth, violence, homelessness, etc.

Having worked with individuals and families experiencing housing instability/homelessness for over ten years, I've heard many stories from a wide range of folks. For example, during my time working with unaccompanied youth who were experiencing housing instability, many shared with me that they were told they must pray and ask for forgiveness for their "sins." According to the non-profit they were seeking assistance from, if a young person found themselves not being cared for by an adult (parent/guardian), it was certainly something they had done to put themselves there as a result of their "sin." The implicit message was that youth should disregard the abuse (physical, sexual, emotional) inflicted on them and tap into their "grit" in order to be strong and endure such trauma(s). Once again, the focus is on meritocracy—work hard and build a skill and somehow the years of trauma endured will dissipate. The rhetoric of charity exploits the good will of others, while meritocracy preys on the desperation of individuals who want stability—stability of housing, living wage incomes, food access, and other critical material needs. This struggle for stability compels individuals to continue their hard work, regardless of whether or not their work results in educational, vocational or general life advancement. Simultaneously, people continue giving in the hopes that their charitable contributions will lift folks out of poverty.

During one of my college-level courses, I show a film on the educational rights promised under the McKinney-Vento Act, a federal policy designed to protect families and their children to their rights in accessing services, ultimately ensuring their educational rights are upheld. Many students after watching the film ask, "If they are homeless, then why did one of the young girls in the film have her nails done?" As if children (or their parents/guardians) who do not have access to consistent, stable housing are somehow "less than" and should not be concerned with their outward presentation. If an individual residing in a shelter is trying to find a job, or secure housing, they will be perceived negatively if they are not dressed or appear a particular way. At the same time, these same individuals are expected to "look poor" in order to prove their situation or deservedness to housing, food or employment services. Our notions of charity often bring about judgment of the person and not of the circumstances in which caused them to experience homelessness. This approach to charity asks the questions of who "deserves" to be helped, who "deserves" access to opportunity, and who "deserves" support and services to address emotional and material needs? The true answer is everyone. Every human being in our nation and across the globe deserves to have their humanity respected, affirmed and cultivated—regardless of their occupation, income, housing status, race/nationality, gender, gender identity, religion, language, previous conviction, or citizenship status.

The underpinnings of many social problems are systematic—meritocracy and charity will not, and cannot eradicate the deep-rooted convictions our current administration endorses. I am not suggesting that people shouldn't work hard or give to others. The fact of the matter is, no matter how hard people work, or how much they give, the current economic, educational and housing structures of society rarely allow for that hard work and/or giving to create significant, long lasting change. Hard work and giving are not the culprits here; it is the systems and structures that allow, and even create conditions that perpetuate poverty and homelessness, despite the efforts of individuals and communities committed to contributing to, and being a part of, the social fabric of this country. We cannot continue to support the notion that hard work and giving will lead to stability, and/or social mobility if we are not also willing to create systems and structures that support greater access to, and fair distribution of, resources to disinvested communities.

No matter how hard one works, a bootstrap approach ultimately fails to disrupt and dismantle ideologies, systems and practices that are hierarchical and divisive; making us all prey to a system that is unconscionable. A system that shows little to no regard for our humanity. A system built on greed. A system that works to sort individuals and communities based on superficial and/or constructed identities in order to make us believe that despite our categorization or position in life, our hard work will one day pay off. In reality, a system of corruption, greed and inequity can knock any one of us down, at any given moment. Further, the current system of charity is not effective in changing social conditions that result in, and perpetuate long standing issues such as poverty, homelessness, violence, incarceration, racism, sexism, ableism, linguicism, etc.

Rather than working hard to get ahead in a system that is not designed for the majority of us to flourish—economically, socially and emotionally—we must instead work towards liberation; eliminating inequitable systems, policies and practices that reproduce conditions of poverty, homelessness and marginalization. The current administration is an explicit reminder of the work we must engage to radically transform systems that will yield tangible results of ample and equitable access to the promise of "liberty and justice for all."

MUSLIM BAN OF THE ANARCHY STATES OF AMERICA

REFLECTIONS ON NARCISSISM: WHAT THE RESEARCH SUGGESTS

CARL C. BELL

Carl C. Bell, M.D. is a clinical Professor of Psychiatry and Public Health, director of the Institute for Juvenile Research (IJR), University of Illinois at Chicago (UIC). He is a National Institute of Mental Health international researcher and an author of more than 400 scientific publications. He is author of *The Sanity of Survival: Reflections on Community Mental Health and Wellness* (Third World Press, 2004).

I was walking somewhere, a car pulled up, and an African-American gentleman rolled down his window and asked if I was Dr. Bell. I told him I was. Next, he asked me if President Donald Trump had issues with narcissism and if he had a narcissistic personality disorder. I told him that it would be unethical for me to comment on such a question because it would be against the ethics of the American Psychiatric Association, of which I was a member. I further explained that there was the "Goldwater rule"[1] which prohibited a psychiatrist from commenting on a public figure, as had been done frequently when Barry Goldwater was running for president of the United States in 1964. He thanked me any way and told me that he thought President Trump was narcissistic and he just wanted confirmation from a Black psychiatrist.

So, at Haki Madhubuti's 75th birthday celebration, when Haki reminded me he needed for me to write something on President Donald Trump for a collection of essays he was pulling together for Third World

Press, I again told him that I did not think American Psychiatric Association ethics would allow it. He told me that he thought the ethical prohibitions may have been relaxed since President Trump's election, so I told him I would check. I checked with the American Psychiatric Association and was told that in fact the "Goldwater rule" had been strengthened since Donald Trump's election because the association did not want psychiatrists to get into the same trouble they had gotten into when Goldwater was running for president.

Apparently, Ralph Ginzburg, published a special issue of *Fact Magazine* on Goldwater entitled "The Unconscious of a Conservative: A Special Issue on the Mind of Barry Goldwater." The thesis of the issue was that Barry Goldwater was mentally unsound to be the President of the United States. The magazine came to this conclusion after they sent thousands of questionnaires to psychiatrists who were certified by the American Board of Psychiatry and Neurology with nearly four-fifths who answered the survey saying Mr. Goldwater was mentally unfit. About one-fifth of respondents to the questionnaire refused to diagnose Mr. Goldwater because they had never done a clinical interview on him, but still went on to say that they thought he would be mentally unfit to be president. Apparently, the Ku Klux Klan supported Mr. Goldwater, which is strange if you think about it, as Goldwater's father was Jewish. However, as they say, politics makes strange bedfellows.

There seem to be some parallels between Mr. Goldwater and Mr. Trump (although one had Jewish ancestry and the other has German ancestry) but it would still be unethical for me to comment on the psychiatric status of someone I have never done a psychiatric evaluation on in real life. The ethics guidelines are clear:

> *"On occasion, psychiatrists are asked for an opinion about an individual who is in the light of public attention or who has disclosed information about himself/herself through public media. In such circumstances, a psychiatrist may share with the public his or her expertise about psychiatric issues in general. However, it is unethical for a psychiatrist to offer a professional opinion unless he or she has conducted an examination and has been granted proper authorization for such a statement."[2]*

Accordingly, I can share my expertise about psychiatric issues in general, and I choose to reflect on the dynamics of narcissism.

Experience with the Issue of Narcissism

I think it is important for someone to document their experience and scholarship about a subject before they open their mouths, because everyone has an opinion, but not everyone has an informed opinion. So, here is evidence of my chops.

After I finished medical school at Meharry Medical College in 1971, I entered into psychiatric residency. At the time, the field of psychiatry had become interested in the area of narcissism.[3] When Freud was writing, he had glossed over the issue of narcissism. Fortunately, for psychiatry Heinz Kohut[4], who I used to call the second coming of Freud, wrote extensively about narcissism to cover what Freud only mentioned briefly. I read Kohut extensively and I could not help but notice there was a relationship between racism and narcissism. So, I made a presentation of my observations to the American Psychiatric Association's Annual Meeting in Chicago in 1979. The paper was entitled "Racism: A Symptom of the Narcissistic Personality Disorder."[5] At that time, if you presented a paper at the American Psychiatric Association, you had to submit it to the *American Journal of Psychiatry*, and it had to be reviewed by peers before it could pass muster and be accepted. The submission got rejected and I got a scathing letter saying that I did not have a clue about the dynamics of narcissism. Not to be shut down, I sent the manuscript to the *Journal of the National Medical Association* and it got published. I was talking to a psychoanalyst about my notions and how the paper got rejected by the *American Journal of Psychiatry*, but accepted and published by the *Journal of the National Medical Association*. He suggested that I send the paper to Dr. Kohut to see what he thought of my thesis. I sent the paper to Dr. Kohut and he wrote back saying that he was 'glad to see the evidence of the applicability of many of his thoughts,' and to keep him on my mailing list to send him more interesting contributions.

Prior to this article, I had written another paper entitled "Racism,

Narcissism, and Integrity," that was published by the *Journal of the National Medical Association* in February 1978.[6] In this essay, I suggested that psychoanalytic models were useful in understanding social phenomena as it seemed to me that racist attitudes might be indicative of a narcissistic personality disorder. Further, I suggested that life experiences, especially near death experiences, and religion were possible aids in transforming primary narcissism (the early, unhealthy narcissism displayed by a child) into secondary narcissism (the healthy narcissism of an adult that reflected a realistic confidence and self-esteem). This paper was noticed and picked up by the *Journal of Continuing Education in Psychiatry*, and I was asked to supply an abstract of the article that was translated into three different languages in September 1978. In 1982, *Psychopathologie Africaine*, published in Senegal, Africa, did a report on "Racism: A Symptom of the Narcissistic Personality Disorder."

Since the early eighties, I have lectured occasionally on the issue of racism and narcissism around the U.S., and wrote an editorial raising the question of whether or not racism was a mental illness.[7] In 2001, I was a guest on ABC's Nightline discussing the issue of whether racism was a mental illness. Somewhere along the line, I hooked-up with a White psychologist, Ed Dunbar who had been studying racist attitudes using the Gough's Prejudice (Pr) scale from the Minnesota Multiphasic Personality Inventory.[8] Ed had been doing work in corporate America working with White executives trying to understand why certain people would set up hostile work environments resulting in various lawsuits. He found that the Gough Prejudice (Pr) scale was a useful way to provide "objective" evidence of an individual's prejudice.

In 2002, I was asked to participate in developing the research agenda for the American Psychiatric Association's *Diagnostic and Statistical Manual* (5th edition)[9] regarding cultural gaps within the manual. I developed language that would hopefully guide scientific inquiry on how to tease out the issue of racism and psychopathology as it was clear behavior was multi-determined, as it was cultural, sociological, psychological and biological.[10] Of course, there was never any funding to look at the issue, but I was assigned to the American Psychiatric Association's Personality Disorders Workgroup from 2002-2009, and I advocated for research into the issue of racism and narcissistic personality disorders. Nothing ever came of it. Fortunately, I was asked to contribute a chapter to the *Oxford Handbook on Personality Disorders,* and with my co-author, Ed Dunbar, we were able to get some of my theoretical and clinical ideas and Dr. Dunbar's actual research into print.[11] I mention all of this not to self-aggrandize, but I understand how critical African-American readers and others can be, so I felt the need to demonstrate my professional expertise on the issue of narcissism before going any further.

Difficulties in Discussing Racism

One of the first observations I like to make about racism is the confusion about racism. Chester M. Pierce, M.D. a professor of psychiatry, public health, and education Harvard and the founder of the Black Psychiatrists of America, wrote about African-American's confusion about racism. Dr. Pierce suggested that psychiatrists not only study defense mechanisms, but they should also study offense mechanisms. Along with his assertion, he noted that there were offensive mechanisms designed to keep Blacks in the inferior, dependent, helpless role. Dr. Pierce had actually studied White people in experimental circumstances and developed the concept of *microaggression* and *microinsults.*[12] Dr. Pierce noted that African-Americans were confused about three things:

1. When, where, and how to resist racism and oppression, versus when, where and how to put up with racism and oppression.

2. Whether they are being tolerated or accepted by Whites.

3. African-Americans lack of ability to make a distinction between the compassionate efforts of individual Whites and the vicious actions of Whites as a group.

I added a 4th confusion, which was whether African-Americans could claim their successes to yourself and their failures to a lack of effort or whether African-Americans could attribute their successes or failures to something outside of our control, i.e. *"the man."*

The other difficult problem with a discussion about racism is the reality of living in America. We Americans believe in our Constitution, which essentially says that people should be judged by the content of their character and not such things as the color of their skin. However, this ideal allows a racist person to say they are not racist, because they are an American. Unfortunately, African-American people are all too often confronted with a reality that we are judged by the color of our skin. This difficulty leads to problems when discussing racism in America. To *"make it plain,"* as Malcolm would do, narcissism and the development of the self has to be explained.

Narcissism and the Development of the Self

The theory of narcissism is complex but I will try to explain it simply. An infant is born with a fragmented self, i.e. a collection of unconnected mental structures and activities. In addition, there is a set of at least seven drives down deep in the brain stem. These drives are there because all vertebrae (i.e. animals with spines) have developed functions to help them survive. These drives have different names depending on who is studying them but they are:

- **Exploration:** all vertebrates have to explore their environment to find what they need to live.

- **Sex:** all vertebrates have a need for sex so the species can survive.

- **Aggression:** all vertebrates need to be able to defend themselves from others that would harm them and threaten their lives.

- **Connectedness:** all vertebrates, especially mammals, need to be attached to one another for at least a time to be nurtured and to continue the species.

- **Fear:** all vertebrates must have a healthy sense of fear so they do not engage in activities that will end their lives.

- **Separation:** all vertebrates, especially mammals, when they are young and vulnerable need to be concerned about being separated from their caregivers as the caregivers help manage the needs of helpless infants and assist the young in getting control over these drives.

- **Play:** Vertebrates have neurologic circuits that drive them to play.

For a long, but worthwhile tutorial on these drives, see *The Animal Within Us* on YouTube.[13]

* * *

As the mother appropriately soothes these drives in an infant, the infant not only gradually learns to control these drives on their own, but they experience empathy from their relationship with their mother (fathers can also fulfill this function). As the mother and child separate from time to time, the child must tolerate this separation and gradually develop a sense of self. However, if the relationship between the mother and child has been unempathic or the separations between the mother and child have been traumatic, then an early defect in relatedness to others occurs. Accompanying this defect in relatedness, is a tendency to develop a "default" way of functioning that is characterized by a fragmented, frustrated, rageful infantile state. We have all seen children "fall apart" and regress to the early level of functioning when frustrated. We all know how cruel and unempathic children can be until they "grow up." One of the characteristics of narcissism is to lack any experience with empathy for the other. Essentially, because the infant or child was not treated with empathy, the child grows up treating others as they themselves have been treated. Put another way, *"hurt people, hurt people."*

Racism and Narcissism

In evaluating and occasionally treating racist individuals, I found many similarities between these patients and murderers that murder multiple people, individuals that habitually abuse and molest children, and sadists. They lack empathy and they are prone to rage. *Others have written profoundly about these issues.*[14] *"Racism is the practice of racial discrimination, segregation, persecution, and domination based on a feeling of racial differences or antagonisms; especially with reference to supposed racial superiority, inferiority or purity."*[15]

Murderous people are very narcissistic, they dehumanize others, and there is no consideration for their needs – there is no empathy for someone, not like the narcissist. I have never seen a racist/narcissist who had any respect for the supposed inferior's territoriality – this, of course, includes men who feel entitled to grope and make unwanted sexual advances toward women. Such behaviors are often seen in immature children and adolescents; there is simply a lack of respect. Most racists I have treated in the past have problems with frustration tolerance and impulse control and they always seemed to have a tendency to "fly off the handle" as we used to say. Patients with Narcissistic Personality Disorders engage in levels of grandiosity, a lack of self-boundaries, and dehumanization and these are very similar characteristics of racists.

However, because behavior is multi-determined and is biological, psychological, sociological, and cultural, it is important to point out that racist attitudes can occur secondarily to social or cultural indoctrination and not a symptom of a Narcissistic Personality Disorder. People with this source of racism are able to relinquish their racist ideas and feelings, with sufficient contact with the "outgroup." The problem comes when society is segregated and there is not sufficient contact to create an understanding of a common humanity. It has also been my experience that confronting one's own mortality often spurs narcissistic feelings to become more tempered. Kohut once said *"Man's capacity to acknowledge the finiteness of his existence and to act in accordance with this painful discovery may well be his greatest psychological achievement."*[16]   It has often been curious to me how it is said, *"Behind every great fortune is a great crime."*[17] Yet, when very wealthy people begin to age and realize they don't have long for this world, they start giving their money away in a charitable manner. I suspect this has to do with the dynamics of narcissism.

Official American Psychiatric Association Criteria for Narcissism

The American Psychiatric Association's criteria for a diagnosis of a Narcissistic Personality Disorder are strikingly similar to the characteristics of racists that I describe above. The criteria for a Narcissistic Personality Disorder in the *DSM-5*[18] are:

> "A pervasive pattern of grandiosity (in fantasy or behavior), need for admiration, and lack of empathy, beginning by early adulthood and present in a variety of contexts, as indicated by five (or more) of the following:
>
> 1. has a grandiose sense of self-importance (e.g., exaggerates achievements and talents, expects to be recognized as superior without commensurate achievements);
>
> 2. is preoccupied with fantasies of unlimited success, power, brilliance, beauty, or ideal love;
>
> 3. believes that he or she is "special" and unique and can only be understood by, or should associate with, other special or high-status people (or institutions);
>
> 4. requires excessive admiration;
>
> 5. has a sense of entitlement, i.e., unreasonable expectations of especially favorable treatment or automatic compliance with his or her expectations;
>
> 6. is interpersonally exploitative, i.e., takes advantage of others to achieve his or her own ends;
>
> 7. lacks empathy: is unwilling to recognize or identify with the feelings and needs of others;
>
> 8. is often envious of others or believes that others are envious of him/her;
>
> 9. shows arrogant, haughty behaviors or attitudes."

The other characteristics that narcissists have in common with racists in the *DSM-5* are they have vulnerable self-esteem issues, which makes them very susceptible to any form of criticism and makes them prone to counter-attack impulsively. They are also prone to being denigrating and rageful toward others.

Accordingly, for all these reasons, I thought it important to do some psychiatric research on the relationship between racism and narcissism, but so far not much serious work has been done, and most of the studies have been anecdotal and clinical.

Dr. Dunbar's concept of Pathological Bias

Dr. Ed Dunbar proposed that we try to broaden the concept of Racism and Narcissism and explore the reality that narcissistic people had symptoms that could be considered Pathological Bias. Based on his research he proposed criteria for Pathological Bias that we hoped would get studied by other researchers. The criteria certainly made sense to me.

Proposed Criteria

1. Cautionary statement

A. Pervasive pattern emergent by early adulthood and present in a variety of contexts, as indicated by one or more of the following:
   i.   Intrusive ideation concerning outgroup persons
   ii. Aversive arousal concerning outgroup ideation & intergroup contact
   iii. Relational disturbance of intergroup contact AND

B. The presence during the past 6 months of three or more of the following:

   i.   Generalized fear or perceived threat of outgroup persons.
   ii. Hostility or rage response toward outgroup persons.
   iii. Expressed victimization by outgroup persons without corroborating evidence of actual harm/victimization.
   iv. Aversive ideation or fearful preoccupation concerning outgroup persons.

    v.   Expressed victimization by outgroup persons with corroborating evidence of actual harm done.

    vi. Emotional lability marked by transient hostility secondary to benign intergroup contact.

    vii. Marked aversive preoccupation with outgroup persons.

    viii. Panic and anxiety secondary to benign contact experiences with outgroup persons.

    ix. Endorsement of beliefs and values promoting intergroup hostility and conflict.

    x. Endorsement of violence as a solution to intergroup problems

    xi. Panic and anxiety secondary to benign contact experiences with outgroup persons.

    xii. Interpersonal provocation of outgroup persons secondary to benign contact experiences.

    xiii. Reported avoidance of or retreat from outgroup persons secondary to benign contact.

C. Criteria for each mental disorder are offered as guidelines for making diagnoses, because it has been demonstrated that the use of such criteria enhances agreement among clinicians and investigators. The proper use of these criteria requires specialized clinical training that provides both a body of knowledge and clinical skills.

D. These diagnostic criteria of pathological bias reflect current formulations of evolving knowledge in our field. They do not encompass, however, all the conditions for which people may be treated or that may be appropriate topics for research efforts.

E. The purpose of this diagnostic model is to provide clear descriptions of diagnostic categories in order to enable clinicians and investigators to diagnose, communicate about, study, and treat people with various mental disorders. It is to be understood that inclusion here, for clinical and research purposes, of a diagnostic category such as pathological bias does not imply that the condition meets legal or other nonmedical criteria for what constitutes mental disease, mental disorder, or mental disability.

F. The clinical and scientific considerations involved in categorization of these conditions as mental disorders may not be wholly relevant to legal judgments, for example, that take into account such issues as environmental stressors (e.g., civil unrest or warfare), cultural norms, disability determination, and legal competency.[19]

Alternative DSM-5 Model for Personality Disorders

Unfortunately, the Personality Disorders Workgroup never got a chance to consider the concept and diagnostic criteria for Pathological Bias nor were they very welcoming of exploring the issue of some forms of racism being a symptom of a Narcissistic Personality Disorder. Despite the plans that were made to study these issues in *DSM-5*, there just was not enough solid research for a legitimate consideration of these issues. Instead, the workgroup went in a different route. They looked at all the legitimate science on Personality Disorders that had been done post – *DSM-4*[20]. After lengthy discussions in the Personality Disorders Workgroup, the group decided to try to make the issue of diagnosing a Personality Disorder simpler.

Accordingly, we proposed that a clinician doing a psychiatric assessment of a patient needed to decide whether a patient had a Personality Disorder or not. Based on reams of research since the publication of *DSM-IV* and lengthy discussions by the workgroup, the Personality Disorders Workgroup of the American Psychiatric Association decided to provide an "Alternative DSM-5 Model for Personality Disorders.[21] A healthy personality at the level of self-functioning was characterized by:

> **Identity:** characterized by an "ongoing awareness of a unique self; maintenance of role-appropriate boundaries; consistent and self-regulated positive self-esteem, with accurate self-appraisal; and the capacity of experiencing, tolerating, and regulating a full range of emotions,"[22] and Self-direction: which is exemplified in a person who "sets and aspires to reasonable goals based on realistic assessment of personal capacities; utilizes appropriate standards of behavior, attaining fulfillment in multiple realms, and can reflect on, and make constructive meaning of, interpersonal experience."[23]

> **Empathy:** a person has healthy empathy for others if he or she is: "capable of accurately understanding others' experiences and motivations in most situations; comprehends and appreciates others' perspectives, even if disagreeing, and is aware of the effect of [his or her]...actions on others."[24]

> **Intimacy:** intimate aspects of a personality are normal if the person is capable of: "maintaining multiple satisfying and enduring relationships in personal and community life; desiring and engaging in a number of

caring, close, and reciprocal relationships; and striving for cooperation and mutual benefit and flexibly responds to a range of others' ideas, emotions, and behaviors."[25]

A Personality Disorder was characterized by "*impairments in personality functioning and pathological personality traits.*"[26] To qualify for a diagnosis of Personality Disorder a person would need to exhibit moderate or greater impairment in personality which was conceived in two categories – self and interpersonal functioning, and to have one or more pathological personality traits. The patient personality functioning and traits would need to be an enduring pattern that would have been present since adolescence or early adulthood. Of course, there were the usual exclusionary diagnostic criteria that the impairments in personality function were not a function of another mental disorder or were not the product of the effects of substances (alcohol or drugs) or a medical condition (e.g. having a severe head injury).

Conclusions

This essay is not a commentary on any current or former politician's potential personality disorder. While, I have evaluated some political figures, at their request, it would be unethical and clinically improper to "diagnose people long distance." Simply because a psychiatrist does not know what motives a person has does not mean that person is not clear about their intentions. You can only determine what is behind a person's behavior by talking to that person about their motives and accessing their personality and psychiatric status directly in a clinical interview.

Everyone "reads" other people. Psychiatrists do an assessment of a person using standard a psychiatric assessment tool - a thorough history and mental status examination. Without doing so directly would only be making assumptions. Accordingly, I cannot comment on Donald Trump's personality or psychiatric condition. However, per American Psychiatric Association's ethics, I can educate the public about various psychiatric disorders, and I have chosen the area of narcissism as I have been studying this area for nearly the past 40 years. I trust with the information the public is better informed about issues of narcissism, racism, and pathological bias.

References:

[1]Wikipedia. Goldwater rule. Online: en.wikipedia.org/wiki/Goldwater_rule. Accessed March 20, 2017.

[2]American Psychiatric Association. The Principles of Medical Ethics with Annotations Especially Applicable to Psychiatry - Principles with Annotations - Section 7, No. 3. Washington, D.C.: American Psychiatric Association, 2010.

[3]Gedo JE, Goldberg A. *Models of the Mind: A Psychoanalytic Theory.* Chicago, IL: University of Chicago Press, 1973.

[4]Kohut H. *The Analysis of the Self.* New York, International Universities Press, 1971.

[5]Bell CC. "Racism: A symptom of the narcissistic personality disorder." In Bell CC. *The Sanity of Survival.* Chicago, IL: Third World Press, 2004, pp. 415–427.

[6]Bell CC. "Racism, narcissism, and integrity." In Bell CC. *The Sanity of Survival.* Chicago, IL: Third World Press, 2004, pp. 405–414.

[7]Bell CC. "Taking Issue - Racism – A Mental Illness?" *Psychiatric Services,* Vol. 55, No. 12: p. 1343, December 2004.

[8]Bell CC and Dunbar E. Racism and Psychopathology. In Widiger TA (ed). *The Oxford Handbook of Personality Disorders.* New York: Oxford University Press, 2012, pp. 694-709.

[9]American Psychiatric Association. *The Diagnostic and Statistical Manual, 5th Edition.* Washington, D.C.: American Psychiatric Press, Inc., 2013. Online: en.wikipedia.org/wiki/DSM-5

[10]First MB, Bell CC, Cuthbert B, Krystal JH, Malison R, Offord D, Reiss D, Shea T, Widiger T, Wisner K. Personality Disorders and Relational Disorders: A Research Agenda for Addressing Critical Gaps in DSM. In DJ Kupfer, MB First, & DA Regier (eds). *American Psychiatric Association Research Agenda for DSM V.* Washington, D.C.: American Psychiatric Press, Inc., 2002, pp. 123–199.

[11]Bell CC and Dunbar E. Racism and Psychopathology. In Widiger TA (ed). *The Oxford Handbook of Personality Disorders.* New York: Oxford University Press, 2012, pp. 694-709.

[12]Bell CC. The Last Word "Finding a Way Through the Maze of Racism" *EMERGE,* Vol. 5, Issue 11, p. 80, September 1994.

[13]Online: youtube.com/watch?v=JfqVIG9bejU

[14]Kohut, H. Thoughts on narcissism and narcissistic rage. *The Psychoanalytic Study of the Child*, 27, pp. 360-400, 1972.

[15]Bell CC. "Racism, narcissism, and integrity." *Journal of the National Medical Association*, Vol. 70, No. 2, pp. 89-92, February 1978, p 90.

[16]Kohut H. "Forms and transformations of narcissism." *Journal of the American Psychoanalytic Association*, Vol. 14, pp. 264-268, 1966.

[17]Online: brainyquote.com/quotes/quotes/h/honoredeba197735.html

[18]American Psychiatric Association. *The Diagnostic and Statistical Manual, 5th Edition.* Washington, D.C.: American Psychiatric Press, Inc., 2013, pp. 669–670.

[19]Bell CC and Dunbar E. Racism and Psychopathology. In Widiger TA (ed). *The Oxford Handbook of Personality Disorders.* New York: Oxford University Press, 2012, p. 705.

[20]American Psychiatric Association. *Diagnostic and Statistical Manual, 4th edition.* Washington, D.C.: American Psychiatric Press, 1994.

[21]American Psychiatric Association. *The Diagnostic and Statistical Manual, 5th Edition.* Washington, D.C.: American Psychiatric Press, Inc., 2013, pp. 761–763.

[22]Bell CC. State of the Art and Science – Dynamic Descriptions of Personality Disorder in the DSM-5. *American Medical Association Journal - Virtual Mentor*, Volume 15, No. 10, pp. 857–859, October 2013. Online: journalofethics.ama-assn.org/2013/10/stas1-1310.html

[23]Bell CC. State of the Art and Science – Dynamic Descriptions of Personality Disorder in the DSM-5. *American Medical Association Journal - Virtual Mentor*, Volume 15, No. 10, pp. 857–859, October 2013. Online: journalofethics.ama-assn.org/2013/10/stas1-1310.html

[24]Bell CC. State of the Art and Science – Dynamic Descriptions of Personality Disorder in the DSM-5. *American Medical Association Journal - Virtual Mentor*, Volume 15, No. 10, pp. 857–859, October 2013. Online: journalofethics.ama-assn.org/2013/10/stas1-1310.html

[25]Bell CC. State of the Art and Science – Dynamic Descriptions of Personality Disorder in the DSM-5. *American Medical Association Journal - Virtual Mentor*, Volume 15, No. 10, pp. 857–859, October 2013. Online: journalofethics.ama-assn.org/2013/10/stas1-1310.html

[26]American Psychiatric Association. *The Diagnostic and Statistical Manual, 5th Edition.* Washington, D.C.: American Psychiatric Press, Inc., 2013, p. 761.

Toronto, Ontario, Canada. 19th Nov, 2016. Hundreds of Canadians take part in a massive protest against American President-elect Donald Trump at Nathan Philips Square in downtown Toronto, Canada. Credit: Creative Touch Imaging Ltd./Alamy Live News

TRUMP, ECO, AND ENEMIES: WHY SUPPORTERS WILL FOLLOW 45 'TIL DEATH

JONITA DAVIS

Jonita Davis is a writer and writing instructor from Michigan City, Indiana. Her work can be found in Creative Nonfiction, the Washington Post, Ravishly, and other publications.

Just a few miles from my house in northern Indiana lives a family who, along with much of their community, voted steadfastly for Trump. These people spat on "Day without an Immigrant" activities in my area and gloated as the rest of us feared the worst—ICE was doing sweeps in our area. The supporters applauded as photos of local families in tears appeared in the media. Families were forever torn apart; a few businesses were closed as the owners were served up for deportation.

Supporters kept repeating the refrains of the election campaign. He was getting rid of the "bad hombres," the criminals that could snatch our kids and rape our women.

Then, ICE arrested a prominent business owner and wealthy area resident. He and his Trump-supporting family were shocked. She admitted to local reporters that she thought trump meant the "bad hombres," not upperclass white folks.

She forgot that her husband was a light-skinned Mexican. He looked white, but that wasn't enough. He was still a person of color, an enemy to the Trump supporter.

Some of us truly believed that such a widely-reported story would change the minds of supporters--around northern Indiana at least. I've always been an optimist, despite living over three decades in my own dark skin. My realist friend, who is also an activist in the local Latino community laughs at my belief that the supporters would change. She even told me, "This isn't going to change anything," in her how-cute-of-you-to-think-so voice.

She was right. Support for Trump and "down with Obamacare" rhetoric blossomed on the eve of the health care vote that would not take place.

The behavior baffled me. Just how much does a man have to do to lose favor with the Indiana Republicans, much less, the ones all over the US? Trump came for one of their beloved community members in Indiana and other parts of the country. The man's own supporters were taken from their homes. It did nothing. Neither did attempting to abolish the Affordable Care Act and raising the premiums in an area already plagued by poverty and unemployment. Many of the residents are elderly, as well. They still support Trump even after he revealed his plan to abolish the EPA. We live in an area that still remembers the Gary/Chicago smog years and the damage done by the Whiting, IN oil leaks. The supporters still stand firm.

Why would people hold such steadfast support for a man who goes against their own wellbeing?

I had to do some studying about this. I think I know the answer, but there had to be something out there in philosophy, psychology, or another field to describe this phenomenon. I do realize that many Republicans will eventually abandon ship. A good deal of them already have. Trump's approval polls at the beginning of April reported only one-third of the country standing behind the man. That third of the American population is still standing behind the hate, misinformation, and chaos the man is creating. Why?

It is simple. Trump does a lot of things for those in white America finding themselves living like the minorities they once looked down on. For a people who are finding that their ideologies are not shared with the majority, and are in fact called unacceptable, Trump provides a place of comfort. That comfort is a warm blanket stitched with fault and blame. He gives the people of America who ironically feel their voices aren't being heard (over the newly voiced POCs and LGBTQs getting more of their deserved share of the spotlight) place to plant all that anger and guilt. Trump supporters need somewhere to lay blame for their post-recession foreclosures, lost pensions, doused retirement dreams, and more. He has identified and even legitimized an enemy—people of color—that hails back to the "good ol' days" of Jim Crow, Japanese internment, and migrant hatred. Enemies the supporters know well, from an era they cherished.

When America was Allegedly "Great"

My conclusions come from reading the writings of Umberto Eco, whose study of modern society created several writings, talks, and lessons in cultural studies. His 2013 book, *Inventing the Enemy*, is a cultural commentary in a collection of essays that begins with an essay on modern society's need to create and cling to a common hatred and enemy. These enemies aren't real threats. Eco describes them as:

> *the people who become our enemies often are not those who directly threaten us…but those whom someone has interest in portraying as a true threat even when they aren't. Rather than the real threat highlighting the ways in which these enemies are different from us, the difference itself becomes a symbol of what we find threatening.*

Here's an example: Remember, those *"bad hombres"* that the wife feared so much, despite having an undocumented husband? They were not real. In fact, several studies have concluded that crimes committed by undocumented immigrants are minimal. Despite the truth, Trump has published lists of alleged crimes committed by "illegals." In reality, the story of the "illegal" trying to invade your home is far from true. According to the FBI, violent crimes like rape, murder, and robbery in the US are largely committed by someone you know. The same goes for the nonviolent. So, Uncle George is probably the one who stole your mower, not some immigrant running around without "papers." Undocumented immigrants like other targets of the administration are just a place set blame because they are foreign, dark, and different.

Let's think about this. For as long as we have been a country, Americans—specifically white Americans—have held themselves as superior to other foreign, dark, and different groups. This attitude goes all the way back to the first settlers. Those first pilgrims and explorers believed that the greater good of the colony and the nation they were building, was best served by slowly pushing the Native Americans inland. After all, they were savages who would kidnap the kids and rape the women, according to the propaganda at the time. Then, the colonists deemed it necessary to move tribe after tribe until their nations were supplanted into plots of desert terrain.

Then, someone got the bright idea to bring African people over to America. The dark people were not much more than dark animals from an unknown continent at the time. The Africans became labor—slaves-- and when it came time to liberate them, the greater good of the economy was often cited. The collapse of the Antebellum South is still blamed, not on the Civil War that cut through the country killing crops and families, but on the mass amount of slave labor that was lost. Jim Crow grew up out of that anger.

But, when it was time to integrate, to finally put all the bad feelings in the history books where they belonged, white America wouldn't move. The races had been separate for much too long. The integration would cause too much economic stress. The women and children couldn't handle the transition.

Every step of the way, there had to be a reason to hate the Black people. They weren't alone. Latinos and Asians also received the backhand treatment by the white majority. The Japanese were rounded up and herded into prisons called Internment Camps over the fear that one amongst them might be a Communist sympathizer. (If this sounds familiar, it should. Look up the treatment of refugees in 2017 America. Doesn't look like we've learned much from history.) The Japanese needed to be contained. They might rape the white women and kidnap the kids.

Together, POCs were portrayed throughout history as being the savages that would tear down that white picket fenced American dream. They would also decimate the All-American Family That delicate dew-eyed porcelain doll called a wife and the precious being that she birthed. Many a white man holds up this image at the first hint of a threat. The thought of a dark-skinned man or boy anywhere near that image is just the thing that fueled racist hatred for well over a century after slavery ended.

The POC is the enemy Trump offered up. That enemy gave his supporters someone to hate during his campaign. Easy enough with the head of the rival party being a Black man and his POC-loving bestie.

Then he won.

Now Trump hangs onto the enemy like a drunken frat boy who already had his key taken and drinks watered all the ways down, but he still insists on staying at the damn bar. He's the one person at the office meeting who is holding everyone hostage with a complaint about paper towel prices when the regular business is wrapped and everyone else is ready to go. He's hanging onto the old enemy propaganda and trying to uphold values that are no longer relevant in this country. Because if he lets go, he and hundreds of thousands of white Americans will finally have to wake up to the fact that America of 1950 is long gone. You need to be more than "young, white and free" to get your way in this country, and those guys kissing over there have just as much right to be in this conversation as you do. After all, statistics show that they probably make more money than you do and are far more educated.

So, Trump supporters in northern Indiana and all over the country cling to a Cheeto with bad hair. Eco's theory on inventing the enemy explains why the supporters need their leader. They will follow him down as he sets fire to female reproductive rights, guts healthcare, drains retirement accounts, squanders tax dollars, and topples the US reputation in the international arena.

And, like mosquitoes to that bug light on the bug light on the porch, those supporters will follow Trump to their own demise, because they can't imagine life in other way.

THE TRUTH ABOUT TRUMP'S FASCIST PROGRAM, WHAT IT MEANS FOR BLACK PEOPLE – AND WHAT MUST BE DONE ABOUT IT!

CARL DIX

Carl Dix is a representative of the Revolutionary Communist Party and an advocate of Bob Avakian's New Synthesis of Communism. In 1970, Carl was one of the Fort Lewis 6, six GIs who refused orders to Vietnam. In 2011 he co-founded, with Cornel West, the Stop Mass Incarceration Network which carried out a campaign of civil disobedience to stop "Stop and Frisk."

In appealing for Black votes (and trying to give other voters the impression that he wasn't a racist) during his presidential campaign, Donald Trump declared: *"What do you (Black people) have to lose?"*
A whole hell of a lot.

      The Trump-Pence regime has unleashed a fascist onslaught on the US and the world. It has begun to demonize and target group after group. Trump has asserted that the truth is whatever he says it is. He has attacked the media and threatened those who criticize him. He has enacted a ban on U.S. funds to health care providers anywhere in the world if they even inform women about abortion. This regime is headed in a clear direction: aiming to reinstate open white supremacy; have the U.S. running amok all over the world; slamming women "back into their place;" persecuting Muslims, immigrants, and gay and trans people; taking away legal and political rights altogether.

A key part of their fascist program is aimed straight at Black people. Trump has threatened to send the feds into Chicago to "fix" the carnage there if city officials can't handle it. This is an attempt to use the horror of young Black men killing each other (and other Black people caught in the crossfire) to advance an overall offensive against Black people. One that aims to wipe out the struggle of Black people against their oppression once and for all.

Trump has promised jobs, but, in reality, the few jobs his people will dole out will be to bribe people to become enforcers of his program: More Blacks in the U.S. army going around the world to kill other oppressed people, more Black police and jail guards and Black people recruited into Trump's deportation squads. This will mean hunting down undocumented immigrants, tearing their families apart and disappearing people. And it brings to mind the Buffalo Soldiers being part of the theft of the land from the native inhabitants of America while Black people in the south were being violently subjugated into conditions that amounted to slavery by another name. The Trump-Pence regime has promised educational reforms. The heart of this was signaled by Trump's false statement that the public schools are "flush with cash." He plans to take money from already underfunded public schools and divert it to private and charter schools. This will come down to gutting public education and funneling students into schools that train them as Christian fundamentalist robots, unable to think critically or to resist.

The sharp edge of this program will be unleashing law enforcement to restore law and order. Trump's Attorney general, Jeff Sessions, has vowed to take the gloves off the police, police who have been caught in video after video murdering and brutalizing Black people. Trump has signed executive orders that aim to fill the prisons even fuller. He told Fox News Commentator, Bill O'Reilly, that Black Lives Matter was: "... essentially calling death to the police." Trump's plan amounts to a reign of terror on top of 400 years of hell for Black people. And there is his threat to send in the feds to fix the problem of violence in Chicago.[1]

Trump is already getting suggestions about what the feds he has threatened to send to Chicago should do. Robert J. Milan, a former Chicago area prosecutor, has authored a plan for a police state clamp down on a predominantly Black South Side neighborhood. He proposes building concrete barriers around an area from 55th St. on the north to 79th St. on the south and State St. on the east to Western Ave. on the west. These barriers would close 75 of the 150 entrances and exits to the area. And his plan would mobilize the National Guard to man the other half of the entrances and exits and impose a curfew from 7PM to 7AM. Anyone entering or leaving the area would have to show their ID and flooding the area with cops.[2]

This plan will make that neighborhood an open air prison under martial law where the residents are subjected to the pass laws of apartheid South Africa. The Gil Scott Heron refrain, *"Let Me See Your ID,"* from the album *Sun City* that built global solidarity with the struggle against apartheid in South Africa will have to be resurrected to oppose apartheid like conditions enforced on Black people in the U.S. And ominously, this open-air prison should raise the specter of the ghettoes Jews were forced into by the Nazis in Europe during World War II. Those ghettos were a step along the way to carting millions of Jewish people off to the death camps.

400 Years of Hell

And let's be clear, Black people have suffered vicious exploitation and savage oppression since the first Africans were dragged to these shores in slave chains. Worked from can't see in the morning to can't see at night as slaves on the plantations. Enslaved people were treated as little more than talking tools. Forced to produce cotton and other products for the world market by a regime so brutal that historians call it the whipping machine. Families were torn apart if the master decided selling someone "down the river" improved the plantation's bottom line. Women could be raped by any white man associated with the plantation. All these horrors were driven by the needs of capitalism. It wasn't that white people were, or are, by nature devils, or "ice people." It's that capitalism arose and created a global market for tobacco, cotton and other products, and this drew all too many white people into acting and thinking in devilish ways. The notions of white supremacy and racism arose on the basis of this material foundation. Even as some white people have stood against this, when there has been leadership that inspired and guided them to do so.

The Civil War led to the abolition of slavery, and during Reconstruction Black people gained citizenship, the right to vote, access to education for the first time and more. But violence by supporters of the defeated confederacy and betrayal by Northern capitalists led to the overthrow of Reconstruction. And Black people were forced into slavery by another name. Most Black people were forced into being sharecroppers, often on the same plantations where they had been enslaved. They were robbed by the plantation owners and subjected to the separate and unequal conditions of Jim Crow segregation for almost a century.

And all this was enforced by the lynchings of 3,959 Black people between 1877 and 1950.[3] Blacks were seized by white mobs and often beaten, set on fire and had their body parts cut off before being killed. Lynchings were public spectacles where white families gathered in a festive atmosphere These families often brought picnic baskets to enjoy the spectacle. Blacks were sometimes forced to watch so the message of intimidation was driven home. Notices of lynchings were posted in newspapers so people could travel from other areas to participate in them.

Again, this continuation of the vicious exploitation and savage oppression of Black people was driven by the needs of capitalism. In particular, by the need to compete with cotton production from the British and French colonies for the global market

Jim Crow segregation and lynch mob terror ended when Black people migrated out of rural south into cities across the country after World War II. The powerful upsurges of Black resistance and the support these inspired from whites and others forced the country's rulers to end those forms of oppression. But this didn't end the oppression. Black people became the bottom tier of the U.S. industrial workforce and were subjected to discrimination in housing, education, healthcare and every other facet of life.

Then, as U.S. capital moved its production facilities to other parts of the globe in search of workers who could be even more viciously exploited than workers in this country, millions of Black people became surplus population; people who were no longer part of the legitimate economy of this country.[4]

Historically, the exploitation of Black labor has played a crucial role in the building up of the wealth of America. At the same time, Black people have been a big problem for this country. The horrors to which they have been subjected expose as a bald-faced lie that America is a land of freedom and democracy. And their resistance has inspired other sections of people to open their eyes, stand up and resist themselves and begin to call into question the whole set up in this country.

What They Fear

This is a great fear that the rulers of this country have been trying to deal with since the 1960s, and today they are dealing with it in a situation where millions of Black people can no longer be profitably exploited by capitalism But, at the same time, Black people remain a potentially explosive section of the people in this country. One whose history is one of rising up in powerful resistance to the abuses they have suffered and, thru this, sparking broader resistance.

The system's response to this has been a program of beating Black people down, penning them in, locking them up and even killing them off. Witness the successive wars on drugs which were really wars on Black (and increasingly Brown) people. President Nixon's Chief of Staff, HR Haldeman, explained Nixon's approach and the thinking behind it: *"The key is to devise a system that recognizes this while not appearing to."*[5]

This criminalizing of Black people, especially the youth, has led to an 800% increase in the numbers of people in prison in the U.S. with most of those incarcerated being Black or Latino. And it has provided justification for an approach to policing which gives a green light to cops to brutalize and even murder Black people with impunity.

This police terror and mass incarceration, combined with the reality that millions of youth in the inner cities across the country are growing up with futures of hopelessness – no legitimate ways to survive, an educational system that's geared to fail them and no way to be somebody outside of the street life and its code of revenge – is the backdrop to the horror of young Black men killing each other, and killing Black people who get caught in their crossfire. And, this police terror and mass incarceration are the spearhead of what I have been calling for 5 years now a slow genocide targeting Black people, one that could easily become a fast genocide. Here I'm not trying to overstate the situation to get people to respond to it. I'm speaking the truth.

The definition of genocide is acting with the intent to destroy a national, ethnic, racial or religious group, in whole or in part.[6] Look at the numbers of Black people in prison, and the even greater number of formerly incarcerated Black people who are unable to find work because they have a prison record. Look at the way the educational system is geared to fail Black youth, putting so many of them on a track to go in and out of prison. Look at the way that jobs and other legitimate ways to survive and raise families have disappeared for so many Black people. Aren't these actions that threaten the survival of Black people as a people?

Barack Obama presided over an approach to dealing with this that was largely a continuation of what had been presided over by Bill Clinton and the two Bushes; continued discrimination enforced by police terror and mass incarceration. To this, he added reforms like putting body cameras on police or early releases from prison for a small number of the people who had been warehoused in the country's prisons. And honeyed words about understanding the problems along with white house conferences to which people got invited to talk about the problems only to find that no solutions were going to come out of them. Try as he might, Obama couldn't cool things out and get Black people to keep accepting this genocidal assault in silence.

Now comes the Trump-Pence regime with a different and more

extreme approach to dealing with America's Black problem. As police continue to kill Black and Brown people with impunity,[7] Trump has signed an executive order he says will "take the gloves off the police" and end the anti police atmosphere that is keeping police from doing their jobs. The Obama administration had stated an intention to phase out use of private prisons for federal prisoners, but Jeff Sessions, Trump's attorney general, reversed it because it *"... impaired the bureau's (Federal Bureau of Prisons) ability to meet the future needs of the federal correctional system."*[8]

And then, there's Trump's threat to send the feds in to "fix" the carnage in Chicago. Here, Trump is seizing on a real horror as an opening to impose a vicious police state clampdown on Black people as part of an overall offensive against Black people, an offensive that aims to wipe out the struggle of Black people against their oppression as a people, once and for all. Trump's program for Black people is one that will divide and degrade people, and turn people against each other in ways not yet seen. If it is not stopped by a massive surge of resistance from Black people and everyone else who opposes injustice, it will become the acceleration of that slow genocide targeting Black people that I talked about above.

This offensive against Black people is part of an overall fascist onslaught. As the "Call to Action" from RefuseFascism.org puts it:

> *Dissent is piece-by-piece criminalized The truth is bludgeoned. Group after group is demonized and targeted along a trajectory that leads to real horrors. All of this has already begun under the Trump regime. History has shown that fascism must be stopped before it becomes too late.*

In the name of humanity the trump-pence regime must be driven from power before it's too late. Driving this fascist regime from power must be approached, not in order to restore the pre Trump status quo. because that status quo was already a horror for the majority of the seven billion people on the planet. The U.S. pre Trump was a country where Black people were subjected to savage oppression; where immigrants were already subjected to deportation raids that tore families apart and disappeared people; where women were treated like punching bags, sex objects and incubators. And we lived in a world where U.S. drone missile strikes and bombing raids destroyed villages and hospitals and, massacred wedding parties; where capitalism's plunder of the earth threatens the environment of the planet we live on, where tens of thousands of children die needlessly every day from starvation and preventable diseases; and where women are trafficked into sexual slavery in horrific numbers.

Even as we must act to oust this fascist regime that would mean unimaginably worse horrors for humanity, we must not go backward to restore that world. Instead we must go forward to making revolution, a revolution aimed at eliminating the exploitation and oppression enforced on humanity by this capitalist/imperialist system.

And what Black people do, or don't do, will play a crucial role in determining whether we can succeed in ousting the Trump-Pence regime, and whether doing that can become part of getting ready for that necessary revolution. The following quote by Bob Avakian, the architect of the new communism and the leader of the Revolutionary Communist Party, expresses this crucial role in a poetic way:

> *There is the potential for something of unprecedented beauty to arise out of unspeakable ugliness: Black people playing a crucial role in putting an end, at long last, to this system which has, for so long, not just exploited but dehumanized, terrorized and tormented them in a thousand ways – putting an end to this in the only way it can be done – by fighting to emancipate humanity, to put an end to the long night in which human society has been divided into masters and slaves, and the masses of humanity have been lashed, beaten, raped, slaughtered, shackled and shrouded in ignorance and misery.*

I want to conclude this essay by speaking to some of the major arguments I've encountered in sounding the alarm on the horrors that the fascist Trump-Pence regime will mean for Black people and what must be done about it, now.

#1 – Things are already horrible for Black people. Trump can't make them much worse, and Black people need to focus their attention on dealing with what they're already up against and leave dealing with Trump to others - This is wrong and wrong. Wrong because we are dealing with a fascist regime, and people have no idea of the horrors that it has in store for Black people, and for all of humanity. The slow genocide this system has targeted Black people with for quite some time could easily become a fast one. And in aiming to do this, Trump can build on the foundation of the criminalization and de-monization of Black people that this system has used for centuries to justify the savage oppression it has enforced on Black people. And the police state measures that have disproportionately targeted Black people.

It is equally wrong to propose leaving dealing with horrific injustice to others. This is the approach people took to dealing with Hitler's Germany and look at how that worked out. Instead of holding back from speaking out because "your people" have not yet come under attack, the approach needs to be one of throwing in to stop the fascist onslaught before it's too late.

#2 – For the moment, Trump is in power, and Black people need to accept and adapt to that. Instead of calling him out or joining the opposition to his regime, Black people need to try to stay on his good side and look for opportunities to make deals with him to get something for Black people from him – When you're talking about the Trump-Pence fascist regime, there is no good side to get on! He has vowed to take the gloves off the police, police who have been caught on video after video murdering and brutalizing Black people. His at-torney general is taking steps to make it possible to incarcerate more people. Is there any reason to think that this increased incarceration won't dispro-portionately hit Black people?

Anyone out to make a deal with Trump to get something for Black people, whether it's Minister Louis Farrakhan of the Nation of Islam, a clown (in a bad way) like Steve Harvey, or the heads of Historically Black Colleges and Universities will be confronted with terms that come down to collabo-rating with Trump's fascist regime as it enforces its overall program of crush-ing the struggle of Black people. We've seen this before. Some Jewish leaders in Nazi Germany thought they could make a deal with Hitler to get something for their people. And look what they got, a chance to sign onto and help facilitate the genocidal program the Nazis carried out against the Jewish people. We must not have a rerun of this horror show.

#3 – Since most white people supported Trump, the idea of driving his regime from power is unrealistic. Isn't an approach of working to reverse the electoral gains of the Republicans in 2018 and 2020 more realistic? – The thing that this view refuses to come to grips with is that we are dealing with a fascist regime, a regime that is unleashing an onslaught that will greatly intensify all the horrors America has enforced on humanity. And that aims to take away legal and political rights altogether. As for looking to electoral strategies in the future, there is no guarantee that upcoming elections won't be so rigged by continued republican efforts to restrict voting rights of Black people, Brown people and young people as to be meaningless.

Tens of millions of people, including millions of white people oppose everything that Donald Trump represents. Many of them have taken to the streets in opposition to the steps the Trump-Pence regime has taken to advance its fascist agenda, like the Muslim travel ban and the deportation raids. If this resistance was taken up to another level, one of taking on the whole fascist program, and if it took to the streets and stayed in the streets, it could force a political crisis that all forces in society would have to respond to. Such a political crisis was forced by mass resistance in South Korea recently, and it led to the ouster of the sitting president there. This is also what went down in Egypt in 2011, when millions of people took to the streets and forced the ouster of the Mubarak regime.

In both of these countries, the ousters were forced by millions of people, different kinds of people with different viewpoints who were united that the regimes they lived under were intolerable, taking independent political action. Some would say this can't happen in a country like the U.S.. But a fascist regime is being consolidated in the U.S., and this makes it necessary for all those who see this for what it is to throw in to do what's necessary to stop it!

IN THE NAME OF HUMANITY, WE MUST REFUSE TO ACCEPT A FASCIST AMERICA!

References:

[1]Dix, Carl. (2017, February 10). The Truth About Trump's Fascist Program, What It Means For Black People – And What Must Be Done About It! *Revolution Newspaper.* Online: revcom.us/a/478/what-the-trump-pence-regime-will-mean-for-black-people-en.html

[2]Kass, J. (2017, February 21). A plan For Trump's reds in Chicago. *Chicago Tribune.* Online: chicagotribune.com/news/columnists/kass/ct-chicago-crime-kass-0222-20170221-column.html

[3]Miles, T. (2016, September 24). U.S. police killings reminiscent of lynching, U.N. group says. Online: reuters.com/article/us-usa-police-un-idUSKCN11T1OS

[4]*Revolution Newspaper.* The oppression of Black people, The crimes of the system and the revolution we need. Online: http://revcom.us/a/144/BNQ-en.html

[5]Alexander M. (2012, February 6). The new jim crow with Michelle Alexander. Interview. Online: archive.org/details/TheNewJimCrowWithMichelleAlexander

[6]United Nations Treaty Collection (1948, December 9). Convention of Prevention and Punishment of the Crime of Genocide. Accessed February 2017. Online: treaties.un.org

[7]Online: killedbypolice.net

[8]Beech, E. (2017, February 23). U.S. reverses Obama-era move to phase out private prisons. Online: reuters.com/article/usa-prisons-idUSL1N1G82FP

WHEN SUGAR CAME IN FIVE- POUND BAGS

VERNITA HALL

*Vernita Hall, a poet and author based in Philadelphia, has published in numerous journals and anthologies. Her poetry chapbook **The Hitchhiking Robot Learns About Philadelphia**, won the 2016 Moonstone Chapbook Contest (judge Afaa Michael Weaver).*

When sugar came in five-pound bags, phone booths were as plentiful as elephants. U.S. water rights belonged to U.S. residents. Groceries were ported in reusable brown paper sacks. A pat of butter was a guilty gustatory pleasure. A can of evaporated milk poured forth a thick stream of cream. Whole milk and soap powder flowed from biodegradable cardboard cartons. Manufactured goods "Made in America" were not yet endangered species. The phrase "American quality" was not yet oxymoronic.

Moronic was the blithe assumption that we would neither notice nor resent the gradual extinctions, the recurrent plastic surgeries on the crow's-footed face of America. A twenty percent reduction in the weight of a bag of sugar. The insidious acquisition of local water rights by supranational conglomerates who sell back to us our own free water. The watering-down of evaporated milk. The sacrifice of cardboard and paper packaging for staples such as eggs, milk, detergent, and groceries on the altar of the pervasive, eco-unfriendly new god—plastic. The conversion of rich buttery flavor to the unsavory taste of cardboard. The sleight-of-hand switch from supposedly impartial Internet search engine results to overt pre-paid commercials. The Machinery feeds us these time-release capsules of accumulated reversals because the American public, it is convinced, will swallow anything.

The Cold War threatened the world with mutually assured destruction by superpowers. Today the Sword of Damocles dangles from dreadlocks of global warming and overpopulation. But no less ominously is it suspended from the taunt of revenant symbols like the swastika, Confederate flag, the sobriquet "Cleveland Indians." From assault by urban noise, vitriolic rhetoric, and political bombast. Ideological extremism. Rampant proliferation of trash, waste, bottled water, and the plague of plastic. The slogan *Je suis Charlie*, which sharply epitomizes the easily bruised sensitivity of what should be a selectively permeable membrane between freedom of individual expression and personal beliefs. Information insecurity. Increasing encroachment on privacy and civil liberties. Enrichment of a select few at the expense of struggling multitudes. Erosion of quality of life. Marginalization of women. Objectification of children. Soaring cost of education, health and elder care. Oppression of the out-of-favor, the out-of-luck, the non-majority stakeholder. Suppression of the middle class. Lack of embrace for those who swim outside the heterosexual mainstream. A tidal wave of obesity. Misuse of medicines. Fragmentation of families. Civil war. The tragedy of the refugee, and the suicide bomber. The desperation of the disaffected. The crucifixion of Islam.

Now playing in the theatre of the absurd: the hubris of man. Who tunnels out the bases of two-thousand-year-old sequoia trees so cars can drive conveniently through the trunks? Who hunts toward the cliff of extinction elephants and rhinos, to drive up the price of private stockpiles of ivory; sharks, to harvest with unmitigated fervor—facilitated by the ignominious glancing of gold-digging government officials—their golden aphrodisiac fins. Who drives away the productive, invested immigrant. Drives over citizens' rights under the pretext of national security. Who builds more nuclear plants to generate more radioactive waste that science still has not been able to devise the means to render non-lethal to life? Who dumps trash into the oceans, out of sight, out of mind? Plastic is the new fish food.

Lacking civility and substance, the airwaves and national dialogue are replete with nuclear narratives, discourse-as-diatribe. Their attempts at shaping the collective conscience too often press the <pause> button on mutual respect and tolerance. However, dramatic consequences ensue. Because the half-life of hatred rivals that of plutonium.

Purposeful, issues-focused debate is a necessary and vital component of democracy, a core element of healthy collaboration. Personal attacks, however, are time-wasting and diversionary (though for some, admittedly entertaining). Political candidates who appear oblivious to the distinction between these two poles have no place at the helm of any constituency. At the ballot box voters should keep this intellectual myopia at the fore of their selection criteria when choosing representatives who can most effectively serve the public interest.

President Donald Trump is not necessarily to blame for the tone of the national dialogue. The Tweeter-in-Chief may be only one carrier of the zeitgeist infection, symptom of a national illness. He was a pre-packaged, shrink-wrapped, ad-libbed, brand-named known quantity—and we bought that package. *Caveat emptor* (let the buyer beware). The 45th president is a different kind of drum major, popularly elected for a 21st century parade. For him the baton is more blunt stick than instrument. Justice, peace, and righteousness do not appear to be audible in his syncopated beat to any discernible degree. It is, however, perhaps instructive to recall another different kind of drum major—the Pied Piper.

As to policy, sabre rattling and Trump-eting a renewed military build-up are hallmarks of a Cold War, backwards-looking mentality. Already we are losing the war we're winning—the war against our own environment. The complexities of 21st century life require reflective thinkers capable of adaptability, flexibility, collaborative engagement, and listening; advisors who appreciate and are guided by the lessons of history; leaders who exercise power with humility and judicious restraint. Whose handshakes do not manhandle. Who grasp the nuances of suggestion, subtlety, and understatement—in short, the art of diplomacy. Who recognize the importance of checks and balances, such as those provided by three separate branches of government—and a free, probing press to ride shotgun.

In any case, let us be clear: the simplistic unraveling by the current administration of works enacted by a previous administration does not constitute a well-considered, forward-thinking program of advancement for this country. Rather, it is an exercise in "not logic," a narrow act of negation, requiring no more creativity or enlightened reasoning than the destruction of ancient artifacts by modern extremists. To create with purpose and ingenuity is the bold work of architects and innovators. Erasure of the past does not constitute a vision for the future. Quite the contrary.

As for copious deregulation, the marriage of profit-driven corporations to long-term public interests is at best a shotgun wedding. Irreconcilable differences between the two concerns compel concerted and dispassionate government oversight. Republican pledges to drastically fold back the umbrella of governmental regulations under the pretext of cost cutting is disingenuous, at best. The profit motive unbridled is a runaway horse. Corporations, aided and abetted by an army of doggedly persistent lobbyist-weather forecasters, are already expert at dancing between the raindrops of regulatory controls without getting their feet wet. Provisioned by the resources of Midas, the arks of Corporate America are watertight luxury liners. Like the soon-to-be-submerged Marshall Islands, the average consumers are the vulnerable water treaders, who will be left barely afloat as sea levels rise. And for anyone, high or low, who draws comfort in telling themselves *Après nous, le déluge* (After us, the flood)—well, the storm is already upon us.

Resources—natural and financial—are not a bottomless pit. But deficits are a sucking black hole, even for countries printing their own money. Someone has to pay. Trash and waste, even if out of immediate sight, must go somewhere. Someone or something lives near it. Someone or something is poisoned by it. "One-use," "disposable"—these are dangerously unsustainable, short-sighted fantasies. The plastics plague must be confronted and contained. What we spend and where it comes from, what we discard and where it goes—to continue to disconnect cause and effect with such blind indifference is mere self-delusion and the apex of illogic. (Have autism rates snowballed simply from improved patient diagnostics and reporting?) This national blindness may be the greatest danger we face—or choose not to.

We owe the frugal husbandry of scarce resources—water, air, land, forests, minerals, flora and fauna—to future generations. Consideration of the interdependencies of global systems must be delicately balanced with parochial priorities. Renewable, sustainable practices must be developed and implemented. Native peoples understood and internalized their harmonic symbiosis with the natural world. They tasted the sweetness of life at its source. Their stewardship bequeathed to their children the same land flowing with milk and honey that they inherited from their ancestors. They fully grasped that we are as separate from nature as the finger is from the hand. To our detriment and our peril, we have forgotten this essential organic linkage.

In the face of all this, what can one person do? We can curb our own wastefulness, check our own tongues. Live more simply, in concert with the land. (What if your trash had to be disposed of on your own property?) We can turn down the noise, and listen more carefully. We can practice living more mindful lives, in constant awareness of the fragility of our freedoms and our blessings. We can pay off our debts, and use credit with discretion. Invest our money and ourselves in a future of possibilities for all. Educate ourselves, that we may channel better informed opinions and assessments into our decision making. We can vote, with our wallets as well as our ballots. We can treat one another with greater kindness. Love one another more openly and fully.

Inspired by the wisdom of our Founding Fathers and the greatest thinkers in literature, faith, science, and history, let us participate mindfully in the growing of our future. Measure our conduct, speech, and priorities with a new yardstick: one of pragmatic good sense. Let us strive toward an ever more perfect union with the residents of these United States and this planet. Let us respond with greater care—gently, respectfully—to one another and to this wondrous world. Let us ponder the challenge of our predecessor President Barack Obama: "We are the change that we seek."

So, let us press on.

THE 45TH PRESIDENT AND THE TRIUMPH OF PREDATORY CAPITALISM

JULIANNE MALVEAUX

Julianne Malveaux is a professor, labor economist, and noted author whose writing has appeared in numerous mainstream publication. During her time as the 15th President of Bennett College for Women, she was the architect of exciting and innovative transformation at America's oldest historically black college for women.

African American people were going continue to experience inequality no matter who won the Presidential race on November 8, 2016. By every economic indicator, we lag the general population, whether we are looking at income, wealth, or employment. In some ways, the 2016 election offered us options about the terms and conditions of battle, yet also confirmed that battle for social and economic justice was all the more necessary after eight years of an African American centrist President did not close some of the gaps that we hoped it would. The election of the 45th President, Donald John Trump (who will be subsequently referred to as 45, given that repeating his name simply serves to inflate an already massive ego), means a step backward, not forward, in the realm of social and economic justice. His election represents the triumph of predatory capitalism and a serious threat to racial economic justice in the United States. In these first few months of 45's Presidency, the level of both petty personal and macroeconomic economic chicanery has been unprecedented. It is entirely appropriate to repudiate the exploitative nature of this presidency and to assert that 45 is not my president, nor is his economy my economy. His approach to the economy does nothing to lift up people at the bottom, or even in the middle. Instead, 45 is insistent on reinforcing the triumph of predatory capitalism and the victory of his own top one-percent class. From the installation of his daughter, Ivanka, and son-in-law, Jared Kushner, into the White House inner circle, to the installation of an out-of-touch, marginally qualified billionaire Cabinet, 45 has indicated that he is unable to hear from the constituency. However, it is also important to explore strategies to resist 45's inclination to run the United States as one of his personal businesses, enriching himself and his family under the guise of doing the business of a nation that some of us only reluctantly claim as our own (even as we exuberantly claim our role in its development, and even in the building of the very White House that 45 uses as the headquarters for his evil empire).

The purpose of this essay is to explore the ways predatory capitalism has triumphed in the early days of the 45 Presidency, and how it will impact workers in United States, especially African American workers. Its further purpose is to examine the sociopolitical climate that makes this administration's racism, misogyny, xenophobia and predatory capitalism acceptable, even to those who are economic losers when 45's policies are implemented. Finally, this essay will explore some possibilities for resistance.

It is important to note that, for many, 45's campaign was simply a repudiation of President Barack Obama's Presidency, and that in the early months of 45's Presidency, his obsession with his predecessor, President Barack Obama has been, at best, inappropriate. Lacking the skills to offer a psychological diagnosis, it would be unsuitable for me to use words like "unstable, unhealthy, or unbalanced" to describe the trove delusional and false Twitter messages that the 45th President has directed toward his honorable predecessor. However, it is clear that 45 has systematically attempted to dismantle the Obama legacy, not only in health care, but also in environmental protection, consumer protection, labor market protection, and other areas, while developing a philosophically inconsistent foreign policy. Those of us who are repelled by 45's leadership are especially repelled because of the ways he has embraced white supremacist rhetoric and actions to erase the solid legacy of a President who attempted, at least, to provide some protections for people at the periphery of economic prosperity.

45's Rhetoric and Reality

While many are appalled and aghast at the actions of 45's Presidency, we should not be surprised about it. The man who lost the popular vote by more than 3 million votes is doing nothing more than he said he would do when he campaigned. He said he would work to reduce the size of government. He said he would cut taxes (he didn't say, though, that he would mostly cut them for the wealthy). He said he would create jobs; a promise that has not yet been realized but that appealed to the working class whites that both voted their race interests and ignored their class interests. He appealed to working class whites by indicating that the "elites" had forgotten about them, and he also bragged about paying little taxes, indicating that he "smartly" used the tax code that most others comply with. His refusal to release his tax returns is indicative of his contempt for those of us who file taxes on time, and pay on time. Yet a core 40 percent of voters support him because he has so skillfully spun "alternative facts" that they consider him a victim.

The genital-grabbing, bombastic, offensive, and inconsistent President has generated a barrage of headlines that, perhaps, obfuscate his true intentions. While he has played the buffoon in summarily firing an FBI director, spontaneously reaching out to foreign leaders, potentially colluding (or at least sharing information) with Russian nationals, too many have ignored the ways he has managed to use the tenets of predatory capitalism to reward those in his top one percent class, and to penalize those who are in the bottom 50 percent. Amidst the flurry of early executive orders, 45 managed, on his very first day in office, to sign an order to advance the repeal of the Affordable Care Act. Why was this a priority? 45 sent a signal – you poor people are going to be attacked.

Every executive order that 45 signed since his installation connects directly to a campaign promise. He said he would roll back President Obama's environmental initiatives, and he has. His "skinny budget", the budget draft released on March 13, 2017, vowed to cut the Environmental Protection Agency by 31.4 percent, eliminating at least 3200 jobs. As egregious as this action is, it is equally egregious that the skinny budget would cut the Department of Labor by 21 percent, and eliminate a series of worker-protecting oversights. Even as 45 courts global conflict with his irresponsible statements, the skinny budget also eliminates centers of global economic stabilization, by curtailing or eliminating the U.S. contribution to the African Development Bank, and other economic global engagement entities.

It is absolutely clear that 45 is doing what he promised to do – shrink government and limit regulation, mangle foreign policy, destroy federal educational systems and attack environmental protections. His attempt to roll back the initiatives of his predecessor is not unusual. The difference between Trump and Reagan, Big Bush and Shrub is that he has attacked the status quo with vigor, fashioning a message that appealed to the working class while developing public policy that clearly and singularly advantages the upper class. While Reagan, Bush 4x and Bush 4x fully embraced conservative principles, they also colored within the lines – acknowledging and attempting to work with political opponents, comporting themselves with civility, governing with (their version of) integrity. 45 has been unable to manage himself in a manner that befits a leader. Instead, even after "winning" the election, he has played the zero-sum game of winners and losers, of retrospective finger-pointing, of promulgating electoral lies, and of attacking both legal and undocumented immigrants. He is doing what he promised to do, and more than a third of our nation's voters support him for it.

Not a Humane Economy

The "skinny budget" that was released on March 2017 (a more comprehensive budget is scheduled to be released in late May) illustrated the callous nature of 45's economic principles. Developed by the Office of Management and Budget (OMB), headed by Mick Mulvaney, the budget cuts almost every government department, except for Defense and Homeland Security. Table One shows. the detail of these budget cuts by department, and makes it clear that those departments that serve people are those that will be hardest hit.

TABLE 1. AMERICA FIRST BUDGET SUMMARY

Department	Percent Change	Dollar Change
Agriculture	-21	-4.7
Commerce	-16	-1.5
Defense	10	52
Education	-13	-9
Energy	-6.6	-28
HHS	-17.9	-15.1
Homeland Security	6.8	2.8
HUD	-13.2	-6.2
Interior	-13.6	-1.6
Justice	-3.8	-1.1
Labor	-21	-1.5
State/USAID	-28	-10.1
Treasure Int'l Program	-35	-0.8
Transportation	-13	-2.4
Treasury	-4.1	-0.5
Veterans	6	4.4
EPA	-31	-2.6
NASA	-0.08	
SBA	-5	0.43

The devil, however, is in the details that are gleaned through understanding the philosophy that 45 and OMB Director Mulvaney bring to the process. Not only would they cut the Department of Labor by 21 percent, but they would particularly cut those regulatory aspects of the department that provided protections to workers. Thus, the Occupational Safety and Health Administration would have a more limited reach, and companies that had violated safety requirements in the past would be allowed to bid on federal contracts in the future, whether or not they had corrected their errors. Workers, the very people that 45 appealed to, are worse off because of the 45 budget.

Not only is the education budget significantly cut, but too many dollars are spent focusing on charter schools. This is not surprising. Education Secretary Betsey DeVos ("DeVoid") is only connected to the education enterprise because of her advocacy for charter schools. She is ignorant about K-12 public education, ignorant about higher education, so myopic that she thinks that she thinks that HBCUs are models of "choice", and ignorant of the importance of Pell grants for student achievement. While 45 has staged a photo-op with those HBCU Presidents who allowed themselves to be used, he and his team also quietly undermined HBCU funding.

The increase in the DOJ budget is troubling. Attorney General Jeff Sessions wants to continue to attack Black and Brown men by continuing to impose the mandatory sentencing that President Obama attempted to roll back. While there is no money to feed people, apparently, there is ample money to jail them. Sessions has embraced the reactionary "law and order" stance that allows judges very little discretion and disproportionately incarcerates Black and Brown men.

Compassionate Capitalism and Predatory Capitalism

A focus on the DOJ and the regenerate Attorney General allows us to "follow the money" and to understand that predatory capitalism is about the exploitation of people at the bottom, no matter where they are. Our capitalistic system is hard-wired into the "American Dream", but there have been times when this system has, at least, responded to the needs of working people. Predatory capitalism is a capitalism that has no response to human needs because its goal is to extract every penny of surplus value from people.

Capitalism is a system of profit maximization. It is a system that says that capital should be paid as much as it can be paid and that other factors of production, especially labor, should be paid as little as can be paid. Profit maximization means expense minimization. Thus, when someone says they will take the lowest bid on a job, they are indicating that they will accept the fact that someone will pay their workers as little as they can. Compassionate capitalists will require that the lowest bid might also include a minimum wage. In his 2016 executive order, as an example, President Obama required federal contractors to provide sick days and also a minimum wage of $10.10, which was higher than the federal minimum wage.

The nature of capitalism is to be exploitive. But when capitalist and government collude, it is possible to maximize the extent of exploitation. Compassionate capitalism, while preserving some aspects of exploitation, often offer relief in the form of responsive regulation. Predatory capitalism offers no relief and indeed, allows corporations to exploit in the name of a "free market".

If capitalism is a profit-maximizing wolf, then government involvement is the dentist. With compassionate capitalism, the wolf's teeth are filed down, and damage to workers, while significant, is minimized. With predatory capitalism, the wolf's teeth are sharpened, and those at the bottom are losers.

If there is fairness in economic cycles, they should be neutral. In other words, people who lose during economic contraction will proportionately gain during economic recovery. Economic structure may work against this. Between recession and recovery, laws may change to advantage, for example, those at the top. Their political influence is such that they have the opportunity to advocate for their economic well-being. No one advocates for those at the bottom, for the African American, the poor, those who are the least and the left out (and this group, by any calculation, is not the bottom 60 percent of the population – more than half!). It is useful then, to consider Table Two (below) and the ways the benefits of economic oscillations have shifted in the last ten years.

TABLE 2. DIVISION OF WEALTH ACCUMULATION DURING ECONOMIC EXPANSIONS
(approximate)

YEAR	BOTTOM 90%	TOP 10%
1949-1951	80	20
1954-1957	75	25
1958-1960	65	35
1961-1969	62	38
1970-1973	58	42
1975-1979	56	44
1982-1990	20	80
1991-2000	25	75
2001-2007	2	98
2009-2012	-15	115

In the recovery that followed the recession of 1970, the bottom 90 percent gained 58 percent of the benefit of recovery. The gain was not a fair share, but it was a gain far more significant than the result of the recovery from the 2008 recession. Then, the bottom 90 percent lost 15 percent even as the economy recovered. The top 90 percent, gained 115 percent, which meant that they were not only made whole, but also benefited from some of the structural changes. Those changes that disadvantaged people on the bottom, did not realize. While Secretary of State and candidate Hillary Rodham Clinton was far from a perfect candidate, her brand of capitalism would have been compassionate capitalism. Her history suggests that she would have favored workers, unions, women, and children. Her economic plan would have protected the environment, provided affordable health care, and supported education. In contrast, 45's brand of capitalism is unfettered predatory capitalism. His intent is to extract every penny of surplus value from those at the bottom and redistribute it to those at the top.

Follow the Money

Many of 45's foci seem to be philosophically grounded. His focus on small government and tax reduction are consistent with his campaign. However, it is important, especially when criminal justice matters are considered, to "follow the money." Who benefits from mass incarceration? A number of corporations, especially those who run private prisons, see people as a simple profit center. While progressive legislator of both parties understand how financially debilitating it is for our nation to incarcerate people at a cost of up to $50,000 per year, it is important to note that someone is benefitting from the cost of incarceration. There has been abundant research about the human rights abuses in prisons, especially private prisons, where people are poorly fed, inadequately housed (with overcrowded cells), ineptly rehabilitated, and never engaged. Of itself, this is a tragedy. That publicly traded stock increase in values when exploitation takes place is a crime.

We must also follow the money when we look at labor regulations, and at who benefits when these regulations are relaxed. We must follow the money when we look at the focus on charter schools, and at the companies whose profits depend on public school expansion. When environmental regulations are weakened, who gains by being able to pollute? When we follow the money see the manifestation of the triumph of predatory capitalism.

It is beyond the scope of this essay to deal with the many ways our health care system has been manipulated for predatory gain. The

Obama-initiated Affordable Care Act (ACA), while imperfect, expanded health care coverage for more than 20 million people, including at least three million African Americans. The Republican-proposed Affordable Health Care Act eliminates many of the beneficial provisions of ACA. Health care would not be on the chopping block but for the fact that it has been described as "Obamacare". Anything Obama, no matter how beneficial, must, of course, be eliminated. 45 has injected a special venom into anything Obama, even as he acknowledges the importance of covering pre-existing conditions and of including young adults on their parents' health care plan. The Republican manipulations around health care are most likely to increase the predatory profits of insurance companies. They surely don't benefit the people.

Following the money leads us to offensive conclusions for the majority of Americans, but those who have blind loyalty to 45 do not care where the money trail leads. They have observed and experienced the ways that predatory capitalism will benefit 45 and his family, and also experienced the ways that the 45 economic plan will disadvantage everyone else. The 45 administration represents a clear paradigm shift from compassionate capitalism (in various degrees) to unfettered predatory capitalism. Following the money reveals the triumph of profits from private prisons, profits from charter schools, and profits that flow from the bottom to the top. Following the money reminds us of a candidate who bragged that he was smart not to pay taxes, sage not to pay vendors, wise to stiff small contractors, and brilliant to make foreign liaisons that may not have been in the best interest of our nation. 45 has not done everything he said he would do, and we are foolish if we expected anything else.

Resistance

If 45 is not our president, then what is he? Those of us who reject his leadership must be clear that he is an aberration, an abomination, an affront to social, political, and economic decency. How do we consistently resist the ways he has enjoyed the triumph of predatory capitalism? First of all, it is important that those who are "woke" eschew all things "Trump", including clothing brands, golf courses, hotels and restaurants, and any-thing else that carries the odious 45 name. If enough people are willing to boycott the 45 brand, it hits the predatory capitalist and his family where they live. If their joy comes with their profits, then we who would steal their joy will minimize their profits.

We can also engage in secondary actions by informing those who carry, for example, Ivanka Trump products, that we will avoid their stores because of the ways they have bought into the Trump version of predatory capitalism. We can engage in social media campaigns to remind people that the President's daughter has been a beneficiary of insider deal-ing. One day she sits next to a Chinese leader. The next day she is granted exclusive rights to trade in her goods. Fair? Hardly. Make it plain.

Raking in profits combines predatory capitalism with racist op-pression. How do we combat that? We can ask pension funds and others to withdraw their investments from private prisons. Union members can be especially effective in insisting that those who invest their funds avoid these instruments. We must also advocate at the federal, state, and local level, to eliminate involvement with private prisons. There are progressive legislators who will carry this message forward if they believe that they have popular support.

Resistance to the reign of 45, but also a resistance to the predatory capitalism that has allowed profits to flow from the bottom to the top. This is a resistance that rejects an economy that penalizes people because they are poor, because they are workers, because they do not hold stock or play the market. Resistance must take us past the concept of compas-sionate capitalism, to a concept of shared prosperity.

45 is not my president, and this is not my economy. An economic paradigm that deals with shared prosperity is an economy that can be embraced. Resisting 45 is the first step toward embracing the ethic of sharing.

CHARLES L. BLOCKSON: BIBLIOPHILE, HISTORIAN, AND COLLECTOR

DIANE D. TURNER

*Diane D. Turner is curator of Temple University's Charles L. Blockson Afro-American Collection, one of the nation's foremost collections of African-American prints, photographs, slave narratives, manuscripts, letters and other materials. She is the author of **My Name is Oney Judge** (2010), her first children's book, and **Feeding the Soul: Black Music, Black Thought** (2011).*

"For we wrestle not against flesh and blood, but against principalities, against powers, against the rulers of the darkness of this world, against spiritual wickedness in high places.

Wherefore take unto you the whole armour of God, that ye may be able to withstand in the evil day, and having done all, to stand."

— (1 Eph. 6:12-13 King James Version)

An important question to address during the 45th presidency of Donald J. Trump is "How do we overcome evil with good?" In these times, where spiritual wickedness translates into greed and the worship of money at the expense of our poor and our working and middle-classes as well as our children, it is our charge is to stand, for righteousness, truth, charity and love. How did our ancestors do this? The answers are available in the Charles L. Blockson Afro-American Collection, Temple University Libraries. Charles L. Blockson, a righteous warrior, has spent his life fighting and agitating against white supremacy and the structural racism developed to support its devastating myths of Black inferiority, Black criminality, Black inhumanity, etc. which are perpetuated by thousands of stereotypes that African Americans have been assaulted with from their inception on these shores.

During these dangerous times of Donald Trump, his white nationalist friends and billionaire colleagues, it is essential to have knowledge of African American history and culture and the African Diaspora. Why? So we are able to determine truth from lies and ensure that our dollars support our poor and our working and middle-classes as well as our youth. Because Charles L. Blockson amassed a Special Collection on African American History and culture and the Africa Diaspora available to students, scholars, researchers and the community as well as cultural and political activist which is free and open to the public, we must place priority on the value of Black experiences and demand that these narratives are incorporated into the national narrative and preserved.

Learning about, understanding and appreciating the history of African peoples is easily accessible because of Mr. Blockson's commitment to collect, preserve and disseminate the Black experience in all its complexities. One can discover role models to emulate and paradigms to develop and expand upon. One can learn that in these United States of America, African peoples have more history in slavery than in freedom. That from the fourteenth century, there were enslaved Africans in Spanish Florida and by 1619, enslaved Africans were brought by the British and resided in Jamestown, Virginia. Thus, Americans of African descent are among the earliest Americans. One can read Michelle Alexander's *The New Jim Crow* and/or view filmmaker Ava DuVernay's 13th which highlights the fact that the Thirteenth Amendment in 1865 did not end slavery but ushered in what has developed into what Angela Davis warned us about for years: the prison industrial complex.

The Charles L. Blockson Afro-American Collection is a significant repository to visit and to support. We must invest our dollars in places like the Blockson Collection and Third World Press Foundation. We have power to do that. We can overcome evil with good through investing in Black institutions, organizations, and businesses and knowing our history. In speaking with Mr. Blockson he constantly encourages us to know our history, never give up and agitate, agitate, agitate. In the following paper, I will highlight aspects of Charles L. Blockson's life that speak to his commitment and dedication and conclude with a recent interview with him. His life provides a model for us to emulate.

> *"I want to eliminate ignorance, which is another—and in many ways a much worse—form of slavery than physical bondage. In today's world, the lack of understanding breeds fear, suspicion, hatred, insecurity, and inferiority—all avoidable evils."*

— **Charles L. Blockson**

* * *

Charles L. Blockson: A Biographical Sketch

For those who have met Charles L. Blockson and/or are knowledgeable about his contributions to African American history and culture and the African Diaspora, he is recognized as a national treasure. He has inspired scores of Black writers, including myself. During April 2017, his lifelong contributions were acknowledged in the city of Philadelphia when it was announced that he is the 2016 recipient of The Philadelphia Award. The award is "among the most cherished, meaningful and prestigious awards" founded by Edward W. Bok in 1921. Every year, a citizen from the Philadelphia region is conferred with the award for outstanding service for advancing "the best and largest interest of the community." Mr. Blockson has spent his career doing what he loves collecting, preserving, documenting and disseminating African American history and culture and the African Diaspora. In the process, thousands of students, faculty, scholars, researchers, the general public and African American communities have learned about the Black experience. However it has not been easy for him. He experienced racism, opposition and numerous obstacles resulting in many battles and struggles as an advocate for the inclusion of the Black experience in the national narrative. His battles were not in vain: they resulted in him becoming a co-founder of the African American Museum in Philadelphia; founding member of the Pennsylvania Black History Committee of the Pennsylvania Historical and Museum Commission; past president of the Pennsylvania Abolition Society; chairman of the National Park Service Underground Railroad Advisory Committee; and director of the Philadelphia African American Pennsylvania State Historical Marker Project (the largest African American marker program in the U.S.).

Blockson is passionate about his life's work. He does not tolerate insincerity nor people who exploit others. He always acknowledges those who paved the way for him, especially his African American ancestors such as Olaudah Equiano, Phillis Wheatley, Harriet Tubman, Paul Cuffee, Nat Turner, Frederick Douglass, Frances Ellen Watkins Harper, William Still, Mary Ann Shadd Carey, Samuel Fraunces, Oney Judge, Carter Godwin Woodson, Paul Laurence Dunbar, W.E.B. DuBois, Paul Robeson and his wife Eslanda Goode Robeson, Gordon Parks and the lineage of prominent as well as little known people of African descent.

Charles Leroy Blockson was born on December 16, 1933. He writes in his memoir *Damn Rare: The Memoirs of An African-American Bibliophile* (1998) that *"according to the lore of the Zodiac, I am a searcher, a seeker of the truth, and a lover of humanity."* These qualities have guided his life. Born to Charles Edward (1915-) and Annie (1914-1987) Blockson and raised in Norristown, PA, he is the oldest of eight children. In 1958, he married Elizabeth Parker. From their union, he has one daughter, Noelle Parker Blockson.

Educated in the Norristown Area School District, Blockson excelled in athletics including football and track and field. He was a star athlete at the Norristown High School and Penn State University. He won state and national honors and participated in the Penn Relays held in Philadelphia, Pennsylvania. His roommate at Penn State University was Rosie Greer. While in high school and college, Blockson would go to bookstores when traveling to participate in sports events. He especially liked to visit the bookstores in Harlem and Greenwich Village while in New York City. Blockson's love for books was influenced by his father who inherited his love of old books and antiques from his mother. Through his father's library, Blockson was introduced to Richard Wright's *Native Son* (1940) and *Black Boy* (1945), Chester Himes' *If He Hollers Let Him Go* (1945), Ann Petry's *The Street* (1946) and other Black authors. Other early reading included black newspapers such as *The Philadelphia Tribune, The Baltimore Afro-American, New York Amsterdam News*, and *The Chicago Defender,* as well as *The Crisis, Negro Digest*, and *Ebony*.

Blockson began collecting at age nine while in the fourth grade. During a history lesson, his White female teacher claimed that Negroes had no history. Her false statement, which reflected a majority of White thinking during that time, commenced his odyssey to unearth, collect, and preserve the history, culture and contributions of Blacks. He began collecting books, pamphlets, photographs, records, postcards, etc. with the subjects of colored, Negro, Black, Afro-American, Afro-Cuban, Haitian, Afro-Brazilian, Ethiopian, Jamaican, Egyptian, Nigerian, etc.

Book-collecting excursions led Blockson to the Salvation Army, antique shops, church bazaars and Philadelphia where he discovered many bookstores. His favorite bookstore was Leary's at 9th and Market Streets where he purchased in the hurt book bin a first edition of William Still's *The Underground Railroad* for $1.00. Blockson became well-known among book and artifact dealers, and his passion for collecting has taken him around the world, inspired him to write books such as *Black Genealogy* (1977), made him one of the foremost experts on the Underground Railroad and put him in the company of leading African American figures like Paul Robeson, Marian Anderson and Rosa Parks.

Today, Blockson has two significant collections related to the study of Africana American history and culture at the Charles L. Blockson Collection of African-Americana and the African Diaspora at the Pennsylvania State University and the Charles L. Blockson Afro-American Collection at Temple University in Philadelphia, Pennsylvania. In 1984, the noted bibliophile and author donated his extraordinary collection to Temple University because the university aggressively attracts a wide ethnic, cultural and racial diversity student body and is situated in the heart of an African American community. He was adamant that the community have access to his collection. The Charles L. Blockson Afro-American Collection now contains more than 500,000 books, documents, and photographs, and is a research center for scholars around the world.

Blockson recently donated Harriet Tubman's signed hymnal and other personal items to the National Museum of African American History and Culture (NAAMHC) at the Smithsonian Institution. Blockson said that when he inherited Harriet Tubman's 39 personal items from Meriline Wilkins, including the shawl that Queen Victoria presented to her, it was the crowning point of his life as a collector. After eight months of housing the items in his bedroom, he decided to donate the items to NAAMHC. When he contacted President and CEO Lonnie Bunch about the Tubman items, Dr. Bunch and several of his curators visited the Blockson Collection in Philadelphia. On March 10, 2010 the following appeared in Newsdesk from the newsroom of the Smithsonian:

"There is something both humbling and sacred found in the personal items of such an iconic person," said Lonnie Bunch, director of NMAAHC. "It is an honor to be able to show the private side of a very public person, a woman whose very work for many years put her in service to countless others. This donation by Charles Blockson is a selfless gesture that ensures that her story will be enshrined forever within the Smithsonian Institution."

The Blockson donation of Tubman items has become a popular attraction at the NAAMHC in Washington, DC.

Among Mr. Blockson's proudest moments was the unveiling a State Historical Marker commemorating The Pennsylvania Slave Trade on August 5, 2016 in partnership with the Independence Seaport Museum. Mr. Blockson researched and submitted an application for the State Historical Marker, approved by the Pennsylvania Historical and Museum Commission and was paid for by him in the amount of $1,625.00. The state historical marker installed near the Independence Seaport Museum on the Delaware River reads:

> *African people, first enslaved by the Dutch and Swedes, survived the brutal voyage from Africa to the Caribbean Islands and the Americas, debarking on the Delaware River waterfront as early as 1639. William Penn, other Quakers, and Philadelphia merchants purchased and enslaved Africans. As the institution of slavery increased, these courageous people persevered and performed integral roles in building Pennsylvania and the nation.*

Blockson is the recipient of numerous awards and honors. He received the Distinguished Alumni Award from Penn State University, and has three honorary doctorate degrees from Lincoln University, Holy Family University and Villanova University. In addition, he served as advisor to the Philadelphia Constitution Center; a member of the Norristown Area School District's Hall of Fame and Hall of Champions; and is instrumental in establishing, along with the Valley Forge Alumni Chapter of Delta Sigma Theta Sorority, the memorial at Valley Forge that honors Revolutionary War soldiers of African descent. He is listed in the *Who's Who in Black America* and is featured, along with his mentor, Arthur Schomburg in the book, *A Gentle Madness: Bibliophiles, Bibliomanes and Eternal Passion for Books* by Nicholas A. Basbanes.

Blockson has lectured across the globe including the Sorbonne in Paris, France (one of his favorite cities) in 1991 at the African Americans in Europe Conference; in the African countries Egypt and Senegal; and in Sweden, Iceland and Denmark with the U.S. Department of the Interior on the subject of the Underground Railroad.

Blockson is the author of 13 books including *Black Genealogy*, *Damn Rare: The Memoirs of an African American Bibliophile*, and *The President's House Revisited Behind the Scenes: The Samuel Fraunces Story*. He has written numerous magazine articles. In 1984, the article he wrote for *National Geographic*, "Escape from Slavery: Underground Railroad," was the first cover story pertaining to African American people, and is one of the most popular stories in the history of the *National Geographic* magazine. As a result, the U.S. State Department commissioned him to lecture on the subject in the Caribbean Islands and South America.

* * *

Interview with Dr. Blockson

Dr. Blockson is Curator Emeritus of the Charles L. Blockson Afro-American Collection, and resides in Gwynedd, Montgomery County, Pennsylvania. I had the pleasure to interview him for this paper as follows:

Diane Turner (DT): Mr. Blockson can you talk about how you became a bibliophile, historian and collector of African and African American history and culture?

Charles Blockson (CLB): My collection goes back to the time when I first started out in the fourth grade when I asked my teacher, "Did Negroes or colored people as we were called then, have a history?" She said, "No, Charles, Negroes were born to serve white people." So from there, I went to the Salvation Army, bookstores, and later discovered, through the help of my parents, it was something to be proud of our history, and we did have a history. And, it was while I was sitting down next to my grandfather, who sang spirituals, coded spirituals about the Underground Railroad. As the years went by, I learned that several members of our family escaped from Southern Delaware, Sussex County through Philadelphia to Canada. So our history was involved with the Underground Railroad. And later, whenever I went to bookstores in Philadelphia; wherever I travelled as an athlete at Penn State, playing football and running track. I went to bookstores all over the country, later into Europe, parts of Africa, South America, and the Caribbean. Wherever I went I started collecting.

DT: Based on the stories that your grandfather shared with you about your history, do you believe that African Americans have a responsibility to tell their own stories? And, if so, why?

CLB: It's important. At an early age my grandfather, my mother's father, they had records of my hero, a lifetime hero, Paul Robeson. He would record, in many of his songs and in his spirituals, his music and folk songs, he sang about our people. Roland Hayes is another great African American Tenor, and let me not forget to mention Marian Anderson, who sang. We had her records. Years later, I would meet Paul Robeson, Marian Anderson, and later Rosa Parks. My book collecting excursions, from an early age, as I said, took me all over. Not only did I collect books, I collected pamphlets, photographs, sheet music, whatever. Later I got into collecting African artifacts.

DT: When did you realize that collecting would be a lifelong pursuit?

CLB: At first, I didn't realize, I just followed my instinct. It was the divine providence that led me to collecting. Each of my books, pamphlets, sheet music, have their own story, not about me so much but about the individual, or individuals, who are in, who are recognized in the photographs, books, and so forth. I learned a lot about our history in different languages, cultures, culture in Haiti, culture in Timbuktu, culture in the Caribbean. It became a part of the African diaspora, which I collected.

DT: What motivated you to continue to collect?

CLB: Well Since I'm 83 now, I was born under the star, the searching star, of Sagittarius. I'm a searcher. And, as long as you're involved with books, you never grow old. There's always something new to learn. And, as I said, I tell people all the time, I'm only a conduit connecting the past, present, and the future together. And when my time comes to pass on someone else will pick it up. It is important that we know our history.

DT: Why did you select Temple University as the place to house your collection?

CLB: The Philadelphia area is where I have lived most of my life. It is the location that I know best and that knows me best. It seemed the logical site for a major repository on African people. Temple University first expressed an interest in purchasing my collection in 1973 and asked for an opportunity to view it. Included in the group who visited my home was Dr. Lawrence D. Reddick, then professor of History at Temple. Dr. Reddick later talked to me about that day and his own frustrations with Temple at that time. He said, "Would you believe it? A university library that boasts of one million volumes does not have one third of the books that are needed for Afro-American Studies." When Temple made its offer to buy the collection, I declined. Years later, I made up my mind to donate my collection to an institution, under the condition that I serve as curator. I resisted all attempts by various individuals and institutions to purchase any of my collected items individually or in small lots. To break up my collection was out of the question considering the lifelong labor of love and pain that had gone into assembling it. My collection was assembled with a view toward showing the strength and stability of the African Diaspora, particularly in the United States. The strength of the collection lies in its comprehensiveness and I expected to continue to add to it after making the donation. Hence, another condition of donation was that the institution had to provide a budget for a constant stream of additional purchases. By 1982, I had decided to donate the collection of over 20,000 books and documents to Temple University. At the time, Temple Black scholars included Sonia Sanchez, David Bradley, Dr. Harry Bailey and Dr. Wilber Roget. Dr. Jessie Carney Smith, the Chief Librarian at Fisk University was chosen to conduct an appraisal of my collection. She estimated a value between $500,000-550,000. The collection is presently worth much more. The Blockson Collection played a significant role in the establishment of the Ph.D. program in African American Studies at Temple University, which is the first in the United States, chaired under Dr. Molefi Kete Asante.

DT: What are some of the most rewarding highlights or memories related to your collecting?

CLB: I have so many. It's like I said: meeting Paul Robeson, meeting Rosa Parks, and other spirits. Connected recently with the new African American History Museum in Washington DC, I was willed, by divine providence, through the grandniece of Harriet Tubman, Ms. Meriline Wilkins, 39 items that belonged to the great freedom fighter Harriet Tubman, leader of the Underground Railroad. I donated the 39 items to the Museum in Washington D.C., the Smithsonian, among the items were the hymn books that she used to sing songs from and the shawl that Queen Victoria presented to her. So, you never know where it's going to take you. It led me also to have my portrait painted four or five times. A sculptor, Antonio Salemme, who did a sculpture of Paul Robeson back in 1925, he did a statue of him as well as a bust, he asked me to pose for him. He did a bust of me, earlier he did a bust of Ike Eisenhower and Ethyl Waters back in the 20s. He said, "Charles, Paul Robeson was the first Negro, black man, I ever did a bust of, and you're the last." He was 98 years old when he did my bust. It was made a part of the collection at Temple.

DT: Mr. Blockson you're always emphasizing African Americans telling their own story. Can you tell me why? Why is it important that we tell our own stories?

CLB: The hand that holds the pen, quill, or pencil controls history. So it's good to control history. So much of our history has been lost, stolen, or strayed. It's been years and years. It was a blessing when Roots came, back in 1977, when Alex Haley published Roots, stimulating interest in African American genealogy. All the time that Alex Haley was writing roots, I was writing my own Genealogy, discovering my African connection with the Igbo of Nigeria and the Native American portion. So, if this truth is prevalent today, it would be a better message of collecting today. People have different avenues to go through but telling your own story is very important. It makes you proud. It also makes you preserve your family history. Telling our stories is not only necessary but also empowering.

DT: What message do you have for the youth?

CLB: Have a curiosity of who you are what you are. Even if you're by yourself. If you believe in becoming a person, find out who you. It'll be your parents or your guardians, some people aren't fortunate enough to have parents, they're adopted or whatever, whoever raised you, record their history, go out and search, do your own, write, search, write, and tell the story through songs, words, poetry, whatever.

DT: I have one last question for you. In the current climate of our society, why is the Charles L. Blockson Afro-American Collection relevant?

CLB: As I said earlier, not to be redundant, it doesn't belong to me; I'm only a conduit. They have you there as the Curator now. And when you'll be going you'll pass it on to others. Someone should always be out there to pick up the baton and lead it on to another generation. It is important to know your history. As our ancestors were interned in the holds of the slave ship, the world thought of them as the "last" of the human race, those upon whom fate and fortune had not smiled. Still, bit by bit they retained their dignity, preserved their history, and passed it on for generations yet unborn but always foretold.

DT: Is there anything else you would like to add?

CLB: A bibliophile never knows whom his or her collection will influence. For me, the glow in the eyes of people who have come to the Collection is a reward beyond measure. As a bibliophile, I discovered many years ago that nothing is more important or difficult than trying to make readers, young and old, feel the past as a vivid reality. I firmly believed that our history was not the history of individuals, but rather a collective endeavor. Every generation reflects on what has come before them. Such is the nature of historical memory. The past is always author to the present, for the simple reason that people look backwards in order to better understand the present. Our ancestors arose through the struggle for freedom and dignity, and participated in every fight where individuals struggled against individuals to be free. Peace and freedom, always, to those preserving the history. Make sure you pass it on.

DT: Any thoughts about Donald Trump?

CLB: He reminds me of Hitler. He's demonic. Who could read the mind of Donald Trump? He a schemer. He represents ignorance. When I started the Blockson Collection I wanted to eliminate ignorance. He is the antithesis of what my Collection stands for. The collection represents freedom.

DT: Thank you.

'AMERICA NEEDS YOU'

ELIZABETH WARREN

Elizabeth Warren (D) is a U.S. Senator for Massachusetts. The following is a transcript of her keynote address at the Undergraduate Commencement of the University of Massachusetts Amherst on Friday, May 12, 2017.

Good afternoon and thank you to Chancellor Subbaswamy and to the Board of Trustees for inviting me to be here with you today.

I always love visiting this campus and seeing the great work being done by students and faculty. I also have a lot of UMass Amherst grads on my staff, so I get to see first-hand exactly how terrific a UMass Amherst education really is. You are turning out a lot of smart people! I know. I hire them!

It's also great to see State Senate President Stan Rosenberg and your state legislative delegation here. What a great team you have working for Western and Central Massachusetts.

I was a law professor for many years, so this is not my first commencement speech. But if I go longer than 20 minutes I know it will be my last. I understand that every extra minute I speak is that much longer before you can hit the bars.

Not that some of us need to hit the bars, of course. Imagine my surprise last week when I got my daily news roundup and right there, the front and center headline was: "Elizabeth Warren's Commencement Speech Drinking Game." I have to say, the timing was perfect. I was suffering from some writer's *block and the drinking game got me going.*

The downside, of course, is that I now know what you're hiding under those robes. So, let's get it out there right from the beginning. If you learn nothing else from this speech, know this: Fireball is a nickname that Donald Trump uses on Twitter, not a beverage to be consumed by distinguished college graduates.

Alright. So let's get to the commencement part of this. First, to the graduates: You worked hard, and we're here to celebrate your success. Congratulations to all of you! Way to go!

And to all of the parents and the grandparents, the family and friends, the teachers and advisors: You helped make this day possible. So congratulations to you as well. Congratulations to all of you!

Graduates, this is a day for celebration. You've earned it. But I know that this is also a day that is tinged with sadness. You've gone to your last party in Southwest. You've had your late-night slice at Antonio's. So a truly existential question bears down upon you: Will you ever feel joy again?

So what does come next? Some of you may be worried that you haven't gotten it all figured out. Believe me, I get it. My own path had plenty of twists and turns. Heck, I dropped out of college, got married at 19 to the first boy I ever dated – so a lot of you are already doing better than I did.

But I'm here today to make a pitch for the work that you do going forward. I'm here to ask you to get more involved in our democracy.

Some of you are already headed into public service. I'm looking out at future teachers and firefighters, nurses and social workers. Some of you will work directly in government, some will work in non-profits. And, of course, many of you will work for small businesses. Many of you will start your own businesses. Many of you will join big corporations. But my pitch is for something different—it's to get more directly involved in the democracy of policy.

Policies matter enormously and I'm just going to give you one small reminder – and yes, this one counts for a small nip of Smirnoff. Anyone here have a student loan? I know, that's like asking does anyone here wear a funny hat. The interest rate on your public loans was set by your elected officials. And your tuition and fees—and how much you needed to borrow to make it to this day—were heavily influenced by the funding your University received from the Commonwealth and from the federal government – funding that is set by your elected officials. As a practical matter, how much you owe, and who has access to the kind of first-rate education you have received here, is set in part by a handful of people who, in a democracy, are supposed to answer directly to you.

It's easy to say, "I don't like politics" or "I don't like any political party." I get it. I never even considered running for student government when I was your age, and I already had grandchildren by the time I ran my first Senate campaign. And believe me: there are days when I leave work so frustrated that I want to spit. But the decisions that get made by your government are important and far reaching. And it is no longer possible to assume that democracy will work if most Americans simply wait until election time to learn a little about the candidates and otherwise ignore what's going on.

I am not here to make a pitch just to Democrats—or to Republicans. Yes, I'm a Democrat. I am a proud Democrat. But my point applies to Ds and Rs—and to independents, and to libertarians, and to vegetarians...and to Big Mac-atarians. The point I want to make is a point about democracy.

Our country – our democracy – is not a machine that will run on its own. It needs you out there fighting for what you believe in. And here's why: If elected officials don't hear from people like you, then the policies will be set by the people they do hear from. And, believe me, they hear plenty from corporate CEOs, from Wall Street, from giant corporations and from others who spend buckets of money to make sure that their interests are heard. And here's the thing, your elected officials are increasingly working only for the few, the very wealthy few, and they are setting policies only to benefit the few, the very wealthy few. And if that doesn't change soon, then this country will fundamentally change. It is your world, your future, that is on the line.

So I am here today to ask you to get engaged. Not engaged like I did back at 19 -- but engaged with some issues. And the kind of issues I'm talking about are policy issues. I know that some of you are already deeply committed to fights that matter to you. And I want to say thank you for that. So my message to you is, please don't quit after you leave school. We need you. But I'm also here to try to expand the circle, to ask more of you—to ask all of you—to expand your post-graduation to-do list to include engagement and advocacy for an issue that you really care about. And I want to give three very serious suggestions for how you might do it.

The first, is start with something that's at the core of who you are. It's a lot easier to engage on an issue if you take the time to think through who you are – if you know what you believe in and if you are willing to fight for it.

Figuring out who you are is not as easy as it sounds. I think Conor was right on this. No one can do it for you. The list of possible issues that move you is long:

- *You can with the cost of college*
- *Free speech*
- *Animal rescue*
- *Nuclear weapons*
- *Access to voting*
- *Free flights to Hawaii. (I put that in to make see if you're still listening. OK back to the real list.)*
- *Criminal justice reform*
- *Military veterans*
- *Clean water*
- *National Parks*
- *Homelessness*
- *Hunger*
- *Bullying*
- *Prenatal care*

And I'm trying to keep this apolitical, but I can't help myself and I have one more – the principle that no one, no one, in this country is above the law. We need a Justice Department, not an Obstruction of Justice Department.

But regardless of who you are politically or who you vote for, you have to think hard about what really matters to you—not to your mom and dad, or to your girlfriend or to your dog— although your dog may have a strong opinion on this. And don't just pick whatever cause that Emma Watson or Taylor Swift are supporting this week – no matter how much you want to be in their squad. No, you've got to figure out what makes your heart flutter and your stomach clench. What makes wake up ready to go and what makes you wish you didn't have to move. (And, no, I'm still not talking about Emma Watson and Taylor Swift.) You are a lot more likely to follow through if you really, deep-down care about an issue. So that's my first.

Second, do a little studying. I know I just made myself the least popular graduation speaker anywhere in America by telling graduates who have just finished your last assignment from your professors and turned in your last research paper, to study a little more, but I'm not trying to win Miss Popularity. I think so long as Mitch McConnell is running the Senate, that's out of reach for me. So I'll say it: study up because knowing something about an issue makes a difference. So go online and read the facts. Not the alternative facts, the real facts. I have to say, I never thought we would need a modifier for "facts" – like how do you distinguish them now: facty facts, or the factiest facts? But you've got to get to the facts.

Third, join with others. Find a group that is engaged on the issues that you care about. A group makes a difference. More good ideas. More information. More ways to get your voice heard. One voice is powerful, but two voices are more than twice as powerful, and ten or ten thousand voices create a force to be reckoned with. It's not as easy to join a group when there aren't weekly club meetings and a table at the campus center concourse. You have to try. Really try. But please do it.

Because America needs you.

Each generation must rebuild democracy to serve its own time and its own needs. The World War II generation faced challenges that were different from those of the Vietnam era generation—and each shaped and rebuilt democracy differently. Your generation faces huge challenges—sharp differences that divide this nation along deep fracture lines, intergenerational challenges that have saddled young people in this country with an unprecedented $1.4 trillion in student loan debt, an economy that is producing great wealth for the top ten percent and locking everyone else out.

If democracy for you simply means leaving it to others, letting others set the terms of the political debate, and surrendering the policy decisions to people faraway in Washington, then our country will work better and better for a smaller and smaller number of people. But if democracy for you means connecting up, studying, making hard decisions and defending them with intelligence and commitment, then this country will flourish.

America needs your commitment, and, here's the thing, you need the commitment. Advocacy— getting involved in issues you care about and fighting for them—can reshape our country, and I guarantee it will reshape you. No matter what other work you do every day, if you find the issues that matter to you and you get in the fight, you will build a life with more heart flutters and fewer "don't make me move" moments. You will build a life that is deeply worthwhile. Take it from me, someone who wakes up every day energized and ready to jump in! Except the morning after I played the Elizabeth Warren drinking game.

Class of 2017, you've built the right foundation for your success with a UMass Amherst education. I believe you can make great things happen. For our country, and for yourselves.

Go UMass.

THE TRUMP DOCTRINE: THE LOSS OF POLITICAL CIVILITY AND PROTECTIONS FOR THE POOR

TED WILLIAMS, III

Ted Williams III is a Political Science professor and current chair of the Social Science Department at Kennedy-King College. He is the former host of WYCC–PBS television's The Professors weekly talk show, has provided political commentary for various news outlets periodicals. He is an accomplished speaker and actor who has appeared in commercials and training videos for Fortune 500 companies.

The election of Donald Trump has taken America into unchartered territory. Of course, the nation has been led by the unapologetically elite and discriminatory before now. In fact, the history of the US is a history of the bourgeoisie abusing power for the purposes of exploiting the weak. Trump's classism, disregard for the marginalized, and xenophobic vision of the US are nothing new. In 1923 President Coolidge restricted immigration from various parts of the world under the pledge that "America must be kept American". President Woodrow Wilson ordered the re-segregation of the federal government and publicly praised the Ku Klux Klan. Andrew Jackson forcibly removed 20,000 Native Americans from their land by gunpoint. These are but a few examples of the use of the American presidency to support an exclusive vision of the American dream. There are two things that make Trump's ascension different, however.

For many, the election of Barack Obama signified a new era in U.S. politics. Millions put faith in the idea that America would embrace a more peaceful path, one that rejected imperialism and military conquest around the world and the subjugation of people of color at home. Both America and the world accepted Barack Obama as a symbol of this hope.

For this reason, the descent into Trump's America has been especially painful. America has selected one of the most ill prepared, overtly bigoted, ethically compromised, and aristocratic presidents this nation has ever seen. Trump's campaign represented a combination of insults, false promises, and the pernicious use of language designed to exploit the racial fears and stereotypes persistent in many parts of this nation. Furthermore, he has rejected the transparency central to the Obama administration. This includes refusing to release his tax returns, ending the Obama-era practice of making the White House visitor log public, and holding clandestine meetings during his massively expensive tax-payer supported vacations at his Florida resort.

For every aspirational policy value that Obama represented, Trump has represented the antithesis. While Obama worked to expand healthcare coverage, Trump has worked to retract it. Obama set new carbon emission standards for power plants. Trump has rejected the idea of global warming and the need for these standards. Obama signed the Dodd-Frank Wall Street Reform and Consumer Protection Act to regulate big banks and prevent abusive lending practices. Trump signed an executive order to gut these regulations. Obama signed the Fair Sentencing Act, which reduced the disparity for sentencing between crack and powdered cocaine. Trump has declared that he wants to revive the war on drugs. Obama's Department of Education strengthened transparency and protections for student loan borrowers. Trump's Education Secretary, Betsy DeVos, immediately rescinded those protections. The Trump presidency is a wholesale rejection of the progress that occurred under Obama. We tragically have reversed course.

Additionally, in this hyper-exposed social media driven era, most assume that the behavior of public officials would be tempered by the accountability of public scrutiny. The idea that anyone's words and actions can be instantly made known to millions has made most public figures cautious. As Howard Dean (who famously yelled during a campaign speech), Mitt Romney (whose hidden comments about the poor were exposed), and Representative Todd Akin (who made controversial comments about legitimate rape) all learned, public gaffes can be fatal for a political career.

Yet, Trump was never phased by traditional political conventions. In a strange twist, the kinds of controversies that ruined the campaigns of many a politician before him only served to fuel Trump's enthusiasts. He memorably remarked that he could *"stand in the middle of Fifth Avenue and shoot somebody"* and still retain support among his base. Though this was not tested, his extreme public insults and unsavory behavior were heavily rewarded through public support.

For as odious as the rhetoric of the 45th president has been, I suggest that this pales in comparison to the offensiveness of his public policy prescriptions. He has conveyed an unambiguous political vision that is classist, prejudiced, and designed to benefit the wealthy. This agenda is where attention must be focused if his presidency is to be effectively rebutted. Not only has he changed how elections are won in this country, but also, he has laid out an agenda to retard the development of this nation in myriad ways. Consequently, my critique of Trump will focus on two areas: the annihilation of political civility, and the promotion of public policies designed to disenfranchise millions.

With respect to public rhetoric, Trump's presidency has been appallingly unique. While America has witnessed tough talk and careless words in the past (most recently in the administration of George W. Bush), it is rare that have we witnessed the brazen ignorance, arrogance, and hypocrisy of this president and this administration. In multiple areas, both his campaign and governing philosophy have been damaging, purposely inflammatory, and full of clear falsehoods. Let's recall a few of his most famed insults and lies:

• He consistently mischaracterized and insulted Mexicans, Muslims,

Jews, women, people of color, and political opponents. On the campaign trail his victims included John McCain, Khizr Khan, Carly Fiorini, Ted Cruz, Jeb Bush, Ben Carson, Meghan Kelly, and a former Miss Universe, to name a few.

• He accused President Obama of not being a U.S. citizen and eventually of wiretapping Trump Tower.

• He repeatedly called for the imprisonment of Hillary Clinton for scandals that have never proven true.

• He has erroneously claimed that millions of illegal residents voted in the presidential election, and that his inauguration crowd size and electoral victories were the largest in history.

This list is in no way exhaustive; however, it displays clearly the tone and tenor of his leadership. His rhetoric served to divide and exclude millions, intensifying the class, racial, and gender schisms so clearly present in the U.S. He capitalized on racism and economic fear, promising to "Make America Great Again". For historically marginalized groups, this language implies that America was better during times in which they had few rights. For historically dominant groups, this language is a clarion call that they can retain their supremacy by reversing decades of minority progress. What has been equally as shocking has been America's acceptance of this conduct. In addition to obvious far right supporters, for whom Trump represented a new savior, many moderate Republicans and Independents fell in line. They exhibited both extreme cowardice and political expediency in their inability to stand against him. Their complicity was as damaging as the fervent encouragement of his most ardent supporters.

If Trump's campaign is the new standard for our politics, I am greatly concerned about what the future will hold. His victory suggests to others that it is advantageous to adopt a strategy of bigotry, classism, and public insults. In a political climate that rewards winning over principle, politicians from both parties are taking note. Why would the average candidate promote civility in this climate when the incentives for the converse are so obvious? Unfortunately, the harm to our political process, already full of acrimony and partisanship, may be irreversible.

As damaging as his presidency has been for the spirit of U.S. politics, it has been equally detrimental for the economically vulnerable among us. Let us begin with his effort to strip healthcare coverage from 20 million Americans with no solid replacement plan. When President Obama was elected, 37 million Americans were uninsured. Medical bills were the number one source of bankruptcy, and insurance companies denied millions access based on pre-existing conditions and lifetime insurance caps. For the truly sick and poor, American healthcare was a nightmare.

Many fail to remember that the Affordable Care Act, Obama's ultimate solution, represents the Republican plan of the 1990's. While President Trump and the Republicans made it the centerpiece of their criticism of Obama, the plan is a compromise that is heavily driven by the private sector, and has been a gift to insurance companies. President Obama's initial healthcare initiative was a public option, an effort that would have created a government-run insurance company for those who couldn't afford participation in the private market. This policy, along with Progressive efforts to move towards a single payer system, were labeled as Socialist, radical, and un-American by those on the right. A series of anger-filled national town hall meetings were reported as evidence of America's opposition to the public option. In response, the Democrats backed off the plan, opting for a supposedly free-market alternative that would require all Americans to purchase coverage.

Following the model for state-based car insurance requirements, the goal was full citizen participation with government subsidies for those unable to pay. The irony of the Republican outrage is that the insurance mandate, the crux of Obamacare, represented a bi-partisan deal. Given the fact that Bob Dole, Mitt Romney, and groups like the Heritage Foundation were both the architects and early adopters of this effort, it is highly hypocritical and disingenuous for these same groups to have rejected it once it was embraced by Obama. Consequently, when Trump rode into office bemoaning the allegedly Socialist Obamacare policy, he quietly supported many of its core principles. These include removing limits on lifetime coverage, preventing discrimination against pre-existing conditions, and allowing students to remain on their parents' health insurance until the age of 26. In fact, Trump's initial proposal was so reliant on the core tenets of the Obama plan that it gained the nickname "Obamacare lite." Republican opposition to the healthcare plan is an example of political comedy. It is pure theater, staged to separate them from Barack Obama, seen as a Socialist, Muslim, Kenyan-born anti-Christ by a large swath of the Republican electorate. Consequently, in principle the Republican leadership rejects Obamacare, yet in practice they support it because it is their creation.

Once Trump was elected, many Republican moderates resisted efforts to repeal the Affordable Care Act due to its popularity among their constituencies. As a result, Republicans in upstate NY fought to keep the Medicare expansion at the core of the policy and were even willing to tax the wealthy to pay for it. Yet Republicans in the South wanted to gut many of the basic essential benefits including ER visits, prescriptions, and preventative care. The Republican Freedom Caucus wanted to remove maternity and mental health coverage. What became clear was a rift in the Republican Party under Trump. The group that had spent 8 years making healthcare reform the centerpiece of their national agenda had no plan for this reform.

In addition to healthcare, his efforts to dismantle public education, block Muslims from entry into the country, and promote tax policies that protect the rich, have all worked to exacerbate inequality in the nation. While Obama's presidency failed to make a significant dent in this nation's economic imbalances, his guarantee of reparations for African American farmers ($1.25 billion), equal pay through the Lilly Ledbetter Act, and the expansion of healthcare coverage for millions all pushed the bar in the right direction. For every one of these efforts to move towards equality, Trump has produced adversative acts to promote inequality. His Education Department is cutting funding to public schools, and his EPA has rolled back protections for clean water. He has directed his cabinet to slash federal programs for the poor in housing, legal aid, and ironically, anti-poverty programs. Furthermore he and Attorney General Jeff Sessions have renewed a commitment to the war on drugs and failed policies of mass incarceration. Harkening back to the era of Nixon, Trump has referred to himself a "law and order" president intending to use imprisonment as his chief anti-crime strategy. Sadly, this approach has only exacerbated the problems faced by our nation's most challenged communities.

With America's prison population being larger than any other nation, the incarceration of more people is not the answer to our crime problems. Crime is a holistic problem that requires a multi-faceted approach. Mass incarceration has failed to work and only serves to disproportionately impact those too poor to secure adequate legal protections. Any leader who has a desire to set the nation on a path towards long-term solutions, will recognize the fallacy of these policies. Trump's carelessness, bravado, and ignorance of history will have a devastating impact for generations to come.

As much as I vehemently disagree with his presidency, even a broken clock is correct twice a day. It would be a strategic mistake to be so blindly partisan that we cannot see this. Poor communities who have been plagued by low business ownership and economic exploitation should take advantage of the possible focus on small businesses and decreased taxes. In a multi-faceted agenda, this may be the sole area for the benefit of these communities. Yet, unfortunately, the bulk of his efforts are toxic as he has shown himself to be wholly unconcerned with the poor, people of color, and promoting equality. In the vast majority of areas, he should be opposed.

The Trump presidency is an important time for our nation. How we respond to him and his agenda will say more about our collective identity, than his. Whether we passively tolerate injustice and fear-inducing rhetoric, or whether we actively and collectively reject them represents a significant test of the character of our democracy. The stakes are high. I hope this nation responds correctly.

Source: altoday.com/wp-content/uploads/2015/07/Donald-Trump-angry.jpg

ONWARD: ACTIVATING CRITICAL RESISTANCE!

PUBLIC AND PRIVATE EDUCATION THAT WORKS FOR THE MAJORITY RATHER THAN THE ACUTE FEW

ALISHIA ATKINS

Alishia M. Atkins, an alumna of Spelman College, is a licensed professional educator and tenured faculty member in the Child Development Studies Program at Kennedy-King College. She serves as the Practicum/Field Site Supervisor, and is a faculty-liaison for numerous community partnerships with early education centers throughout Chicago.

One of the foundational purposes of education is to provide opportunities for individuals to become independent thinkers, who are able to create innovative ideologies where they do not currently exist. More importantly, the acquisition of knowledge, which can be used to further improve the conditions of a group of people, community, or society, is at the heart of being an enlightened individual.

However, in order for one to discover new ideas, he or she must understand the origins of his or her identity. A foundational principle of teachers and institutions truly seeking to address the educational needs of the masses is their commitment to become pupils of the children they serve, which can occur by familiarizing themselves with the backgrounds, languages, and experiences of the students entrusted in their care. Such intentionality can ensure the learning experiences offered are relevant and authentic thus, enabling each student to make a connection with the content to which they are exposed in schools. This perspective is consistent with the concept of "cultural congruence", which signifies the ways in which teachers alter their speech patterns, communication styles, and participation structures to resemble more closely those of the students' own culture (Ladson-Billings, 1994, p.16).

The use of children's cultural, racial, and/or ethnic identities can be used as a gateway to new knowledge, which can make learning more meaningful. However, far too often, students from diverse backgrounds are limited, and are the product of missed instructional opportunities, as a result of an educational system that is designed to serve the few, while neglecting the masses. So, what is the purpose of education? Education in many of today's schools is often associated with *"the rules of the culture of power, and are a reflection of the rules of the culture of those who have power"* (Delpit, 1995, p.25).

Today's Educational Climate

The educational climate, from a national perspective, is one of uncertainty as a result of the appointment of Mrs. Betsy DeVos, the recently confirmed Secretary of Education of the United States. The recommendation of Mrs. DeVos is one of contention for many educators, parents, advocacy groups, professional organizations, and legislators alike, due to Ms. DeVos's lack of experience in education. This point was proven, as indicated by the Senate's division on Mrs. DeVos's appointment, which led to the tie-breaking vote cast by Vice-President Pence for her confirmation (Huetteman & Alcindor, 2017). This appointment will certainly impact the trajectory of education today, and in the near future. Specifically, Mrs. DeVos's educational philosophy in regards to growth versus proficiency on performance assessment measurements saliently demonstrated her limited knowledge of a poignant educational issue (Strauss, 2017). In addition, the Secretary of Education's support of public charter schools and private school vouchers is evident based on her financial contributions (Turner, 2017). More importantly, Secretary DeVos has indicated her belief in public charter schools, but has not offered an alternative course of action when questioned about the possibility of public charter schools performing at lower-levels than traditional public schools, and would not commit to a budget void of depleting public education funding (Strauss, 2017). The hope is for the leadership in the Department of Education to seek council and guidance from countless practitioners, researchers, legislators, and other education professionals who possess the expertise to positively influence the American educational landscape.

One of the primary items on Mrs. DeVos's agenda, as the Secretary of the Department of Education, is school choice. Secretary DeVos seeks to offer parents opportunities to provide high-quality public and private educational options for their children. However, a recent AP NORC poll indicates many Americans are unfamiliar with school choice. *"There were 58 percent of respondents saying they know little or nothing at all about charter schools, and 66 percent reporting the same about private school voucher programs, according to the poll conducted by The Associated Press-NORC Center for Public Affairs Research"* (Danilova & Swanson, 2017). This lack of knowledge among the general population can lead to an erred perception of what is best for the education of their children. For instance, misinformation, and an increased focus on today's rhetoric about the condition of public education across the country can lead an individual to believe all public schools are of poor quality; thus, leaving private or charter schools as a primary alternative.

Trump's Education Secretary, Betsy DeVos, is a champion of school choice. However, based on the Secretary of Education's first 100 days in office, there has been little movement on a school choice proposal that comprehensively outlines plans for the entire country (Phenicie, 2017). Is it Mrs. DeVos's lack of experience in education, or the vacancies she has yet to fill in the Department of Education's staff? One of the primary goals of President Donald Trump's administration, with the assistance of the current Education Secretary, is to decrease the department's budget by $9 billion for the 2018 fiscal year, while adding a $1.4 billion increase to the budget for school choice (Phenicie, 2017). However, there has been no release of plans for school choice to date, which is concerning given the fact that funds are allocated for a plan that does not currently exist, or has yet to be released. *"It's no secret that expanding school choice is the Trump administration's favorite K-12 policy; but, the administration has yet to release a detailed proposal explaining how it plans to make that a reality"* (Klein, 2017). More importantly, there is a plan to remove funding from current federal provisions. For example, among the anticipated budget cuts, or decreases in funding are Title II grants, which support things like teacher training; furthermore, the 21st Century Community Learning Centers, which fund before and after school programs are also at risk (Phenicie, 2017). The indisputable fact is the removal of funding impacts the quality of education. The two aforementioned areas will certainly have a significant impact on public education.

To believe in school choice is one thing, but to keep the playing field unleveled by defunding key educational programs and initiatives is unacceptable, and harms public education. Essentially, the plan to fund school choice, while significantly defunding public education will have detrimental effects. Offering vouchers and private school options will not remedy the education system in the United States. The voucher system is based on providing scholarships to low-income children to have the option to attend private schools of choice, using tax dollars. However, every family may not meet the income requirements to receive tuition funding, which provides school options for some, but limits quality options for others.

The Federal Government: Education Provisions

The federal government makes provisions to provide support to states as each entity endeavors to offer quality educational opportunities for children. For example, the Every Student Succeeds Act (ESSA), which was signed into law by President Trump's predecessor, is designed to reauthorize the Elementary and Secondary Education Act. Some key provisions of the Act, which reauthorizes the programs in the Elementary and Secondary Education Act for four years requires the following: state-wide technical assistance and support for local education agencies; the alignment of challenging academic content and achievement standards; English language proficiency standards; academic assessments disaggregated within each state and school by racial/ethnic group, economically disadvantaged and non-disadvantaged students, children with and without disabilities, English proficiency, gender, and migrant status (National Conference of State Legislatures, 2017, p.3). A philosophical provision of the Act is to provide resources to State and Local Education Agencies (LEAs) that may need additional support to provide high-quality educational experiences to all students regardless of race, class, social-economic background, or exceptionality. However, the budget cuts to the U.S. Department of Education's budget, proposed by the Trump administration, can make these provisions difficult to meet.

Under DeVos, many of the key provisions and oversights of the ESSA are being repealed. The Senate recently voted to block Obama administration accountability rules governing how states rate and improve schools under the Every Student Succeeds Act (Phenicie, 2017). The more extensive oversight of education at the state-level is an idea that will likely be supported and further extended by the Trump administration, based on the hands-off approach demonstrated by Mrs. DeVos thus far. *"Federal funding is critical to supporting state education systems and making sure every child receives a high-quality education, no matter their family background or zip code"* (The Council of Chief State School Officers, 2017).

Despite the provisions of federal legislation like the ESSA, the proposed decrease in staff, funding for education, and removal of accountability rules throughout the U.S. Department of Education, can lead to continued challenges in the delivery of quality at the state and local education levels, especially for high-risk populations. This leads one to question, is the goal really to improve, fund, and increase the quality of educational options for all children in the United States?

Educational Equity, Higher-Education and Globalization

The fact remains, all schools must be created with equity to increase the likelihood that quality will exist. According to Merriam Webster (2017), equity is, "Justice according to the natural law, or right, specifically: freedom from bias or favoritism". When a lack of equity exists, as it does throughout many education systems, it is impossible to uphold the provisions of landmark cases like Brown vs. Board of Education, which ruled separate, but equal schools unlawful (United States Courts, 2017). As a result of funding disparities, which are sure to persists with the current regime at the federal level, separate, unequal, and inequitable schools are a harsh reality.

Students, faculty, staff, and families throughout elementary, secondary, and post-secondary educational institutions are aware of Mrs. DeVos's appointment, and are making their voices heard through resistance. Recently, during a commencement address at a Historically Black College and University (HBCU) in Daytona Beach, Florida, DeVos was invited as the commencement speaker. As Education Secretary DeVos began her address, the graduates booed, stood, and turned their backs away from the stage as she made the address (Phenicie, 2017). DeVos's statement in regards to Black Colleges being champions of school choice was met with significant criticism (The Associated Press, 2017). Essentially, the statement revealed Secretary's DeVos's lack of understanding and knowledge of the origins, and philosophy of why such institutions were founded, which primarily began as a grassroots movement to educate children of color in response to Jim Crow laws.

During DeVos' short stint as the highest ranked educational officer of the land, she has been met consistently by protesters during scheduled school visits (Phenicie, 2017). The protests are a glaring example of our nation's stand against nepotism and tyranny. It is also reflective of the lack of judgement of President Trump to make a qualified appointment to one of the most influential educational positions in the country, which will significantly impact our nation's children. The fact that President Trump actually appointed an unqualified candidate, who is clearly out of touch with the American educational landscape is insulting, and disheartening. The future of our nation's schools rests on the advocacy of all citizens of the nation working towards providing well-equipped places of learning for the masses, while resisting the ignorance and lack of respect for our nation's most vulnerable residents…children.

Options for the Future

Despite the challenges discussed, it is important to keep parents and the American population accurately informed about what is occurring in education. An important idea to consider is parent education classes, or workshops throughout the academic year based on current events in education, as a mandatory part of a school's parent engagement initiative. These workshops can be offered in a city or municipality at designated times throughout the year. Through the workshops, parents can learn how local and national educational decisions will impact their children and communities. The more knowledgeable individuals are the greater ability they will have to make informed decisions, while becoming powerful advocates for their children. Another option is to offer teachers, administrators, and policymakers incentives to serve as leaders of such parent education workshops, or classes.

An additional alternative is to create the schools we desire for our children. For example, it can be helpful to utilize any aspect of the grassroots movement that established countless Historically Black Colleges and Universities (HBCUs), as a resource for developing independent elementary and secondary schools nationwide, which are funded by the families and communities they serve. In addition, these established schools must have a comprehensive system of accountability in which all stakeholders have a voice in the way in which the schools are governed. Finally, it is important to cultivate the quality of teachers and administrators envisioned for these schools. Moreover, it is imperative for various communities and stakeholders (parents, community members, students, legislators, practitioners, educational researchers, child advocates, administrators, etc.), to have a seat at the table in the preparation of teachers.

It is critical for teachers and administrators to have the skills and knowledge to interact with, and relate to children and families in today's schools in culturally sensitive ways, and to ensure the curriculum and climate of schools are reflective of the diversity of our country. It is the responsibility of all citizens, and will require commitment from the U.S Department of Education, and the President of these United States to ensure quality, equity, and access for the masses rather than merely the few.

References:

Council of Chief State School Officers. (2017). CCSSO expresses concern with president's budget proposal. Washington, DC: U.S. Online: ccsso.org/News_and_Events/Press_Releases/CCSSO_Expresses_Concern_with_Presidents_Budget_Proposal_.html

Darling-Hammond, L, & McCloskey, L. (2008). Assessment for Learning Around the World: What Would It Mean to Be Internationally Competitive? *Phi Delta Kappan*, 90 (4), pp. 263-272.

Delpit, L. (1995). *Other People's Children: Cultural Conflict in the Classroom*. New York: The New Press.

Danilova, M. & Swanson, E. (2017, May 15). AP-NORC Poll: Most Americans Feel Fine About School Choice. The Associated Press, 132 (96). Online: memphisdailynews.com/news/2017/may/15/ap-norc-poll-most-americans-feel-fine-about-school-choice

Huetteman, E & Alcindor, Y. (2017, February 7). DeVos confirmed as education secretary; Pence breaks tie. *New York Times*. Online: nytimes.com/2017/02/07/us/politics/betsy-devos-education-secretary-confirmed.html?_r=0

Klein, A. (2017, May 9). Betsy DeVos: federal progress on school choice coming soon. *Education Week*. Online: blogs.edweek.org.

Ladson-Billings, G. (1994). *The Dream keepers: Successful teachers of African American children*. California: Jossey-Bass.

National Conference of State Legislatures. (2017). Summary of the every student succeeds act, legislation reauthorizing the elementary and secondary education act. Washington, DC: Online: ncsl.org/documents/educ/ESSA_summary_NCSL.pdf

Phenicie, C. (2017, March 20). Effective, efficient — and limited: DeVos lays out her vision of federal role to state schools chiefs. *The 74 Million*. Online: the74million.org/article/effective-efficient-and-limited-devos-lays-out-her-vision-of-federal-role-to-state-schools-chief

Phenicie, C. (2017, May 15). The first 100 days for the new education secretary: How DeVos stacks up against her predecessors. *The 74 Million*. Online: the74million.org/article/the-first-100-days-for-the-new-education-secretary-how-devos-stacks-up-against-her-predecessors

United States Courts. (2017). *History-brown v. board of education re-enactment.* Online: uscourts.gov/educational-resources/educational-activities/history-brown-v-board-education-re-enactment

Strauss, V. (2017, January 18). Six astonishing things Betsy DeVos said-and refused to say-at her confirmation hearing. Washington Post, Online: washingtonpost.com/news/answer-sheet/wp/2017/01/18/six-astonishing-things-betsy-devos-said-and-refused-to-say-at-her-confirma

The Associated Press (2017, March 1). Trump signs executive order on historically black colleges.

Turner, C. (2017, January 1). At DeVos' senate hearing, questions of choice, charters, other options (National Public Radio Broadcast). Online: npr.org

U.S. Department of Education. (2009). Race to the top fund. Washington, D.C.

WHAT ARE OUR BRIGHT TOMORROWS? VISION FOR A NEW AMERICA

APRIL BERNARD & SOKONI KARANJA

April Bernard is a scholar–activist who has taught at universities in the U.S. and internationally. She has written in the areas of critical criminology, transformative justice, and feminist theory. A consultant on crime, youth, and gender program and policy initiatives, she has worked with local and international organizations, including the United Nations.

Sokoni Karanja, founder and former President and CEO of Centers for New Horizons, is the President of 2016 Ma'AT, an initiative which aims to eliminate violence by strengthening unity in Chicago's communities of color. He is the recipient of numerous awards for his community service and leadership including the MacArthur Foundation's Genius Award.

There is hope for a brighter tomorrow. Hope beckons as we see ourselves in the eyes of our children. Hope calls from the horizon with the voices of the Ancestors, those whose blood fills the land of Freedom they worshiped, those stripped of their mothers' land by force, and those who repent and seek to repair the harm caused. Hope knows there is life after Donald Trump. What that life will be depends on whether we choose to unite and put an end to the cycles of madness that have sorted, divided, and distanced us into believing that our fragmented selves are greater than the intersections that bind us together. This essay provides a prescription for a New America based in part on Mindy Thompson Fullilove's Book *Urban Alchemy* (2013) and offers the reasons why envisioning a post-Trump world through unity's lens is the only way toward a brighter tomorrow.

Fullilove describes the madness of a sorting process that combines a series of thorny racially-biased strategies to create a fragmented society. The sorting process, both past and present, are known by their effect, the creation or increase of physical, social, economic and ideological distance between groups. The sorting process is the impetus for the development (and redevelopment) of fragmented urban spaces. Fullilove, builds on the work of Wallace (1998) and others in listing the following as strategies in the sorting process: redlining, urban renewal, rapid deindustrialization in urban spaces, community disorganization, and mass criminalization of residents in the marginalized communities that the sorting process created. Together, these strategies, that included intentional unresponsiveness to crisis in Brown and Black communities, such as shutting down fire stations in the Bronx and allowing homes and commercial buildings to burn as a tactic to scare individuals from communities and cut demolition costs, have contributed to urban blight, crime, violence, generational poverty and targeted inequality.

The sorting process creates physical distance between groups by establishing divisions such as expressways, train tracks, and industrial districts that separate and isolate neighborhoods deemed by planners as higher risk or less valuable in terms of investment. Sorting adds physical distance between groups through urban renewal strategies that causes displacement of low income residential areas by demolishing homes without adequate replacement housing, and creating vacant land or other dysfunctional or non-functional spaces with limited utility. Rapid deindustrialization, such as the closing of manufacturing companies in the heart of the nation's urban communities contributed to mass unemployment and limited access to viable and stable economic opportunities. The loss of well-paying, semi-skilled manufacturing jobs, as Chicago shifted from an industrial economy with jobs that were dispersed across the south and west sides to a service economy with livable wage paying job opportunities concentrated in or near the city center, contributed to a black unemployment rate of nearly 20% today which is over four times greater than the rate for whites and a poverty rate among blacks (at over 30%) that is more than three times that of whites (Hendricks, 2017).

High rates of housing mobility, neighborhood decay, unemployment and poverty contributed to community disorganization, crime and death. The continued mass criminalization of residents in these communities reinforces social, economic, and especially ideological differences by suggesting that persons most marginalized in the sorting process and their communities are "high risk" and deserve to be devalued and eternally stigmatized, because of their alleged inability to pull themselves up and out of their circumstances.

The Trump presidency provides an additional layer of complexity to the sorting process by reinforcing ideological divisions between groups, particularly the wealthiest 1% and those they label "high risk." Trump, with his dystopian and divisive rhetoric, has also interrupted the comfort level for people who uncritically danced between the intersections of privilege and oppression that define the myth of their assimilated melting pot all men are born equal existence. Some believed the Obama presidency signaled an end to racism and the rise to colorblindness and assumed that we have overcome the barriers that would prevent a Black man from becoming commander and chief in America's White House, yet the hateful rhetoric and events of the Trump campaign and his current efforts as president to reverse and repeal the signature initiatives of the former president and first lady's (Barack and Michelle Obama) reveal the extent to which unresolved issues with color continue to bind our nation's progress.

While Trump supporters exist, the majority of the 300 million people in America have responded to his presidency with fear, frustration, and disappointment. Through their protests for abortion rights, equal pay for women, public school education, environmental protection, immigration, and an end to police terrorism the majority of Americans are demanding an alternative. The Trump presidency is causing individuals in America to come to terms and out of the closet holding signs bearing their group membership, by triggering feelings of fear, frustration, or fraternity. Despite the early failures the Trump presidency, history will note that Trump has thus far been overwhelmingly successful at drawing upon the existence of multiple traumas in the plural American psyche.

The intensive, targeted, persistent, and collective impact of the sorting strategies over time is greater than what each could achieve individually. Together these sorting strategies combine into one overarching and debilitating process that functions to traumatize a dominant aspect of the American psyche into accepting arbitrary reasons for differences in the use of and relationships to power. How easy it must be for those most privileged to grab on to hegemonic justifications for perceiving and treating some as more or less deserving, valued, or at-risk, rather than looking in the mirror and accepting inadequacy, immorality, and inhumanity, or is it? Do questions arise when a feeling of comfort follows the deliberate turn of the page to words and images that suggest the poor due to their own generationally transferred laziness, drug addiction, and willful seduction into the lure of street-culture are to blame for their experiences of chronic isolation, lack, and want? Could the trauma of resisting and denying the facts of one's vile existence cause the creation of "alternative facts" to the point of eradicating egalitarian legacies that could result in subsequent generations of the privileged class questioning the validity of their "inheritance" and "entitlements"?

Trauma also affects those whose acceptance of their schizophrenia enables them to deal with their reality of navigating multiple realities. The reality of multiple realities includes an acknowledgement of the perceived benefits of adhering to the meritocratic principles built into the hegemonic perspective that requires all to simply follow the rules of capitalism and pull yourself up by your bootstraps to become "successful" while not questioning why someone above you is holding on to the bootstraps of those at higher rungs while reaching for yours and those below you as well.

Not having access to minimal basic needs and opportunities is also traumatizing. The crime, violence, disorganization that result are not only symptoms of a traumatized individual psyche, but also of a community, city, and societal psyche that fails to demand equity, redistribution, reparations, and preservation. Not using one's voice to protect and demand fairness for all races, classes, genders and ethnicities contributes to the building and fortification of the Collective Vile Self, which gives birth to and nurtures shared immorality, oppression, and denial that both exist. Irrespective of one's use of or relationship to power, whether the oppressed or the oppressor, the racist or racialized, the trauma of living an increasingly fragmented, divided, and individualized existence in America must be healed.

The prescription begins with acknowledging that the sorting process began before Trump became president. Both democrats and republicans, local, state, and national were and continue to be complicit actors. In Chicago, like Philadelphia, Boston, New Orleans, and other urban areas across the nation the culpability of both democratic and republican politicians continues to contribute to the separation between high risk/less valued communities and those of the wealthy. Federal housing policy drove urban renewal strategies and the dismantling of public housing. Limited corporate incentives followed with deindustrialization. The war on drugs and welfare reform became a war on the most vulnerable. Local investment an increase in social, economic, and political power in one community contrasted with devastating disinvestment and social, economic and political isolation in another. All of these strategies were in place decades before Trump took office.

Structural violence in the form of racial segregation and persistent inequality kills poor urban Blacks in communities throughout the U.S. The interpersonal violence that follows segregation and inequality through the sorting process is only one form of violence leading to death among the urban poor. Decades of racial segregation, discrimination, and economic exploitation have not only led to Blacks living in the poorest and sickest neighborhoods, but have caused disparaging health outcomes for Blacks, including death (Wallace, 2011; Ansell, 2017). Inequality is a disease causing poor urban Blacks to die from health related ailments at alarming rates and have a life expectancy that is up to 35 years less than that of wealthy whites (Ansell, 2017).

While the sorting process has devastated historically African American communities, until recently some immigrant communities have demonstrated resilience. The shared native language, familial bonds, and customs of close knit immigrant communities helps to strengthen social bonds that act as a buffer to the threat of the sorting process. Since his presidency Trump has created an atmosphere of fear among the immigrant population. Whether Latino, Arab, Asian, Caribbean, or African, Trump with his threats to build a wall separating Mexico and the U.S. and expand travel bans has made some immigrants fear they will be subject to arrest or deportation. Out of concerns for their own safety and with an understanding of how their mere presence contributes to their familial and community unity and stability, some immigrants have opted to quit their jobs, forfeit their efforts to advance their education, and keep their children home from school. This atmosphere of fear underpins the sorting process by reducing the social and economic viability of communities, forcing some to stay home rather than work, and vilifying of people color as bad hombres, high risk, and less valued members of society.

The Trump presidency as a nuanced contributing factor to the sorting process has occurred within a supportive context. The failure to address the consequences of decades of sanctioned, pervasive, entrenched, blatant, and yet subtle institutional and interpersonal forms of discrimination provided the perfect compost for an emerging Trump presidency. The ineptness of the Democratic Party to back a convincing agenda in opposition to blatant inequality and social injustice stemming from decades of global-local Neoliberalism, the dismantling of the social safety net, punitive criminal justice legislation, and a history of sorting urban communities significantly contributed to Trump's successful candidacy. While the divided mind of the Republic Party (e.g. conservatives, progressives, vs. Tea Party) was on full display for the American and global public, the incongruities in the rhetoric of the Democratic Party leadership persisted and they failed to produce a viable and convincing agenda for the American public. In this context, the Trump presidency emerged with divisive rhetoric, plans for building walls, bombing nations, objectifying women, and violating the most intimate spaces of our collective moral consciousness.

The prescription recommended here is not a response to Trump, but to the context and history of oppression that has given rise to a Trump presidency, one that is explicit in its intention to pin multiple groups against one another. There are also lessons to be learned from the history of social movements and community development about planning, organizing, and unity that can help guide the way forward. Fullilove suggests that to stop the madness of the sorting process, we must align our ideas, create the spaces (cities) we want, and connect ourselves to others. A key step in this prescription is to take the lessons learned from the past to align our ideas with the goal to value the intersections.

Fullilove defines the concept of community based on physical boundaries established through the sorting process and views the community as one part of the main target for change, the city. The problem is that this two dimensional definition of community boundaries limits the exploration of intersections that go beyond physical places. Ideally the definition of community would be based on shared action, ritual, language and customs that intersect multiple dimensions, factors, or spaces (e.g. race, class, gender, ethnicity, etc). By valuing and celebrating the ways in which our individual and collective identities intersect we create shared knowledge and experiences of our proximity to, perspectives on, and use of power (Bernard & Agozino, 2012).

The process of valuing the exploration of intersections is not simply a matter of going across the tracks to have tea with the more or less valued. Instead this step of the prescription requires radical confrontation of our own prejudice, fears, animosity, and trauma by acknowledging that the redlines we have become accustomed to using to define our existence are fictitious. Redlined communities literally do not exist on planning maps and they should not in our minds. The term 'redlining' has been conjured to mean a separation of the affluent from those with less. Redlining exists in our minds and comes with assumptions about our own value and that of others.

At most, the physical boundaries we use to describe neighborhoods or communities should be used to acknowledge their representation of the historical, institutional, and racially motivated social, political, and economic sanctioned realities of disinvestment. These boundaries represent the degree to which those in power and their descendants have worked to protect their "inheritance" while circumscribing the identity and legacy of others. To blur these physical boundaries between communities we should seek opportunities to share intersection stories, language and rituals that foster a new shared reality and understanding of the effects and use of power. We cannot use the master's tools to dismantle the master's house (Lorde, 1979). Redlines in our minds are tools that must be dismantled and replaced with new concepts, ideology, strategies, and processes to repair and heal our fragmented selves, places, and spaces.

The redlining also occurs among those who have been most marginalized through the sorting process as well. The internalization of the legitimacy of redlining and the outcomes of the sorting process has led to the suppression of criticism of societal messages among some who desire to separate themselves from those that have been labeled as less valued and higher risk. An aim in the process of valuing intersections is to challenge our understanding and use of power in our everyday interactions.

To blur the red-lines separating our communities, we must begin by erasing them in our minds. Creating space, rituals, and opportunities for exploring the ways in which our experiences in relation to power are shared or not. Dialoging about how to strategically foster more equitable or egalitarian experiences should begin in elementary school and continue into our workspaces, social, civic, and religious organizations, and homes. Shared language, rituals and experiences must be emphasized to create shared spaces. African Americans and other ethnic groups in America should learn multiple languages, including Spanish, Swahili, Hebrew, Arabic, and Mandarin enough to communicate with their local and global brothers and sisters. Shared language(s) creates space for shared ritual, culture, and expressions of shared solidarity in opposition to the misuse of power and social injustice and in support of local and global efforts to heal the trauma that results.

As we build an expanded notion of community, Fullilove recommends that we find out what we are for. Identifying a change agenda is difficult without achieving meaningful progress in the previous step of challenging the redlines in our minds. The #BlacklivesMatter Movement and most recently the Women's March demonstrated that when there is a blurring of the redlines, individuals representing the shared intersections, perspectives on and experiences of the misuse of power and social injustice can come together spontaneously or intentionally to fight power and heal together.

Healing rituals, however large or small, are essential components of this prescription or vision for a new America, but we must not become complacent with rituals that do not lead to policy, legislative, and space (community) changes. While acknowledging their importance, doing a collective garden, a protest march, or peace vigil may not result in immediate or radical legislative or policy changes toward insuring that every American has access to resources to meet their basic needs, employment with livable wages, education for their children, healthcare, and social security. These efforts cannot continue to function as a proxy for emphasizing the development of a common agenda aligned with a political party and local, state and national representatives that are willing to be held accountable for responding to our vote for ending the madness and moving toward a more egalitarian society. These efforts must engage the institutions within and near physical community spaces, such as the schools, hospitals, police departments, and employers to respond to the data that suggests that structural violence has contributed to racial disparity in the health, educational, employment, housing and criminal justice outcomes that are most detrimental to those who are black and brown in America.

Hope beckons, but to move toward the call beyond the horizon, we must fight an ongoing fight for justice, peace, unity, and freedom for all. History has shown that freedom is a guiding post, not a fixed state that can be granted by legislation alone. Along with the myths of capitalism we must bury the myth that freedom can be won at another's expense. Instead, we must prepare ourselves and our children to link arms with similar and disparate others and continue to fight for that right.

References:

Ansell, David. 2017. *The Death Gap: How Inequality Kills.* Chicago: University of Chicago Press.

Bernard, April and Onwubiko Agozino. 2012. Free Space and Inner Space: A Place for Reconstructing Self and Other. *Journal of Pan African Studies* 5 (6): 56-74.

Fullilove, Mindy Thompson. 2013. *Urban Alchemy: Restoring Joy in America's Sorted Out Communities.* New York: New Village Press.

Drake, St. Claire. 1945. *Black Metropolis: A Study of Negro Life in a Northern City.* New York: Harcourt.

Hendricks, K., Lewis, A., Arenas, I., and D. Lewis. 2017. *A Tale of Three Cities: The State of Racial Justice in Chicago. Chicago: Institute for Research on Race and Public Policy,* University of Illinois at Chicago.

Lemann, Nicholas. 1991. *The Promised Land: The Great Black Migration and How it Changed America.* New York: A.A. Knopf.

Lorde, Audre. Master's Tools Will Never Dismantle The Master's House: Comments At "the Personal And The Political" Panel: (second Sex Conference, October 29, 1979).

Wallace, Deborah. 2011. Discriminatory Mass De-Housing and Low-Weight Births: Scales of Geography, Time and Level. *Journal of Urban Health.* 88: 454-68.

Wallace, Deborah and Rodrick Wallace. 1998. *A Plague on Your Houses: How New York was Burned Down and National Public Health Crumbled.* New York: Verso Press.

BLACK WOMEN AT THE CENTER OF OUR BRIGHT TOMORROWS: UNDERSTANDING POLITICAL INTERSECTIONALITY FOR COALITION-BUILDING

THEODOREA REGINA BERRY

*Theodorea Regina Berry is Associate Dean and Associate Professor of Curriculum Studies at the University of Texas at San Antonio. She is a pioneer scholar on critical race feminism and her research appears in such journals as the **Journal of Curriculum Theorizing, Race, Ethnicity, and Education, and Urban Review**. She is a contributing author of **From Oppression to Grace: Women of Color and their Dilemmas Within the Academy** (2006), and co-editor of **The Evolving Significance of Race in Education: Living, Learning, and Teaching** (2012).*

While this particular season of authoritarian, elitist government may feel especially new to many people in this country, those who have been positioned as "pushed out" or "othered" recognize this political climate quite well. History has born witness to the ways in which enslaved African people in the United States fought side by side with revolutionaries in the war for this country's independence yet the newly organized Congress debated the freedom of these individuals. Black women have survived and thrived amidst political turmoil for the entire existence of U.S. government. And, in some cases, we have been asked to choose sides, to be Black or woman. Black activist-scholar Angela Yvonne Davis (1981) chronicles the dismantling of the coalition between White woman suffrages and

Black activists concerning voting rights.

The coalition formed at the Seneca Falls New York convention fell apart when it became clear that politicians would support voting rights for one group or the other but not both. Black women like Sojourner Truth were being asked to choose sides. In the original transcription of her famous speech given at the Women's Rights Convention of 1851 in Akron Ohio, Truth clearly states "I am a woman's rights" and situates herself on the side of gender rather than race. In the end, Black men acquire the right to vote through the passage of the Fifteenth Amendment. The suffrage movement for women's right to vote included the participation of Black women through such Black women's activist groups as the National Association of Colored Women (Davis, 1981) and Delta Sigma Theta Sorority, Inc. (Giddings, 1988). Yet, the efforts of the Black women organizations to support the cause of suffrage were seldom acknowledged by White women. Women, and implicitly Black women, were not granted the right to vote in the United States until the passage of the Nineteenth Amendment in 1920. In the sixties, Black women found themselves discontent with the Women's Movement while marginalized in the Civil Rights Movement that yielded legislation that would serve as the foundation for women's rights (Giddings, 1984). In recent years, Black women have been significant in the movement for Black lives, including Black Lives Matter. This movement is centered on the end of violence and disrespect toward Black people by White authorities and systems. A major discussion in the movement is centered on the murders of Black men by White people (Berry & Stovall, 2013), specifically White police officers. Sadly, little to no discussion has been maintained concerning the violence against Black women by White people. Balancing our multiple and intersecting identities in a hostile political climate has provided us with distinguishable, unique ways of seeing the world, understanding complex multilayered issues, and addressing issues that serve to meet the needs of various groups of people. Our intersectional identities serve us well.

As someone who subscribes to and advocates for critical race feminism (CRF), intersectionality is central to my way of understanding the world. Introduced by Richard Delgado (1995), CRF is an outgrowth of Critical Race Theory (CRT) and espouses all of its tenets: (1) the normalness and ordinariness and race and racism; (2) white-over-color ascendency which includes "color-blind conceptions of equality" (Delgado & Stefancic, 2001, p. 7) (also known as a critique of liberalism), and interest convergence; (3) race as a social construction; (4) differential racialization and revisionist interpretations of history; (5) anti-essentialism and intersectionality; (6) uniqueness of the voices of color. Among these tenets, CRF focuses on anti-essentialism and intersectionality as well as the uniqueness of voices of color. Additionally, CRF includes notions of multi-dimensionality, multiplicative praxis, and multiple consciousness. Multi-dimensionality is the way in which our multiple identities inform one another (Berry & Stovall, 2013). Legal scholar Mari Matsuda refers to multiple consciousness "to describe intersectional identities of women of color... who view the world simultaneously from both gendered and racialized perspectives" (Wing, 2015, 0. 165). Multiplicative praxis is theory, action, and reflection used "to push forward social policy that allows black women to capitalize on their richness and strength..." (Wing, 1997, p. 32). It is a praxis that takes all of who we are and the lessons we garner from our multiple and intersecting identities to serve the greater good. This multiplicative praxis integrates critical race praxis. CRF endorses "critical race praxis, the combination of theory and practice" (Wing, 2015, p. 164) which promotes scholarship in conjunction with service to the community.

These assets positions Black women as ideal agents of change in a political climate that does not value those who are not White, male, wealth-classed, heterosexual, Anglo-protestant Christian, and able-bodied. Kimberle Williams Crenshaw identifies political intersectionality as a key concept toward understanding Black women's positions in this current political climate. Crenshaw (1995) notes:

> the concept of political intersectionality highlights the fact that women of color are situated within at least two subordinated groups that frequently pursue conflicting agendas. The need to split one's po-

litical energies between two sometimes opposing groups is a dimension of intersectional disempowerment that men of color and white
women seldom confront
(p. 1252).

To this point, I will address two significant events where political
intersectionality exists and the ways in which Black women have used our
multiple consciousness and multiplicative praxis to benefit others in this
political climate: Black Lives Matter and Women's March 2017.

Black Lives Matter was founded by three Black women: Alicia
Garza, Patrisse Cullors, and Opal Tometi. These women started the movement after the murder of Trayvon Martin during the trial of his killer,
George Zimmerman. After the subsequent murders of Jordan Davis,
Michael Brown, Eric Garner, one thing became clear: Black women are
leading the charge for justice in response to Black men who have died "at
the hands of police, in police custody or from gun violence" (Drabold,
2016, n.p.). Identified as the "Mothers of the Movement" during the 2016
Democratic National Convention, several Black women spoke during
prime time television viewing hours of the convention, including the fol-
lowing: Gwen Carr, mother of Eric Garner; Sybrina Fulton, mother of
Trayvon Martin and co-founder of the Trayvon Martin Foundation,
Maria Hamilton, mother of Dontre Hamilton and creator of Mothers for
Justice United; Lucia (Lucy) McBath, mother of Jordan Davis; Lesley
McSpadden, mother of Michael Brown. Upon closer investigation, the
seven largest cities in the United States have active chapters of Black Lives
Matter and five of those chapters are led by Black women.

January 21, 2017, one day after the inauguration of the 45th president of the United States, a Women's March on Washington DC was
held to advocate for policies and legislation to support human rights issues
including women's rights. The march was held in direct response to the
electoral college's selection of Donald Trump as the 45th president of the
United States. Two Black women served in key leadership positions to
organize the march and the movement: Tamika D. Mallory, Co-President
and national co-chair for the march, and Janaye Ingram, Secretary and

Head of Logistics for the march. Key components of the mission statement for the Women's March and Movement align with some of the guiding principles of Black Lives Matter:

Women's March and Movement Mission Statement	Black Lives Matter Guiding Principles
Women's rights are human rights, regardless of a woman's race, ethnicity, religion, immigration status, sexual identity, gender expression, economic status, age or disability.	*Diversity:* commitment to acknowledging, respecting and celebrating differences and commonalities.
We practice empathy with the intent to learn about the intersecting identities of each other.	*Empathy:* Commitment to the practice of empathy.
We will suspend our first judgment and do our best to lead without ego.	*Loving Engagement:* committed to embodying and practicing justice, liberation and peace in our engagements with one another.

Not unlike the history of Black people in the United States, the future of Black lives in the United States will continue to rely heavily on the participation and leadership of Black women. In her seminal work, *When and Where I Enter: The Impact of Black Women on Race and Sex in America*, Paula Giddings (1984) chronicles the history of Black women's contributions to U.S. society, particularly as they connect to issues of race and gender. Black women were significant to the freedom of enslaved African people through support and leadership. Black women were central to the education of Black people pre-Civil War and post-Reconstruction. As stated earlier, Black women participated in the women's suffrage movement, despite their marginalization. Black women formed organizations to address political, social, and educational issues within the Black community. Black women engaged in the development and implementation of the early Civil Rights Movement. We remained vigilantly active during the modern Civil Rights Movement and the Black Power movement, enduring the marginalization of sexism within and outside the movement. Black women began to take leadership in political and social movements. Shirley Chisolm, Barbara Jordan, and Fannie Lou Hamer are clear examples of Black women living in the space of political intersectionality as they addressed issues of race as women.

Central to the work of the Student Non-violent Coordinating Committee (SNCC), Fannie Lou Hamer balanced her civil rights activism with her roles as spouse and mother. This balancing was contrary to the lives of women as described in Betty Friedan's (1963) The Feminine Mystique. But when White women were determined to be a distraction to the organization by Black men, Hamer and other Black women chose to side with Black men in demoting and marginalizing the White women who had been actively engaging with SNCC. The existence of political intersectionality promoted the necessity of this choice. As candidate for President of the United States, the campaign for Congresswoman Shirley Chisholm (NY) indicated "shortcomings of both the Black and the feminist movements" (Giddings, 1984, p. 337). As an early member of the National Organization of Women (NOW), she garnered support from student groups; As a principal architect of the National Women's Political Caucus (with Gloria Steinem, Betty Friedan, and New York Representative Bella Abzug), she was disappointed by their lack of support and resigned from the Caucus (Giddings, 1984). Black (male) leadership overwhelmingly failed to support Chisholm; the only male-led Black group to endorse her were the Black Panthers. Chisholm could balance her roles as a leading politician representing the interests of the Black community while maintaining her beliefs and efforts in women's equality (Lerner, 1972). She was a pioneer in the struggle for political intersectionality. Congresswoman Barbara Jordan was the first Black women elected to the Texas State Senate and the first Black Texan in Congress. In her run for Congress, Barbara Jordan yielded 80 percent of the vote in her district, garnering support from the Black community as well as women (Rogers, 1998).

The struggles of political intersectionality remain with us today. While the Black Lives Matter movement has centered the voices of mothers in the discussion regarding the murders of Black men, discussions regarding the murders of Black women is limited. At times, Black women who attempt to center this discussion are labeled as unsupportive. An abundance of research exists regarding the marginalization of Black boys in schools. Recently, scholars like Venus Evans-Winters (2005) have addressed the ways in which Black girls have been marginalized, entering the school-to-prison pipeline faster than many Black boys. Former First Lady Michelle Obama held a summit that focused on Black women and girls. But this work suffered critical fire from both scholars on Black boys and White feminists, each demanding its own allegiance.

The experiences of our past and present have provided us with the knowledge that positions us to lead our beloved community into our tomorrow. In this political climate, White supremacist, alt-right ultra conservatives, segregationists, protectionists, and isolationists resist engaging in dialogue that is not aligned with their own ideologies. This leaves all people of color and, in many cases, white women on the margins of the social norm. The neo-liberal project ascribes to equality (rather than equity) and respectability politics in ways that align to interest convergence. This phenomenon allows most people placed as socially marginalized to be made to feel equal if they ascribe to certain conditions deemed respectable. However, the guiding principles of both the Black Lives Matter movement and the Women's March Movement clearly indicate the ways political intersectionality that exists for Black women not only does not have to work in opposition to one another but also articulates the ways in which our intersecting identities have served us well on many fronts in this present moment.

But what Black women are experiencing in this political climate is not unlike what we have experienced in the past. Given our ability to exist in a political intersectionality, we are poised to prove central to the social, political, and educational future of the Black community. Black women can support the interests of both the Black community as well as critical feminists for social justice. Black women are poised to call into question multiple oppressions from multiple fronts. Living at the intersections of race and gender, we understand a discourse that demands multiple ways of knowing and functioning that embody justice, equity, and empathy. Our past and present experiences position us as leaders of a bright tomorrow that pushes aside our current divisive discourse against one another within this nation and against other nations, making room for collaborations and conversations of inclusion. We have traveled this road many times before today, this political moment. And while we may not have always been recognized for our efforts or have been successful in these efforts, we have learned the importance of recognizing, acknowledging, respecting, and supporting the multiple and intersecting identities of all people, but most especially those who have been socially marginalized in this country.

Understanding political intersectionality in the ways that many Black women have lived through such a phenomenon could prove beneficial in coalition building amongst such groups as the Women's March Movement and the Black Lives Matter Movement. The guiding principles of both groups align with one another that speak to the intersecting identities of the groups' leadership. Through his understanding, such coalitions could thwart the divisive discourses of a political climate set upon the maintenance of White supremacist capitalist patriarchal (hooks, 1994) actions and reactions that support structures of dominance in a society that has consistently promoted White (male) privilege (McIntosh, 1986). Working from the position of citizens who are neither exploiter nor oppressor, placing Black women at the center of coalition building can lead this country toward a future as a more perfect union, a true union where everyone's voices matter. Black women have led us in the past; Black women and our understanding of political intersectionality can lead coalition building for a bright tomorrow.

References:

Berry, T.R. & Stovall, D.O. (2013). Trayvon Martin and the curriculum of tragedy: Critical race lesson for education. *Race, Ethnicity, and Education*, 16(4), 587-602.

Crenshaw, K.W. (1995). Mapping the margins: Intersectionality, identities politics, and violence against women of color. *Stanford Law Review*, 43(6), 1241-1299.

Davis, A.Y. (1981). *Women, race, and class.* New York: Vintage Books.

Drabold, W. (2016). Meet the mothers of the movement speaking at the democratic convention. *Time*, Online: time.com/4423920/dnc-mothers-movement-speakers/

Evans-Winters, V. (2005). *Teaching Black girls: Resiliency in urban classrooms.* New York: Peter Lang.

Friedan, B. (1963). *The feminine mystique.* New York: W.W. Norton.

Giddings, P. (1984). *When and where I enter: The impact of Black women on race and sex in America.* New York: William Morrow.

Giddings, P. (1988). *In search of sisterhood: Delta Sigma Theta and the challenge of the Black sorority movement.* New York: William Morrow.

hooks, b. (1994). *Teaching to transgress: Education as the practice of freedom.* New York: Routledge.

McIntosh, P. (1986). White and male privilege: A personal account of coming to see correspondences through work in Women's Studies. Paper presentation at the annual meeting of the American Educational Research Association, Boston, MA.

Rogers, M. B. (1998). *Barbara Jordan: American hero.* New York: Bantam.

Wing, A.K. (2015) Critical race feminism. In K. Murji & J. Solomos (Eds.) *Theories of Race and Ethnicity: Contemporary Debates and Perspectives* (pp.162-179). Cambridge, UK: Cambridge University Press.

Wing, A.K. (1997). Brief reflections toward a multiplicative theory and praxis of being. In A.K.Wing (Ed.) *Critical Race Feminism: A Reader* (pp.27-34). New York: New York University Press.

RE-LITERACY AND AFRICAN POWER IN THE TRUMP ERA

GREG KIMATHI CARR

Greg Kimathi Carr is Chair of Afro-American Studies Department at Howard University and Adjunct Faculty at the Howard School of Law. He is First Vice President of the Association for the Study of Classical African Civilizations and Editor-in-Chief of The Compass: The Journal of ASCAC. He blogs at drgregcarr.com , can be found on Twitter at @AfricanaCarr and can be reached at gcarr@howard.edu

Donald John Trump could conceivably be the catalyst that Africans in America and those willing to make common cause with us for a better world have been waiting for. At the center of our multi-racial, multi-class and multi-national coalition politics, Africans in America and beyond must now renew and extend our discrete cultural, political and economic bonds. Learning from the best of our network building efforts over the last several centuries, with particular focus on institution building and organizational efforts undertaken during the Black Power era, the historical ties that bind us must be rediscovered, renewed and repurposed.

At the center of this work is deep study. We must reject the lure of symbolic posture and/or easy answers in favor of collective reading, debate, planning and executing. This is the major lesson of the so-called Civil Rights and Black Power eras and formations, from the Citizenship and Freedom Schools to the Independent School and Black Studies movements, among many others. A handful of deeply flawed ideologues, symbolized by figures such as Stephen Kevin Bannon, now threaten out-sized influence over the direction of the world's most powerful, dangerous and potentially transformative nation state. Jacob Hudson Carruthers's (Djedi Shemsw Djehuty) clarion call for Africans to prepare themselves for intellectual warfare and Asa Grant Hilliard's (Nana Baffour Amankwatia II) call for Africans to "do our homework" must now inform our daily regimen and political practice. We must meet the Trump era with deep, collective "re-literacy."

A century from now, if we do not experience a leveling natural or humanity-triggered event, the United States of America could well have reached a form and configuration we cannot currently recognize. Those unfamiliar with Neely Fuller's thesis on the systemic power of White Supremacy will strain to identify exactly when "Alt-Right populism" [White Nationalism] overwhelmed the fragile corrective capacity of the country's federal structure. Africans, well versed in the indelible presence and power of racism/White Supremacy in modern world and post-enslavement American life, are clear. We have been at least since the betrayal of the Reconstruction amendments that forced us to wage a Second Reconstruction a century later. And we remain clear in the wake of the long, steady assault on the hard-won legislative victories for all secured mostly with the blood of Africans.

Still, even the unclear will no doubt point to the 2016 federal election as a "tipping point" in the long march to this country's fundamental renegotiation. It would be in this national election that just over a quarter of registered voters, driven largely by overt post-Barack Obama contempt to mirror their local and state level efforts at political race redemption, stupidly unleashed craven ideologues who reversed New Deal and Great Society era legislative and judicial progress, unfettering their owners, unregulated, anti-labor transnational capital.

In a best case scenario, the more fortunate occupants of this future America might think and work in networked collaborative spaces, safely bypassing the continent's blotches of suffering red dystopia. These geographical pockets would be well resourced by local, state and regional economies powered by renewable energy and well-educated and politically organized labor. Spanish, Mandarin, Cantonese, Yoruba, Farsi, Lakhota and other languages will have been elevated alongside English as "official" languages in these places, following pioneering statutory efforts of multi-lingual, truly multi-cultural states like South Africa. Assaults on rights and protections afforded by the federal constitution will have been checked by powerful counterweights from more creative, corrective and transformative manifestations of "states rights." In other words, the White settler state will have Balkanized after falling victim to overplaying its hand at its last stand.

No longer "minority" groups, non-white citizens in these large swaths of a perpetually negotiated nation will leverage demography to their collective benefit. California, the finally reconstructed South and the international East Coast will have stitched their polyglot fortunes together. The past victims of American Apartheid will have ceased to be pleading wards before the altar of 18th century Enlightenment-era White political ghosts and the federal republic for which they stood.

The last clingers to the federal nation-state mythology may concede that airbrushing racist, sexist and elitist conceits and sins of the "Founding Fathers" had doomed the settler colonies-turned nation-state experiment from its inception. At any rate, new narratives will have emerged to subsume older, whiter, elite male ones. The world, no longer organized around Western centers and non-Western peripheries, would still face major challenges, but with no one country dominating international arrangements. And the United States would finally be dislodged as the enduring centerpiece of the receding Age of Europe and its former colonies.

If such a reconfiguration becomes the case, it will be cause for either lament or celebration. It would simply be one possible scenario for a country founded on dispossessions and genocide and fed and strengthened on the largest forced migration and serial attempted dehumanization in history. Many in its borders would still suffer unnecessarily as they clung to the old myths of a common national culture with whiteness at its center.

This is only one possible scenario. It presumes that human progress is perhaps the natural arc of history, a debatable proposition certainly not shared by anti-statist xenophobes like Bannon. Among other scenarios of course, would be a geographical American state completely given over to international finance capital and its wholly-owned local employees, federal, state and local politicians. Protected from the most desperate of the aggrieved by a ruthless military populated by segments of the underclasses, the well-educated and resourced beneficiaries of transnational capital will occupy bastions of status, fenced off from teeming and economically obsolete masses.

This is hardly unimaginable: This scenario follows the dystopia that twentieth/twenty-first century Europeans have long ago ensconced as a central thematic obsession in their art, from canonical novels such as 1984 and Brave New World to cannibalistic books/movies from Planet of the Apes and Soylent Green to the Hunger Games and the Scorch Trials. Some Africans, like the lawyer/activist Randall Robinson, tap into this preoccupation to depict similar landscapes in books like *The Reckoning: What Blacks Owe to Each Other*.

These polar opposite scenarios emerge from a common reality: The current global and national arrangement of people and institutions cannot and will not endure. Human societies are completing an expansion of movement that began with goods, continued with people, and now converges with "flat world" force of technology, communication and ideas. If humanity is to survive as a group, brittle "blood" loyalties baked into the Western-style order of imagined nation-state communities must embrace what writers like Wole Soyinka and Ngugi wa Thiongo have called a "politics of knowing" that identifies the power to be found when different peoples contribute culturally-derived lessons for improving the human condition. The African must now speak to the world on her own terms, knowledge and experiences. But we must study to discern and test the best of what we have known against what we must now know.

Faced with the inevitable death of old political arrangements,

America's White Nationalists of all classes have rejected the embrace of the other as a structural proposition, preferring the adornment of symbolic diversity and rallying instead to what may amount to their best last stand. With no independent coalition political parties of sufficient critical mass to intervene, corporate-funded Democrats and Republicans continue to double down on old strategies for holding and managing local, state and federal power. Public education, never universally superior and increasingly fragmented, has rendered the likelihood of a deeply informed electorate more unlikely than perhaps at any time since the 1960s.

Elected as a direct consequence of the harnessing and subsequent neutering of Black political movements of the 1960s-1980s, Barack Obama attempted to somehow enact modest expansions of access to capital, education, housing and health care while simultaneously projecting hyper-nationalist American hard and soft power. Embracing a tactical mix of moderate political positions, code-switching racial signals and a meteoric, technology abetted electoral rise, Obama captured the cultural imagination of a diverse, viscerally hopeful and largely ill-informed general electorate. He benefitted from the thrust of Black political participation unleashed after the Second Reconstruction's Voting Rights Act of 1965, a subsequent surge in Black elected officials culminating at the national level with the Jesse Jackson presidential campaigns of 1984 and 1988, and the finance capital-subsidized Democratic pivot toward white working class voters by William J. Clinton in 1992 and 1996.

If impoverished, working poor and lower middle class White Nationalists had been able to overcome their visceral rejection of anything even remotely African, they would have seen that the drone-wielding, immigrant deporting Obama posed no threat to the American international political order and even sought to improve their domestic opportunities. Instead, like previous waves of Whites driven to political madness by racial illogic, they mounted "Tea Party" insurgencies, aided and abetted by billionaires who viewed Obama as a minor threat to their God-given right to unfettered profit. Wholly owned politician subsidiaries of capital used the culturally driven White Nationalists to seize state and local power, enacting disastrous fiscal policy in states like Kansas and Indiana while vowing, on the national level, to oppose everything Obama attempted and represented. In bizarre acts of political self-flagellation, White poor and working class voters continued to vote for their own civic evisceration, their gaze fixed inexorably on the "foreigner" in their White House.

White American Nationalism, unlike Black (Inter)nationalism, is not Pan-European. Black (Inter)nationalists, while acknowledging local political and economic ties as well as cultural and historical experiences, have an expansive view of Black identity that generally embraces global networks of African culture, politics and economics. For the White American Nationalist, however, there is no commitment to global or economic political white identity beyond vague notions of a "common Western heritage" that eschews non-whites and occasional select non-Protestant white groups. Many White American Nationalists anchor race contempt in a vision of a U.S. settler state in which non-whites, however long they have been in the country, can never be fully "American." Especially not a child of an African father, regardless of his mother's white (if ultimately complex) identity.

In early 2011, the scion of a wealthy New York builder who had successfully parlayed his inheritance into a "success brand" that belied his serial business failures entered the anti-Obama fray. Donald Trump was always alert for the next opportunity to elevate the Trump name brand. By then he was best known to those beyond New York for his celebrity venture capitalist "reality" show on NBC, The Apprentice. Trump began to dabble, then to lead, the "birther" movement, arguing that Obama had not in fact been born in the United States.

Five years later, and very likely in opposition to his simple wishes to expand his brand and perhaps become the billionaire he had pretended to be for years, Donald Trump was propelled by White Nationalist populism to the Presidency of the United States. He has shown no real interest in the position beyond the accouterments of power. Time may reveal the bargains with various national and international partners that he entered, knowingly and unknowingly, to sustain his campaign while attempting to leverage it for his likely real goals. And, should his endlessly reckless streams of self-sabotage prove politically (and perhaps legally) fatal, Republican "Plan A1" is already in place. In the religious demagogue Michael Richard Pence, Trump is fenced in by true right-wing political operatives with an insurance policy more reliable even than any he negotiated for his own projects as a businessman.

Still, White Supremacy is an unstable concoction. Trump, the ultimate political wild card loose in the federal bureaucracy, has staffed his largely hollow government at the highest levels with pure political incompetents from the billionaire class. Finance capital is no longer just influencing the federal government. As in the 1980s dystopian film *The Running Ma*n, it is running it as a wholly owned subsidiary.

Steven Mnuchin at Treasury and Wilbur Ross at Commerce represent the worst elements of finance capital and anti-labor in corporate America. Elizabeth Dee (Betsy) DeVos and Benjamin Solomon Carson at Education and Housing and Urban Development are textbook examples of Trump-style Affirmative Action. Rex Wayne Tillerson presides over a hollowing out and largely mute Department of State. And the rest of the cabinet, from anti-environmentalist Scott Pruitt at the Environmental Protection Agency to anti-health care Tom Price at Health and Human Services to anti-information Rick Perry at Energy represent a cognitive dissonance that threatens to render the term "ironic" inert.

For Africans, the most dangerous member of Trump's cabinet is Selma, Alabama's Jefferson Beauregard Sessions III. A third generation namesake of American traitors Confederate States of America President Jefferson Davis and General Pierre Gustave Toutant Beauregard, Sessions represents a familiar concoction of southern civility and intolerance. As U.S. Attorney General, Sessions has moved swiftly to exert federal influence in and over states and municipalities in ways he fought against as a faithful "states rights" member of the U.S. Senate. There is no contradiction, to be sure: Sessions's fidelity is to The Lost Cause: To the restoration of the Order of Things as They Were. It is easy to understand why he was the first Senator to endorse and campaign for Trump, wearing the bright red "Make America Great Again" hat. In the words of Pan African Internationalist and Labor stalwart Bill Fletcher, Sessions and his miserable colleagues such as the Kentucky obstructionist Mitch McConnell would like nothing better than to roll back the twentieth century.

This overpowering right-wing coalition of politically ensconced billionaires, xenophobes and religious and/or political ideologues are stitched together in a marriage of convenience with Republican majorities in both chambers of the national legislature. Led in the House of Representatives by a feckless and completely overmatched Speaker, Paul Ryan and in the Senate by the baldly race and sex baiting McConnell, this group has been exposed as having one consistent goal: To pass legislation that funnels trillions of dollars into the hands of their corporate donors. If we are fortunate, future scholars may only point to the appointment of Neil Gorsuch to the U.S. Supreme Court as the most lasting domestic damage of the Trump Presidency. Gorsuch will provide a reliable vote to the John Roberts wing that decided in their 2010 Citizens United v. Federal Election Commission, that political spending by corporations is a form of protected speech under the First Amendment.

The African must not surrender to a sense that nothing can be done to build in the wake of recent American political developments. It is in this specific regard—deploying deep study and acting on what is discovered—that what Cheikh Anta Diop called "the serenity to appreciate the facts as they are" will operate to neutralize despair.

At this late juncture in world history, Africans and others must once again rise to the opportunity to build transformative networks beyond national boundaries and imaginary allegiances to oppressive states. The International Community of European-style nation-states, steadily destabilizing in the wake of irrepressible movements of ideas and information, must yield to international networks of people of good will and righteous indignation. Africans, the human engine for the rise of the Modern World System, will avoid being fodder for the worst impulses of human nature only by deliberate, concerted, connected, studied action.

Trump is a welcome accelerant to the flammable ingredients of the American settler colonies-turned-state. As Brother Malcolm famously remarked on Valentine's Day 1965 in Detroit, the week before he was killed:

> "You can't say that you're not going to have an explosion and you leave the condition, the ingredients, still here. As long as those ingredients, explosive ingredients, remain, then you're going to have the potential for explosion on your hands."

Sixty eight years earlier, W.E.B. Du Bois, writing near the beginning of the McKinley presidency and the first stirrings of America's Caribbean and Pacific Ocean "empire of color," also identified the explosive potential of unaddressed moral challenges in his first book, *The Suppression of the African Slave Trade to the United States of America*:

> "It behooves the United States, therefore, in the interest both of scientific truth and of future social reform, carefully to study such chapters of her history as that of the suppression of the slave-trade. The most obvious question which this study suggests is: How far in a State can a recognized moral wrong safely be compromised? And although this chapter of history can give us no definite answer suited to the ever-varying aspects of political life, yet it would seem to warn any nation from allowing, through carelessness and moral cowardice, any social evil to grow."

The lesson to be learned from Malcolm, Du Bois, and many other astute African students of and commentators on American and world history, is that very little of what unfolds in American history is not predictable. As technology has shortened our attention spans, we are called upon to renew the eagle's view, to discern the patterns of history so that we might collectively intervene and alter its course. Or be doomed to confront it again.

Technology has rendered much of the work of previous generations accessible with little effort. We must make a renewed study of the nineteenth century. Any study group that spent one month with Du Bois's

Black Reconstruction in America would understand the rise of Trump perhaps better than Amiri Baraka understood the tumultuous 1960s after having read it two full generations ago. For good measure, a read of Du Bois's fictional Black Flame Trilogy will find the student identifying every stock character currently being misinterpreted or ignored in social media, on television and radio news commentary, and in the newspapers and news websites.

This was one of the strengths of the intellectual and artistic arm and thrust of the Black Power movement. That movement has sometimes been sanitized and twisted by academics into an inaccessible and nevertheless deliberately misread American story that sticks in the throats of some of the current generation in search of liberation and connection. Some have been taught to regard the era as fraught with irredeemable contradictions of class and sex, or as one dimensional by people who wouldn't be caught dead with the subjects they claim to be experts on.

The Heritage Foundation provides an overwhelmed Child-in-Chief, his face an increasingly doughy strawberry pillow festooned by a thinning nest of yellow and grey hair, with thoroughly researched and vetted lists for judicial appointments. The serial comedy of the Trump White House is a distraction that is moving quickly through popular culture from fertile mine for comedy to numbing, banal disinterest. But the agenda of our open enemies remains focused. The effort to remake the federal judiciary is perhaps the single most important domestic element for the remaking—and potential balkanization—of the American state. And they are well on their way.

And where are our think tanks? They exist, to be sure, from the Joint Center for Political and Economic Studies to the NAACP Legal Defense and Education Fund and many others. But what of the Black Internationalist formations? When was the last time the reader supported the National Coalition of Blacks for Reparations in America or the Association for the Study of Classical African Civilizations?

Meanwhile, we have lost memory of the work of the Institute of the Black World, the Institute of Positive Education, the Institute for the

Arts and the Humanities and the Communiversity. Our presses continue to function, from Third World Press Foundation to Africa World Press to Black Classic Press. Yet we turn from literacy at the very moment when our language must be unearthed, read slowly, digested, debated and extended as roadmaps and action plans. In the age of trump, we must become fearlessly re-literate. We must search the pages of Black World/Negro Digest/First World to discern the parallels and historical rhythms behind the movements of the 1960s, 70s and 80s and today. This is not nostalgia. It is the practice of weaponized literacy. It is, in the words of Amen em Hat, the 12th dynasty Pharaoh quoted by Jacob Carruthers, a weheme mesu, a "repetition of the birth."

We still cannot intelligently discuss, dissect and build on the specific policy advancements of the Barack Obama presidency without laying bare his full body of work. We must develop the serenity to appreciate the facts as they are. As the new National Museum of African American History and Culture settles into its permanent presence on the National Mall, Black vendors still sell "never can say goodbye" bags with the beautiful Obama family depicted. But there are many books on the Obama presidency already written that transcend the childish politics of symbol to present us with the challenge to learn and grow collectively. We have not read them. We do not teach them. So we, the American African remain, in some ways, like a race of children.

I walk the museum regularly. On every occasion, I see more than a handful of white children wearing "Make America Great Again" caps and shirt. I cannot imagine what they must think that phrase refers to. But I cringe at the thought that, one day, I may encounter an African child wearing the paraphernalia, which I regard as more dangerous than the overt symbol of hatred of a noose. If a noose is rightly perceived as a direct threat, how then to interpret the school children touring the Museum and the National Mall in "Make America great Again" caps and shirts?

While Trump and the GOP rode birther hate speech and the White Nationalist vein it tapped to power, the irony is that the Obama they have created bears little resemblance to the Obama of reality.

Trump's self-proclaimed travel ban twists itself to argue that it builds on Obama's 2011 extreme vetting policy. Trump's immigration raids build on momentum from the Obama presidency that had many label him the "Deporter in Chief." Trump's anti education work follows in the wake of Obamas race to the top, dalliances with charters and acquiescence to D.C. vouchers. And the confused politics of conservatism found thirteen percent of Black men voting for Trump. I wonder how many of them were religious conservatives who cheered when Obama underplayed structural White Supremacy in favor of lectures to Black men to pull their pants up. After all, in our former President we found a man who took the pardon pen to liberate non-violent drug offenders and to pardon Chelsea Manning but could not sign a pardon for Marcus Garvey. We failed Obama by not requiring that he become something other than what he became. We failed ourselves as well.

We fail each other, every day, through our fatigue, through our temporary suspension of belief, even through our desire to look away and lose ourselves in momentary distractions. Still, somehow, in this learning spaces which we were bequeathed by our Ancestors to maintain for our future, we rise anew each day to renew our purpose and will, becoming stronger in the broken places.

We must read more. We need to study and understand more. We need to respect ourselves enough to redouble our efforts, supporting the best of those efforts and finding it within ourselves to improve, day-by-day. As Asa G. Hilliard used to say, there is no mystery to creating excellence in African education. It takes love of learners and learning, content mastery, and master teaching. Those who think that this cannot be done to scale should cease their lament long enough to turn their eyes and ears in the direction of the places where it has been done and where it is being done.

The Black scholars who created the first languages, alphabets, arts and sciences in world history sent their children across the oceans only yesterday. We survived that temporary trauma, and must now look to those who studied deeply in order to form our genealogy of resistance.

The thinkers who resisted the counterrevolutions of Europe's colonies, whether they be the Haitians, the Maroons of Jamaica, Suriname, or the Dismal Swamp. Those who theorized and fought for liberation in the early American period, from Prince Hall and William Cooper Nell to Maria Stewart, David Walker and Sarah and Richard Allen.

Those who found and represented Africa as they negotiated the war to consolidate American white supremacy, from Martin Delany, Fred Douglass, Mary Ann Shadd, Henry Highland Garnet to Henry McNeil Turner, Orishatukeh Fadumah and Edward Wilmot Blyden. The culture keepers who studied and staffed the great African organizations that emerged at the turn of the twentieth century and beyond, from Marcus Garvey and Hubert Henry Harrison to Nannie Helen Burroughs, Carter Godwin Woodson and Arturo Schomburg, the great keeper of texts. Those who emerged in the 1950s and 1960s to connect the entire genealogy, from Cheikh Anta Diop to Dudley Randall, Toni Cade Bambara and Hoyt Fuller.

It is our children who will now shape the stories that must be told within the next circles of meaning. As W.E.B. Du Bois once wrote, we must now out-think and out-flank the white owners of the world, realizing that our oppression is all-too-frequently with our consent. The future is ours if we will stand, fortified by our long memory and far-reaching vision, to shape it.

While Russia continues to match or exceed U.S. meddling in foreign elections and affairs, our people get sucked into watching television news like it is a sporting event. This is a direct consequence of not having studied even recent history. Convene a small circle of friends and explore the history of Russia, the Soviet Union and then Russia. And the relationship of Russia to African people, good and bad. Include African-Americans, from Ira Aldridge, Paul Robeson, Cyril Briggs, Claude McKay and Oliver Gordon to the scholarship of Allison Blakey and Joy Carew and the commentary of Yelena Khanga. Look at the rise of Communism and Ben Davis, Louise Thompson and William Patterson, James and Esther Cooper Jackson, and so many more. Every student should know the name and work of the peerless Black Internationalist historian Gerald Horne, and be familiar with contemporary columnists and Russia experts such as Terrell J. Starr.

What good are the millions upon millions of pages of words produced by our best thinkers over millennia if they cannot be mined now for collective advancement? At a time when our children are convinced of their infallibility by a consumer culture that confuses desire with vision, the very nature and purpose of literacy is being renegotiated. As Douglass noted in the years before Civil War, power concedes nothing without a demand. Education has been the primary source of Black power from the dawn of humanity through our recent oppressions and liberation struggles. And, in the moment of Trump, education remains the conduit to liberation.

Deep learning transforms wordplay into poetry. Study of past battles, victories and losses transforms organizing into transformation. Informed writing generates fresh ideas that connect to deeper rhythms of meaning. Trump and the brutal forces that enable and sustain his kind are neither original nor difficult to comprehend. They are, however, the battlefield we find ourselves on at the moment. Let us study. Let us fight. Let us win.

"YOU'RE FIRED!"

ERICA R. DÁVILA

Erica R. Dávila *is an Associate Professor of Educational Leadership at Lewis University in Illinois, where she teaches in a doctoral program focused on social justice and transformative leadership. Her research and published articles examine Latinx critical studies, critical race theory, and urban education.*

I am Woman, I am of color, I am a teacher, I am a warrior, I am here.

Nation-states have to fight for the creation and maintenance of unnatural borders. The United States is not excluded from this grim reality. This nation and its colonies were built on stolen land with slave labor. These United States were founded on war, slavery, genocide and rape. As I reflect on this sociohistorical reality, I think of my ancestors and the ways they evolved within this reality. Despite the history of slavery and genocide our ancestors resisted. In this personal narrative, I situate my identity as an Afro Puerto Rican woman who is proud of my ancestral Warriorship, but critical of the colonial project that sparked my warrior stance.

I Am Everything He is Not...and Thank God for That

In this framing of my identity I am purposefully othering our current president, known as 45 in this essay. I am everything he is *NOT* and I am very intentional about this opposition. Like many, I first learned of 45 when he hosted a reality TV show, and in this show he was known to fire contestants and the catch phrase "you're fired" quickly became synonymous with 45. To understand that this was his claim to fame is a critical reality check because the phrase "you're fired" is rooted in a deeper and important history of a country that thrives on the backs of those in the position to be fired.

Personally, I grew up in a community and family who were in that vulnerable state of "being fired" unlike 45 and the many who inhabit cabinet spaces within his administration. Our vulnerability was rooted in the history of this country, as Puerto Ricans our very existence was embedded in the colonial project. And in my early years, I grew up in a neighborhood in Chicago that was being quickly gentrified, making our presence as people of color who rarely spoke English in public, one of "other" and simply disposable. This lived reality of the structure of power at the root of our nation keeps folks in this vulnerable state of losing their job and being pushed out of their communities. I used this as an example of how distinct 45's lived experience is directly in contrast to many in this country who struggle to acquire, maintain and thrive in their respective careers. He has never known what it means to *NEED* a job to feed your family thus using this catch phrase without understanding the weight or connotation it entails.

For the entire history of this country, people have fought and continue to fight against the reality of unemployment and underemployment, which is part of a larger historical context that has been created to keep folks poor and others rich. It is important to note that our country is designed to enforce social classes under a colonial model and we have yet to experience leadership that effectively seeks to change the landscape of social inequity of Americans.

The reality TV show host-turned-president awakened something in many around this nation. He awakened his base, those who were/are feeling that people of color were diluting their power especially since his predecessor is a Black man. And he awakened or reminded those who never experienced the power that the former group feels they lost and are now a part of the resistance. I am proud to be a part of the latter group although not easy, just like my ancestors, I will resist. I will share my positionality as part of the critical resistance, specifically as a critical educator fighting for my voice and with my people to be heard.

I recall being a college student studying Sociology and Education at a university in Chicago. I am a product of the Chicago Public Schools (CPS). Neither of my parents completed high school and we survived thanks to public aid. This reality led me to analyze the sociological frameworks I was studying in college in a real and grounded way, I kept thinking they are trying to tell me all of this poverty was engineered. At first, I was pissed off and could not wrap my head around that reality. But after a continued reflective path and much reading and dialoging I started to understand that the schools I attended were set up to keep us as the working poor. I was born to parents who were already labeled in this society as deficit as missing things like a formal education or material things like a home instead of seeing everything they did (and do) contribute. My parents demonstrated what it meant to have unconditional love, compassion and humanity, but these values do not carry the same currency in our society. What I came to understand was that most people on welfare actually needed it because they have been set up to fail from the start; being born into a lower socioeconomic class with limited access to basic human needs like quality health care and quality education.

However, this was not the narrative I grew up understanding. Although my parents instilled a strong pride in my Puerto Rican identity and history, they shared the narrative of meritocracy and the "American Dream" that they were fed. They internalized the message that if you just work hard you will succeed. Ironically, 45 actually provoked their resistance, as well and now (so many years later) they have revisited the validity of the "American Dream."

Whiteness as Exclusionary

When I first started studying race and racism, one of the moments I recall clearly was reading Haney-López's, *White by Law*. It helped me understand how certain folks were given their "whiteness" by the court of law. This idea was transformative in my mind because it helped me understand the social construction of race, but more importantly the legal construction and the ways they intertwined in these United States.

Whiteness was created to exclude people of color, and this exclusion is being maintained throughout history with reminders for folks of color, that we are "other." The courts and the law are part of the structures that created the racial divide, and yet we continue to turn to those very courts for racial justice. This conundrum continues, and in many ways, is exacerbated by Trump's admistration and policies.

Racism has been at the forefront of his campaign and now his time in the White House. The main slogan of 45's administration is to "Make America Great Again", which was also used by the Reagan campaign. Many have argued that there is another message at the root, which is to "Make America White Again."

Recently, a candidate running for Congress in Tennessee, Rick Tyler, used this very phrase. He was not the only one reading 45's slogan with this revision from "Great" to "White." In fact, many in 45's base are aiming for this very goal. He and others have demonstrated this belief in many attempted political moves such as but not limited to, the fascination with building a wall on our southern border. There have been many attempts to ban folks from mostly Muslim countries, despite their many contributions to our country. The resistance has been strong and undying.

When 45 attempted to keep folks detained at airports, thousands flooded many major airports demanding their release. Lawyers who fight for justice were literally in the trenches setting up offices inside the airports, and while 45's ban impacted the lives of many folks, the resistance fought to keep that impact to a minimum. While 45's platform have been front and center in the media, including the border wall and the Muslim ban, there have been so many other ripples of his platform impacting so many people in this country. For example, the "slow violence" happening in public spaces, for example public schools.

Over the last 40 years, we have seen many public school student suffer from policies that leave children of color at the margins, curriculum and testing methods that have been proven to be ineffective year after year, a decrease of school counselors, an increase in police presence that leads to hyperdiscipline. Activists and concerned parents are fighting against these types policies and fighting to save public schools that serve our children well. I am an advocate for public schools and I will fight against the state and federal attempts to eliminate them.

Schools as Public Space

In another attempt to create the "other," our public schools are under attack in many levels. Schools in the U.S. function as sites of struggle where teachers should critically explore their emancipatory potential as educators and public intellectuals. The political nature of classrooms are entrenched in traditional notions of power, knowledge and truth that reproduce social categories of inequality. These spaces provide the context for a need of transformative intellectuals in schools at every level, from early childhood through higher education.

Thus, critical educators at all levels of schooling must create/re-create and question the discourse around public intellectuals by reflecting on ideas that can rupture the anti-intellectualism that is woven in the current structure of public schools. The profession of teaching has been contested in various forms throughout history, but the current context for teachers (especially in public schools) is hostile. We need to fight to keep public schools alive and thriving, we have seen a rapid demise of public schooling, and one of the most horrific examples is right in my home town of Chicago where 49 schools closed in just one summer, and these schools were mostly serving children of color and many are the working poor.

This is not an accident. The problem with having a private system ready to discard students based on subjective policies and practices is that they keep many children at the margins and literally never given an equitable chance of succeeding. Millions of children who have the legal right to services in public schools, such as the right to an Individualized Education Plan (IEP) due to their special needs or students whose first language is not English and who under federal law need a bilingual education are dismissed in a private system and framed as disposable.

Do Not Say His Name

I have noticed that even some in the mainstream media refuse to say his name and instead refer to our current president as solely 45 - this includes many white people who are in a higher socioeconomic class. I believe some might have even voted for him and then regretted it, but the bottom line is they will not even use his name. As I reflect on this technique, it makes me feel empowered because for too many years throughout history so many of our people have been stripped of their names and for many stripped of their whole identity. One of the most important examples and I believe the one that set up the impetus for all other examples of this un-naming is slavery. I still recall learning about enslaved persons having to sign an 'X' because their so-called masters attempted to keep them illiterate and that the law actually stated that these humans were only a fraction of a human. This practice speaks volumes about humanity and the fear of losing power, which we still see and experience in current politics and practices, such as mass incarceration. Research has demonstrated that many folks are incarcerated due to a system that thrives on locking people up and the stripping of their humanity, identifying them by a number and stripping them of their rights even after their release.

However, we are resisting. There are folks on the outside and inside fighting this narrative and building despite the project of mass incarceration. We are flipping the script on 45 and using the tactic of not naming him to strip him of some power. He is a reflection and symbol of this very fabric we must resist. Objectifying him by not naming him allows us to understand that this is larger than him and really about a system. I believe history is everything that matters and informs why and how I am even here and who I am in this space.

I have heard some of 45's base argue that history is not relevant, which is how he can rationalize his platform because *ANY* sense of history will pull their platform from right under their feet. My history is that I am part of a lineage of folks who were innovators and leaned into their ancestry, into their otherness, into their blackness, into their indigenous roots and in this space they survived, and defied genocide and collectivity birthed a generation of fighters. Genocide does not just kill in a physical sense; the colonial project attempts to kill the spirit of the indigenous people who breathed this very land into existence. The make up of the land, the flowers that bloomed, the food that grew the life threatens the very root of the colonial project. The colonial project came to extinguish entire cultures.

Throughout history, folks born out of this struggle have resisted the colonial project, warriors who fought to keep their physical and spiritual selves alive are passed on from one generation to the next. We are the benefactors of their Warriorship and they have passed down the tools to be able to function in this "post" colonial space where we are given smoke and mirrors of liberation and freedom. We know that at every turn, there is another state-sponsored booby trap to continue the colonial project, which has guided politics and practices in these United States. However, just as the title of this anthology states "we [the resisters] are the clear majority in [45's] stolen land." This collective critical resistance will be echoed for the duration of this presidency, and as long as the colonial project attempts to other and silence our people of this country.

While I resist, I recognize where my Warrior stance comes from and it is from a history rooted in isms - racism, classism, sexism that my ancestors fought and while some may argue they lost I believe we are still fighting and will continue to do so.

My very presence (and the collective of people writing for this anthology) is part of the fight, part of the critical resistance. It is important to understand the impetus for this fight has been violent acts on our people; we are not defiant because we enjoy it, we are defiant to survive and thrive in a country built on exclusion while touting a narrative of inclusion.

LET'S GET FREE! A CALL FOR HIP-HOP ACTIVISM IN THE TRUMP ERA

DANIEL R. DAVIS

__Daniel Ryan Davis__ is a public speaker, author, educational consultant, urban historian, and Africana Studies professor. His primary research interests are 20th Century African American History, African American education, Hip Hop/urban culture, and the enslavement era. His most recent publication is entitled __Sustained Inequality: African American Education in a 'Post-Racial' Nation.__

"You could name practically any problem in the hood and there'd be a rap song for you."
— Jay-Z

During a lecture in my Spring 2015 *African American Studies 214: Hip Hop Culture and Politics* course I had a meltdown. A profanity laced, "why are we even talking about this shit?" "this is all bullshit!" style meltdown. Imagine the scene, a 30-year old scholar activist with a doctorate degree in "Black" Studies wearing black Timberland boots and a black hoodie at a 90% Black college located in a 95% Black community plagued by extreme poverty, crime, and educational underachievement emphatically bashing the culture that he, much of his class, and the community he's teaching in represents. Not to mention I just battle rapped against a student in the previous week's class. As a young Black male from the "hood," born in the hip hop generation and a true to life "hip hop head," I realized in that moment that I was hurting.

I felt guilty about romanticizing the genius, power, and influence of a culture that I proudly boasted "was created by us" when I knew inside that this culture wasn't truly serving a pragmatic purpose regarding the collective condition of African Americans. I felt academically irresponsible discussing this art form as if it were something more meaningful. I ranted that hip hop was simply cultural expression and entertainment and not a vehicle for change or Black uplift. My class stared at me, somewhat startled as I shouted that I would never teach this class again because it's useless if we're honestly trying to better ourselves as a community. In that moment, I meant every word, but again, I was hurting.

After class, several of my students came to me saying that they "felt me," but reiterated that learning about hip hop was indeed important. They disagreed with my assertion that it was pointless because it was so influential to our community. After sitting in my office that afternoon and reflecting on what just happened and after even more reflection on the drive home while Young Jeezy's Trap or Die mixtape blasted through my speakers, I settled in the realization that I was just "having a moment." I understood that I was just frustrated by the pain, suffering, and hopelessness I confronted daily doing this work, and when you're upset the thing you love most and that's closest to you often bears the brunt of your emotions. The reality was that I understood then, as I do today, that we have a tool in our hands that can possibly fix many of the problems in Black America. We simply aren't utilizing its corrective and healing qualities.

Music has always fueled Black America's will to compete, joyfully proclaimed its' victories, and woefully expressed its' defeats. At their most rudimentary level, musical artists have always encapsulated the pulse of Black America. Due to our horrific introduction to the United States as chattel slaves, exacerbated by centuries of sustained oppression, marginalization, and unequal treatment, African Americans have been forced to adroitly create coping mechanisms and alternate approaches to psychological uplift and social mobility. Namely, in response to circumstances created and maintained by White supremacy, African Americans have excessively looked to the arts, specifically music, as a panacea. This charge is not a criticism, it simply serves as an acknowledgement of African Americans' survivalist spirit, resiliency, and the power of our artistic genius.

When then 32-year-old R&B/Soul legend Marvin Gaye serenaded the world with his iconic hit record "What's Going On (1971)," it was clear to any listener that this song was more than just words and sounds. When Marvin started the song singing *"Mother, mother, there's too many of you crying/brother, brother, brother, there's far too many of you dying"* it was a knock at the door of millions of hearts, anxiously, yet unknowingly, anticipating his arrival. Mr. Gaye himself, speaking about the social climate during the song's release, stated that *"people were confused and needed reassurance. God was offering that reassurance through his music. I was privileged to be the instrument."*

"What's Going On" was released at the intersection of three particularly impactful and historic moments in the United States. The year, 1971, immediately followed the Civil Rights Movement, an over decade long period defined by intense racial confrontations and continuous peaceful protests in the form of sit-ins, marches, boycotts, and trajectory altering legal battles for the full citizenship of African Americans; this was a period that witnessed the desegregation of public schools and the rise of Dr. Martin Luther King, Jr. This year also resided in the early stages of the Black Power era, which was heavily informed by the spirit of Black pride and a more bellicose resistance to racial oppression. Just as requisite to the definition of this space in time was the controversial Vietnam War. This was a time of mass protest, national skepticism, uncertainty, and hippie altruism. Adeptly, Marvin was able to capture the spirit of each of these societal "goings on" using smooth melody, soul, and deliberate word selection. The song was, and still is, verbal acupuncture—a sonic balm for those in discomfort.

Moreover, Marvin goes on to say "father, father- we don't need to escalate/ war is not the answer/ for only love can conquer hate." Here Marvin simultaneously provides a prescription (love) for the ills of racial tension and international warfare while reinforcing the basic yet immense value and necessity of the family as he has, at this point, spoken to "mother, brother, and father." It is this type of rhetorical offering, cloaked with the fervor of the collective human spirit that's been molested by life's circumstances, that illustrates the infinite capacity and potential of music. This potentiality has been exhibited for generations by artistic healers of yesteryear. These now antique ventriloquists for the human spirit such as Lead Belly, Billie Holiday, Bob Dylan, Bob Marley, Johnny Cash, Donnie Hathaway, John Lennon, Curtis Mayfield, James Brown, and many others made songs that were not only pleasurable to the ear, but also soothing to the soul, comforting to the spirit, stirring for the young, cautionary to the powers that be, and prescriptive to society.

The aforementioned artists, housed within multiple musical genres, each understood the power of their musical gifts and their celebrity platforms. The African American musical canon, particularly, beginning with the work songs on the plantation fields of the southern United States, has a tradition of art informing life and vice versa, that dates back centuries. Marvin Gaye's "What's Going On," while masterfully performed, is but another example of this musical custom. These artists of the past lacked the political, corporate, and economic clout enjoyed by African American artists today. Despite this, many of these artists still understood and accepted their social responsibility and offered the community emotional and spiritual activism—a sort of musical philanthropy.

In the 1960's when then 36-year-old James Brown screamed "Say it loud—I'm Black and I'm proud," that was activism. When he released the song "Don't Be a Drop-out" at 34 years of age and donated the royalties to a drop-out prevention charity—that was activism. When Ray Charles refused to perform in a segregated venue because his people were forced to sit in the back—that was activism. Many other early to mid-twentieth century artists, some previously mentioned, have also contributed dutifully to this artistic expectation.

Today, in the surreal "Trump Era," the African American community needs its most influential, talented, and resourceful musical artists to live up to their musical heritage. We need our gifted modern day *griots* to help us through this moment of confusion, valid pessimism, escalating overt racism, extreme economic inequality, and relative political chaos. We need them to speak progress and productivity in their music, as well as aide us with economic support while using their political voice. In 2017, it's imperative that our artist, who we have blessed with our fandom, with economic prosperity, and with the luxury to exercise their respective passions, to help us not only figure out "what's going on" today, but also what we can do about it. It's within these contexts, the African American musical canon and the present "Trump Era," that we must examine the societal contributions, motivations, and responsibilities of contemporary artists stationed within our most current and possibly most impactful musical era—hip hop.

What is Hip Hop?

At its inception, hip hop was a positive, socially conscious, party culture. The youth who founded this culture, naturally merged each of these characteristics into what would become a global phenomenon. In fact, a phenomenon may not be the appropriate term to describe hip hop; that word implies the occurrence or presence of a remarkable wonder with a temporary existence-hip hop is here to stay.

Hip hop generationers are generally considered to be individuals born between 1965-1984. These "hip hoppers" were socialized after hip hop culture's genesis and introduction to the world in the 1970s. Therefore, the historical perspectives, social experiences, political happenings, etc. of the 1970s-90s, are all shared by residents of this hip hop era. What is also shared is hip hop generationers' historical placement in a post-civil rights and de-industrialized world that endured the crack epidemic, the birth of the prison industrial complex (New Jim Crowism), a controversial federal welfare system, rampant fatherlessness, and a computer technology boom whose significance will be discussed later. It's from this collective purview that musical and cultural legends were born and continue to be produced.

Today, the wealthiest, most admired, and most powerful individuals we have in Black America are hip hop artists and moguls. Shawn Carter, a.k.a. Jay-Z, Sean Combs a.k.a. "P-Diddy," "Puff Daddy," "Diddy," and "Puffy," and Andre Young a.k.a. Dr. Dre have a net worth of $550 million, $750 million, and $700 million dollars respectively. Additionally, each of these hip hop power brokers have huge communication platforms under their control: Jay-Z – Tidal Streaming Service, Roc Nation Media Company; Puff Daddy – Revolt Television Network, Dr. Dre – Apple Music, Aftermath Records. Below is a list of some of hip hop's "cash kings:

Rapper/Entertainer/ Entrepreneur	Net Wealth (millions)
Master P	$350
Russell Simmons	$325
Ronald Slim Williams	$170
50 Cent	$155
Birdman	$150
Pharrell Williams	$150
Lil Wayne	$150
Kanye West	$147
Snopp Dogg	$143
Ice Cube	$120
LL Cool J	$100

Source: Inquisitr.com (2016)

Combined, the 14 aforementioned hip hop artists and executives have a sum net worth of approximately $4 billion dollars! Unquestionably, these artists, along with a multitude of others, have benefited greatly from the loyal support and adulation of the African American community.

Where is the reciprocity?

In this contemporary climate, with Donald J. Trump serving as commander in chief, the African American/hip hop community, along with other groups of color, is quite frankly under blatant attack. Ironically, the call for the African American artist community to step up is coming at a time when Trump wants to cut funding for the National Endowment for the Arts which supports art, artists, and programs to nurture artists. It's no secret that President Trump has been lauded as at best, "racially insensitive" and at worst (and perhaps most accurately) a complete bigot. President Trump's emphatic pledge to remove illegal immigrants, and simultaneously demean Mexican culture, ban multiple countries that are predominately Muslim from traveling to the United States, and his repeatedly racist comments targeting African Americans— "what the hell do you have to lose," "look at my African American over here," etc., are clear signs of his racist and xenophobic ideologies. Trump also plans to cut funding for the Minority Business Development Agency (MBDA) which supports minority owned business by helping them gain capital and contracts. Combined with his insultingly patronizing interactions with Black ministers and celebrities, overwhelmingly White cabinet appointees, history of discriminatory practices as a businessman, and endorsement of stop and frisk, a severely discriminatory police policy which encourages overt racial profiling, it's clear what we as African Americans are up against under his "rule."

This historical moment amplifies the African American communities' call for action to our musical artists and cultural leaders. Without question, these artists also serve as our key cultural/political influencers, economic leaders, entrepreneurial resources, media controllers, community advocates, philosophers, and youth role models. Quite frankly, in many respects, given the current political and economic climate, they may just serve as our hope.

In recent years, despite Puff Daddy spearheading the very popular 'Vote or Die' movement and several big name rappers, including Jay-Z and Young Jeezy among many others, publicly supporting the presidential candidacy of Barack Obama and Hilary Clinton, we have unfortunately seen our hope or our elder statesmen of hip hop appear hopeless and useless as vehicles for African Americans' collective progress. In 2016, hip hop legend Lil Wayne, one of hip hop's most listened to and revered artists, was quoted as saying "there's no such thing as racism." Later that year, while being interviewed on ABC's Nightline, when asked about Black Lives Matter, he shockingly stated "What is that? What do you mean? It just sounds weird…I am a young Black rich motherfucker, if that don't let you know that America understand Black lives matter these days I don't know what it is, don't come at me with that dumb shit ma'am, my life matters, especially to my bitches." When probed by the interviewer, "do you separate yourself from it [Black Lives Matter]?" he replied "I don't feel connected to a damned thing that ain't got nothing to do with me, if you do you crazy as shit, you, I'm connected to this motherfucking flag right here (takes a red flag from his pocket which represents the infamous Bloods street gang, which he allegedly joined after becoming a multi-millionaire adult rapper) cuz I'm connected, I'm a gang banger man, I'm connected" and after the interview, while angrily removing his microphone he stated *"I ain't no (inaudible) politician."*

In a 2013 Los Angeles Times article titled "Jay-Z on Social Responsibility: 'My Presence is Charity,'" when asked about African American artists of today, noted activist and legendary entertainer Harry Belafonte stated "I think one of the great abuses of this modern time is that we should have had such high-profile artists, powerful celebrities… but they have turned their back on social responsibility. That goes for Jay-Z and Beyoncé, for example. Give me Bruce Springsteen, and now you're talking. I really think he is black." In response to this critique, Jay-Z responded "I'm offended by that because first of all, and this is going to sound arrogant, but my presence is charity. Just who I am," he said. "Just like Obama's is. Obama provides hope. Whether he does anything, the hope that he provides for a nation, and outside of America is enough." To add insult to injury, Jay-Z later responded to this slight in a song and called then 86 year old civil rights hero Harry Belafonte "boy."

What Must Be Done?

Optimistically, hip hop artists and/or rap generationers have a unique opportunity to be purveyors of change and revolution. The direct to consumer/fan capability provided by social media and YouTube, without the middle men of cable networks, radio stations, record labels, publicists, etc., allows an artist to influence his or her legions of loyal followers to an astounding degree. The present marketing capability that social media and YouTube provides should liberate artists. No longer do they need to appease their proverbial "masters." Artists no longer need to worry about "embarrassing" or "upsetting" their record label by speaking out on an issue, participating in a protest, leading a boycott, or creating content that is true to themselves. More than ever, our creative geniuses of today can be the emotional, political, and social leaders we need them to be in harmony with our academic thinkers, journalists, businessmen, street level activists, politicians, and religious leaders. Fortunately, many hip hop artists are already presently active within this frame of thought. Well known artists such as: Kendrick Lamar, Nas, J Cole, Talib Kweli, Common, Mos Def, KRS-1, Lupe Fiasco, David Banner, T.I. (as of late), and others are speaking truth to power, participating in boots on the ground protests, and using their artistic gift to uplift their community in song.

In addition to leading by example and providing thoughtful commentary on society, we need our hip hop power brokers to invest in the Black community. Self-reliance, within the context of Black America, is more than individuals holding themselves accountable for their individual actions. While this is certainly mandatory, it's also necessary for successful members of the community to "lift as they climb." We need more than thoughtful lyrics, token philanthropy, rhetoric, and celebratory anthems to better our collective condition in this time of Trump especially.

We are in desperate need of educational and social service institutions designed to both address our psychological, geographical, emotional, and economic deficits while promoting and expanding upon our natural and learned gifts, cultural knowledge base, talents, strengths, and aspirations; this requires funding. We need professional training programs for those of us who don't attend traditional colleges and/or universities. We need programs and workshops designed to encourage entrepreneurship in our community. Additionally, we need investors to support these entrepreneurs with capital and mentorship; this requires funding. We need more programs that target convicted felons designed to assist them with their transition back into the "free" world. This requires funding. We need more media controlled by members of the community. This means radio, television, and print. We must be agents of our own change and uplift. We must tell our own story and portray our culture, lived experiences, and history ourselves; this requires funding. Our hip hop artists and executives have the ability to galvanize and provide funding for many of these initiatives. The collective will of our hip hop artists simply does not seem to be there.

It's embarrassing that we, as African Americans and the hip hop community specifically, have so many resources at our disposal, yet we still have so many needs that haven't been properly addressed. We, the fans, the consumer, the congratulator, the spectator, are tasked with the responsibility of holding our gifted artists accountable. Our unconditional support is at our own peril. How ridiculous is it to enthusiastically support those who have at best forgot about you and at worst actively contribute to your lowly condition and the demise of our youth? The academic community must extend our hands to the artist community and provide theoretical frameworks, philosophical approaches, and historical perspective to supplement their pragmatic efforts.

We must realize that "only us can save us," so in the spirit of notable activist hip hop group Dead Prez, LET"S GET FREE!

References:

Jay-Z. 2011. *Decoded.* New York: Spiegel & Grau. p. 203.

Gaye, Marvin. (1971). What's going on [Recorded by Marvin Gaye]. Detroit, MI: Motown Records.

Ritz, D. 1991. *Divided soul: The life of Marvin Gaye.* Cambridge: Da Capo Press. p. 151.

ABCNews Nightline]. (2016, November 2). Lil Wayne on Black lives matter [Video File]. Online: youtube.com/watch?v=L6mBZSQdGCE&t=2s. Accessed: April 22, 2017.

Brown, A. (2013, July 26). Jay Z on social responsibility: 'My presence is charity'. *Los Angeles Times.* Online: articles.latimes.com/2013/jul/26/entertainment/la-et-ms-jay-z-on-social-responsibility-my-presence-is-charity-20130726

Anthony, J. (2008, November 4). Soulja Boy gives shout out to slave masters. *The Guardian.* Online: theguardian.com/music/2008/nov/04/soulja-boy-slavery

Nas. (2002). Black Zombie. [Recorded by Nasir Jones]. New York: Columbia Records.

Sicat, P. (2016, June 29). Rappers: Net Worth of Rap Music Artists. *Inquisitr.* Online: inquisitr.com/3255691/rappers-the-net-worth-of-rap-music-artists

FLESH ON THE GROUND IN THE TRUMP ERA

TALIB KWELI GREENE

Talib Kweli Greene is a Hip-Hop recording artist, entrepreneur, and so-cial activist. He is the son of professional educators. In 2011, Kweli founded Javotti Media, which is self-defined as: "a platform for independ-ent thinkers and doers. His website is: talibkweli.com

If you grew up in New York City in the 1980s, avoiding the orange phe-nomenon known as Donald Trump was damn near impossible. He was everywhere, attending parties and premieres, dating fashion models. His first mention in the mainstream media ever was a 1973 story in the New York Times about how he was being sued for housing discrimination. Much like the gaudy, decadent television show *Lifestyles Of The Rich and Famous*, Donald Trump represented every stereotype the poor and work-ing class masses had about rich people in the 80s. That spoiled, entitled, hyper-violent, sexist villain seen in so many 80s teen comedies? Donald Trump was a father figure to that caricature. And it was fine, because as long as all he was doing was making sure poor New Yorkers of color had a hard time living in his buildings, he was tolerated. Scratch that, he was celebrated. Donald Trump, son of a billionaire slumlord and Ku Klux Klan supporter, was seen as a symbol of the American Dream, the physical embodiment of wealth itself.

So, when Donald Trump took out a full-page ad in the *New York Post* demanding that the Central Park Five, black teenagers who were later exonerated by DNA testing, and set free, should be given the death penalty for a crime they had yet to be found guilty of, it was dismissed by mainstream media as Trump just being Trump. When reports began to surface about Donald Trump saying things like "laziness is a trait in the blacks" and "the only kind of people I want counting my money are short guys that wear yarmulkes every day," they were dismissed as Trump just being Trump.

Personally, I always recognized Donald Trump's racist dog whistles. I would cringe whenever my favorite rappers would mention him in lyrics as a symbol of opulence. When he began doing reality TV, while overseeing failed business venture after failed business venture, while declaring bankruptcy four times, Trump began to make more sense to me. He was a clown, a court jester, an empty suit. I was fine with letting him pretend to be the boss, fake firing people on TV. Donald Trump's tangible effect on my life wasn't realized by me until he was triggered by the election of the first black president in United States history, Barack Hussein Obama.

And triggered he was. There was something about Obama that just didn't sit right with Donald Trump, and being a famous white man he was given an incredible platform to speak on this at length on Fox News, often. As the world's most famous birther, Donald Trump went out of his way to normalize the very racist lie that Obama was not born in America. According to Trump, Obama had to be lying. He offered no proof of this, other than Obama seemed foreign to his sensibilities. If you grew up the son of a billionaire Ku Klux Klan supporter, you were promised a world in which no black man would ever have authority over you. Barack Obama's mere existence destroyed Donald Trump's world, and so he made disparaging Obama his main focus.

Dedicating his life to destroying Obama's credibility made Donald Trump a darling of the far right and the Tea Party. The party of no now had a celebrity spokesman, one who was fun to watch whether he made sense or not. And as long as Trump was anti-Obama, it didn't matter whether he aligned with so-called conservative Christian values. Being anti-Obama was all that was needed to elevate Trump from reality TV show star to serious GOP presidential contender.

Like many left-leaning progressives, I was naive to how much of a shot Donald Trump truly had. As a working artist, I'm blessed to travel the world seeing humanity at its very best. The people who come to my shows are compassionate, intelligent and they stand for justice. I am blessed to choose who I want to work with and be around. My friends who aren't artists for a living don't have this luxury. They are forced to commute daily to jobs that help some boss get richer than them while working around people they may not even like. These people had a more realistic view of Trump's chances. My friend Seth Byrd, a plumber by trade, told me Trump had the election in the bag. I bet him a dollar Trump would lose. I still owe him that dollar.

When Trump started his campaign by saying Mexicans are rapists and kicking Mexican reporters out of his press conferences, he was exhibiting the same behavior I saw him exhibiting when he demonized the Central Park Five. When he bullied Elizabeth Warren with that Pocahontas slur and disrespected Ghazala Khan, a Gold Star mother, I saw the same misogynist who had been famously busting into girls dressing rooms unannounced at his pageants for years. Despite this sordid history, the GOP handed Donald Trump the nomination. Soon after, Trump would hire the executive chair of Breitbart News Inc. as his campaign manager. Steve Bannon is notorious for his advocacy of white supremacy. He is on record publicly advocating for white nationalism over and over again. He is anti-diversity, anti-immigrant and anti-Muslim. He has been accused of saying he didn't want his children to attend school with "whiny jews.' So when Donald Trump himself RT'd neo-nazi accounts over 75 times during his campaign and then hired an admitted white nationalist to run said campaign, that wasn't just coincidence.

Even if people missed Steve Bannon's love of white supremacy, it was impossible to miss how Breitbart.com became a Trump cheerleading site while they weren't printing stories about how *"Gays Need to Get Back In The Closet," "Renegade Jews," "How Birth Control Makes Women Crazy"* and how the confederate flag has a *"Proud And Glorious Heritage."* This is not hyperbole, these are actual Breitbart headlines. Between Breitbart.com and its louder, dumber cousin Infowars (run by Alex Jones) Trump had the only news outlets he needed. It didn't matter that Infowars posted stories about Obama being a demon who smelled of sulfur and hard-hitting pieces about how the Sandy Hook massacre was staged. As long as they said good things about Trump, he considered them his primary sources of info. Everything else was ironically dumbed fake news. By using his Twitter account to spread the lies he read on Breitbart and Info Wars, Trump effectively reached his core base without having to deal with the fact checkers and investigative journalists who would call him on his bullshit. While we went high and ignored the trolls as they went low, they used Twitter and Facebook to spread enough lies to help win Trump the election. Especially the Russian sock accounts. America elected a troll for president.

By the time the tape surfaced of Trump bragging about sexual assault, I had learned my lesson. Trump's base would support him no matter what he said or did, and his base was a very vocal minority that chose social media as their venue while mainstream media was busy patting itself on the back. I could no longer afford to dismiss Trump as a joke. The man was caught on tape saying he gets to "grab them by the pussy" without permission because he's a star, and it somehow made him more popular with his core, family values supporters. These people would clearly do whatever it took to win this election, even if it meant contradicting everything they claimed to stand for. Racist white people in America knew that making the most famous birther in the world president would be the ultimate fuck you to Obama. They relished the thought of electing Trump to stick it to the *nigger* president with unabashed glee.

There are those who say that Hillary Clinton and Barack Obama are at least as bad, maybe worse, than Donald Trump. There are Bernie

Sanders supporters who began to support Trump after Bernie lost the primary. Fact is, every presidential candidate who has ever had a real shot at the presidency has been an imperialist, because America has always used imperialism to support its interests around the world. So yes, Obama utilized the very immoral drone program more than any President and deported many immigrants. Yes, Hillary Clinton supported, then later apologized for her support of, mass incarceration policies. However, these politicians, including Bernie Sanders, respected the system of checks and balances that keep our country from descending into dictatorship.

When I see former GOP president George Bush — who I could've sworn was the most evil president we'd ever seen until Trump — also challenge Trump's knack for fascist rhetoric, I know it's not just my lefty bias that is making me see Trump as a far worse existential threat to democracy than any American "politician" that has come before him. Many say that Bernie Sanders was cheated out of the DNC nomination. What Bernie Sanders himself said was that he would campaign for and support Hillary Clinton for president, because he acknowledged where we were, not where he wanted us to be. Did Sanders want to be the nominee? Of course. Did he deserve to be the nominee over Hillary? Quite possibly. But he wasn't. Blame that on money in politics and the two-party system. But in the meantime, Bernie knew that the work to stop Trump still needed to be done. He knew that Hillary Clinton was the only politician with a chance to defeat Trump. Sadly, many of Bernie's supporters only supported Bernie as long as they thought Bernie could be president. Once Sanders didn't get the nomination, they were all too willing to hand Trump the presidency out of spite for Hillary Clinton, which was the exact opposite of Bernie's messaging post-primaries.

I have always hesitated to compare Trump to Hitler. It can come off as petty and dramatic and undermine otherwise sound arguments to jump to Hitler comparisons. However, Donald Trump has without a doubt consistently displayed the traits of a narcissistic fascist who doesn't understand the difference between president of a democracy that has governmental checks and balances and a dictator. When I saw his first unhinged press conference, in which he disrespected a black journalist, silenced a Jewish journalist, and told bold faced, very unnecessary lies about the margin of his victory over Hillary Clinton, I knew I was watching a Hitler moment. It wasn't good enough that Trump won the election, he very badly needed us to believe that he won bigger than anyone in history. This is so far from being true it's amazing that he even fixed his lips to trot this lie out, but lie he did. Bigly.

When challenged on this lie by a journalist from NBC, Trump's response amounted to *"well that's what I had heard, so..."* When no other journalist pressed the issue, when Trump was simply allowed to tell lies to the American people from that podium, when Trump was allowed to say that the buck shouldn't stop with him as president, I knew we were in bigger trouble than I thought. The politicians, Hillary, Bernie, they failed to stop Trump. The journalists are now failing to correct Trump and hold him accountable. The media has completely failed us.

The right-wing media insisted for almost weeks that Hillary Clinton was under criminal investigation over emails, when she wasn't. Obama was criticized for everything from asking about the price of arugula during a campaign stop to mentioning that his blackness helped him relate to Trayvon Martin. GOP congressman Joe Wilson literally yelled "liar" at Obama during a speech in 2009, while Obama was the president. The double standard that is applied to Trump is unacceptable. Donald Trump built his political career on a racist lie about Obama being born in Kenya. Why is nobody yelling "liar" at Trump? If the politicians and the media refuse to hold the Trump administration accountable, the people have no choice but to.

How do we fight back? We show solidarity with marginalized groups that will be further marginalized in Trump's America. We stand with the family of Ben Keita, a black American Muslim who was lynched in Seattle. We stand with the families of Srinivas Kuchibhotla and Alok Madasani, the Indian men shot by a white supremacist in Kansas. We show solidarity with the women who marched on Washington during 2017's historic women's march. We show solidarity with Jewish people whose communities and cemeteries are currently under attack by white supremacists. We stand with the Native Americans who are protecting Standing Rock from the DAPL pipeline. We say no to mass incarceration. We say no to the over-policing that leads to over-criminalization of communities of color. We say no to the travel ban, we say no to the wall, we say no to Donald Trump, loudly and often.

These are the reasons I decided to show up in Washington on Monday, March 6th. I was inspired by the Green Revolution, by Occupy Wall Street, by the Ferguson Uprising. Hashtags and RTs are cute and make us feel all warm and fuzzy inside, but without actual flesh on the ground, there is no movement. Many working class people say that they do not have the luxury to take time away from their lives to resist Trump, but we are now at the point where we don't have the luxury not to. So I will do what you can't.

As an artist and my own boss, I can determine my schedule easier than someone who has a boss. So I will put my flesh in these streets as much as I can. I don't know what this is about to be, as I have never done anything like this before. But I can't just sit around and do nothing. I am not rich, I still have to work for a living, and I still will. But when I'm not getting that bag, I will be in these streets showing solidarity for as long as I can be.

For two weeks, I invited those who wanted to resist to meet us at Rock Creek Park, 24th and P St. NW, Washington D.C., at noon. We held our ground, demanding that the House Of Representatives begin the impeachment process of Donald Trump, staring with his violation of the Emolument clause, a release of his tax returns and a call for an independent bipartisan investigation into the Donald Trump's Russian connections.

THE REPUBLICAN PARTY OF HUSTLERS AND PIMPS: TRUMP, THE ULTIMATE HUSTLER/PIMP

AMINIFU R. HARVEY

Aminifu R. Harvey is a retired professor of social work from Fayetteville State University. He was tenured associate professor at the University of Maryland, and co-founded and founded Afro-centric youth and family institutions in the early 1980s. He is among those responsible for bringing Afrocentric theory and practice to social work.

The fool is obstinate, and doubts not; knowing all but their own ignorance.

— **Teachings of Imhotep**

What is a *hustler?* What is a *pimp?* Let's just start off with the truth. The Republican Party is both a hustler and a pimp. A hustler's aim is to "run game" to trick you into believing falsehoods. A hustler's aim is to feed on your weaknesses/your desire for something to be which is not. The hustler's goal is to cheat you out of something of value (in this case, your vote for Donald Trump). The hustler makes promises that you believe will benefit you, knowing he has no intention of delivering on those promises.

Look at the gender composition of the U.S. Congress. What about the composition of Trump's cabinet? Mostly old, white conservative males. The exceptions are Ben Carson, Secretary of Housing and Urban Development, who it seems to me would have expertise as the Surgeon General; Betsy DeVos, Secretary of Education, a conservative supporter of independent, private religious schools and anti-public education; Linda McMahon, head of the Small Business Administration, the CEO of World Wrestling Entertainment—you have got to be kidding me; and Elaine Chao, Secretary of Transportation, a Taiwanese American who served as Secretary of Labor under the last Bush administration and has a history of high public private positions and whose bio reads as if she would be best to head up the Small Business Administration. The latter are the exceptions by race and gender, but not by wealth. Ms. DeVos might be better in no position or maybe the Secretary of Social Affairs. Can you image what happens to children of color? More specifically, if states determine the education of children in this country and there is no higher authority to appeal to concerning the miseducation of our children, we as Black people will be in deep manure. What will be the content of courses? As it is now, little of the truth about the continuous attempts to eliminate Native American culture exists. And where is the history of the contributions to the development of America in the existing course material. Who will the teachers be? What ethnicity? Will they have to cite the entire Declaration of Independence in order to qualify for a teaching position? You can bet your bottom dollar that the wealthy Betsy DeVos, who was approved by Congress to head up the Department of Education, will not fight for its existence. Remember her inability to answer questions at her confirmation hearing? She's being pimped and loves it.

Trump's cabinet is composed of seven billionaires and ten multi-millionaires. What is your annual income? Are these the class of folk who live in your neighborhood and come to your backyard parties? They have no idea what your present life style and needs are. So we have a cabinet that is 86% white, 82% male, and 77% white males. It is the least diverse cabinet since Ronald Reagan.

The hustler lies to you, that is, makes promises about doing things that you will benefit from, knowing that he is unable to deliver. But he knows your weaknesses and will feed upon them, *"I will make American great again."* (A white male supremacist America?) *"I will create jobs and bring jobs back to America." I will stop those criminal Mexicans from crossing the border by building a wall that the Mexican government will have to pay for."* Well, by now we know that the Mexican government has flat out said they will not pay for the wall. If this building ever happens, it will probably be contracted out by the federal government to one of his wealthy construction company friends, or maybe to a company he has some financial interest in. And the federal government will pay for it out of our tax money! What is bewildering to me is Trump's and the Republican Party's obsession with anti-isms of foreigners of color and of non-Judeo-Christian religions. He really has such an obsession with Mexicans. What is it? They usually work the jobs that Americans do not want and most are low-wage, hard working laborers. In North Carolina, for example, they have revitalized economically suffering communities with their culturally oriented businesses. Remember, any purchase has taxes associated with the purchase. This goes for a house to an automobile to a piece of candy, which increases local and state revenue for sure.

In urban areas they work in mostly low paying jobs as janitors, house maids, dishwashers, at car washes, and as menial under the table construction workers. Many still work as farm laborers. To export them is a major step in destroying the economy. If he and the Republican Party were really interested in the economy, they would establish constructive programs allowing their group to become citizens of the U.S., if they are illegal and have committed non-felony crimes. There would be programs for those who have committed minor felony type crimes. There is no doubt in my mind that Trump and the old, white, male Republican Party are playing on the fears of those who believe America belongs solely to Caucasians. It is a known fact that in a few years people of color will out-number the white population, and the non-white Hispanics are the largest population of this group. And even if one is "illegal," if their children are born in the United States, their children are citizens. Of all the ethnic populations, including Caucasians, the non-white Hispanic population has the highest birth rate. Caucasians have the lowest. Perhaps this focus on illegals is a diversion from the real issues of the move to increase the control and wealth of the richest 1% of Americans, who are white males. Or perhaps Trump is in collusion with Russia to destroy the economy of the United States in order to have Russia as the preeminent world financial power as Vladimir Putin wants. Maybe this is why Trump has initiated the phrase "false news," so the public will actually believe that the journalists and other news media are not providing the public with real news (criticizing him for his lying and false statistics (alternative facts)). Then he can control information to his and the Republican Party's benefit. This is what fascist governments do. Don't be hustled!!!

Another view is that this is the Confederacy still fighting the Civil War with an emphasis on states' rights over the federal government. Yes, the Republican Party wants to drastically reduce the control of federal agencies such as the Environmental Protection Agency and possibly eliminate the Department of Education and the Consumer Finance Protection Bureau. This party as a whole does not support climate change, even though all the scientific evidence demonstrates its validity. They do not believe in climate change, even though it has been proven scientifically. Well, a hustler will always misrepresent the truth and make up his/her own information and statistics (Kellyanne Conway's alternative information/facts, better known as lies) as if it is the truth. That is because he/she knows what the victim/sucker wants to hear/believe. Trump ran on a platform of creating and bringing jobs back to America. So far all he has done is propose to eliminate jobs, which will have the effect of disrupting the national economy. He proposed to upgrade the infrastructure of America; now he says he will put that off until next year. America you have been hustled!!!

Pimped

What is a pimp? A pimp is a person who works in collaboration with another person and is the front person to conduct an immoral, unethical or illegal activity. The front person is led to believe that even if he/she gets caught in this immoral, unethical or illegal activity, nothing or only minor punishments or sanctions will be imposed. The best example of this so far in the Trump administration is the case of retired Lieutenant General Michael Flynn. Flynn was appointed as national security advisor. It was discovered that he had spoken with the Russian Ambassador about security issues before Trump was elected and, thus, before he was officially appointed as national security advisor. It is illegal for a civilian to discuss such official security issues. It was later ascertained that he misinformed Vice President Pence about his conversation. You can bet that Trump probably directed or at least encouraged this conversation and its content. Flynn, the front man, is fired by Trump and, thus, becomes the fall guy. Pimped!!!

Another person who has allowed himself to get pimped is Senator Tim Scott, the Senate's lone African American Republican. He is a South Carolina conservative. He is supporting Jeff Sessions for the office of Attorney General. In his early political career Sessions was known as an avowed civil rights opponent. Can people change their political views? Yes, and Scott says Sessions has and is now fair and impartial in his political decision making. Is this true? Maybe, but why run the risk with someone who has a history, no matter how long ago, of being a racist. There are too many young and qualified persons to support an old, historically proven racist. Tim Scott you just got Pimped!!!

For those of you who voted for the Republican Party and 45, if you don't know by now that you are being hustled because you thought he would bring jobs to American, let me explain this to you. Those lower class white women and poor, non-college, non-skilled white males, if you ain't got a job now you probably will not get one, unless it is at Walmart as a greeter. There are few if any labor intense industrial jobs left in America. Those that were sent overseas you probably will refuse to take because they are physically hard, stressful, monotonous, and non-livable wage paying jobs with limited benefits, if any. (What about health insurance? Oh well, let's get rid of Obamacare. Hustled and pimped, America). The Republicans and Trump know this. There are no more labor intense jobs: cars are assembled by robots and you have to be a techie to be able to inspect the robots' work. Are you a techie? And there are not a lot of these positions left. Who makes telephone directories anymore, and who uses secretaries anymore? Computers have reduced, if not almost eliminated, secretarial positions. That is why they are now called administrative assistants. And to those 42–47 % of you who did not vote and those of you who voted for Mickey Mouse, you just got Pimped!!!

Yes, Donald Trump is both a hustler and pimp—and maybe a smart one in the business arena, but a smart hustler stays in the arena he knows. Trump made the mistake of taking his hustler/pimp strategies and tactics into the government arena and attacking the integrity of the general public. As president everyone is your constituency, and not everyone is an easy mark nor will they agree to be your front person. He never counted on the backlash he and the Republicans are receiving from the general public (Women's March), celebrities (NBA players), and businesses such as Google, Apple, and Nordstrom. "What about my daughter's clothing line?" Most people do not like misogynist and blatant racists. Trump has demonstrated his disregard for the Black community by disregarding the written request from the Congressional Black Caucus to meet with him. As of this writing he has not even had the courtesy to respond to their letter requesting a meeting. When asked by a Black female correspondent if he planned on meeting with the CBC, he asked if she was friends with the Caucus and if she could set up the meeting. How insulting.

A New Day

This is a new day and age, especially for younger citizens. It is important to have anti-Trump rallies and reactions to his executive orders. For example, the courts placed a ban on his immigration policies, fostered by such public behavior. My deeper worries, though, concerning Trump and this Republican administration are their gestapo and Hitler-like behaviors. Trump makes statements as if the statements are true but with no supporting evidence. Yet many people believe him due to his position of authority. He has stated that illegal immigrants from Mexico are criminals and rape American women, a fear tactic. Just as Hitler said Jews were responsible for the economic problems in Germany, thus justifying their deportation to prison camps and physical deprivation and murder, accomplished by going house to house and arresting them with no real legal justification. Not too farfetched from what we see Immigration and Customs Enforcement (ICE) doing now. As of February 11, 2017, ICE conducted raids at homes and work places in Atlanta, Chicago, New York, North Carolina, South Carolina, Kansa, Florida, Texas, and Virginia. As Angela Davis said, They come for me now in the day, they will come for you in the night.

Trump and the Republican Party have already stated that they will hire 5,000 more ICE personnel and 3,000 more Border Patrol personnel. Oh, these are the new jobs Trump promised. Are you young enough to qualify, old, white poor males, and is this the job you have been waiting for, young people, with your college degrees? A friend of mine said his fear of the singling out of Chicago as a city with the highest crime rate by Trump is that he will impose oppressive tactics to "clean up the crime," stop and search. My question is, On what basis has he chosen Chicago? According to the FBI's 2015 Uniform Crime Report the following are the cities with the highest crime rates per 100,000: Kansas City, Missouri; Oakland, California; Little Rock, Arkansas; Baltimore, Maryland; Rockford, Illinois; Milwaukee, Wisconsin; Memphis, Tennessee; Birmingham, Alabama; Detroit, Michigan; and St. Louis, Missouri. Chicago, Illinois does not even rank in the top 30 of cities with the highest murder rate. East Chicago, Indiana, ranks 28th, but this is not the Chicago that Trump is referring to. The neighborhood of Altgeld Gardens in Chicago does have the 3rd highest violent crime rate in the U. S., but that certainly is not all of Chicago nor the South Side of Chicago. So, why does Trump select Chicago? Is it to embarrass the progressive Black leadership who reside in Chicago: Jesse Jackson, Minister Farrakhan, Rev Jeremiah Wright, ex-president Obama, Haki Madhubuti, and a plethora of cultural scholars and social activists who reside in Chicago? Or is it a test case to see how oppressive and Nazi-like one can be under the guise of implementing law and order.

If one wants to truly eliminate violence, then eliminate poverty. When one has some true investment in their lives and community, they are less likely to risk the loss of these important and valuable commodities. An ethical and humanitarian administration would: place health and welfare services into these under privileged communities; eliminate food deserts; place more social services programs for youths; provide well-structured and culturally competent afterschool programs in the community; update the instructional materials and equipment in schools; pay teachers a livable wage and have culturally competent elevation instruments; and employ the culturally competent teaching philosophies, methods, and techniques that have been researched and tested for African American children.

Speaking of getting pimped and or hustled, a friend of mine told me that her friend's African American son told her that he and many of his friends voted for Trump because he said he would provide jobs. These young African Americans are college educated. Mis-educated again; Carter G. Woodson must be rolling over in his grave. (How many of you know who he is and/or have red his classical work?) Have they ever sung the Black National Anthem? In the last stanza it says to the native land be true. If one were to be true to their native land, Africa, they would know and be grounded in the moral and ethical principles of Ma'at and the 42 Declarations of Innocence. The African American community needs to institute mechanisms to insure our protégés know these moral and ethical principles and, thus, would not have allowed many of our children to be bamboozled. We do have models to be replicated, such as our Pan-African schools and African American rites of passage programs.

Culture

Children who had character based on Ma'at, The Seven Cardinal Virtues (order, balance, harmony, compassion, reciprocity, justice, and truth) are less likely to be hustled and or pimped. Trump and the present Republican Party have not demonstrated any of these Virtues, but then hustlers and pimps never do. That is why they are immoral and unethical.

It seems to me that the essence of a culture is the development of moral human beings that have the obligation to live in harmony and cooperatively with each other and nature and to enhance the welfare of the community. This philosophy is epitomized in the 42 Declarations of Innocence that the ancient Egyptians employed as guides for their moral behavior. In the introduction to *The Husia: Sacred Wisdom of Ancient Egypt*, Jacob H. Carruthers states that the people of the Nile Valley had a tradition of holy or sacred writings which acted as governance for their daily life and that these works predate the *Torah*, the *Holy Bible* and the *Holy Q'uran*. These holy works include *The Book of Knowing the Creations*, *The Book of Prayers and Scared Praises*, *The Book of the Moral Narrative*, *The Books of Wise Instruction*, *The Book of Contemplation*, and *The Book of Declarations of Virtues*, and *The Books of Rising Like Ra*. All of these works contain moral imperatives. The text that is most widely known is *The Book of the Coming Forth by Day*, which contains the 42 Declarations of Innocence and lays the foundation for The Ten Commandments.

In reading the Declarations of Innocence, one sees reflected Ma'at's Seven Cardinal Virtues: **Order, Balance, Harmony, Compassion** (sometimes known as righteousness) **Reciprocity, Justice, and Truth**. In Kemtian culture, these Virtues and Declarations were the guidelines providing an ethical way of life for the individual, family, and entire society. Additionally, they provided the guidelines for an ecologically balanced relationship with nature. The following are examples of the Declarations:

1. I have not done evil against people.
2. I have not mistreated my family and associates.
3. I have not told lies.
4. I have not associated with evil or worthless persons.
5. I have not begun a day by demanding more than I was due.
6. I have not defrauded the poor of their property.
7. I have not slandered a servant to his superior.
8. I have not caused anyone to be hungry.

9. I have not caused anyone to suffer.
10. I have not taken milk from the mouth of children.
11. I have not stopped the flow of water in its season.
12. I have not been greedy.
13. I have not engaged in violence.
14. I have not discriminated against others.
15. I have not violated the law.
16. I have not dealt deceitfully.
17. I have not terrorized anyone.
18. I have not been hot tempered.
19. I have not quarreled.
20. I have not been aggressive.
21. I have not caused strive.
22. I have not been impatient.
23. I have not been talkative.
24. I have not been false.
25. I have not stolen.
26. I have not polluted the waters.
27. I have not exalted myself.

One fights immorality and unethical behavior with moral fortitude and ethics. The question I put forth is, Are you a person of morality and are you ethical? If so, then you have no other option than to stand for Truth and Justice and declare war on the Republican Party of which Donald Trump represents.

Here's a suggestion: Have a party and guess which ones of the Declarations have the Republican Party and Trump not violated. Then have a discussion concerning the implications of each Declaration for the people of this country. You can also evaluate yourself, employing the examples of the Declarations. Then evaluate the Republican Party and Trump on the Seven Cardinal Virtues. These are some suggested actions:

1. Your actions must be directed to the Republican Party, and not only focused on Trump.

2. Stop reacting solely to Trump's personality and character.

3. Focus on policies that the Republican Party are trying to enact.

4. Remember that local elections are as important as the presidential election.

5. Trump is a billionaire businessman; he is not a politician, and cares less about any kind of political future. Your state and federal Representatives and Senators are politicians and depend on their constituency to reelect them. Therefore, your power lies in the fact that you have the organizational power not to reelect them.

6. Telephone your state and federal congressional elected officials. Text your zip code to **520-200-2223** to receive the names and phone numbers of your state and federal officials.

7. Host a pro-truth and justice telethon and host a card-a-thon party.

8. Demonstrate in front of the homes of your Representatives and Senators on a continuous and regular basis.

9. Hold sit-ins at your Representatives' and Senators' local and federal offices.

10. Follow their voting record and let them know that you are evaluating their voting record.

11. Let Congress know you are deeply concerned with Trump's relationship with Russia and see him as a possible threat to national security.

12. Begin to choose someone to oppose public officials when they are up for reelection.

13. Develop your own policy on education, juvenile and adult justice, economic policy, women's rights, etc. and present this policy to officials in-person and demand a response.

14. Organize voting in your area. Get the vote out.

15. Even though there is supposed to be a separation of church and state, ministers, imams, rabbis, priests, and all spiritual leaders need to constantly address the issues of moral and ethical social justice to their congregations.

16. Boycott businesses that support Trump administration policies and visually support businesses that oppose this administration's policies.

17. For African Americans, we need to call for a national conference of the African American organizations, such as the NAACP, the National Urban league, Black Lives Matter, the Black Police organization, and all the Black professional organizations and religious conferences and organizations, to decide one person to run for office for all the upcoming elections on a local, state, and national level.

18. At the above conference, legislation/policy needs to be developed to address the issues facing Black America, such as LGBTQ concerns, criminal justice, health and welfare, and community development.

19. Distribute leaflets with the Seven Cardinal Virtues and the Declarations of Innocence, asking how the Republican Party and Trump fare. Then ask the question, Is this the party you want to reflect the values of America?

After Trump's first national address, many journalists and news commentators stated that his address was presidential. Well, that might be true but the content of his address were al lies, when you review the policies related to his statements. For example, he says he believes every citizen should have clean drinking water but his policy allows for the dumping of coal ash into our rivers. Remember hustlers and pimps are liars and immoral and unethical. Don't get hustled or pimped.

ACTIVATING CRITICAL RESISTANCE: BEING THE CHANGE WE SEEK

LASANA KAZEMBE

*Lasana Kazembe is a proud papa, poet, and professor. His areas of research include urban education, critical pedagogy, and arts-based literacy. He recently edited a poetry anthology entitled **Write to Be: Poetry by Stateville Writers**. He is an Assistant Professor of Education at Indiana University-Indianapolis.*

"If we could construct a psychiatric Frankenstein monster, we could not create a leader more dangerously mentally ill than Donald Trump," Gartner began. "He is a paranoid, psychopathic, narcissist who is divorced from reality and lashes out impulsively at his imagined enemies. And this is someone, as you said, who is handling the nuclear codes."

— John Gartner, Ph.D, Harvard

Several months before the announcement of the victor of the 2016 presidential election (which Noam Chomsky calls the *'quadrennial circus'*), I made a statement to my Africana Studies students which shocked some, angered others, and frightened more than a few. I told them to get ready because, by my analysis, Donald J. Trump was going to, in fact, become the next president of the United States of America. Many of them (mouths agape) were probably (silently) questioning my credentials, my sanity, and wondering if they had picked the right instructor.

I had arrived at that sad conclusion prior to learning about American University political historian Allan Lichtman's scientific analysis method (which he calls the '13 Keys') for predicting the outcome of U.S. presidential elections. It should be noted that Lichtman has successfully predicted the winner in every U.S. presidential election since 1984. It should be further noted that this distinguished professor of history has (very early) predicted Trump's impeachment and has shared his analysis in a new book, *The Case for Impeachment* (2017).

I had based my own prediction of Trump's victory on my observation of similar phenomena occurring around the world. The phenomena in question can be described as the growing political popularity and rise of ultra-far-right, white nationalist parties and politicians in several countries including France (Jean and Marie LePen), Hungary (Viktor Orgun), Netherlands (Geert Wilders), Greece (Nikolaos Michaloliakos), and Italy (Matteo Salvini). Like the Euro American Trump, ultra-right-wing Europeans around the globe were spouting highly-racialized rhetoric laced with racism, xenophobia, and militant sentiment. Like Trump's, their rhetoric found swift appeal among a broad, and growing swath of white, economically-challenged citizens in their respective countries who had felt the sting of globalization, the echo of China, and the impact of growing numbers of (largely) Black and Brown people, both citizen and immigrant alike. And while this creeping white nationalism was initially blamed on a global economic downturn, more perceptive scholars and political thinkers have identified the true source: white racism. And as the flailing body of disgruntled poor and working-class masses was being hastily assembled, all it needed was a talking head to be attached. Robert Mercer and other shadowy billionaires supplied seemingly endless cash to stimulate that body's development, even as the electrified words of Trump and others fed the head (while poisoning the heart). And now, that body has risen from the gurney prepared to sew global mayhem and wreak national havoc on the townspeople.

It is a sad fact that most U.S. politicians on the left and right are bought and bossed by the ultra-rich. This critique is often leveled against

Republicans, but more and more corporate Democrats (and their neoliberal puppeteers) are beginning to be exposed and indicted for their part in running a political shill game that disfigures the very democratic principles which they espouse. Notable exceptions such as Maxine Waters and Elizabeth Warren are typically positioned by media as lone dissenters crying aloud in the wilderness. As for clergy, their most prominent spokespersons have either fallen silent, or have been offered starring roles in the Trump circus. A critique of the collusion and cooptation of Black clergy would call for a separate book. Progressive academicians who have been critical of Trump have either been silenced, marginalized, or ignored altogether. For its part, the Democratic Party is rightly under intense scrutiny owing to the collusion of its leadership in undermining and derailing the 2016 campaign of presidential-hopeful, Senator Bernie Sanders. A progressive sign of encouragement is the pending class-action lawsuit filed against the DNC and its former DNC head, Debbie Wasserman Schultz accusing both parties of massive election fraud and attempting to disenfranchise supporters of Senator Bernie Sanders. Such actions are on par with the very worst of racist, terroristic pogroms committed by 'un-Reconstructed' politicians, police, and judges against Black Americans since the Reconstruction era and coming forward. Meanwhile, in Trump's America, and across the spectrum, ordinary people continue to pay the price for having put their faith in seductive, charismatic leaders.

That leaves us. We, the people. My analysis of our American moment boils down to two introspective questions which I pose and which drive my thinking on this book's purpose:

1) What understanding(s) should we be taking from this situation?
2) What understanding(s) should we be giving to this situation?

American satirist, H.L. Mencken once wrote "no one ever went broke underestimating the intelligence of the American people." Mencken's acerbic wit rings even truer alongside the fact that we are living in an age of conscious forgetting bracketed by what late philosopher Sheldon Wolin termed *"inverted totalitarianism."* That is, in ways both overt and subtle, people have become their own oppressors, tormentors, and jailers.

Given our current situation, it would be extremely easy (and useless) for average Americans to become cynical and jaded to the point of numbness. Nor would it be practical for us to completely disengage from participating in this system. Neither of these options, in my view, represent what we should be taking (i.e., learning) from this situation.

Deeper Historical Knowledge and Political Clarity

Sadly, U.S. citizens are renown (and frequently mocked) for possessing short historical memories and (in sadder instances) an absolute lack of historical knowledge. These days, attitudes of indifference or callous apathy often accompany the historical ignorance. This is not good, and only serves to worsen our situation. Average citizens of this country have been grossly miseducated concerning its origins.

A good starting place would be to wean ourselves from the "non-nutritious" diet of American exceptionalism, White nationalism (masking as patriotism), and subaltern, reductive Black history. As critical historians have mentioned, the United States' two birth defects are the genocide campaign against the Native Americans and the enslavement of the African Americans. Our political vision, so obscured by a daily diet of social media and mundane spectacle, has made it extremely difficult for most to distinguish fact from fiction, and to understand, recognize, and resist a creeping fascism and neoliberalism which has been gaining momentum during the last thirty years. Writers such as Lerone Bennett, Jr., Cedric Robinson, and Gerald Horne have dedicated themselves to presenting a more accurate, truth-bearing U.S. history.

Deeper Engagement and Understanding of the Electoral Process

Shockingly (or maybe not so), many Americans had never heard of the Electoral College, and many still have little to no understanding of how it works. Many these days have extreme difficulty distinguishing between fact and opinion. As a means of increasing their civic literacy, and before running out to merely cast votes, Americans should strive to learn to engage important aspects of the electoral process. These include:

- issue education (ex., climate change, fracking, education policy);
- candidate education (who are the funders? lobbyists? SuperPACs?);
- basic civic literacy (names and platforms of one's political reps);
- lobbying (forming coalitions of progressive, informed voters);
- participation in developing and advocating policy.

Deeper Awareness and Scrutiny of Political Issues

Let us not be so bedazzled by the shock and awe of Trump, that we fail to see the broader functioning of White supremacy. It should be noted that at the time of this writing, intense (and, in many cases, violent) clashes are underway following decisions in several southern cities to re-move Confederate monuments and statuary from the vicinity of U.S. parks, courthouses, and other public spaces. In one American city after another, multicultural majorities who favor removal of these icons of what New Orleans Mayor Mitch Landrieu recently called "the lost cause", are being harangued, vilified, and physically attacked by numerical minorities of Confederate-flag waving, torch-wielding White Americans who har-bor deep affection and emotional connection to the likes of Robert E. Lee, Benjamin Tilmon, and Ku Klux Klan founder, Nathan Bedford For-rest. The sheer numbers of Americans who opt to not protest, but still disfavor Colin Kaepernick, yet favor the presence of Confederate statuary cannot be known.

Indeed, in these illustrative examples, the preservation of white-ness, as well as that of white physical and psychic space is at the beating center of the heart of spectacle of Trump, the removal of Confederate statuary, and the nation's sharp lurch toward fascism. Indeed, developing such critical awareness takes time and serious commitment. Americans of all stripes may benefit from less time on Facebook, and more time fac-ing a book.

While I do not share the blanket critique of all news being fake news, I do feel that Americans' overreliance on mainstream, corporate news sources is contributing to our political ignorance and miseducation. As a means of developing and expanding their worldview, Americans should seek out alternative (non-corporate) news sources. A few include:

- *Alternet* - alternet.org
- *The Real News Network* – therealnews.com
- *Crooks and Liars* - crooksandliars.com
- *Blacklisted News* - blacklistednews.com
- *Richard Prinze's Journalisms* - mije.org/richardprince
- *Mother Jones* - motherjones.com
- *Truth Out* - truthout.org
- *The Intercept* - intercept.com
- *In These Times* - inthesetimes.com
- *Black Agenda Report* - blackagendareport.com
- *The Weekly Standard* - weeklystandard.com
- *Al Jazeera America* - aljazeera.com
- *The Guardian* - theguardian.com
- *The BrownWatch* - brown-watch.com
- *The Times of India* - timesofindia.indiatimes.com
- *Counterpunch* - counterpunch.org
- *Christian Science Monitor* - csmonitor.com
- *The Jerusalem Post* - jpost.com

In their recent (2014) study, "On the Precipice of a "Majority-Minority" America: Perceived Status Threat from the Racial Demographic Shift Affects White Americans' Political Ideology", Craig and Richeson identify what they term 'perceived status threat' to explain the emergence of increasingly conservative attitudes among white Americans. Flowing from this increasing conservatism, is a resilient and measurable retrenchment of White supremacy across all areas of American society. Here are just a few telling examples:

- According to a 2016 study from the Sentencing Project ("The Color of Justice: Racial and Ethnic Disparity in State Prisons"), Black Americans are incarcerated in state prisons across the country at more than five times the rate of whites, and at least ten times the rate in five states (sentencingproject.org);

- Near daily instances of White male terrorists either harming, killing, or attempting to harm and/or kill Black Americans. These include Dylann Roof (South Carolina church shooter), Peter Selis (killed Black and Brown folk at San Diego pool party), James Harris Jackson (drove 200 miles by bus from Baltimore to New York to specifically hunt and kill Black men), Sean C. Urbanski (stabbed Black student at University of Maryland). Jeremy Christian (Portland, OR - stabbed two people fatally who intervened as he was harassing two Muslim women on a train).

NOTE: A critical takeaway from these cases is the near total reluctance on the part of police officials to describe these cases as race-motivated, which would then classify them as racial hate crimes. Relatedly, we should pay attention to the inattention that such crimes are subject to receive from the new U.S. Attorney General, the infamous Jeff Sessions.

- The aforementioned may constitute an expanded type of White interest convergence that seems to occur often between White male terrorists and the White law enforcement officials with whom they interact with. Such as how police in Charleston bought Burger King for Dylann Roof while he was in their custody. Apparently, he had worked up quite the appetite mere hours after he had gunned down nine Black people inside a historic Black church in Charleston.

- The May 24, 2017 appearance of U.S. Secretary of Education, Betsy Dee DeVos (i.e, the notorious BDD) at a hearing with the U.S. House of Representatives Appropriations subcommittee. As she was being questioned by Rep. Katherine Clark (D-MASS), DeVos was literally 'all smiles' as she defended her school-choice, pro-charter philosophy and quite literally (and liberally) endorsed states' rights to discriminate against students in U.S. schools. This includes Black, Latino, Asian, LGBTQ, and disabled children. Those familiar with the U.S. Civil War, Plessy v. Ferguson, and other glaring examples, will recall the 'states' rights' refrain as the popular justification by unreconstructed White southerners and northerners alike, for imposing White supremacist laws, codes, policies, restrictions, etc. in order to protect white space, property, and privilege. What several U.S. Representatives described as DeVos' advocating of discrimination, DeVos, herself, described it as 'state flexibility.' In his recent interview with Armstrong Williams, HUD Director Ben Carson struck a similar troubling tone, when he stated *"poverty is a state of mind."*

- Indeed, the cabinet level appoints of Jeff Sessions, Betsy Dee DeVos, Dr. Ben Carson (Department of Housing & Urban Development) and Sherriff David Clarke (Department of Homeland Security) (these last two, a classic example of White interest convergence)

Earlier, I mentioned Chomsky's reference to the *'quadrennial circus.'* Of course, his was a tongue-in-cheek reference to the American presidential election. Chomsky went on to state that for the demos, our real work lies not in becoming distracted, seduced, or preoccupied with the circus. I think it is impractical to think that progressive (i.e., anti-Trumpist) folks are going to disengage en masse from the U.S. electoral process. Similarly, it is impractical to expect an attitude adjustment and/or change in disposition of right-wing, alt-right, etc.

One of the purposes of this book is to invite everyday people to the work of dismantling the system of White supremacy and replacing it with a system based on truth, justice, and liberation for the masses. In his brilliant essay, "To Remake the World: Slavery, Racial Capitalism, and Justice" for the *Boston Review Forum I* (2016), Harvard Historian Walter Johnson channels W.E.B. Du Bois who gives us our charge:

> In *The Suppression of the African Slave Trade to the United States of America* (1896), an extended description of the various heartless and cynical prevarications through which the United States evaded the suppression of the Atlantic slave trade, Du Bois made an argument about the character of historical time. There were, in his view, moments that were propitious for change, moments when it was possible—with courageous and concerted action—to remake the world in its own better image. The cost, for Du Bois, of missing those moments could only be reckoned in the blood of the subsequent generations who paid the price for their forebears' failures. Perhaps we should heed his warning. (*Boston Review, Forum I*, p. 30-31).

RESILIENCE AS RESISTANCE: BUILDING COMMUNITY IN TIMES OF SOCIAL DISSOLUTION

DOMINICA McBRIDE

Dominica McBride is an award–winning evaluator and champion of culturally responsive evaluation and development. She has published articles and chapters on evaluation, cultural competence, and prevention of risky behaviors in youth. Her website is becomecenter.org

We are now in a time of heightened fragmentation and social distance, with people and communities falling through the proverbial crack because of a lack of empathy, compassion, foresight, and engagement. These voids were present pre-Trump, manifested in the murders of black men at the hands of police, in a healthcare system steeped in capitalism, and in an education system sorely lacking cultural sensitivity and responsiveness. However, the Trump presidency has inaugurated a virtual *kakistocracy*[1], exacerbating these phenomena to the point of lasting harm, and more ominously, to a point of no return. For example: reputable and once financially viable hospitals are drastically cutting budgets; police are given more liberty with less accountability; and educational youth programs are being suffocated. The yawning space between persons and institutions, citizens and policymakers, is abysmal, and growing. The answer, however, is not simply in blaming others or the system. Resistance is essential, but it is not enough.

The diagnosis and remedy for what ails US society today – underlying our current societal problems, our persistent systemic injustice, even our catastrophes – is to be found in the 'space between.' It is the space between thought and action, between persons, between communities; between the grassroots and institutions, between informal and formal leadership, between doubt and vision. When we're able to bridge this 'space between' with understanding, mutual care, and nation-building, then clarity, conviction and hope emerges – all vital elements of community resilience.

The crisis of infant mortality in Auburn Gresham, a neighborhood struggling with violence and poverty on the south side of Chicago, is a case in point. Once a community characterized by "neighborly bonds," the neighborhood now has one of the highest violence rates among 77 neighborhoods in the city. In talking with 15 unrelated parents about the causes of infant mortality, most said it was rooted in the stress and sickness of the social environment, in the non-existent or unhealthy relations between neighbors. Into that chasm comes fear, and in that fear were seeds of violence and isolation. None of this is surprising. Over half of residents rarely, if ever, engage in community activities. Only about a third are regularly active in community affairs. Though many residents have access to resources, most are 'silo-ed' by their fear and sense of isolation, and the despair that follows. Consequently, residents were not tapping into opportunities to build strong relationships with one another and to contribute to their neighborhoods to become a humane and vibrant community. Resilience sits at this dynamic's antithesis.

For example, an afterschool program in an elementary school in Auburn Gresham experienced the murder of one of their member's brother. The murder happened in the alleyway of the school, so both the student and his peers experienced the trauma. While they felt the fear, anger, and sadness of this type of loss, the young people decided to come together and throw a surprise celebration for their fellow student, to support him and each other through this difficult time. These young people not only showed flexibility and contractibility, but also compassion, thoughtfulness, and growth. Unfortunately, this instance is one of few, and instead fragmentation characterizes many communities across the country today.

I am a program evaluator by trade, a community and counseling psychologist by training, and a community organizer at heart. I believe that the malady and the remedy lies in the 'space between.' So, I strive to engage the practical work of healing the wounds, starting where people are, support grassroots efforts to build community, and cultivate that often intangible but very real sense of social cohesion. When committed people and responsible organizations, guided by the right conscious and subconscious notions of human relations and community, bridge the 'space between,' constructive and sustainable progress and substantive resilience are typically the result. However, in any given context where division is the predominant experience and the focus is pathological, even the most evidence-backed approach, undertaken by people with the best of intentions and skill, can falter.

Resilience can be thought of as a safety net. A safety net absorbs some of the inertia of the falling object and creates more time for the object to come to zero velocity.[2] Even though the object still decreases below the stagnant net, it is able to bring the object back to that original orientation because the strings expand and contract. The net has both flexibility and contractibility. These dynamics are central to resilience. If the strings of the net expanded too much, the object would fall through. If they did not come back together, the object would hit the ground. This closeness and ability to come back together is key in creating resilience. Resilience is the ability to experience stress or trauma and not only return to status quo but even move beyond and grow.[3] We need to take responsibility for moving forward, in building resilience within ourselves, our communities, and our society.

Crucial to this understanding of resilience are relationships. Relationships are not only the glue of humanity but they are the constitutive basis for every single human being. Outside of autonomic functions, the only area of our brain that does not 'sleep' is that which is social[4]. In other words, we are inextricably connected to one another. This social area of our brain governs not only our relationship to other human beings, it constitutes our relationship to our own selves, our values, and our world-view. Relationships, then, serve as a barometer for resilience. Relationships can be identified, described, even measured, and most importantly, intentionally cultivated.

Here are the ways in which relationships are present in, and essential for, the relational, cultural, and structural elements of community resilience, and how we can nurture and grow in each area.

Relational Resilience

Relational resilience is the cohesion between people. It's how neighbors regard one another and what one neighbor is willing do for another. It's the extent that a neighbor is willing to share, trust, and support. How do we go from a sense of isolation and fear, to actually knowing our neighbors, even to the point of this kind of respect, care, and engagement? In short: we encounter, we talk, we relate.

Re-evaluation Counseling (RC)[5] offers powerful lessons for how to build relational resilience. We must first see each other differently. Into this 'space between,' we bring distorted perceptions of 'the other' – the other group, the stranger, the neighbor, sometimes even our own family members. RC poses that underneath the grime of trauma, pains, slights, and misperceptions, each person has value and positive human potential, and is worthy of respect and care. Carl Rogers would call this "unconditional positive regard." In brushing off this 'dirt' of life, we can see and affirm this depth of humanness in ourselves and 'the other.'

This happens through a particular quality of encounter, conversation, and interchange. To make this happen, we need to have deep, non-judgmental, compassionate listening; and we need to exhibit a brave, vulnerable, honest, emotive, and reflective expression. The talker's job is to dig deep, cry, laugh, shout, share, and be willing to see how the past and greater context influences their feelings, thoughts, and perceptions. Through this necessary discharge of emotional energy, the person is able to come to a clearer understanding of themselves and the world around them. With this clarity, the person is able to let go of the past, forgive, see themselves as that which is beyond thinking and trouble, and move in the world with a clear purpose, positive intention and "right action".[6] They are better able to challenge oppression and make change in their community. Then, the talker gives the listener the same opportunity – a space to "be" themselves and be accepted.

To cultivate relational resilience, we need to be there for each other, and to be there in this way: While our elected officials and institutional leaders can and should take part in this with the community, it is our job first to do it with each other. We must weave our own social fabric, block by block, in our neighborhoods and in our families. At the very least, we can be listening ears for each other. We can even offer a shoulder to cry upon, become prayer or meditation partners, or financial tenders. We can help our neighbors navigate through and overcome tribulations and empower and uplift both temporarily and permanently. When we are cohesive, we are better able to create the reality we want and need regardless of any outside decisions and actions that impact us and our community. In this way, we are better equipped to mold our own culture – the tangible and intangible environment that shapes how we live our lives.

Cultural Resilience

Culture is how people in a group relate to things (objects, models, ideas) and others. In this way, culture is, by definition, shared amongst a group of people, be it in the form of a religious community, an ethnicity, a nation, a neighborhood, or an organization. It manifests through common norms, values, language, beliefs, practices, rituals, and traditions. Cultural resilience is the intentional identification and consistent application of a set of values, norms and practices that help foster and maintain the unity and vitality of a group. As a result, cultural pride has been shown to be a protective factor, helping to build individual resilience, constructive behavior, and success in life.[7] And, similar to relational resilience, developing this cultural aspect of community resilience requires a paradigm shift.

In 2009, I explored how culture could be used to contribute to family health through a study conducted in partnership with 80 African American community members in Phoenix, Arizona. To revitalize their oppressed and fragmented community, these members became convinced of the necessity of seeing others differently – no longer as strangers or distant associates, but as an extended family. Most of the community members (89%) valued their extended family as important and positive in their lives.

This notion of extended family was a cultural anchor, a mender and healer, a powerful tool for social change, and a way to engender individual and community resilience. Extended family transcended the physical ties of blood. Friends, fellow worshippers at church, mosque, and temple, and neighbors were considered family.

Clearly, the concept of community as extended family has transcendent potential, with the ability to uplift and empower. Extended family can give a sense of an expanded self, a self that extends from the past, is more expansive in the present, and has larger impacts for the future. In this way, the 'extended family' encompasses ancestry, collective memories and historical actions, and timeless, familial stories.

Further, this change in thinking meant treating the 'new' extended family as 'the whole exceeding the sum of the parts.' It served as a tool to integrate and perpetuate identified and cultivated cultural strengths, such as valuing collectivism and practicing interdependence. According to these community members, focusing on building extended family was one of the most potent means of developing resilience. Community as extended family endowed persons with a sense of physical and emotional security. With this sense of belonging, participants noted that feelings of loneliness or isolation dissipated. One participant concisely represented what extended family is in action: "…when someone in the family really have a need, all of them get together…makes me feel better." In many instances, neighbors can assume familial roles and 'look out' for one another in addition to simply spending time together on porches, in houses, and on neighborhood streets. Quality time together made difficult life circumstances more tolerable, not only enhancing the present but bringing hope for the future. Based on this notion of quality time, they suggested that neighborhoods change their language and instead of something like a block party, they have regular "family reunions."

By embracing such a paradigm shift, changing our perceptions of our neighbors, re-orienting the direction of our local actions, and altering the language to describe it all, we can create a vital culture that promotes cohesiveness in the community, and fosters resilience. The next step, then, is to build structural resilience, ensuring the longevity of our hard-earned collective wellbeing, and maintaining our sanity in the insanity of the wider society.

Structural Resilience

In the 1990s, Dr. Amos Wilson sent a call to the African American community to do "nation-building." In building a "nation," a community needs systems that work for them, such as a culturally responsive education system, a restorative justice system, and an infrastructure of wellbeing dedicated to optimal physical, emotional, and social functioning. With the current support structures deteriorating, and more people losing their resources and livelihoods, there is every reason to build these new systems from the grassroots up.

Structural resilience is characterized by institutions, organizations, initiatives, and programs that bolster the resilience and vitality of the people, especially those who are marginalized economically, socially, and psychologically. This may sound like a complex and exhausting feat; however, everything needed to create these structures is already present – in and with each other. In the African American community, for instance, 'family' and 'neighborhood' and 'community' consists of formal and informal teachers, counselors, health providers, and spiritual guides; socially conscious businesspeople, social entrepreneurs, religious leaders, and community organizers. There is untapped talent in engineering, agriculture, culinary arts, construction, business development, and conflict meditation. There are idealistic young people and wise elders, former gang-bangers and returning military veterans.

Consider how the Trauma Response and Intervention Movement[8] in Chicago is preventing and eradicating trauma eight blocks at a time, starting with training resident leaders as first responders. This eight block model offers multiple pathways to structural resilience. Grassroots education systems could be developed in eight block sectors, following in the footsteps of Marva Collins, who founded a highly effective school housed in the top floor of her home. By utilizing access to information through the internet and personal and professional networks, formal and informal teachers could hone their skills and get to work in their own locales. We can learn from history, as the 'village,' as a whole, cared for the children. Everyone in the neighborhood could raise the children, serving as role models, mentors, and protectors.

In all these ways, we can create the institutional structures that undergird an edifying social environment, and serve as the springboard towards an enlightening and prosperous future for all concerned. To do this, we employ an asset-based – not problem-and-solution based – approach.

We begin with a skills and talents inventory on our blocks, learning who can do what, discovering what activates and drives them, urging them to pursue their shared hopes and vision for their lives and community. In all likelihood, there is at least one inherent 'instigator' in each community to prod, facilitate, and sustain the effort needed for such nation-building. Together, as a 'family,' the community can decide on the values and principles by which to design the blueprint of the emerging social infrastructure, and then, build it together.

Conclusion

In the current kakistocracy, there is very little chance the privileged and 'powerful' will listen and respond to the majority of Americans, let alone marginalized communities. While resistance in the form of protests and advocacy serves important purposes, more is needed. We must demand of each other the time and energy necessary for intentionally weaving a strong safety net and building community resilience. We must commit to relationships with each other, to our value system, and to the institutions that truly work for and with us, on our behalf. There is really no alternative at this point. We have no choice now but to care for our communities – not only to survive, but to thrive.

References:

[1]Wikipedia defines kakistocracy as "a state or country run by the worst, least qualified, or most unscrupulous citizens."

[2]Wikipedia (2017). Safety Net. Online: wikipedia.org/wiki/Safety_net

[3]Kulig, J.C. (2000). *Community resiliency: The potential for community health nursing theory development*. Public Health Nursing 17:374-385.

[4]Goleman, D (2006). *Social Intelligence: The Revolutionary New Science of Human Relationships*. New York, NY: Bantam Books.

[5]Online: rc.org

[6]O'Brien, B (2016). Right Action: Right Action and the Eightfold Path. Online: thoughtco.com/right-action-450068

[7]Caughy, MO, Campo, PJO, Randolph, SM, Nickerson, K (2002). *The influence of racial socialization practices on the cognitive and behavioral competence of African American preschoolers. Child Development*. 73:1611-1625.

[8]Online: tr4im.org

BLACK MOTHERING IN A TIME OF WAR

jessica Care moore

jessica Care moore is is an internationally renowned poet, playwright, performance artist, and producer, She is the CEO of Moore Black Press, Executive Producer of Black WOMEN Rock!, and founder of the literacy-driven, Jess Care Moore Foundation. Her published works include: The Words Don't Fit in My Mouth, The Alphabet Verses The Ghetto, God is Not an American.

When my 10-year old son, King was just a baby, he would see an American Flag and point at it and yell, *"Obama, Obama!"* I remember feeling a small sense of joy from the naivety of my beautiful child and his relationship with the country he was born into in 2006. President Barack Obama was his president, and despite my years of writing poems about the oppressive, systemic racism of this country, protesting loudly in the streets as a student, and traveling to meet other professional artivists to give voice to these violent post-racial realities, I loved that my son was born with the *"audacity of hope."*

Our 44th president was a revered, recognizable black male role model for my son I was raising without a present father. King grew up believing he could be absolutely be The President of the United States one day, and I knew i would forever be praying he would never want to run. The idea solidified in his psyche even more after meeting Vice President Joe Biden at 9-years old at the Detroit Annual NAACP Freedom

Fund Dinner, and Biden referred to King as "the president," several times and told him not to forget about him when he got in office.

President Obama was also my mothers president, who was often denied service at restaurants when she left Canada at 17 to marry my Alabama raised, Detroit daddy on the other side of the river. My mother who had to go to court in his defense when police accused my daddy of kidnapping my mother and his own children. My mother who after the assassinations of Martin Luther King Jr and John F. Kennedy decided to not become an American citizen, considered changing her citizenship so she could vote for the charismatic, handsome Senator from Chicago, I would jokingly refer to as her "boyfriend." This moment in history was for her and my daddy, Tom "T.D, Moore, who would didn't live long enough to witness it.

During the primary election, King grew fond of the candidate he called "Grandpa Bernie," but said he also thought it would be cool for a woman to finally be president for the very first time. What temporarily shifted in my son's spirit was remarkable for me as mother, poet and activist raising a black son to be free and self empowered. To love all people, but most importantly, to love himself and to serve his community. My son, who when asked, "Who does mommy work for," proudly answered, "Mommy works for mommy."

My son was coming home from his 5th grade classroom, telling me about students who were "for" the wall being built to keep out Mexicans. He heard about students in a Michigan suburb chanting "build that wall" while others brown students cried. He was shook by the popularity of someone who he heard say disrespectful comments about women on repeats on cable news stations.

"Mommy, how can someone like this become the President?"

I'll never forget a few weeks after 45 was in office, King, lying in his bed looking distraught, nearly in tears. He told me, "I'm scared of becoming a teenager when he's president." And there it was. A small bit of my son's childhood innocence stolen. My fearless son full of countless dreams, and possibilities for success weekly, now reduced to speaking about his uncertain future. It was a deep cut into my heart to hear my beautiful spirited child speak this way. The profundity of him recognizing that he would indefinitely grow taller, and wiser and into something even more powerful, small thinking men like Trump would inevitably fear. King knew Trump referred to dead children who looked like him in Chicago, as simply carnage.

I was interviewed on numerous occasions asking for my perspective as a black woman on Senator Hilary Clinton. Many of us had grown distrustful of the American system and also wanted something new. Only a few of my associates thought that Donald Trump had any slight chance of winning. Trump was the celebrity rich guy that would come into NYC parties in the 90's with a blond woman on each arm, and drink with the rest of the crowd. No one imagined the possibility of this country sinking so low in character that a man who spoke about women in such vile ways would win the hearts of Americans. Racist white men have historically shown hate and repression to their own women since the beginning of recorded time, perhaps even equal too, if not more than the way they loathe, envy and are fearful of black men.

Still, outdated racial ignorance and a continuous lack of respect for women would somehow galvanize this character with no political experience into The White House, making it not only a house painted white, but white supremacist and highly dangerous. In 2016, the United States of Europe, the KKK and the purposely undereducated were reenergized, but for what cause? The beautiful image of that black American family for 8 years overwhelmed the racist construct of white America that was propagating a demise of the "white male" through racial intermixing and the reality that they would soon not just be the global minority, but an American minority as well.

In the year before my birth Nikki Giovanni interviewed Lena Horne about black women and survival. Horne said, *"I didn't know about my grandmothers migration story until I was in my 40's. But, they survived. So it's in us, it must be in us, to survive."*

I remember the collective feeling of sadness and even a deep depression that seemed to sweep across the consciousness of many of the brilliant, fearless black mothers in my life. How will we survive this? What do we tell our children? Even my radical thinking women friends had moments of caution.How do we not go mad? How do we protect ourselves from tyranny? How do we find joy and tell our indigo children to continue, and never give one man that much power over their lives, their spirits, or their humanity.

When Trump was elected president, I was in Rio De Janeiro, Brazil, speaking and reading poetry at an FLUPP International Literary Festival. Poets from South Africa, Portugal, Spain, Germany, Brazil, France, Cuba, all participated. I was the only American poet on the bill. When I entered the lobby of the Olympic-renovated hotel the morning after the election, I was met with deep hugs of sadness, as if someone in my family had suddenly died. Maybe something had died. Maybe we needed a reason to protest. Maybe we became to complacent during the Obama Administration, and forgot the genocide, rape, and slave labor on which this country was built.

I told my fellow international poets that the hug should be a large group one, because America had long tentacles. I was embarrassed, the same way I was embarrassed when traveling during the second Bush administration. You have to explain why this leadership is in place, you have to represent the country that has never made you feel equally represented. President Obama made international travel fantastic for nearly a decade. He was the first American President I ever considered writing a poem for, without extreme criticism.

I returned home several days home to a different America. People in the airports looked distraught and some of us were just quiet. You didn't know who to trust. Did the pilot vote for Trump? The person next to you in business class? The flight attendant?!

I was happy to return to a country that was finally protesting again! I loved watching the different cities erupt in unison against this republican regime, threatening the livelihood of muslims, women, girls, gays, all people of color, our strong indigenous family, the poor and the elderly.

During the Woman's March, I decided to drink tea and watch and support the beautiful sea of protestors in spirit from afar. I wondered where all these women with pink vagina shaped hats were when the police lined up and began charging a peaceful demonstration for Michael Brown in Missouri. When I was forced to lie my body face down onto the ground in Ferguson with Rosa Clemente and Talib Kweli, when we were simply walking. When I read a poem in the place where Michael Browns body laid for hours, blood filling the cement, the same way our bodies were lynched in broad daylight and left to publicly hang to further impose psychological warfare onto our community. Did they rock black hoodies for Trayvon Martin? Did they travel to Cleveland after Tamir Rice was murdered in a park in seconds by police? What about the breath of life stolen from Eric Gardner on film?

As Black mothers, there is always more to consider than just our own bodies. We provide the spiritual armor for our families lives too. As a black woman mothering in a time of war, I wanted to know what my black sons' lives were worth. Did they matter as much as abortion rights? I was not alone. Composer, vocalist and scholar, Imani Uzuri, gave so many of us displaced, frustrated sisters a voice by simply writing on social media, "My pussy is not pink." Black women who did not publicly applaud or were critical of the march were suddenly being labeled "divisive." We must come together now, I wondered? Now? Black women's backs have been showing up for the rights of women since before Sojourner Truth asked her prophetic four-word question, "Ain't I A Woman?!" Black mothers who raise their daughters, and pray their sons just make it home from school, no longer want to have to ask that question. The fight for us did not just begin.

We don't have anything to prove. Even if we may not have been in love with Senator Hilary Clinton, we did our jobs on Nov 4th 2016 and voted for her in a dominate way. We showed our strength. We did what was best for the country. Still, madness, sexism, racism and fear had already tornadoed through those rural communities anyone sane knows Donald Trump could care less about.

In 2016, the U.S. began slipping back in time. The only option for surviving this crisis is genuine institution building. The narcissism of republican white men is uncanny. You can't make this stuff up. The only option we have is to build institutions that support our mission. To create our own moral laws and live by them. To create commerce in our own communities and support artists. Black mothering in a time of war, means writing letters to teachers to explain to them we are clear there is a conspiracy to destroy black boys' spirits, but the ones in this classroom will not be damaged. We must remember we are the first teachers. Some of us will need to homeschool and educate our children together if we must. Build our own schools of resistance. Women must find ways to support our village in stronger non western ways. We must be our own healthcare system.

I ultimately told my son, I am the president of my own universe. No government reigns over me. I reminded him that we don't allow fear to permeate into our thinking. There was no place for it. I reminded him that his generation must become the real change agents to make this world better. I also began to organize nationwide "Sister-Fire" events to bring women from different walks of life together for conversation, art, strategy, self care, networking, mothering, and healing in a safe place. Our voices at the forefront, not an after-thought or sideline position.

This is what we do in a time of spiritual warfare.

We light candles.
We meditate
We organize
We speak with our ancestors
We remember our power
We raise our children with self determination

We build a beautiful, resilient fire

With Love & Struggle,

The President

APPENDIX

HAKI R. MADHUBUTI

DONALD TRUMP IS *NOT* MY PRESIDENT:

The Republican Party is a Criminal Enterprise Controlled by the Billionaires (.01%) and the Democratic Party as well as the DNC that Continues to Bring a Toenail Clipper to a Gunfight

Note: This essay was originally written in 2016, and published in the *South Shore Current* newspaper (Dec. 2017). The original essay gave us the idea and inspiration for this book.

It must now be an accepted fact that we do not live in a post-racial America. Racism or more accurately white supremacy, is not only alive and well in the United States, it is indeed a growth industry. Most people of all cultures who think, read, survey, and analyze world conditions understand that the Black and Brown peoples (mainly men) fear factor helped elect an unqualified, egomaniacal, psychopath to the highest office in the land. Donald Trump is not just the tip of the white spear; he is the bullet in the cannon.

Most Black activists and progressives from the sixties and seventies, who have lived and struggled over the last fifty years, were not caught up in the white liberal rope-a-dope of the Democratic National Committee (DNC) and the Democratic Party. It is clear to us, most certainly since the presidency of Nixon, that the Republican Party and the Republican National Committee (RNC) are for sale to the highest bidder. It is a party of corporate money. We have seen this movie before during the election of and tenure of Ronald Reagan—remember he kicked off his presidential campaign in Philadelphia, MS, thereby signaling to white supremacists that he's aboard the same confederate train. Once elected, Reagan went immediately anti-worker and anti-union by systematically dismantling the Professional Air Traffic Controllers Organization (PATCO).

Then there was/is Bush II, with a brain that is unmeasurable because it can't be found. He turned his presidency over to vice-president Dick Cheney and the neocons, who illegally took us into wars in Iraq and Afghanistan costing us over 3 trillion dollars and growing. Bush II also gave us the worst financial meltdown since the Great Depression. As a result of Bush II and the neocons, their false analysis, lies, and physical destruction of the Middle East led to the creation of the Islamic State. After his failed presidency, Bush II immediately went into hiding in Texas only to come out to support his brother Jeb in his failed attempt to win the nomination. However, over the last eight years, the Republican Party, RNC, and Republican Congress have attempted (with much success) to blame the coming of the end of the world on President Barack Obama.

Trump destroyed his Republican primary opponents with innuendo, outright lies, insults, and race-based fear tactics that had not been used in such a blatant white supremacist way since Reconstruction. However, it was Trump's outright promise to deport 11 million undocumented migrants from the US and his call to temporarily ban all Muslims from entering the country, his call to reinstate "Stop and Frisk" laws, Law and Order, building a wall between Mexico and the U.S., and bringing back illegal torture of perceived enemies that cemented his hero status among the Alt-right. Trump's unabashed announcement that he knows more than the generals and would defeat the Islamic State as his first order of business was in keeping with his coded use of Black and Brown men as major enemies of the United States. Also, his mixture of misogynist, homophobic rhetoric as well as his mocking impersonation of a disabled reporter in addition to his failure to issue any serious policy papers relegated his fight against Hillary Clinton to that of character assassination, rumor, and name calling. Clearly, these tactics made his run for the presidency a reality show not unlike his popular Celebrity Apprentice.

Remember, the CEO of CBS was caught on mic stating that Donald Trump may not be good for America, but he was excellent for CBS or words to that effect. The Clinton Campaign, Democratic Party, and DNC were outmaneuvered at every turn. They believed in their own entitled, inflated polls that continued to show Hillary Clinton four to seven points ahead depending upon what happened that week. After all, this was her time. This was a woman's time. Except, no one told Donald Trump and his supporters the news. They didn't get the telegram.

For the last five years or so, whenever I had to speak in a radius of 500 miles or less from Chicago, I would drive. Thereby, traveling to colleges, universities, bookstores, community centers, libraries, retreats, men's conferences and urban schools in Illinois, Michigan, Ohio, Iowa, Indiana, Wisconsin, and Kentucky—my biggest fears were confirmed. What I discovered was that there were about 400 rabid right-wing white supremacist radio stations across the land. And it is very clear that the nation moves on 18-wheel trucks and there are millions of white truck drivers crisscrossing the country listening to this right-wing white supremacist neo-fascist drivel and accepting it as gospel. Therefore, we have millions of white men and some women, going home each week confirmed in their misinformation and ignorance. Their fears confirmed to them daily by the likes of Alex Jones, Rush Limbaugh, Bill O'Reilly, Sean Hannity, and others. It has been proven that their ahistorical animosities, playground accusations, and lies need no facts to survive and thrive because no one out there on the road or the airwaves (except for the four or five progressive radio stations) challenged their inaccurate worldview. Do the math. If you have a minimum of 4 million white drivers crisscrossing the country per week—each with families and extended families—we're talking about a voting population between 20-25 million who believe in Trump, and over half of that populace are women.

The DNC shot itself in its foot by favoring Clinton over Sanders. Its disgraced former director, Representative Debbie Wasserman

Schultz, clearly used backroom tactics to support Clinton over Bernie Sanders and tried in many ways, directly and indirectly, to disrupt the national progressive movement that Bernie Sanders had awakened among young people, African Americans, Latinos, women and those defined as the other. They all felt the Bern and were fired up as Bernie Sanders filled stadium after stadium across the country. And if all was fair, he could have possibly won the nomination. The Clinton campaign never completely won over those who felt that the DNC had cheated them out of the nomination. However, what is not clearly talked about is that the forces who really defeated Hillary Clinton were:

1. Hillary Clinton, herself, in her failure to inspire;
2. Bill Clinton's history with women and the Clinton Foundation's contradictions;
3. White working, middle class, and unemployed men;
4. White women (educated, less-educated, and ill-educated);
5. Which should probably be first, billions of dollars from numerous PACs, corporate, and 'dark money' sources;
6. The national Democrats did not show up.

What is not acknowledged, is that the fear factor of Black and Brown men flooding white communities, putting white women at-risk was the underlying message from Trump. His slogan "Make America Great Again" is really coded language for make America white again.

Keep in mind, that according to The New York Times and other publications, Mr. Trump received over 2 billion dollars worth of free media. And finally, by galvanizing the white ethnic vote, Mr. Trump continued to talk about the election being rigged and stolen, which of course, energized and stimulated his white political base. However, that which is true, there was serious voter suppression in Black, Brown and poor communities, and in at least 33 states with Republican governors and legislatures. The best evidence for this is Greg Palast's book, *The Best Democracy Money Can Buy* and his film of the same title. Mr. Palast documents the corporate, political, and on-the-ground Republican workers, suppression of Black, Brown, and poor people's votes. In addition, Trump's repeated vilification of Black Lives Matter along with his and Speaker Paul Ryan's push for privatization of everything that is a part of the Commons such as: healthcare, water, transportation, climate damage, etc. These parasitic actions and others are the perfect example of Donald Trump's effective use of white male privilege.

As the New York Times columnist, Nicholas Kristoff, clearly points out in his recent column, "Of What Ifs?", that if Hillary Clinton had committed any one of the many disqualifying, illegal, childish, insulting, harmful, hateful spoiled brat incidents over a lifetime that the Donald joyfully lived for she would not have been considered for the nomination or had had such a stellar career in public service. The hands on the p- comment on the bus or his serial marriages and adulterous lifestyle should have disqualified him months ago. Yet, this highly unfit, ignorant, very rich white male has been able to ride his white male privilege, his daddy's money, his media fame "blame NBC", his connection to the very rich, the Alt-right "Stephen Bannon former head of Breitbart News", the maddening birtherism and disinformation campaign and anger against President Obama aided by eight years of spiteful speech by the Republican Congress, right-radio, and Fox News, that 24/7 also preached deep fear of Black, Brown, and other men in the form of urban street thugs, Islamic state killings, rapists from across the southern borders, coming for white women and the ultimate prize - the American nation that only this white savior, Donald Trump could save. You can't make this stuff up! It is absolutely surreal and yes frightening to those who did not grow up suffering such demeaning activities for centuries in this country - Black people. For once, white Americans, may understand daily the enslaving reality of a racist, misogynist, anti-Semitic, anti-LGBTQ put-downs from whites that question everything from Black IQ to the legality of our full citizenship.

In the West, most certainly in the United States, white people never, I say never, have to think about being white. Being white is an accepted, normal, and privileged existence. However, Black people everywhere in the world, especially in the United States, must think about and deal with being Black every day of the year, and this is amplified in the darker one's complexion. Dark-skinned Black men and women have a storm to negotiate each day they step outside their family or comfort zones. All the white systems of organizations, control and definition have been put in place to keep Black men out. To reduce Black people's struggles and the definition of their race to "people of color" is to display an ignorance reserved for newborn babies. We must never diminish the critical power that "Black" carries in a white supremacist culture.

If all 42-million plus Black people in the United States disappeared tomorrow, there is not one job, position, appointment, post, function, manager, executive, professorship, CEO, CFO, general of the military, etc., now held by Black people, including the President of the United States, that could not be filled within a week by white people. In a nation of over 314 million people, the Black population is 42 million according to Black Stats by Monique W. Morris. In a nation with a surplus of PhDs, MBAs, lawyers, MFAs, medical doctors, technical non-degree positions and others, too many white young people are jobless. There are millions of white people standing in line and submitting similar resumes from the basements of their parents' homes where they have been forced to move back to after undergraduate school or technical training because of the "recession" of 2008-2009 that is still with us. They are unable to find employment.

Bottom line: Black people are no longer essential to America's economic labor force.

This is the core fact of our existence in this country and unless we recognize it and plan accordingly, the future will remain a question mark. Little, if any substantial change politically, socially, culturally, economically, educationally, and spiritually for Black boys, men, people will occur in the world or the United States until there is an unfiltered, honest conversation—with correctives and programs that work under the deadly effects—locally, nationally and internationally of white skin privileges and its underpinnings white nationalism, white supremacy, i.e., white power.

FASCISM ANYONE?: THE 14 DEFINING CHARACTERISTICS OF FASCISM

LAWRENCE W. BRITT

Dr. Lawrence W. Britt has examined the fascist regimes of Hitler (Germany), Mussolini (Italy), Franco (Spain), Suharto (Indonesia) and several Latin American regimes. Britt found 14 defining characteristics common to each. The following article is reprinted from Free Inquiry magazine, Spring 2003 (23)2.

1. Powerful and Continuing Nationalism: *Fascist regimes tend to make constant use of patriotic mottos, slogans, symbols, songs, and other paraphernalia. Flags are seen everywhere, as are flag symbols on clothing and in public displays.*

2. Disdain for the Recognition of Human Rights: *Because of fear of enemies and the need for security, the people in fascist regimes are persuaded that human rights can be ignored in certain cases because of "need." The people tend to look the other way or even approve of torture, summary executions, assassinations, long incarcerations of prisoners, etc.*

3. Identification of Enemies/Scapegoats as a Unifying Cause: *The people are rallied into a unifying patriotic frenzy over the need to eliminate a perceived common threat or foe: racial , ethnic or religious minorities; liberals; communists; socialists, terrorists, etc.*

4. Supremacy of the Military: *Even when there are widespread domestic problems, the military is given a disproportionate amount of government funding, and the domestic agenda is neglected. Soldiers and military service are glamorized.*

5. Rampant Sexism: *The governments of fascist nations tend to be almost exclusively male-dominated. Under fascist regimes, traditional gender roles are made more rigid. Divorce, abortion and homosexuality are suppressed and the state is represented as the ultimate guardian of the family institution.*

6. Controlled Mass Media: *Sometimes to media is directly controlled by the government, but in other cases, the media is indirectly controlled by government regulation, or sympathetic media spokespeople and executives. Censorship, especially in war time, is very common.*

7. Obsession with National Security: *Fear is used as a motivational tool by the government over the masses.*

8. Religion and Government are Intertwined: *Governments in fascist nations tend to use the most common religion in the nation as a tool to manipulate public opinion. Religious rhetoric and terminology is common from government leaders, even when the major tenets of the religion are diametrically opposed to the government's policies or actions.*

9. Corporate Power is Protected: *The industrial and business aristocracy of a fascist nation often are the ones who put the government leaders into power, creating a mutually beneficial business/government relationship and power elite.*

10. Labor Power is Suppressed: *Because the organizing power of labor is the only real threat to a fascist government, labor unions are either eliminated entirely, or are severely suppressed.*

11. Disdain for Intellectuals and the Arts: *Fascist nations tend to promote and tolerate open hostility to higher education, and academia. It is not uncommon for professors and other academics to be censored or even arrested. Free expression in the arts and letters is openly attacked.*

12. Obsession with Crime and Punishment: *Under fascist regimes, the police are given almost limitless power to enforce laws. The people are often willing to overlook police abuses and even forego civil liberties in the name of patriotism. There is often a national police force with virtually unlimited power in fascist nations.*

13. Rampant Cronyism and Corruption: *Fascist regimes almost always are governed by groups of friends and associates who appoint each other to government positions and use governmental power and authority to protect their friends from accountability. It is not uncommon in fascist regimes for national resources and even treasures to be appropriated or even outright stolen by government leaders.*

14. Fraudulent Elections: *Sometimes elections in fascist nations are a complete sham. Other times elections are manipulated by smear campaigns against or even assassination of opposition candidates, use of legislation to control voting numbers or political district boundaries, and manipulation of the media. Fascist nations also typically use their judiciaries to manipulate or control elections.*